*Wood engraving of the Statue of Liberty
in the Rue de Chazelles. The statue was erected
at the foundry site, 1881-84.
On Sundays, crowds gathered to admire it.
Wine was served from trestles in the street.
The statue was dismantled at the end of 1884
and shipped to America.
(See page 44.)*

AMERICANS IN PARIS

Brian N. Morton

Quill
William Morrow
New York

Americans Abroad Series by Brian N. Morton

Americans in London (August 1986)
Americans in Venice (in preparation)

Library of Congress Catalog Card Number: 85-63392

ISBN: 0-688-06509-0

Printed in the United States of America

First Quill Edition
1 2 3 4 5 6 7 8 9 10

Contents

Introduction

A few years ago I spent a week in Paris with 50 American undergraduates beginning their junior year abroad. Each morning a tour bus came to our hotel and five minutes later the guide arrived. Each morning the students listened dutifully to his recital of French history as we paused before the Madeleine, the Sorbonne, and the Palais de Justice. But their early enthusiasm soon waned. The French names were strange, the events unfamiliar. On the last morning the bus arrived but the guide did not appear. I anxiously pointed this out to the driver. "C'est impossible, Monsieur," he said. But the impossible had happened and soon our bus was blocking the frenetic Parisian rush-hour traffic. In desperation I took the guide's place, warning my weary audience that I would talk not about the French in Paris, but rather about Americans in Paris. For the next two hours, I told them about Thomas Jefferson browsing for books along the quays, amassing a collection which later became the Library of Congress; Aaron Burr's constant need for "a lady of the night"; Robert Fulton's first steamboat trial on the Seine; Whistler's portrait of his mother, quickly purchased by the French government; Thomas Edison's immense success with his phonograph; George Gershwin's taxi horns; and Buster Keaton's return to the limelight, as the leading circus clown in Paris. The morning was soon over, the students delighted, the "guide" pleasantly surprised; the idea for this book was born.

Thomas Jefferson once remarked that every man has two countries, his own and France, and by France he meant Paris, where since 1776, an active American community has thrived. Americans have come to study, to paint, to sculpt, to dance, to sing, to write, to love—in a word, to live. What Paris gave them was a sense of personal and artistic freedom, and the experience of a very different way of life. In New York to be penniless writing poetry was a humiliation; in Paris it was a respected tradition.

This book is a record of the American experience in Paris from 1776 until the present. It aims to guide you, street by street, to the houses where Americans lived and worked, and to the haunts they frequented. As you saunter along the Rue Jacob, you will be able to retrace the footsteps of Benjamin Franklin, John Adams, and John Jay and learn what brought them here. And if you put up in the Hôtel d'Angleterre on the same 17th-century street, you may compare your impressions of the hotel's courtyard garden with those recorded by Washington Irving, Sherwood Anderson, and Ernest Hemingway, who also stayed there.

The List of Americans will help you follow the path of James Fenimore Cooper, who came to Paris in 1826 for one year and stayed on for seven; or of George Catlin who, in 1845, opened a gallery of Indian portraits with fourteen Ioway Indians performing tableaux vivants on the fashionable Rue St.-Honoré. Everyone admired but no one bought. Catlin, soon penniless, took refuge on Rue Tronchet near the Madeleine, where he described himself as "destitute, despondent and deaf but still without bitterness." Or you may accompany P.T. Barnum through Paris late in the evening after his show, when he would have to "take a cab to carry [his] bag of silver home at night."

But if you do not have the good fortune to be in Paris, you can sit at home and wander through the city with your favorite Americans, and discover others whom you hadn't dreamt of meeting there, such as Samuel Morse, Hart Crane, John Dos Passos, Cole Porter, Mary Pickford, Edna St. Vincent Millay, Aaron Copland, and Orville and Wilbur Wright.

The first Americans in Paris were diplomats. Silas Deane of Connecticut arrived on 5 July 1776, unaware of the signing of the Declaration of Independence, but armed with instructions from the Continental Congress to secure French military and financial aid for the war. The declaration of 4 July 1776 had created American citizenship for those whom the British called rebels. Thus Deane became the first official American citizen to set foot in Paris.

Deane was well received and was followed by Benjamin Franklin and his successor Thomas Jefferson, both of whom impressed the Parisians with their worldliness. Each spoke French and charmed the ladies and the gentlemen at Versailles. British diplomats, though competent, were little match for their American counterparts. The Americans and the New World they represented caught the imagination of the French, beginning a love affair which has survived these two centuries.

By 1795, after the chaos brought about by the French Revolution, American merchants were selling grain to the starving nation and with their handsome profits buying up mansions abandoned by the French aristocracy. Here they lived fancily with coaches and footmen.

In the 1830s French medical schools drew American doctors for advanced work, among them Oliver Wendell Holmes, father of the future chief justice, and Mary Putnam, daughter of the New York publisher. During the Civil War, bitterly divided Americans in Paris tried to win Napoleon III's support for their respective causes. But when Prussia invaded France in 1870, volunteers from the two American factions joined forces and fought alongside the French.

Toward the end of the 19th century, American technology gained international recognition, especially in the vast Paris Universal Exhibitions, where men like Thomas Edison displayed their inventions and peddled their patents.

After World War I, many doughboys, like John Dos Passos and Cole Porter, stayed on to study. American writers and artists had always been drawn to Paris, but it was the 1920s which brought the biggest influx of all.

After World War II, the GI Bill provided four years of support for painters Ellsworth Kelly and Robert Rauschenburg. Humorist Art Buchwald, like so many others, studied at the Alliance Française to collect his 75 dollars a month, but in truth honed his writing skills at the *Herald Tribune*. Man Ray returned to Paris from Hollywood; Richard Wright and James Baldwin came to escape racial prejudice; and Mary McCarthy and James Jones also took up residence in Paris.

I have tried to present the widest possible selection from the rich and varied history of two centuries of Americans in Paris. The more than 350 Americans in this guide have been chosen for their achievements and for the influence Paris had on their lives and work. A few have been selected thanks to a charming anecdote or because their stay in Paris sheds light on Franco-American relations.

Faced by the problem of deciding who was an American, I have been arbitrary. I have included Thomas Paine, although he arrived in America in 1774 at the age of 37, returned to England thirteen years later, and then fled to France in 1792. When he died in America he had spent less than one-third of his life there, yet he was an American political writer and was strongly influenced by the French Revolution. On the other hand, Jacques Lipchitz, like many European refugees, was 50 years old when he arrived in America.

His work was also influenced by his stay in France, but he was not American at the time and receives only brief mention.

The addresses of Americans now living and working in Paris are not included in this book in order to protect their privacy.

Quotations in this book have been reproduced verbatim. As a result, some variations in spelling and punctuation occur.

Subsequent editions would be enriched by readers sharing their interests and knowledge with the author. Any corrections or suggestions for additional entries will be gratefully received and fully acknowledged whenever possible.

About the Author

Brian N. Morton was born in London, England. He did his graduate studies at Columbia University, New York. He taught at Williams College, Massachusetts, and since 1969 has been teaching French literature at the University of Michigan, Ann Arbor. His forthcoming book, *Beaumarchais and the American Revolution,* deals with secret French aid to America from 1776 to 1778. Together with his French wife and two children, he divides his time between Ann Arbor and Paris.

About the Guide

This guide is organized by streets in alphabetical order.

You can discover the Americans who lived in Paris by reading through the street entries. Next to the house number, you will find the story which links it to an American. House numbers in bold type indicate that the original building is still standing, even though its use may have changed. House numbers in parentheses indicate the site where the original building once stood. The symbol ⚜ separates entries at the same address.

You can choose someone of interest from the *List of Americans* (p. xv). This List identifies by profession most of the Americans appearing in the guide and gives the address, or addresses, linked to their stay in Paris. When there is more than one address, these are listed in chronological order. For example,

Benjamin Franklin   2 Rue de l'Université
        52 Rue Jacob
        62 Rue Raynouard

When you read the Franklin entry on the above streets, you will be able to meet him on his arrival in Paris in December 1776 on Rue de l'Université, move with him a few days later to Rue Jacob, and finally enjoy with him the eight years he spent on Rue Raynouard.

This guide also has a comprehensive index (p. 275).

After the street name the *arrondissement* is given in parentheses. A map reference follows for streets appearing on one of the area maps, or a métro stop for streets off the beaten track. (Sites of buildings which no longer exist have no map or métro reference.)

There are maps of those areas of Paris where many Americans have lived (p. 291). If you are in Paris, these will help you plan walks.

Street Names

Paris street names change. When Thomas Jefferson arrived in Paris in August 1784, he took chambers at the Hôtel d'Orléans on Rue des Petits-Augustins. Today you can see the original building, although it is no longer a hotel and the street has become Rue Bonaparte. During the French Revolution many names were changed; Rue Notre-Dame, for instance, became Rue de la Raison. In the 19th century, with the modernization of thoroughfares carried out by Baron Haussmann, many of the older streets disappeared. Recently Place de l'Etoile became Place du Général de Gaulle.

House Numbers

The numbering of houses in Paris was first introduced in the 18th century. Parisians, suspecting that its real purpose was to help tax collectors find them, refused to cooperate. The aristocracy were also uncooperative because their names were used as their addresses. An orderly and logical numbering system was imposed by Napoleon, which, with few exceptions, holds true today. Throughout this guide, street names and numbers in use in 1983 have been listed.

Currency Terms

In 18th-century France, the terms *livre* and *franc* were interchangeable. There were approximately 23 livres to the pound sterling, which was the currency generally referred to by Americans. A livre in 1776 roughly equalled one dollar today.

French Terms

Salon. A living room or library in which receptions are held on a regular basis. *Salon* can also be used to refer to official art exhibits held in Paris.

Hôtel particulier. A private mansion. This term was common in the 17th and 18th centuries, less so in the 19th, and is rarely used today.

Bis or *ter.* Suffixes occasionally used after a house number. Rather than renumbering all the houses on a street, the *bis* or *ter* was used after a house number when an additional house was built or a single house was divided in two. The American equivalent of 21 *bis,* 21 *ter* is 21 A, 21 B.

List of Illustrations

List of Americans

Addresses for each American are listed in chronological order.

Adventurers
Lindbergh, Charles	2 Avenue d'Iéna
Peary, Robert Edwin	Place de la Sorbonne

Architects
Bulfinch, Charles	9 Quai Anatole-France
Hood, Raymond	14 Rue Bonaparte
Hunt, Richard Morris	14 Rue Bonaparte
Maybeck, Bernard Ralph	14 Rue Bonaparte
Richardson, Henry Hobson	14 Rue Bonaparte
Sullivan, Louis	14 Rue Bonaparte

Bankers
Morgan, John Pierpont	3 Place Vendôme
Welles, Samuel	24 Rue Taitbout

Clergymen
Brooks, Phillips	2 Rue Scribe
Dana, William	Place de la Madeleine
Graham, Billy	8 Boulevard de Grenelle
King, Martin Luther	14 Rue Monsieur-le-Prince
	65 Quai d'Orsay
Parker, Theodore	13 Rue de la Paix

Composers, musicians, and singers
Antheil, George	12 Rue de l'Odéon
	13 Avenue Montaigne
Armstrong, Louis	252 Rue du Faubourg St.-Honoré
Bechet, Sidney	13 Avenue Montaigne
	21 Rue du Vieux-Colombier
Copland, Aaron	30 Rue de Vaugirard
	36 Rue Ballu
	207 Boulevard Raspail

Ellington, Duke	31 Avenue George-Cinq
	252 Rue du Faubourg St.-Honoré
	Place du Trocadéro
	62 Rue Mazarine
Garden, Mary	Place Boieldieu
Gershwin, George	19 Avenue Kléber
	25 Rue de Mogador
Homer, Louise	1 Place du Châtelet
	3 bis Rue Jean-Ferrandi
Moore, Grace	133 Avenue des Champs-Elysées
	Place Boieldieu
Payne, John Howard	156 Place du Palais-Royal
	89 Rue de Richelieu
Piston, Walter	52 Rue Broca
Porter, Cole	269 Rue St.-Jacques
	13 Rue Monsieur
Rodgers, Richard	133 Avenue des Champs-Elysées
Rorem, Ned	11 Place des Etats-Unis
Sousa, John Philip	Place des Etats-Unis
Thomson, Virgil	20 Rue de Berne
	9 Rue Médéric
	36 Rue Ballu
	17 Quai Voltaire

Diplomats and statesmen

Adams, John	17 Rue de Richelieu
	62 Rue Raynouard
	Pont Royal
	56 Rue Jacob
	43-7 Rue d'Auteuil
Adams, John Quincy	97 Rue de Richelieu
Bigelow, John	Avenue des Champs-Elysées
	Bois de Boulogne
Burr, Aaron	7 Rue de Grenelle
	7 Rue du Croissant
	Place du Palais-Royal
	Jardin des Tuileries
Deane, Silas	47 Rue Vieille-du-Temple

Franklin, Benjamin	2 Rue de l'Université
	52 Rue Jacob
	62 Rue Raynouard
	Rue du Louvre
	56 Rue Jacob
	Place de la Concorde
Gallatin, Albert	21 Rue de l'Université
Gerry, Elbridge	2-20 Boulevard Beaumarchais
Grant, Ulysses S.	112 Rue du Faubourg St.-Honoré
Harriman, Averell	2 Rue St.-Florentin
Herrick, Myron T.	2 Avenue d'Iéna
Herter, Christian	109 Rue Notre-Dame-des-Champs
Jay, John	17 Rue Bonaparte
	56 Rue Jacob
Jefferson, Thomas	30 Rue de Richelieu
	17 Rue Bonaparte
	Boulevard Haussmann
	1 Rue de Berri
	21 Quai des Grands-Augustins
	78 Rue de Varenne
	17 Place Vendôme
	11 Quai de Conti
	36 Rue Geoffroy-St.-Hilaire
Kennedy, John F.	37 Quai d'Orsay
Marshall, John	2-20 Boulevard Beaumarchais
Monroe, James	95 Rue de Richelieu
Morris, Gouverneur	63 Rue de Richelieu
	Esplanade des Invalides
Pinckney, Charles C.	2-20 Boulevard Beaumarchais
Rives, William C.	82 Rue de l'Université
Roosevelt, Franklin D.	239 Rue St.-Honoré
	37 Avenue George-Cinq
	2 Rue de Richelieu
	15 Place Vendôme
Roosevelt, Theodore	Esplanade des Invalides
Skipwith, Fulwar	102 Rue de Grenelle
	17 Quai Voltaire

Slidell, John	4 Place Vendôme
	25 Avenue Franklin-D.-Roosevelt
	4 Rue Monsigny
Sumner, Charles	108 Rue de Richelieu
	25 Rue de l'Odéon
	10 Rue de la Paix
Wilson, Woodrow	28 Rue de Monceau
	11 Place des Etats-Unis

Doctors and dentists

Earle, Pliny	6 Place de l'Odéon
Evans, Thomas	41 Avenue Foch
Holmes, Oliver Wendell	55 Rue Monsieur-le-Prince
	6 Rue Daunou
	13 Rue de l'Ancienne-Comédie
	Place du Panthéon
Parker, Willard	13 Rue St.-Sulpice
	39 Rue des Saints-Pères
	Rue Léon-Jouhaux
	1 Place du Parvis-Notre-Dame
	49 Rue Vivienne
	Avenue Rachel
Putnam, Mary	39 Rue Monsieur-le-Prince
	12 Rue de l'Ecole-de-Médecine
	47 Boulevard de l'Hôpital
	16 Rue de Vaugirard
Stewart, Campbell	1 Place du Parvis-Notre-Dame

Entertainers

Astaire, Fred	10 Place de la Concorde
	1 Place Vendôme
	15 Place Vendôme
Baker, Josephine	23 Boulevard des Batignolles
	13 Avenue Montaigne
	32 Rue Richer
	112 Rue du Faubourg-St.-Honoré
	Place de la Madeleine
Barnum, P.T.	24 Rue de Rivoli
	49 Rue Vivienne

Cody, William "Buffalo Bill"	Porte des Ternes
	Champs-de-Mars
Dolly Sisters	82 Boulevard de Clichy
Duncan, Isadora	4 Rue de la Gaité
	45 Avenue de Villiers
	5 Rue Danton
	99 Rue de la Pompe
	9 Rue Delambre
	25 Rue de Mogador
Fairbanks, Douglas	10 Place de la Concorde
Fuller, Loïe	32 Rue Richer
Houdini	28 Boulevard des Capucines
Keaton, Buster	63 Boulevard de Rochechouart
Pickford, Mary	10 Place de la Concorde
Swanson, Gloria	10 Place des Etats-Unis
Thumb, General Tom	24 Rue de Rivoli
	49 Rue Vivienne
Vander, Clyde "Barbette"	63 Boulevard de Rochechouart
Welles, Orson	8 Place Edouard-VII

Inventors

Edison, Thomas	23 Quai de Conti
	La Tour Eiffel
	Place de l'Opéra
Fulton, Robert	102 Rue du Bac
	50 Rue de Vaugirard
	Passage des Panoramas
	Avenue de New York
Morse, Samuel	9 Rue des Mathurins
	108 Rue St.-Lazare
	Place du Palais-Royal
Peirce, Charles Sander	Avenue de l'Observatoire
Thomson, Elihu	La Tour Eiffel
Wright, Wilbur and Orville	228 Rue de Rivoli

Journalists

Bennett, James Gordon	120 Avenue des Champs-Elysées

Buchwald, Art	135 Boulevard du Montparnasse
	24 Rue du Boccador
	83 Quai d'Orsay
	52 Rue de Monceau
Calmer, Edgar	4 Rue de Vaugirard
Hearst, William Randolph	10 Place de la Concorde
Flanner, Janet	36 Rue Bonaparte
	13 Avenue Montaigne
Goodrich, Samuel	23 Quai de Conti
	1 Place du Parvis-Notre-Dame
Liebling, A.J.	1 Rue Lulli
Lippmann, Walter	18 Quai d'Orléans
	228 Rue de Rivoli
Paul, Elliot	28 Rue de la Huchette
	40 ter Rue Fabert
Sevareid, Eric	1 Place de la Sorbonne
Shirer, William L.	85 Boulevard de Port-Royal
	4 Rue de Vaugirard
	5 Rue Lamartine
	49 Rue des Ecoles
	27 Rue de Fleurus
Sulzberger, Arthur	15 Place Vendôme
White, Theodore	24 Rue du Boccador
Willis, Nathaniel	1 Rue Notre-Dame-des-Victoires
	15 Rue Vivienne
	Place du Palais-Royal
	Le cimetière du Père-Lachaise

Merchants

Barlow, Joel	7 Rue Danielle-Casanova
	22 Rue Jacob
	102 Rue du Bac
	50 Rue de Vaugirard
Bingham, William	43 Rue d'Auteuil
Codman, Richard	28 Rue Bayen
Singer, Isaac	83 Boulevard Malesherbes
Vans, William	24 Rue de l'Université

Military and naval officers

Eisenhower, Dwight D.   133 Avenue des Champs-Elysées

Jones, John Paul
- 62 Rue Raynouard
- 43 Rue d'Auteuil
- 19 Rue de Tournon
- 41 Rue des Ecluses-St.-Martin
- 23 Avenue George-Cinq

Patton, George   25 Avenue Montaigne

Pershing, John
- 35 Rue de Picpus
- 10 Place de la Concorde

Novelists, poets, and writers

Adams, Henry
- 206 Rue de Rivoli
- 23 Avenue Foch
- 16 Rue Christophe-Colomb

Anderson, Sherwood   44 Rue Jacob

Baldwin, James   170 Boulevard St.-Germain

Barney, Natalie Clifford   20 Rue Jacob

Benét, Stephen Vincent   36 Rue de Longchamp

Burroughs, William   9 Rue Gît-le-Coeur

Capote, Truman   7 Rue Montalembert

Cather, Willa   19 Quai Voltaire

Cooper, James Fenimore
- 12 Rue de l'Abbé-Grégoire
- 29 Rue de Verneuil
- 22 Rue d'Aguesseau
- 13 Rue St.-Florentin
- 59 Rue St.-Dominique
- Rue du Louvre

Crane, Hart   Rue de la Santé

Cummings, E.E.
- 7 Rue François-Premier
- 13 Rue Du Sommerard
- 45 Rue St.-André-des-Arts
- Rue Gît-le-Coeur
- Rue du Dragon
- Rue du Douanier

Dos Passos, John
- Rue Descartes
- 45 Quai de la Tournelle
- 37 Quai d'Anjou
- 171 Boulevard du Montparnasse

Eliot, T.S.	9 Rue de l'Université
Emerson, Ralph Waldo	Passage des Panoramas
	13 Rue de l'Ancienne-Comédie
	15 Rue Bonaparte
	16 Rue Notre-Dame-des-Victoires
	2 Rue de Richelieu
	7 Rue de Beaune
Faulkner, William	26 Rue Servandoni
	82 Boulevard de Clichy
Ferlinghetti, Lawrence	89 Rue de Vaugirard
	52 Rue de Seine
Fitzgerald, F. Scott	14 Rue de Tilsitt
	171 Boulevard du Montparnasse
	58 Rue de Vaugirard
	10 Rue Pergolèse
Fuller, Margaret	4 Cité Rougemont
	Place du Palais-Bourbon
Harte, Bret	39 Avenue de l'Opéra
Hawthorne, Nathaniel	164 Rue de Rivoli
Hemingway, Ernest	44 Rue Jacob
	108 Boulevard du Montparnasse
	30 Rue Bonaparte
	74 Rue du Cardinal-Lemoine
	39 Rue Descartes
	8 Boulevard de Grenelle
	113 Rue Notre-Dame-des-Champs
	171 Boulevard du Montparnasse
	6 Rue Férou
	69 Rue Froidevaux
	12 Rue de l'Odéon
Howells, William Dean	164 Rue de Rivoli
Hughes, Langston	15 Rue Nollet
Irving, Washington	69 Rue de Richelieu
	44 Rue Jacob
	4 Rue du Mont-Thabor
	89 Rue de Richelieu

James, Henry	13 Rue de la Paix
	19 Rue La Boétie
	29 Rue Cambon
	2 Rue Scribe
	20 Rue de la Paix
	228 Rue de Rivoli
Jones, James	10 Quai d'Orléans
Keller, Helen	7 Rue de Berri
	77 Rue de Varenne
	Place du Panthéon
Kerouac, Jack	28 Rue St.-André-des-Arts
Lewis, Sinclair	211 Rue St.-Honoré
	2 Avenue Montaigne
	112 Rue du Faubourg-St.-Honoré
	108 Boulevard du Montparnasse
Longfellow, Henry Wadsworth	49 Rue Monsieur-le-Prince
	Jardin du Luxembourg
	5 Rue Racine
	228 Rue de Rivoli
Lowell, James Russell	7 Rue de Beaune
MacLeish, Archibald	23 Rue Las-Cases
	41 Avenue Foch
	44 Rue du Bac
McCullers, Carson	239 Rue St.-Honoré
Melville, Herman	228 Rue de Rivoli
Millay, Edna St. Vincent	65 Rue des Saints-Pères
	50 Rue de l'Université
	159 Boulevard du Montparnasse
	105 Boulevard du Montparnasse
	5 Rue Benjamin-Godard
Miller, Henry	24 Rue Bonaparte
	36 Rue Bonaparte
	60 Rue Raymond-Losserand
	2 Rue Auguste-Bartholdi
	Rue de Furstenberg
	100 Rue de la Tombe-Issoire

Paine, Thomas	22 Rue Jacob
	Palais du Luxembourg
	95 Rue de Richelieu
	2 Rue de l'Odéon
Porter, Katherine Anne	166 Boulevard du Montparnasse
	70 bis Rue Notre-Dame-des-Champs
Pound, Ezra	9 Rue de Beaune
	59 Rue des Saints-Pères
	70 bis Rue Notre-Dame-des-Champs
	252 Rue du Faubourg-St.-Honoré
Rice, Elmer	Rue Bonaparte
	59 Rue de Lille
Saroyan, William	74 Rue Taitbout
Seeger, Alan	17 Rue Du Sommerard
Shaw, Irwin	24 Rue du Boccador
Skinner, Cornelia Otis	239 Rue St.-Honoré
	6 Rue Pierre-Demours
Stanton, Elizabeth Cady	Esplanade des Invalides
	Jardin des Tuileries
Stearns, Harold	108 Boulevard du Montparnasse
	50 Rue Vavin
Stein, Gertrude	27 Rue de Fleurus
	5 Rue Christine
Steinbeck, John	7 Rue de Berri
	1 Avenue de Marigny
Stowe, Harriet Beecher	53 Rue de Verneuil
Tarkington, Booth	9 Rue de Tournon
Tate, Allan	32 Rue de Vaugirard
	6 Place de l'Odéon
Thurber, James	10 Place de la Concorde
	5 Rue Lamartine
	24 Rue St.-Benoît
Twain, Mark	164 Rue de Rivoli
	Esplanade des Invalides
	7 Rue de l'Echelle
	169 Rue de l'Université
Van Doren, Mark	5 Rue Corneille

West, Nathanael	43 Boulevard Raspail
	9 Rue de la Grande-Chaumière
Wharton, Edith	58 Rue de Varenne
	53 Rue de Varenne
Wilder, Thornton	151 Boulevard St.-Germain
Williams, Tennessee	22 Rue de l'Université
Williams, William Carlos	43 Boulevard Raspail
Wilson, Edmund	58 Rue de Richelieu
Wilson, Harry Leon	137 Boulevard du Montparnasse
Wolfe, Thomas	13 Rue des Beaux-Arts
	8 Rue Duphot
	29 Boulevard Poissonnière
Wright, Richard	1 bis Rue de Vaugirard
	38 Boulevard St.-Michel
	9 Rue de Lille
	14 Rue Monsieur-le-Prince
	170 Boulevard St.-Germain
	4 Rue Régis

Painters

Alcott, May	11 Rue Mansart
Biddle, George	84 Rue d'Assas
	31 Rue du Dragon
Breer, Robert	9 Rue de la Grande-Chaumière
	31 Rue du Dragon
Bruce, Patrick Henry	33 Boulevard des Invalides
Cassatt, Mary	13 Avenue Trudaine
	10 Rue de Marignan
Catlin, George	3 Rue Chauveau-Lagarde
	Avenue du Général-Lemonnier
	251 Rue St.-Honoré
	24 Rue Tronchet
Davis, Stuart	50 Rue Vercingétorix
Dewing, Thomas Wilmer	Passage des Panoramas
Eakins, Thomas	46 Rue de Vaugirard
	14 Rue Bonaparte
	64 Rue de l'Ouest
	116 Rue d'Assas

Gibson, Charles Dana	48 Rue Fabert
	Passage des Panoramas
Hassam, Childe	Passage des Panoramas
Hayter, William Stanley	17 Rue Campagne-Première
Homer, Winslow	49 Avenue Montaigne
Hovenden, Thomas	14 Rue Bonaparte
Hunt, William Morris	3 Rue Pigalle
Kelly, Ellsworth	31 Rue St.-Louis-en-l'Ile
Metcalf, Willard Leroy	Passage des Panoramas
Morse, Samuel	29 Rue de Turenne
	Rue du Louvre
Pach, Walter	Boulevard des Invalides
Prendergast, Maurice	31 Rue du Dragon
Rauschenberg, Robert	31 Rue du Dragon
	8 Rue de Miromesnil
	37 Quai des Grands-Augustins
Ray, Man	22 Rue de La Condamine
	15 Rue Delambre
	5 Avenue de Lowendal
	31 bis Rue Campagne-Première
	44 Rue Hamelin
	29 Rue Campagne-Première
	16 Rue Jacques-Callot
	8 Rue du Val-de-Grâce
	2 bis Rue Férou
Robinson, Theodore	14 Rue Bonaparte
Sargent, John Singer	52 Rue La Boétie
	81 Boulevard du Montparnasse
	135 Boulevard du Montparnasse
	73 Rue Notre-Dame-des-Champs
	41 Boulevard Berthier
Trumbull, John	1 Rue de Berri
	9 Quai Anatole-France
	Esplanade des Invalides
	Place du Panthéon
	Place St.-Sulpice
	Place de la Sorbonne
	69 Rue de Varenne

Twachtman, John Henry	Passage des Panoramas
Vanderlyn, John	70 Rue de Vaugirard
Weir, Julian Alden	14 Rue Bonaparte
Wendel, Theodore	Passage des Panoramas
Whistler, James McNeill	5 Rue Corneille
	1 Rue de Bourbon-le-Château
	3 Rue Campagne-Première
	171 Rue St.-Jacques
	22 Rue Monsieur-le-Prince
	64 Rue des Saints-Pères
	86 Rue Notre-Dame-des-Champs
	110 Rue du Bac

Patrons

Carnegie, Andrew	Place de la Sorbonne
Lehr, Mrs. Henry Symes	52 Rue des Saints-Pères
Singer, Winnaretta	83 Boulevard Malesherbes
	43 Avenue Georges-Mandel
Stein, Michael and Sarah	58 Rue Madame
	33 Boulevard des Invalides

Publishers and editors

Anderson, Margaret	15 Rue de Beaujolais
Beach, Sylvia	15 Rue de Beaujolais
	8 Rue Dupuytren
	12 Rue de l'Odéon
	18 Rue de l'Odéon
	93 Boulevard St.-Michel
Bird, William	29 Quai d'Anjou
Bradley, William Aspenwall	5 Rue St.-Louis-en-l'Ile
Crosby, Harry and Caresse	2 Rue Cardinale
	19 Rue de Lille
Harrison, Barbara	30 Rue de Montpensier
Jolas, Eugene	6 Rue de Verneuil
	40 ter Rue Fabert
Matthiessen, Peter	14 Rue de Perceval
McAlmon, Robert	8 Rue de l'Odéon
Plimpton, George	14 Rue de Perceval

Putnam, George Palmer	164 Rue de Rivoli
Titus, Edward	4 Rue Delambre
	216 Boulevard Raspail

Sculptors
Calder, Alexander	60 Boulevard du Montparnasse
	22 Rue Daguerre
	14 Rue de la Grande-Chaumière
	7 Rue Cels
	7 Villa Brune
	14 Rue de la Colonie
Davidson, Jo	108 Rue St.-Lazare
	7 Rue d'Arsonval
	39 Rue Delambre
	14 Avenue du Maine
	44 Rue du Bac
Hoffman, Malvina	Rue de la Grande-Chaumière
	17 Rue Campagne-Première
	72 Rue Notre-Dame-des-Champs
	Jardin du Luxembourg
	25 Villa Santos-Dumont
MacMonnies, Frederick William	16 Rue Antoine-Bourdelle
Scudder, Janet	4 Rue de Chevreuse
	16 Rue Antoine-Bourdelle
St. Gaudens, Augustus	233 Rue du Faubourg St.-Honoré
	49 Rue Notre-Dame-des-Champs
	3 bis Rue Jean-Ferrandi

Travel writers
Jewett, Isaac Appleton	Boulevard des Italiens
	Boulevard du Palais
	Place du Palais-Royal
Kirkland, Caroline	228 Rue de Rivoli
	2 Rue de Richelieu
	Place du Palais-Royal
Thomas, Ebenezer Smith	228 Rue de Rivoli
	Place Denfert-Rochereau
	Place du Palais-Royal
	292 Rue St.-Martin
Witmer, Theodore	Place St.-Jacques

Miscellaneous

Duncan, Raymond	45 Rue de Villiers
	31 Rue de Seine
Farley, Lillian	7 Quai Anatole-France
Rubinstein, Helena	4 Rue Delambre
	24 Quai de Béthune
Tuck, Edward	82 Avenue des Champs-Elysées
Tunney, Gene	151 Boulevard St.-Germain

STREETS OF PARIS

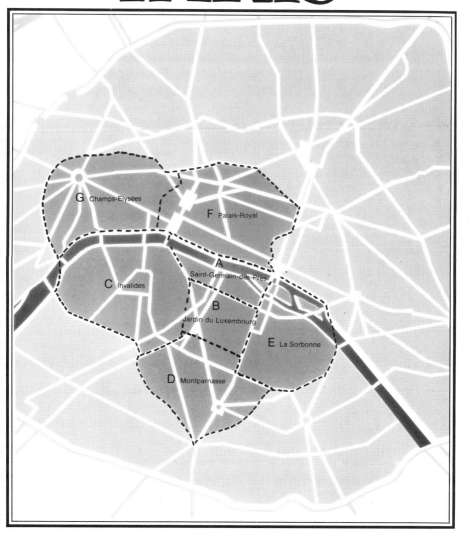

G Champs-Elysées

F Palais-Royal

A Saint-Germain-des-Prés

C Invalides

B

Jardin du Luxembourg

E La Sorbonne

D Montparnasse

Rue de l'Abbé-Grégoire (6th) Map B

12 Hôtel Jumilhac. Little has changed since James Fenimore Cooper, his wife, and five children took an apartment on the third floor of this convent in late July 1826. The massive 17th-century doors still stand guard, while the original lock, weighing some twelve pounds, remains in use. The cobblestones in the front courtyard are a little more worn, but the chestnut trees in the spacious walled garden in the back continue to provide a charming panoply for the Sisters of St. Maur. A few days after his arrival, Cooper described the apartment in a letter to his sister Nancy:

> We have the whole of what you would call the third story, but which here is called *au seconde*—The two lower stories are a school, in which we have placed all the girls, at about $200 a year (apiece) each including board, washing and instruction—The school is genteel and I suppose as good as these places ever are— The children will be with us every night, and at any time in the day, that we may wish—Our *appartement*, consists of a *salle à manger*, about fifteen feet square, or perhaps 18—*an ante chambre, a Salon*, a *cabinet* or library, and two bed rooms, with a kitchen, all on the same floor—There is also a considerable garden to walk in—We pay for these rooms furnished genteelly, about $600 a year—This is the manner that all people of a certain sort, live in Paris, who are not very affluent—A French Duke might live in our Appartement, for instance—Our Predecessor is a Baron, who lets me the rooms, and takes a pavillion in the garden for himself—There is an unaccountable mixture of gentility and meanness, of tawdriness and dirt, in all that I have yet seen in France—Adieu.

The school run by L'Ordre de l'Enfant Jésus des Dames de St. Maur, under the guidance of Mother Liégault, had been open only two years when the Cooper children were enrolled. (Today, Mother Liégault's portrait looks down on the nuns and their students from the wall of the refectory.)

Cooper's *The Last of the Mohicans,* published early in 1826, was already popular in Europe and had established him, at age 37, as the first American writer to be recognized in France. This gave him entrée into French society.

In a letter to a friend written in his usual casual and conversational tone, Cooper described how, on the morning of 3 November 1826, he received an unexpected visitor:

Well, about a week ago I was descending the stairs of our hotel, which you know are common property to everybody that inhabits the building, when I met an old man ascending, as I thought, with a good deal of difficulty. There was a carriage in the court, and from something in his countenance as well as from his air and the circumstance of the coach, I thought he was coming to see me. Indeed, I fancied I knew the face, though I could not remember the name. We passed each other, looking hard and bowing, and I was just going out of the door when the stranger suddenly stopped and said in French:

"Est-ce monsieur Cooper que j'ai l'honneur de voir?"

"Monsieur, je m'appelle Cooper."

"Je suis Walter Scott."

Here was an introduction for you! worth a thousand letters, or the most formal presentations. We shook hands. I expressed my thanks for the honor, and he passed an hour with me in my cabinet. I am delighted with him. He treated me like a younger brother and spoke in the kindest and most encouraging manner. The next two days I breakfasted with him. He then paid me another visit, and we met once more at the Princess Gallitzin's, who gave him a famous soiree.

Cooper would speak in his correspondence of returning to America after one year, but he soon began to feel at home in France and spent the next seven years in Europe, mainly in Paris.

Rue des Acacias (17th)

Elsa Maxwell, newspaper columnist and society hostess, teamed up with the British fashion designer Edward Molyneux and opened the nightclub "Les Acacias" in 1921. Nightclubs, or *boîtes* as they were called, did not enjoy respectability among Parisians at the time, but Elsa became the social overseer and the club soon became a highly fashionable spot, where international celebrities flocked because "everybody" went there. Clifton Webb and the Dolly Sisters, who created the "pony dance" (a popular society dance of the twenties), were the main performers. (House number unknown.)

Rue d'Aguesseau (8th) Métro: Champs-Elysées-Clemenceau

22   Hôtel de Mars. James Fenimore Cooper and family moved here on 1 September 1830 and stayed for four months. Political turmoil had enveloped France the previous month. King Charles X had fled to England and had been replaced by Louis-Philippe, known as the Bourgeois King. The most popular and perhaps most influential man in France at that moment was the aged Lafayette, who as commander of the revived National Guards, remained an idol of the Republicans. Among Lafayette's American friends was Cooper, who recorded in his *Journal* for 19 September 1830: "About 2 o'clock, Gen La Fayette came and sat with me some time." The two men discussed the new French constitution and Cooper's audience with Louis-Philippe, which was to take place that evening. Cooper continued in his *Journal:* "In the evening at 7 o'clock Gen La Fayette came for me in his carriage ... we then went to the Palais Royal to be presented." The king spoke to him with pleasure of his own visit to America using "courteous and unaffected language," as Cooper later recalled.

Quai Anatole-France (7th) Map A

7   Hôtel Palais d'Orsay. Lillian Farley, aged 22, and five other American girls, each 5 foot 10 and "thin, thin, thin," arrived in Paris in 1924. They were put up in this hotel with rooms overlooking the Seine by the French couturier Jean Patou. He brought the long-legged models over to challenge Coco Chanel's seeming monopoly of the American market. Patou felt that having Americans model his clothes in Paris would give potential buyers a better idea of how they would look. In any event it turned out to be a superb publicity stunt. As soon as the girls disembarked from *La Savoie* after an eight-day crossing they were met by a sea of French photographers. One photo shows the six girls in *cloches* and fur-trimmed hats, with a dapper Patou in spats, linking arms; another catches the six models on a park bench in the Tuileries with their legs crossed at the ankles and their feet, encased in Jazz Age T-straps, pointed in a perfect line. During the 1920s, the models would parade through the rooms of the salon which were absolutely silent except for a woman perched on a high stool who would announce the number of each outfit (there was no stage). Elsa Maxwell found the atmosphere dull and convinced Patou to set up the salon to resemble a nightclub. Tables seating three or four were placed in all the rooms, each with an ice bucket and a magnum of champagne. The 84-year-old Lillian Farley recalled: "We drank nothing but champagne—at the Ritz and at Harry's New York Bar." Evenings,

escorted by *comtes* and *vicomtes,* they headed for Le Jardin de ma Soeur, Bricktop's, or went to watch Josephine Baker at the Folies. At dawn they continued on to Montmartre, to Mitchell's for breakfast, or to Les Halles for onion soup. Asked if she ever got tired, Lillian Farley smiled and asked: "Tired? When you're twenty-two, and the toast of Paris?"

9   Palais de la Légion d'honneur, formerly Hôtel de Salm. This building, which was to have a powerful influence on American architecture, was being finished when Thomas Jefferson arrived in Paris in 1784. The American minister was "violently smitten" with it. The *hôtel* possessed two fronts. The one facing the river Jefferson admired from the terrace of the Jardin des Tuileries. The other looked out on Rue de Lille. At number 123 stood Lafayette's home, from which Jefferson, a frequent guest, could admire the building at closer range. The two fronts of the Hôtel de Salm were among those "celebrated fronts of modern buildings" which might serve as models for America, wrote Jefferson to the French architect Pierre L'Enfant, who later designed the new Federal City of Washington. One summer afternoon, Jefferson was delighted to show the building to fellow Americans Charles Bulfinch and John Trumbull. Bulfinch, a 21-year-old architect, went on to design University Hall at Harvard (1815) and, five years later, Massachusetts General Hospital. John Trumbull, aged 30, was already an accomplished painter (*The Surrender of General Burgoyne at Saratoga,* 1832, Yale University Art Gallery, New Haven, Conn.) and was greatly admired by Jefferson. All three men were influenced by this magnificent example of French neoclassical architecture; Jefferson in his designs for Monticello; Bulfinch in his James Swan House in Boston (1796); and Trumbull in his plans for buildings in his birthplace of Lebanon, Connecticut. When Bulfinch completed the Capitol in Washington (1818-1830), an aging Trumbull received his long-cherished commission to do four paintings for the Capitol rotunda. Trumbull had seen the rotunda as a place to hang and highlight his massive historical paintings. To this end, in 1817 he submitted plans for such a building, but it was Bulfinch's design which prevailed. In November 1826 Trumbull's four paintings were completed and installed.

Early in the 19th century, the Hôtel de Salm was acquired by the Grande Chancellerie de la Légion d'honneur. Names and portraits of Americans who have received this decoration are displayed on the top floor. This museum is open to the public.

Rue de l'Ancienne-Comédie (6th) Map A

13 Café Procope. The oldest café in Paris was opened in 1670 by a Sicilian, Francesco Procopio dei Coltelli. Its success was assured when, in 1689, the Comédie Française opened its new theater opposite at number 14, hence the name of the street. Frequented by actors, theatergoers, critics, writers, and chess players, it became one of the most famous Parisian cafés in the 18th century. Its clientele included Voltaire, Rousseau, Benjamin Franklin, Thomas Jefferson, John Paul Jones, and Henry Wadsworth Longfellow. Diderot and D'Alembert agreed upon the publication of the monumental *Encyclopédie* at this café, and on the evening of 27 April 1784 Beaumarchais anxiously awaited the reaction to his new comedy *The Marriage of Figaro*. During the French Revolution, Danton, Marat, and Camille Desmoulins met here, while in the era of Romanticism George Sand, Musset, Gautier, and Balzac were seen at its tables.

In 1832, 30-year-old Ralph Waldo Emerson was a frequent patron, recording in his *Journal:* "The cafés are not to be forgotten, filled with newspapers, blazing with light.... One in Paris who would keep himself up with events must read every day about twelve newspapers of the two hundred that are printed here." The following year another Bostonian, 24-year-old Oliver Wendell Holmes (father of the future chief justice), arrived in Paris to study medicine. Like most students, he was an habitué of the cafés of the Left Bank. Half a century later, retired as dean of the Harvard Medical School, he came back to Paris on a sentimental trip, and recorded:

> I entered the café, which was nearly or quite empty, the usual breakfast hour being past. "Garçon! Une tasse de café." "Cinq sous," was his answer. By the laws of sentiment, I ought to have made the ignoble sum five francs, at least. But if I had done so, the waiter would undoubtedly have thought I had just come from Charenton [French insane asylum]. Besides, why should I violate the simple habits and traditions of the place, where generation after generation of poor students and threadbare Bohemians had taken their morning coffee and pocketed their two lumps of

sugar? It was with a feeling of virile sanity and Roman self-conquest that I paid my five sous, with the small additional fraction which I supposed the waiter to expect, and no more.

Holmes sat and reminisced about the golden days of the two years he had spent in Paris, and particularly about his first breakfast taken at a café:

> Paris as seen by the morning sun of three or four and twenty and Paris in the twilight of the superfluous decade cannot be expected to look exactly alike. I well remember my first breakfast at a Parisian café in the spring of 1833. It was in the Place de la Bourse, on a beautiful sunshiny morning. The coffee was nectar, the *flûte* [French bread] was ambrosia, the *brioche* [cake] was more than good enough for the Olympians. Such an experience could not repeat itself fifty years later....Nothing looked more nearly the same as of old than the bridges. The Pont Neuf did not seem to me altered. Though we had read in the papers that it was in ruins or seriously injured in consequence of a great flood. The statues had been removed from the Pont Royal, one or two new bridges had been built, but all was natural enough, and I was tempted to look for the old woman, at the end of the Pont des Arts, who used to sell me a bunch of violets for two or three sous—such as would cost me a quarter of a dollar in Boston. I did not see the three objects which a popular saying alleges are always to be met on the Pont Neuf: a priest, a soldier, and a white horse.

Quai d'Anjou (4th) Map E

29   Using a hand printing press with a full series of Caslon type, William Bird set up his Three Mountains Press here in 1922. He took the name from Psalm 121, "Levavi oculos meos in montes" (I shall lift mine eyes unto the hills) and the three hills of Paris: Ste Geneviève, Montmartre, and Montparnasse. Bird asked Ezra Pound to be his editor. They announced their series, in editions limited to 300 or less, as a "manifest of the present state of English prose." The first book was Pound's *Indiscretions,* which appeared in March 1923. It was an autobiography of the author's first sixteen years, and added little to the "present state of English prose." This was followed by Ford Madox Ford's *Women and Men,* which appeared with a label pasted onto the title page reading "Contact Editions, 29 Quai d'Anjou, Paris." Contact Editions was the plaything of Robert McAlmon, who moved his publishing house here from Rue de l'Odéon and took over the floor above Bird.

In 1924, Bird printed *In Our Time* by Ernest Hemingway, with a run of 170 perfect copies and 50 flawed copies, which Bird gave to Hemingway to send out for review. Happily, Bird placed much more importance on the quality of the book he printed than on profits, for there were none. A small edition of Pound's *XVI Cantos* was followed by *Distinguished Air,* three short stories by McAlmon. Bird abandoned publishing in 1929.

37   John Dos Passos, who had just returned to France with his friend E.E. Cummings, rented an upstairs room at this address in 1921. Dos Passos's first successful novel, *Three Soldiers,* was about to appear in New York after rejections by fourteen publishers.

Rue Antoine-Bourdelle (15th)   Map D

16   Montparnasse had become popular with artists by the 1870s and in time replaced Montmartre. This street was opened in 1913 and received its present name after the death of French sculptor Antoine Bourdelle, who had his studio here. This studio is now a museum and well worth a visit. In 1878, American sculptor Augustus St. Gaudens also had a studio on this street. After the First World War another American sculptor, Jo Davidson, took a studio nearby on Avenue du Maine. He had an atelier on Rue Antoine-Bourdelle for stonecutting and dropped in frequently at Bourdelle's studio.

Brooklyn-born Frederick William MacMonnies had his studio at this address. He studied with St. Gaudens in New York and then with Falguière in Paris. His fountain for the Court of Honor at the World's Columbian Exposition in Chicago in 1893 had made him famous. A young American girl by the name of Janet Scudder had come to the fair, seen the fountain, and decided there and then that this was the man with whom she wished to study. One year later he took her on as an assistant in his studio in Paris while he worked on *Victory* for the battle monument at West Point and *Bacchante* for the Luxembourg Gardens. Scudder went on to become a major sculptress. Her fountains, garden figures, and playful children grace the collections of the Metropolitan Museum, New York *(Frog Fountain),* the Peabody Institute, Baltimore *(Tortoise Fountain),* the Art Institute, Chicago *(Fighting Boy Fountain),* and those of many private estates.

Place d'Anvers (9th)

This square, created in 1871, covers what used to be the *abattoir de Montmartre,* in use from 1809 until 1867, when it was pulled down. In 1837, Dr. Willard Parker of New Hampshire, who was in Paris studying surgical techniques, visited the slaughterhouse. He noted in his *Journal:*

> We visited one of the Abatoires of this City. There are 4 of these establishments which belong to the city. They are magnificent slaughter houses—we went through the Abat. de Mont Martre— It is 389 yards long—140 broad. Altho the day has been excessively hot the whole establishment was perfectly sweet. 100 oxen 3 or 400 Calves—1000 or more sheep killed every week. There are compartments where the animals are kept. Fountains are so arranged that water passes through & washes at pleasure. We may take a good lesson here.

Rue d'Arsonval (15th)

(7)   In 1907, sculptor Jo Davidson took a studio at this address. He purchased furniture for 50 francs and was given his kitchen utensils by the famous anarchist Emma Goldman. He enrolled in the Ecole des Beaux-Arts. One evening at the Café du Dôme Davidson met an American who agreed to pose for him. He was John Marin, who was to become famous as a painter of Maine landscapes and New York City skylines.

Rue d'Assas (6th) Maps B & D

59   Lycée Montaigne. Forty-seven boy scouts from California spent a week at the Lycée in June 1913. They were interviewed by a reporter from *Le Figaro* who recorded their impressions, which were typical of the many American tourists who came to Paris in the early part of this century. They admired the Eiffel Tower, the politeness of the Parisian gendarmes, the uniformity of the six-floor apartment houses, the red trousers of the soldiers, the French bread or *baguette,* and the three knocks announcing the beginning of a play.

(84)   Painter George Biddle, who had come to France in 1911 to study, took a studio here. He recalled in *An American Artist's Story* a party with Soutine as guest of honor. Chagall, Léger, Marsden Hartley, Jules Pascin, and Chana Orloff were also present.

116   Painter Thomas Eakins moved here in summer 1868, but kept his studio on nearby Rue de l'Ouest. Eakins felt that he had nothing more to learn from Jean-Léon Gérôme, with whom he had studied the previous year at the Ecole des Beaux-Arts, and he moved to the atelier of Léon Bonnat. Eakins left Paris in June 1870, after four years in Europe.

Rue Auguste-Bartholdi (15th) Métro: Dupleix

2   During his first winter in Paris in 1930, Henry Miller came close to starving. Sleeping in a different place nightly, cadging meals whenever possible, he chanced upon Richard Osborn, an American lawyer, who gave him a free room in his apartment. It was a seventh-floor walk-up with 129 steps, wrote Miller, overlooking the Eiffel Tower. Each morning Osborn left ten francs on the kitchen table. When he came home in the evening in their place he found Miller's writing for the day. One evening he found a review of Luis Buñuel's film *L'Age d'or,* which he passed on to Anaïs Nin. It was this which led to a long friendship between Miller and Nin.

Quai d'Austerlitz (13th) Métro: Gare d'Austerlitz

55   La Gare d'Austerlitz. At 7:30 a.m. on Tuesday, 3 July 1917, a train arrived bringing the Second Battalion of the Sixteenth Infantry Regiment, the first American soldiers to arrive in Paris. They were greeted by a crowd of 50,000. On the following morning, American Independence Day, they assembled in the courtyard of the Invalides and then marched to the cemetery in Rue de Picpus, where General Pershing gave a speech at Lafayette's tomb. That evening there was a banquet for 400 men at the Palais d'Orsay, followed by a gala performance at the Comédie Française. On 5 July, a large crowd gathered at the Gare de l'Est to see the first American contingent leave for the front.

Rue d'Auteuil (16th) Métro: Michel Ange-Auteuil

43-47   Hôtel Antier ou des demoiselles de Verrières. This elegant mansion with its spacious courtyard and garden has changed little since the John Adams family moved in during the first week of September 1784. Adams was accompanied by his wife Abigail and their two grown children, Nabby and John Quincy. It was a large, imposing, comfortable mansion, but with its 30 bedrooms and several odd apartments, it was a housekeeper's nightmare. Red tile floors in France could not be cleaned with water. A manservant, called *un frotteur* (from the verb *frotter,* to rub), was employed to whirl around the rooms with brushes strapped to his feet, "dancing here and there like a Merry Andrew," wrote Abigail. Worst of all were the number of servants who had to be employed. "Each servant," she said, "has a certain etiquette and one will by no means intrude upon the department of the other." The cook would not conceive of rinsing a dish; the coiffeuse would not consider dusting a bedroom. Two American domestics did whatever the six French staff refused to do.

The Hôtel Antier, with eight servants, horses, and two carriages, was expensive to maintain. Adams requested larger allowances for American representatives overseas, and told Congress that foreigners were not concerned whether he was "qualified for his office but how many domestics and horses" he could afford. When the Dutch minister called on him, he arrived in a coach drawn by six horses and attended by five liveried servants. But John and Abigail were happy here, for they were finally living together after years of separation while John had been a United States representative in Europe.

The Adamses' first American visitors were Thomas Jefferson and his daughter, followed by the dashing young naval officer John Paul Jones. On 23 September 1779, Jones, commanding the *Bonhomme Richard,* had taken on the British frigate H.M.S *Serapis* mounting 50 guns. After two hours of deadly fighting, the British captain called out, "Has your ship struck?" to which Jones replied: "I have not yet begun to fight." Ninety minutes later, the British ship surrendered, but not before 150 of Jones's crew were dead or wounded. Feted in Paris, decorated by Louis XVI, his bust modeled by Houdon, his handsome figure did not go unnoticed by the ladies, both French and American. But it was Abigail who, in a letter to her sister some years later, left us the best picture of the American naval hero:

> From the intrepid character he justly supported in the American Navy, I expected to have seen a rough, stout, warlike Roman— instead of that I should sooner think of wrapping him up in cotton

wool and putting him in my pocket, than sending him to contend with cannon balls. He is of small stature, well proportioned, soft in his speech, easy in his address, polite in his manner, vastly civil, understands all the etiquette of a lady's toilette as perfectly as he does the mast, sails and rigging of his ship. Under all this appearance of softness he is bold, enterprising, ambitious and active. He has been here often and dined with us several times; he is said to be a man of gallantry and a favorite amongst the French ladies, whom he is frequently commending for the neatness of their persons, their easy manners and their taste in dress. He knows how often the ladies use baths, what color best suits a lady's complexion, what cosmetics are most favorable to the skin.

Other houseguests included William Bingham, who had made his fortune in the West Indies as a military-supply agent in the American Revolution. He was accompanied by the new Mrs. Bingham, a 16-year-old American beauty. The couple typified the new class of socially ambitious Americans, buying antiques, commissioning portraits, and above all, seeking introductions to the royal courts of Europe.

The Adamses, in spite of their staid New England backgrounds, thoroughly enjoyed the latest fads in Paris during the summer of 1784. They went to the gardens of the Tuileries, where they watched the Montgolfier brothers disappear above the rooftops of Paris in their great, egg-shaped, silk-taffeta balloon. At the Comédie Française they saw the newest comedy in Paris, *The Marriage of Figaro* by Caron de Beaumarchais. Although John found it to be "a piece of studied deception and intrigue" (i.e., typically French), Abigail was seduced by its charm, and both admitted that the talent of the French lay in masking the scandalous with gaiety and laughter.

Less amusing were Beaumarchais's repeated requests to be paid for military supplies he had had shipped to America between 1776 and 1778. Adams wisely avoided this issue and left it to the new American minister, Thomas Jefferson.

The Adamses were delighted with their large garden and its fine views. John could stride through "his woods," the Bois de Boulogne, or walk the mile to Passy to see, if he had to, Benjamin Franklin. But he was thrilled by his new appointment as the first American ambassador to the Court of St. James. The news, which he had so long awaited, arrived in spring 1785. Upon leaving France, Adams confided to a friend: "What shall I do in London for *my* garden, *my* park, *my* river, and *my* plain? You see I call all the environs of Auteuil mine, and with good reason, for I will lay a wager they have given me more pleasure in the last nine months than they ever afforded their legal and royal proprietors for a century." A plaque on the front of this *hôtel,* which is a historical monument, commemorates the sojourn here of the Adams family.

Rue du Bac (7th) Maps A & C

44   Sculptor Jo Davidson lived here in the 1920s and had a studio on Avenue du Maine.

Archibald MacLeish bought an apartment in this house in 1927. The following spring, the author of *The Hamlet of A. MacLeish* set about decorating his apartment. He had barely finished, when he decided to take his family back home after five years in Europe. It seems to have been much aggravation for nothing. As he told his friend, the publisher Harry Crosby, "we sold the goddam aptmt."

(102)   In 1795, Joel Barlow, writer and diplomat, and his wife moved into the pension of *la citoyenne Hilaire.* They were joined by their friend Robert Fulton. It was from this address on 13 December 1797 that Fulton submitted to the French government his plan to build a submarine. War had broken out between France and England, and Fulton began, "Considering the great importance of diminishing the Power of the British Fleets, I have contemplated the Construction of a Mechanical Nautilus. A Machine which flatters me with much hope of being able to Annihilate their Navy." The six paragraphs that followed this optimistic opening dealt with costs, compensation, and practical application of the submarine. He asked for 400 francs per gun for each British ship over 40 guns sunk by his submarine, and 12,000 francs for ships under 40 guns. As an American citizen he also asked the French to agree never to use his invention against the American fleet.

At 11:00 a.m. on 2 August 1798, a commission of French experts called on Fulton on Rue du Bac to examine his project. Their report was encouraging and he received permission to go ahead with his underwater ship, but at his own expense. Finally, on the afternoon of 13 June 1800, a small group of scientists and one cabinet minister gathered on the bank of the Seine, close to the Perier brothers' steam pump (opposite 2 Quai de New York), and watched the river intently. After 45 minutes a metallic hump broke the surface, and when the top opened, out stepped Robert Fulton and two sailors. Monsieur Forfait, minister of the navy, wrote to Napoleon to say that "their faces showed no alteration" and that the American invention, while still far from perfect, showed great promise. Fulton had already spent 28,000 francs of his own money, earned from his patent on the Passage des Panoramas, and Napoleon agreed to an advance payment of 10,000 francs. The *Nautilus* was tried out by Fulton and Barlow the following month at Le Havre. There had been so much publicity during its trials that when it was finally ready to attack the British fleet blockading the port, the British simply put out to sea. The attack never took place and Napoleon promptly branded Fulton just another money-seeking adventurer.

110   In 1893, James McNeill Whistler lived here with his wife Trixie. The portrait *The Artist's Mother* had been purchased by the French government upon the advice of Clemenceau and was on display at the Musée du Luxembourg in Paris. Whistler was famous and had been made an Officier de la Légion d'honneur. His ground-floor apartment with its blue-and-white door was spacious, and opened onto a bright little courtyard. In the rear lay a large, tree-shaded garden where in the summer Whistler's guests included Manet, Toulouse-Lautrec, Degas, Mallarmé, Beardsley, and Henry James. The apartment today is much the same as in Whistler's time. It is approached through a *porte-cochère* (carriage entrance) and a long, dark passageway with a disused drinking fountain on the left. This leads to the small, attractive courtyard in front of the house.

Rue Ballu (9th) Métro: Place de Clichy

36   For over half a century, American students of music came to this modest apartment building to study with Nadia Boulanger, who lived on the fourth floor. One of the foremost teachers of composition in France, she exerted a major influence on contemporary American music. Aaron Copland, for instance, arrived in Paris in June 1921 to study at the American School of Music in Fontainebleau. He spent the summer making an important decision. Should he or should he not study under a woman the following year? "No one to my knowledge had ever before thought of studying composition with a woman," wrote Copland. "Everyone knows that the world has never produced a first-rate woman composer; so it follows that no woman could possibly hope to teach composition." But the most bothersome question for the 21-year-old Copland that summer was, how would it sound to the folks back home? Copland took the plunge and became one of the first of Nadia Boulanger's American students. He was soon joined by Melville Smith, Virgil Thomson, Elliot Carter, Walter Piston, and Roger Sessions.

In Boulanger's apartment her students found a chamber organ and two grand pianos. Virgil Thomson described an individual lesson:

> The lessons take place with the teacher at the piano, the student in a chair at her right. She reads the score before her silently at first, then little by little begins to comment, spontaneously admiring here and there a detail of musical syntax or sound, expressing temporary reservations about another. Suddenly she will start playing (and perfectly, for she is a fabulous sight-reader) some passage that she needs to hear out loud or that she wishes the student to hear as illustration to her remarks.

Weekly gatherings on Wednesday afternoon were held by invitation only. Students listened to piano recitals and analyses of most modern scores of the time (Stravinsky, Schönberg, and Mahler). Students met Maurice Ravel, Igor Stravinsky, Albert Roussel, Darius Milhaud, Arthur Honegger, Francis Poulenc, and Georges Auric. Other visitors, including Paul Valéry and Paul Claudel, discussed the works of Mann, Gide, and Proust. Thus, 36 Rue Ballu provided more than a musical education for the young Americans of the twenties; it was a personal introduction to the culture of Western Europe.

In 1924, Aaron Copland, after three years of lessons with Nadia Boulanger, was given a farewell party at her apartment. Together they played a four-hand arrangement of *Grogh,* a ballet by Copland. The following year, she introduced his music in the United States by playing his Symphony for Organ and Orchestra.

Boulanger's second wave of American students, in the thirties and forties, included Robert Russell Bennett, Arthur Berger, Marc Blitzstein, Paul Bowles, Israel Citkowitz, David Diamond, Irving Fine, Ross Lee Finney, Alexei Haieff, John Lessard, Harold Shapero, Elie Siegmeister, Howard Swanson, Louise Talma, and John Vincent. Leonard Bernstein was a close friend and a frequent visitor of Nadia Boulanger, who died here in 1977 at the age of 92.

Boulevard des Batignolles (17th) Métro: Rome

23 Formerly Hôtel Fournet. The cast of *La Revue Nègre,* which was performing at the Théâtre des Champs-Elysées, lived at this hotel in November 1925. Josephine Baker, who had previously shared simple rooming-house accommodations, enjoyed a suite of two bedrooms, living room, and bath. Her companion, French poster artist Paul Colin, was appalled at her menagerie: a parakeet, a parrot, two baby rabbits, a snake, and a baby pig, all of whom shared the living space. The hotel management, however, was bewitched by Josephine and graciously accepted all her companions, human and four-footed.

Rue Bayen (17th) Métro: Ternes

28 Le Château de Ternes (Fondation Gombaud-Darnaud). During the Middle Ages the Bishop of Paris owned a farm on this site; its name on the manuscript deed was Villa Externa. Over the next 500 years, the word *externa* became *estern,* and finally Ternes (hence the nearby Place des Ternes). The present château was built in 1718 and abandoned by its owners during the French Revolution. Richard Codman, a merchant from Boston, bought the château in about 1800 and restored it. He replaced the statues in the park, which had been smashed by the Paris mobs, and planted Scotch pines and red cedars, some of which can still be seen today. Like any good New Englander, he planted a kitchen garden and an orchard, and laid out flower beds.

Codman was among those enterprising American merchants, frequently wealthy sea captains, who came to France around 1795 and made their fortunes during the next decade. Thanks to the war between France and England, the Americans exported desperately needed wheat and other food supplies and imported wines and superb French furniture, much of it from abandoned châteaux. During these troubled years, the French government began to print paper money *assignats,* which soon lost value as inflation grew. The collapse of a paper currency was new in France, but since the Americans had already seen their own currency collapse toward the end of the American Revolution, they profited handsomely by buying with *assignats* and selling against hard money, that is, gold or silver.

Rue de Beaujolais (1st) Map F

15 Formerly Hôtel Beaujolais. Margaret Anderson, editor of the *Little Review,* moved to France in 1923 and lived in a room overlooking the gardens of the Palais-Royal. In 1920, the U.S. Post Office had burned four issues of the review containing excerpts from James Joyce's *Ulysses.* Anderson was fined and fingerprinted for publishing obscene matter.

In 1917, Sylvia Beach and her actress sister Cyprian took rooms here for the summer. Their windows overlooked Rodin's statue of Victor Hugo in the gardens of the Palais-Royal.

Boulevard Beaumarchais (11th)

(2-20)   Site of the magnificent Italianate private house of French dramatist Caron de Beaumarchais. Built in 1787 at a cost of 1,660,000 francs, the mansion had grounds of 6,000 square meters and was a Paris showplace.

It was here that part of what became known as the XYZ affair took place. In 1797, John Adams, president of the United States, alarmed at the French refusal to receive the American minister, Charles Cotesworth Pinckney, decided to send two additional envoys to Paris to convince the French of the seriousness of the American peace mission. Both countries had been seizing each other's ships in the West Indies. John Marshall, a lawyer from Virginia and future chief justice, and Elbridge Gerry, future governor of Massachusetts, were selected as envoys. During their first week in Paris, in October 1797, the three Americans asked for a meeting with the new French foreign minister, Talleyrand. They were well received, but a week later when Pinckney met with Talleyrand's representative he was told that the negotiations could not continue unless the American agreed to slip 50,000 pounds sterling into the foreign minister's pocket. Pinckney could not believe his ears, but two additional representatives confirmed the request. (In their letters to Congress, the American envoys designated the three Frenchmen as XYZ.) On 7 November Beaumarchais wrote to John Marshall, stating that he was delighted to learn of his presence in Paris and inviting the three Americans to dinner in his splendid home. (Marshall had represented Beaumarchais in his suit against the state of Virginia for 150,000 pounds sterling for arms which Beaumarchais had shipped to Virginia during the War of Independence, and which remained unpaid twenty years later.) After an excellent dinner, Beaumarchais assured his American guests that they should not be so concerned over the payment of 50,000 pounds, and that if awarded his claim against the state of Virginia, which was about to be decided on appeal, he would sacrifice 50,000 pounds sterling and thus the American envoys could line Talleyrand's pockets at no cost whatsoever to the American government. For John Marshall, it was a delicate evening, and he confided his thoughts and misgivings to his *Journal*. In his entry for 17 December 1797, he noted that they might agree to such a payment, but only in exchange for a "full and entire recognition of the claims of our citizens." This was in stark contrast to Pinckney's alleged reply to the request for a bribe, which was quoted extensively in America: "No, no, not a sixpence." But nothing came of these negotiations and in summer 1798, the three envoys returned home. Beaumarchais's claims for reimbursement for supplies shipped to America during the War of Independence were settled by Congress in 1832, 33 years after the dramatist's death

Rue de Beaune (7th) Map A

7   Formerly Hôtel de France et de Lorraine. One evening in early November 1872, Henry James left his lodgings on the Right Bank and walked across the Pont Royal to this hotel. The river, he noted, was at flood level and looked like "a civilized Mississippi." He had come to call upon the Lowells, who were spending the winter at the Hôtel de France et de Lorraine. James Russell Lowell had published the *Bigelow Papers* and served as editor of the *Atlantic Monthly* while teaching at Harvard. In the Lowells' sitting room James discovered Ralph Waldo Emerson and his daughter Ellen, who were also staying in the hotel before going on to Italy and Egypt. It was, he wrote, "a little Cambridge by the Seine." The two men agreed to visit the Louvre and spent two hours there on the morning of 19 November. They enjoyed the paintings as much as one another's company and Ellen Emerson wrote to Concord, "Father came home delighted." James derived less pleasure from a similar visit a few weeks later with art historian Charles Eliot Norton, recording that Norton "takes art altogether too hard for me to follow him." During November and December it rained

constantly, but this did not prevent the 29-year-old James and the 53-year-old Lowell from taking ten-mile walks through the city, browsing through the bookstores and along the quays. Lowell, a true Yankee, took delight, noted James, in driving bargains with the antiquarians.

9   Hôtel Elysée. Ezra Pound lived at the Elysée with his English wife Dorothy Shakespear in summer 1920. He had recently met James Joyce in Sirmione, Italy, and had persuaded the author of *A Portrait of the Artist as a Young Man* to leave Trieste and settle in Paris. When Joyce and his family arrived in July, Pound found them lodgings nearby in a private hotel at 9 Rue de l'Université, which reminded Joyce of Dublin.

Rue des Beaux-Arts (6th) Map A

13   L'Hôtel, formerly Hôtel d'Alsace. Thomas Wolfe, 25, took up residence in this hotel in 1925. He had come to Paris "to settle down and write." This year in Paris provided material for his semiautobiographical novel *Of Time and the River* (1935), published as a sequel to *Look Homeward, Angel.* Wolfe, like many Americans in Paris, used the Morgan Guaranty Trust as his mailing address. As a result his real Paris address eluded this writer until he came across Chapter LXVII in *Of Time and the River,* which begins: "That was a fine life that he [the protagonist] had that year. He lived in a little hotel in the Rue des Beaux-Arts. He had a good room there which cost him twelve francs a day. It was a good hotel, and was the place where Oscar Wilde had died." This was the clue which identified this small hotel on a well-known street rich in such hotels. Indeed, Oscar Wilde moved here in 1899, after his imprisonment in Reading Jail, England. He died in this hotel the following year, commenting, "I am dying beyond my means."

Rue Benjamin-Godard (16th) Métro: Pompe

5   Edna St. Vincent Millay spent the month of June 1932 at this address. She was delighted to discover her friend Mary Kennedy living "just around the corner." Both women went to Natalie Clifford Barney's salon on Rue Jacob. Millay had just published *Fatal Interview,* a sonnet cycle in the Elizabethan manner.

Rue de Berne (8th) Métro: Rome

20   Virgil Thomson arrived in France as a member of the Harvard Glee Club in June 1921. In the fall, he moved to Rue de Berne and spent the year studying with Nadia Boulanger. His modest fifth-floor room had its advantages, for his neighbors were mainly *filles de joie*. "I valued its freedom to make music at night," wrote Thomson later, "when my neighbors were out, dining late or dancing, love-time for kept girls being afternoon." His room contained a grand piano, "mounted on blocks and fitted with organ pedals." Thomson continued: "This I had procured on hire; and at this I worked out fugues by Bach, perfected later in practice at church. Here too, since the leg supporting blocks that gave room for the pedal keyboard also raised the height, I used to compose or write counterpoint standing up, using for a desk the piano's level top."

Thomson returned to Harvard in fall 1922, but came back to Paris and to this room in 1925, saying that if he were going to starve to death, he preferred to starve where the food was good. By 1926, his skill as a pianist was appreciated, and among the guests who came to hear him were Gertrude Stein and Alice B. Toklas. Gertrude Stein later found Thomson an apartment on the Quai Voltaire, where he moved in 1927.

Rue de Berri (8th) Map G

(1)   Thomas Jefferson took up residence at the Hôtel de Langeac on 17 October 1785. The *hôtel* was situated on the corner of Rue des Champs-Elysées (today number 92), just within the city walls at the Grille de Chaillot or city gate. Jefferson had arrived one year earlier to join Benjamin Franklin and John Adams in the negotiation of trade treaties with the European powers. In 1785, he succeeded Franklin as minister to France. He noted that the usual question put to him in his new role was: "C'est vous, Monsieur, qui remplacez le Docteur Franklin?" "I generally answered," wrote Jefferson, "that no one can replace him, Sir, I am only his successor." His new position required a residence large enough in which to entertain. Designed by the eminent architect Jean Chalgrin, the *hôtel* had barely been completed when Jefferson, its first tenant, moved in. The rent was 7,500 livres per year, unfurnished. A larger staff was required than in his previous residence on Rue Taitbout, and he added a coachman, a gardener, and an additional cook.

Besides many official visitors, Jefferson received French veterans of the American Revolution inquiring about back pay owed to them by a reluctant Congress. He also received American seamen stranded abroad, Europeans anxious to settle in the New World, inventors wishing to sell their ideas to America, American travellers who needed letters of introduction, and the inevitable artists and authors who imagined their work would be better appreciated in the land of liberty than in France. They were long but interesting days, and Jefferson passed his 42nd to his 46th year here.

One of his great joys was the large garden of the Hôtel de Langeac. "I cultivate in my garden," he wrote, "Indian corn for the use of my own table, to eat green in our manner." He asked Colonel Nicholas Lewis of Albemarle, North Carolina, to send him an ear of the "small ripe corn we call hominy corn," as well as seeds of the common sweet potato, watermelon, canteloupe, and acorns of all sorts.

Jefferson loved to walk and noted that in fair weather he covered four to five miles a day. From his house he observed that it was "820 double steps" down the Champs-Elysées to the statue of Louis XV in the middle of Place Louis XV (today Place de la Concorde, where the statue has been replaced by the Obelisk).

One of Jefferson's favorite guests was the young painter John Trumbull, son of the governor of Connecticut. They had met for the first time in March 1786 in London. Jefferson was interested in Trumbull's "national work" commemorating the great events of the American Revolution, and invited him to come to Paris and "to make his house his home." Later that summer, with the "information and advice" of his host, Trumbull began his *Declaration of Independence* (Yale University Art Gallery, New Haven, Conn.), a work he completed eleven years later. For two months, beginning in December 1787, Trumbull worked on *The Surrender of Cornwallis at Yorktown*. Generals Rochambeau and Chastellux and Admirals de Grasse and Barras, all veterans of the War of Independence, sat for him in Jefferson's home.

7   Hôtel Lancaster. Helen Keller arrived here on 28 January 1937 and stayed for four days. She had come for the unveiling of Gutzon Borglum's statue of Thomas Paine, but this was delayed and the sculptor accompanied her instead on a memorable visit to the Rodin Museum.

☙

John Steinbeck stayed here upon his arrival from Spain in May 1954. He spent two weeks seeking "a pretty little house right in the center of Paris," and found it nearby on Avenue de Marigny.

Boulevard Berthier (17th)

(41)   John Singer Sargent took a small house here early in 1884. At the time, only the east side of the boulevard had been built up, which ensured sunlight for his new studio. At his studio on Rue Notre-Dame-des-Champs his increasingly wealthy clientele had been forced to climb five flights of dark stairs, but here carriages had room to stop and wait. He hired a cook and an Italian servant.

The rent was 3,000 francs a year, three times that of his former studio, but Sargent was certain he would become one of the most famous portrait painters in Paris. After all, his teacher Carolus-Duran had become famous overnight with his portrait of *The Lady with the Glove*. Sargent's portrait of the famous and beautiful Madame Gautreau was already being talked about, though it had yet to appear in the Salon of that year.

The exhibition opened on Sunday, 1 May, in the vast Palais des Champs-Elysées. The day was clear and warm and by 5:00 p.m. there had been some 12,000 visitors. The portrait of Madame Gautreau (listed as the *Portrait of Madame "X"*) drew crowds. Sargent had laid bare her beauty and had revealed her subtle but extensive use of make-up. In a word, she had been exposed. In front of the portrait her rivals finally had the chance to express their malice in public. At the end of the afternoon, Madame Gautreau and her mother turned up at Sargent's new studio demanding that the portrait be withdrawn. The scene was humiliating, with the mother crying that her daughter was ruined and had become the laughing stock of Paris. Sargent, barely controlling his temper, pointed out that no picture once exhibited could be withdrawn. It remained on display for two weeks.

Sargent spent the summer in the country and returned to Paris in the fall, full of confidence. But no new commissions came. In lieu of paying the rent, he painted his landlord's daughter and next the landlord's wife. Finally he upped and left for England; his ten years in France were over. Within a short time in London he was to know fame and fortune. Today, the *Portrait of Madame "X"* hangs in the Metropolitan Museum in New York.

Numbers 43, 45, and 47 remain three-story houses with ateliers on the top floor.

Quai de Béthune (4th) Map E

24 In 1930 Helena Rubinstein bought one of the most beautiful *hôtels particuliers* on Ile St.-Louis. Built in 1642, it had enjoyed an illustrious succession of owners beginning with Denys Hasselin, director of the Royal Ballet. It took Miss Rubinstein five years to evict her tenants before she tore down the *hôtel* in 1935. She replaced it with an art deco building topped with a roof garden complete with fountains, cascades, flower beds, and evergreens. She lived in the top flat on the rare occasions she visited Paris. (The original front door has been saved.)

Rue du Boccador (8th) Map G

24 Theodore H. White lived at this address from 1948 until 1953. White had been chief of the China bureau of *Time* (1939-45) and had published *Thunder Out of China* (1946). He left *Time* in order to finish a novel about World War II. Much of *The Mountain Road* (1958, Pulitzer Prize) was written on Rue du Boccador.

This was a lively apartment house with a constant flow of journalists, novelists, French starlets (including Brigitte Bardot), and, as Irwin Shaw who also lived here wrote, "aspiring Ivy League writers who later turned out to be CIA agents but who didn't let it spoil their fun." Shaw's novel *The Young Lions* (1948) had made him the most affluent of the Americans in this handsome five-story building.

The house also sheltered Art Buchwald, who was writing the "Paris after Dark" column for the *Herald Tribune*. From his studio on the fifth floor Buchwald had merely to step out onto the balcony and tap on the window of the studio next door to take tea with his charming young neighbor Ann McGarry, whom he later married.

The building was owned by two elderly French ladies and managed by their nephew. In true French fashion many modes of life were permitted, but there was one rule. The elevator could be used for going up but never for coming down. Spot checks were made when the owners heard "the sorrowful creaking of the cables in the elevator shaft," recorded Shaw. Threats of legal action were among the lesser forms of reprimand. One day, Irwin Shaw and his wife took the elevator down, only to be confronted by the enraged nephew, who was waiting on the ground floor. Before the nephew could finish his tirade, Shaw interrupted him to show him his wife's leg which was in a cast, the result of a skiing accident. The nephew apologized. The following week Shaw's rent was raised. When he objected, the nephew said that he would go to a lawyer and Shaw countered with the same threat. If their lawyers reached a satisfactory compromise, added the nephew, he would ask Shaw to do him the honor of autographing a copy of his latest book.

Place Boieldieu (2nd) Map F

L'Opéra Comique. The present playhouse dates from 1898. On the evening of 13 April 1900, a packed house was listening to *Louise* by Gustave Charpentier, when suddenly, after the second act, the diva was unable to continue. Her understudy was a 23-year-old American soprano who took over for the final act. Mary Garden's performance was hailed by the entire French press. She sang the role for the following 100 performances.

Two years later, the operatic event of the season was the premiere of Debussy's opera *Pelléas et Mélisande.* The librettist Maeterlinck had proposed his mistress Georgette Leblanc for the role of Mélisande. He withdrew all support when he learned that Mary Garden had been chosen to sing the role. Her performance was described by leading French critics as *merveilleux,* and she was seen as *idéalement belle.*

Mary Garden had begun at the Opéra Comique at a monthly salary of 250 francs (about 50 dollars). By 1907, the year she returned to New York's Manhattan Opera Company, she was earning 7,500 francs per month, a fortune at the time. In 1926, she returned to Paris from the Chicago Opera to sing a farewell performance of *Louise.*

Garden was followed in this role three years later by fellow American Grace Moore. After coaching from Gustave Charpentier, the young American soprano sang *Louise* but, although successful, she was never as popular as Mary Garden.

Bois-de-Boulogne (16th) Métro: Porte Dauphine

On 4 July 1865, the American consul general in France, John Bigelow, invited all American residents of Paris to a fête champêtre to celebrate the ending of the Civil War. The minister also hoped that the celebration would help heal the bitter divisions which had marked American society in Paris for the previous four years. As consul general, Bigelow had played an important part in helping swing French sentiment away from the Confederacy. The picnic was held in the Pré Catalan with "193 ladies, 227 gentlemen, 108 children and their nurses" present. While the elders chatted, young couples danced in the pavilion and the children watched a show by a wizard. After the meal, they all sang "The Star Spangled Banner" and then listened to a Mr. Home who recited a poem about Mobile Bay so eloquently that "ladies burst into tears and men tossed their hats in satisfaction." The day ended with a firework display. Above the tent floated a banner bearing an American eagle and Daniel Webster's motto, "The Union now and forever, one and inseparable."

Rue Boissy-d'Anglas (8th) Métro: Concorde

28 Formerly the nightclub Le Boeuf sur le toit. For the opening on 10 January 1922, Jean Cocteau gave a party at the club for Max Beerbohm, Marie Laurencin, Constantin Brancusi, Raymond Radiguet, and Pablo and Olga Picasso. For the next six years, Le Boeuf was the headquarters of the Paris avant-garde. The orchestra was led by black American saxophonist Vance Lowry, who introduced the music of Fletcher Henderson. Here, for the first time, the French heard the music of George Gershwin, Vincent Youmans, and Jerome Kern. Edmund Wilson described it in *Vanity Fair* as one of the centers of a new kind of music in France—jazz.

Rue Bonaparte (6th) Map A

9 Formerly Gosselin, bookseller and publisher. In October 1826, Gosselin agreed to pay James Fenimore Cooper 2,000 francs for rights to publish a French translation of *The Prairie*. He would ultimately translate and publish almost all of Cooper's work but paid royalties only from 1826 to 1833, while Cooper lived in Europe.

14   Ecole des Beaux-Arts. John Vanderlyn, who enrolled at the Beaux-Arts in 1796, was the first American painter of note to study here. The 21-year-old Vanderlyn was sent to Paris with funds provided by Aaron Burr, who had been particularly impressed by the young man's work and noted that Paris was the place for him "to cultivate his genius." Burr had been correct in selecting Vanderlyn, who later received a gold medal from Napoleon. Vanderlyn returned to America and became a successful portrait and historical painter.

Richard Morris Hunt was the first American to study architecture at the Ecole des Beaux-Arts. Hunt was born in 1827 in Brattleboro, Vermont, and arrived in Paris at the age of 16. He was accompanied by his mother, his brother William (destined to become a painter), and another brother John, who studied medicine in Paris and eventually settled there. Hunt began work in the atelier of the well-known French architect Hector Martin Lefuel. After two years of preparation, he was accepted at the Beaux Arts. The first year was spent in practical design work in nearby ateliers and at lectures in the school, which few students attended. There was no single style; the school stressed the principles of Renaissance classicism to solve the problems of modern architectural design. Every other month, students had to submit drawings for assigned projects; during alternate months, there were daylong competitions when students had twelve hours to turn out detailed drawings for a structure. The results were judged by jury: students were permitted to advance, repeat the exercise, or were dropped. Although Hunt won no prizes, he received several honorable mentions in the five and one-half years he spent here. After his return to the United States in 1855, Hunt became known for the mansions on Fifth Avenue he designed for the Vanderbilts and the Astors. Hunt had clearly been inspired by the châteaux of the Loire Valley, which he had visited and sketched.

Thomas Eakins's first day at the Ecole des Beaux-Arts was Monday, 29 October 1866. He was 22 and had spent the previous two years at the Pennsylvania Academy of Fine Arts. He was thrilled with the idea of working under Jean-Léon Gérôme, who was at the height of his fame and one of the most popular painters of the day. Augustus St. Gaudens, who came here the following year to study sculpture, recalled his excitement at seeing a Gérôme canvas in New York: "When, as a boy, I stopped evening after evening at Goupil's window on Broadway and adored Gérôme's *Death of Caesar.*" Eakins wrote to his sister that he was always at the school by 7:00 a.m., and that in November it got dark soon after he returned to his room on Rue Vaugirard.

If you come in the main entrance to the Beaux-Arts, turn right and pass through a doorway over which is marked "Ateliers d'Architecture et de Peinture." Here, on the first floor facing the Quay Malaquais, was Gérôme's atelier. It was large, accommodating some 70 students on six rows of wooden benches around the raised platform for the model. (Today, the room has seats for 35 students, including easels.) Young Eakins was impressed by his teacher: "Gérôme is very kind to me and has much patience because he knows I am trying to learn, and if I stay away he always asks after me." Eakins spent three years working in Gérôme's atelier, until he felt he had nothing more to learn. He moved on to work with Léon Bonnat and finally with sculptor Augustin Alexandre Dumont, whose statue *Blanche de Castille* was seen by everyone in the Luxembourg Gardens. Eakins visited Spain in 1869 and returned to Philadelphia the following year.

Julian Weir, whose father taught drawing at West Point, arrived in Paris in the summer of 1873 at the age of 21. He took rooms at 63 Rue de Seine and was accepted in Gérôme's atelier that October. He moved to 3 bis Rue des Beaux-Arts while studying at the Beaux-Arts. He soon became one of the earliest American Impressionist painters, his work reflecting increasingly subtle gradations of light and tone. His painting *Portrait of a Young Girl* was purchased by the Luxembourg Museum, Paris. His other works include *Idle Hours, The Green Bodice,* and *The Red Bridge* (The Metropolitan Museum, New York).

Thomas Hovenden, 30, arrived in Paris in 1874. He took lodgings at 15 Rue Jacob and enrolled in the atelier of Alexandre Cabanel that October. The following summer he joined fellow American painters in Brittany at Pont-Aven, where he painted genre subjects featuring the peasants. He exhibited in the Salons of

1876 and 1878. Two years later he returned to America, where he taught painting at the Pennsylvania Academy of Fine Arts (*Breaking Home Ties,* Philadelphia Museum of Fine Art).

Louis Sullivan, influenced by a talk with Richard Morris Hunt, decided to learn French and to go to Paris. In October 1874 he was accepted at the Beaux-Arts and enrolled with the well-known architect Vaudremer. A year later he returned home, bringing with him one important principle learned in France, namely, that in a building the outward form should faithfully express the function beneath. His designs in Chicago include the Stock Exchange Building and the Gage Building.

Theodore Robinson, 24, arrived in Paris in 1876 and took rooms at 54 Rue Madame. He began studying with Carolus-Duran but transferred to Gérôme's atelier the following year. His first painting at the Ecole des Beaux-Arts was accepted at the Salon of 1878. After finishing his studies on Rue Bonaparte, Robinson remained in France, and in 1888 he struck up a friendship with Claude Monet at Giverny. Robinson's painting, under Monet's guidance, began to reveal a brighter palette and looser brushwork. He returned to New York to paint and teach, but died of asthma at the age of 44, just as his increasingly impressionistic style was beginning to mature.

Bernard Ralph Maybeck was born in New York City in 1862 and arrived in Paris at 19 to work as an apprentice to a furniture maker. One day he visited the Church of St.-Germain-des-Prés where he was awed by the structure and the "sincerity" of the anonymous builders who had created the masterpiece 800 years earlier. He entered the Beaux-Arts the following year and worked in the atelier of Jules-Louis André. Here he encountered the Romanesque and listened to Henri Lemmonier lecture on the Gothic. During the summer he wandered with his sketchbook through the churches of Le Puy and Vézelay. He returned to America and began to teach design at the University of California at Berkeley in 1892. Equally important, he urged his students at Berkeley to study at the Ecole des Beaux-Arts. Thus John Bakewell and Arthur Brown came to Rue Bonaparte before returning to design the San Francisco City

Hall, the ultimate expression of the Beaux-Arts baroque in America. One of Maybeck's students, Julia Morgan, became the first woman to be admitted to the Beaux-Arts and returned to California to supervise the building of Hearst's Casa Grande at San Simeon.

Maybeck worked extensively for the Hearsts, designing mansions such as "Wyntoon" (reminiscent of the castles of the Black Forest), on the McCloud River in California.

Frederick MacMonnies was born in Brooklyn in 1863 and studied sculpture in New York with Augustus St. Gaudens. MacMonnies moved to Paris in 1886 where he was accepted at the Beaux-Arts. In Paris he studied sculpture with Falguière before establishing himself in the Rue Antoine-Bourdelle, where Janet Scudder became his assistant. He lived nearby at 23 Rue Delambre.

Raymond Hood was born in Pawtucket, Rhode Island, in 1881. At 23 he failed the entrance exam to the Ecole des Beaux-Arts. He was finally accepted after a year's preparation. His French landlady, unable to pronounce the name *Monsieur Ood,* called him *le jeune homme.* When *le jeune homme* was afraid to enter the Cathedral of Notre-Dame because he was a Baptist, it was the landlady who finally succeeded in allaying his fears. Hood graduated from the Beaux-Arts in 1911. Eleven years later, with his partner John Mead Howells, he won a 50,000 dollar first prize for the design for the Chicago Tribune Tower. He also designed the Daily News Building on 41st Street in New York City. In an article in the November 1930 issue of *Architectural Forum,* Hood wrote:

> Naturally, the exterior of the News Building is so simple that a great many things could be done to it, but whenever I wanted to do anything, I never knew where to begin or where to stop; and I took comfort from a remark that Laloux (a Beaux-Arts teacher) made occasionally to a student who was at a loss as to what sort of ornament to use in a particular place. Laloux's remark was: "Why not try nothing?"

A major Whistler exhibition was held here in summer of 1908. On 15 June, Marcel Proust visited the exhibit and was impressed by the landscapes of "Venice in turquoise, Holland in topaz, Brittany in opal." He sent his mother a long list of paintings she should see.

❧

After World War II, former GIs studying at the Beaux-Arts included Jack Youngerman and Ellsworth Kelly.

(15)   Ralph Waldo Emerson spent the month of May 1848 in a suite of rooms on the second floor, for 90 francs a month. He recorded in his journal that "the fine trees" along the boulevards had been cut down in the Revolution of February which had forced Louis-Philippe to abdicate. "At the end of a year we shall take account," wrote Emerson, "and see if the Revolution was worth the trees." He enjoyed the city, its population, its pleasures, noting: "Paris has great merits as a city. Its river is made the greatest pleasure to the eye by the quays and bridges; its fountains are noble and copious; its gardens or parks are far more available to the pleasure of the people than those of London.... What a luxury it is to have a cheap wine for the national beverage."

17   Formerly Hôtel d'Orléans. John Jay took rooms at this hotel in June 1782 and stayed for one year. He had come from his post as United States representative in Madrid to help negotiate peace with England. The issues concerned the boundaries of the United States, navigational rights on the Mississippi, fishing rights off Newfound-land, and the collection of lawful debts by each nation's creditors. The other two American negotiators were Benjamin Franklin and John Adams, although Adams did not arrive in Paris until the fall. On Monday evening, 28 October 1782, the Adams family dined with the Jays and, after dinner, the two diplomats withdrew to private rooms where Jay apprised his guest of the tortuous state of the negotiations with the former mother country. Jay offered his own "conjectures as to the views of France and Spain" and told Adams of the close ties between Franklin and the French foreign minister Vergennes. Adams and Jay were united in their distrust of the ever-popular Franklin, the crusty Adams remarking, "after the usage I have received from him, I cannot bear to go near him." However, faced by the British, the American commissioners had no choice but to present a united front and, on 31 October 1782, they sat down opposite their British counterparts, Richard Oswald and Henry Strachey at the Hôtel d'Orléans. Day and night sessions followed on Rue Bonaparte, at Franklin's mansion in Passy, at Adams' lodgings near the Louvre, and at Oswald's lodgings at the Grand Hôtel Moscovite, just up the street at 38 Rue Bonaparte.

One month later, all was ready and the signing took place in Oswald's rooms on Saturday, 20 November. Since the American Congress had solemnly promised the French government that America would neither negotiate nor conclude a separate agreement with England, Franklin informed Vergennes of the signing on the previous Friday evening and promised the foreign minister a copy of the articles. Thus, while the Americans had taken it upon themselves to violate their instructions from Congress, the concessions they obtained from Great Britain were excellent. When Vergennes learned of them, he commented that the British had not negotiated peace but had bought it. This preliminary treaty became the final peace treaty of 3 September 1783, signed at 56 Rue Jacob, just around the corner.

Thomas Jefferson took rooms at the Hôtel d'Orléans on 11 August 1784, a few days after his arrival in Paris. In his Account Book he noted the cost of "20 louis a month my rooms." He hired a valet and set about finding a home and a suitable school for his daughter Patsy. Two months later, a school had been found on Rue de Grenelle and a house in the cul-de-sac Taitbout.

24   Formerly Hôtel de Paris. Henry Miller and his wife June stayed here in April and May 1928. Miller taught June how to ride a bike on nearby Rue Visconti in preparation for a bicycle tour through the south of France.

30   Le Pré aux Clercs restaurant. When Ernest Hemingway arrived in Paris in December 1921, he wrote to Sherwood Anderson to thank him for recommending the Hôtel Jacob et d'Angleterre on Rue Jacob. The hotel was "good and cheap," said Hemingway: "The Restaurant of the Pré aux Clercs at the corner of the Rue Bonaparte and the Rue Jacob is our regular eating place. Two can get a high grade dinner there, with wine, a la carte for 12 francs." At the time, Hemingway mentioned getting fourteen francs to the dollar. With his wife Hadley he spent his time looking for an apartment, which they eventually found on Rue du Cardinal-Lemoine.

36   Hôtel St.-Germain-des-Prés. Janet Flanner moved into a room here in 1925 which became her home for many years. On 10 October 1925, her first "Letter from Paris" appeared in the *New*

Yorker. When she saw the published copy, she was surprised to see the column signed "Genêt," a nom de plume chosen for her by the editor Harold Ross. His only instructions had been, "I don't want to know what you think about what goes on in Paris. I want to know what the French think." Over the next half-century she would publish over 700 fortnightly letters covering not only Paris, but also the rest of Europe. Her first profile appeared in the *New Yorker* on 1 January 1927. Devoted to Isadora Duncan, it praised her innovative techniques: "Two decades before, her art, animated by her extraordinary public personality, came as close to founding an aesthetic renaissance as American morality would allow." The profile concluded that Duncan's

> ideals of human liberty are not unsimilar to those of Plato, to those of Shelley, to those of Lord Byron, which led him to die dramatically in Greece. All they gained for Isadora were the loss of her passport and the presence of the constabulary on the stage of the Indianapolis Opera House, where the chief of police watched for sedition in the movement of Isadora's knees.

In autumn 1935, Janet Flanner submitted a 10,000 word, three-part letter devoted to a certain Adolf Hitler. There was doubt among the editors as to whether he merited such space, but her judgment was trusted, and the letter appeared. In it she wrote that Hitler's "brain is instinctive, not logical," and that he belonged "to the dangerous, small class of sublimators from which fanatics are frequently drawn." Flanner's closest literary friendship was with Hemingway, who frequently dropped by to discuss his writing with her. In her 1972 memoir, she recalled F. Scott Fitzgerald: "When Scott was in Paris he had an eccentric, friendly habit of coming to my hotel to discuss literature at two o'clock in the morning, either with me or with Margaret Anderson if she happened to be stopping there at the time." Flanner wrote her last letter in 1975, at the age of 83, when she returned to New York.

⚜

Henry Miller took a room for 500 francs a month (20 dollars) in the Hôtel St.-Germain-des-Prés in February 1930. From his garret, five floors up, under the mansard roof, Miller wrote to a friend: "I love it here, I want to stay forever....I will write here. I will live quietly and quite alone. And each day I will see a little more of Paris, study it, learn it as I would a book. It is worth the effort....The streets sing, the stones talk. The houses drip history, glory, romance."

(80)   Site of the Masonic Lodge of the Nine Sisters. In 1778, Voltaire, aged 84, returned to Paris after an absence of 28 years. On 9 April, he was initiated into this lodge and entered on the arm of Benjamin Franklin. Exhausted by the tumultuous welcome which Paris had accorded him, he died the following month. On 28 November, Franklin attended a ceremony here in honor of the author of *Candide*. In the darkened hall there were addresses and music; then a sudden light revealed a massive painting by Gauget of Voltaire rising up from his tomb to be presented by Truth and Beneficence to Molière, Corneille, and Racine. Lalande, the astronomer, and Greuze, the court painter, placed crowns on the heads of Gauget and Franklin, who in turn laid them at the foot of Voltaire's portrait.

During the banquet which followed, 200 guests toasted the United States and its representative, Benjamin Franklin. (France was the first country in Europe to recognize the independence of the United States.) Franklin was chosen grand master of the lodge for the following year. During the 18th century in America, freemasonry tended to be local and social and had little influence in politics, but in France the freemasons were opposed to absolutism and favored freethinking. Franklin felt at home here and distributed copies of American state constitutions, which were regarded as models of liberty, to his fellow masons.

In spring 1780, Captain John Paul Jones of the United States Navy became a member. The lodge engaged a fellow member, Houdon, to model his bust. On Monday, 1 May 1780, a feast was given here in Jones's honor.

In 1929, playwright Elmer Rice took a third-floor apartment on Rue Bonaparte for the summer. "A three minute walk from the quais in one direction and from St.-Germain-des-Prés in the other," wrote Rice. "Up a magnificent spiral staircase in an eighteenth-century house, it contained six high-ceilinged rooms, amply furnished in bourgeois fashion. There was an improvised bathroom, and quaintly situated off the imposing foyer, a water closet." The rent was 75 dollars per month. (House number unknown.)

Rue de Bourbon-le-Château (6th) Map A

1 James McNeill Whistler lived here at age 21 in 1855. Frequently penniless, he eked out a living copying paintings at the Louvre for American travellers at 25 dollars each. Happily, his model Fumette had become his mistress, which helped reduce expenses, or so he imagined.

Rue Broca (5th) Métro: Gobelins

52 Walter Piston and his wife Kathryn, a painter, took an apartment at this address in 1924, when they arrived in Paris. Piston began studying composition with Paul Dukas and counterpoint with Nadia Boulanger. Both taught at the Ecole Normale de Musique on Rue Jouffroy, and Boulanger lived downstairs from Dukas at 36 Rue Ballu. Piston wrote his first published work, Three Pieces for Flute, Clarinet and Bassoon, while living here. It was successfully premiered on 8 May 1925 at a concert given by the Société Musicale Indépendante.

Villa Brune (14th) Métro: Alésia

7 In 1929, Alexander Calder and his wife took a studio directly above the front door of number 7. The building consisted of eight studios which could be reached by going through the black door and continuing for twenty yards into a garden surrounded by ateliers. Calder, who was forever creating gadgets, gave a circus show of his animals, which helped pay the rent. He recalled, "I had rigged up doors with a string and I could even open my front door from the bathtub without moving a hand."

Rue Cambon (1st) Map F

29 Henry James returned to Paris in November 1875. He took a third-floor apartment consisting of a parlor, two bedrooms, an antechamber (which served as a dining room), and a kitchen filled with shining casseroles. The rent was 65 dollars a month. He liked the apartment for the sounds of city life, the light click of the passing cab horses "with its sharpness of detonation between the high houses." Each morning, a magnificent troop of plumed, uniformed cuirassiers trotted down the street to the barracks of one of the ministries which looked onto the Place Vendôme. It was all he could do to remain at his writing table when he heard the sound of the horses' hooves.

James had returned to France as the Paris correspondent of the *New York Tribune*. He had agreed to submit a weekly letter on a subject of his choosing for 20 dollars each. The *Tribune* heralded his writing as "Paris through Fresh Eyes." He wrote on George Sand, Chartres, and the Opera, but soon discovered that it was one thing to review a book and quite another to be "chatty" about Paris and Parisians. In a city teeming with stories, he complained to his mother that "subjects are woefully scarce." After twenty letters, he stopped. Although James moved in an increasingly cosmopolitan enclave of English, American, and Russian writers, and despite his fluency in French, he was well aware that he had not succeeded in penetrating French society. But this did not bother him. In May 1876, at age 33, he wrote to a friend from the Rue Cambon:

> I am turning into an old, and very contented, Parisian: I feel as if I had struck roots into the Parisian soil, and were likely to let them grow tangled and tenacious there. It is a very comfortable and profitable place, on the whole—I mean, especially, on its general and cosmopolitan side. Of pure Parisianism I see absolutely nothing. The great merit of the place is that one can arrange one's life here exactly as one pleases—that there are facilities for every kind of habit and taste, and that everything is accepted and understood. Paris itself meanwhile is a sort of painted background which keeps shifting and changing, and which is always there, to be looked at when you please, and to be most easily and comfortably ignored when you don't.

It was here that James worked on *The American* (1877), a novel set in France. On 22 November of that year one of the most important meetings of James's life took place. He made his way to Montmartre, climbed its hill, and found a three-story house at 50 Rue de Douai. On the second floor he was ushered into the rooms of Ivan Turgenev. He recorded his impressions: There was beauty in the face, it was clearly Russian, his expression, James wrote, "had a singular softness, with a touch of Slav languor, and his eye, the kindest of eyes, was deep and melancholy." The Russian author was 57, yet he treated his young American disciple with respect and returned his visit promptly, later inviting him to meet Flaubert and George Sand.

Rue Campagne-Première (14th) Map D

3   James McNeill Whistler took a room at this address in 1856 while studying with the well-known French painter Charles Gabriel Gleyre. He was still earning money by doing copies of famous paintings in the Louvre, and had one excellent client, a Captain Williams whom he had already painted in Stonington, Connecticut. "Stonington Bill," as he was known, came to Paris and asked Whistler to do as many copies in the Louvre as he wished for 25 dollars each.

17   Sculptress Malvina Hoffman took a studio on the second floor in June 1910. Her neighbors were three American sculptors, Andrew O'Connor, Mahouri Young, and Paul Dougherty.

Painter William Stanley Hayter also lived here. At the start of World War II, he moved his "Atelier 17," an etching shop, to New York City, where he was joined by Joan Miró, Jackson Pollock, and Robert Motherwell.

29   Hôtel Istria. By November 1923, Man Ray could finally afford to move out of his photography studio next door and take rooms here, which gave his studio a more professional air.

31 bis   Man Ray moved into this studio in July 1922, and stayed for several years. The well-known Montparnasse model Kiki, who had posed for Soutine, Utrillo, Chagall, Derain, Modigliani, Foujita et al., had become his mistress and lived with him for six years. Her memoirs, published in French, were translated into English with a foreword by Ernest Hemingway.

Boulevard des Capucines (9th) Map F

28   The Olympia Music-Hall opened in 1893. Houdini performed here in 1901 under a contract which ran for ten weeks at what was then the highest salary ever paid a foreign performer in Paris.

Rue Cardinale (6th) Map A

2   Black Sun Press. Harry and Caresse Crosby were among the beautiful people in Paris in the 1920s. Boston-born, Harvard-educated, Harry was the nephew of J.P. Morgan. The young couple had lived in Paris for four years, chiefly writing poetry to each other. When they discovered master printer Roger Lescaret in his modest shop on Rue Cardinale, they rented the floor above and set up the Black Sun Press. They took the name from a poem by Archibald MacLeish (their good friend) called "No Lamp Has Ever Shown Us Where to Look." The last lines read, "Still fixed upon impenetrable skies/The small, black circle of the sun."

   The Crosbys began by publishing their own poetry. In 1927, they met D.H. Lawrence and, granting advance royalties of five "twenty dollar gold pieces" specially shipped to Paris from America, they published his story "Sun." That fall, Harry Crosby inherited a superb 8,000-volume private library and correspondence from his cousin, Walter Van Rensselaer Berry. Among the treasures were 47 letters from Proust and 16 letters from Henry James, all to Berry. The Crosbys published both collections and added their own translation of Proust's letters. In January 1929, Hart Crane drifted into Paris and within a few weeks, Harry and Hart were mutual admirers. Harry recognized the brilliance of Hart's long, unfinished poem *The Bridge* (Hart had published *White Buildings* in 1926), and Hart accepted Harry's offer of accommodations in which to finish the poem, which would be published by the Black Sun Press. In 1929, the Crosbys went to New York, where Harry committed suicide. Caresse Crosby returned to Paris and brought out Hart's poem in 1930. (Two years later Crane committed suicide in New York.) Caresse Crosby continued publishing with *New Found Land: Fourteen Poems* by Archibald MacLeish, followed, in 1938, by *Devil in the Flesh* by Raymond Radiguet, and *Night Flight* by Saint-Exupéry, translated by Stuart Gilbert, with a preface by André Gide. Caresse Crosby returned to the United States and continued to publish intermittently in New York, but the heyday of the Black Sun Press was over.

Rue du Cardinal-Lemoine (5th) Map E

74   On 9 January 1922, Ernest Hemingway and his wife Hadley took an apartment on the fourth floor. It was here that he showed his short story "Up in Michigan" to his new friend Gertrude Stein.

Next door on the ground floor was a *bal musette* (popular dance hall), while around the corner stood the Café des Amateurs, "the cesspool of the Rue Mouffetard," as Hemingway called it.

Rue Cels (14th) Map D

7   Alexander Calder worked in a ground-floor studio in this building in 1927. He recalled that during the winter he would leave his window open all night and "the postman would stick his head through in the morning and marvel at my endurance." It was here that Calder created his miniature circus. A piece of green carpet was unrolled and the ring was laid out, while poles supported the trapeze for the aerial act. From a phonograph, a record played: "Mesdames et Messieurs, je vous présente…." Trained dogs, acrobats, tumblers, lion-tamers, and trapeze acts made up the show of marionettes whose movement made them lifelike. Spectators, who sat on Calder's bed, included Jean Cocteau, Fernand Léger, and Joan Miró. His circus was soon known throughout Paris, but almost no one recognized the full promise of Calder's figures and delicately balanced models. In 1928, Calder visited the studio of Mondrian and began his own abstract painting. To the suggestion made later that his art was truly American, Calder replied, "I got the impulse for doing things my way in Paris." Today Calder's circus is on permanent display in the Whitney Museum in New York City.

Le Champs-de-Mars (15th) Map C

Dominated today by the Eiffel Tower, this was the former parade ground of the Ecole Militaire. During the 18th century, as many as 10,000 troops were reviewed here. The Montgolfier brothers took off from this spot in their hot-air balloon, watched by Benjamin Franklin standing on his terrace in Passy.

In October 1826, a few months after his arrival in France, James Fenimore Cooper attended the races here, but was far more impressed by the presence of the royal family headed by Charles X, the brother of Louis XVI. After describing the royal pavilion in a letter to Mrs. Peter Augustus Jay, the daughter-in-law of John Jay of New York City, Cooper continued:

I then went to take a look of the Royal equipages—There is something exceedingly imposing in the state of a King—There were five coaches, richly gilded, and gorgeously decorated otherwise, that were drawn by eight horses each—Nothing could be finer than the forms and action of the beasts. All the appointments were perfect, except they drew by Dutch collars. The Coachmen were gross looking men, fat, well fed, with cock'd hats, and in the blue and silver of the Court, and the postillions were the same. The Coachmen drove six in hand, there being only one postillion to each carriage.—Two of these carriages were cased—it being part of the Royal etiquette that the King never stirs without an extra coach, in case of accidents; on the present occasion, there were two, as the family was all present. There was a little chariot and six, and a post chaise and four that went off empty, so I cannot say to whom they belonged—When the King left the ground I saw him of course—I took a stand, where I could see the whole train pass—The carriages are very large, and in proportion to their teams—They mov'd by, at about ten miles the hour, some of the horses, occasionally galloping—A troop of cuirassiers of the guard preceded and closed the procession, and there was a Multitude of Mounted footmen, in the Royal liveries—

There, Madam, is a famous dish of gossip for you! Princes, Dukes, Ministers &c. &c.—without end—

The use of these grounds as a racetrack was abandoned in 1855 with the opening of Longchamp in the Bois de Boulogne.

The Champs-de-Mars was chosen as the site for the Great Universal Exhibition of 1889. Many elaborately designed halls were erected to house the various exhibits. One such hall was the Galerie des Machines. (See also La Tour Eiffel.)

Barnum and Bailey's "Greatest Show on Earth" opened a triumphant fifteen-week stand at the Galerie des Machines on 30 November 1901. The show employed more than 1,000 men, women, and children, and had three rings, each with its own herd of elephants and camels, and 500 horses.

Early in 1905, posters appeared throughout France announcing the return of Buffalo Bill's Wild West Show. The poster had a buffalo and a portrait of Colonel W.F. Cody with the inscription *Je viens* (I'm coming). Parisians had not seen Buffalo Bill since his triumph in the Great Universal Exhibition of 1889 when his troop performed at the Porte des Ternes. His Wild West Show performed here in the Galerie des Machines from 1 April until 30 May 1905 before going on to Lyon and Marseille. In his memoirs, Buffalo Bill described this engagement as "the most prosperous in tent history."

Fortunately, the Galerie des Machines, which completely blocked the facade of the Ecole Militaire, was torn down in 1909.

Avenue des Champs-Elysées (8th) Map G

Americans have always been struck by the ability of Parisians to simply sit and gaze upon the passing world. Accustomed to working hard, playing hard, and to life having a constant purpose, Americans, at first, perceive this French habit as both incomprehensible and aggravating, symbolic of French laziness. What is worse, it is contagious.

John Bigelow, author, editor of the *New York Evening Post,* and a future American consul to France, was such an American. After seven years of "continuous and most arduous work" in New York, he decided to visit Europe and arrived in Paris in November 1858. In his autobiography, with the revealing title *Retrospections of an Active Life,* he noted:

> Of course I was very much interested by what I saw, heard, and read in Paris. To an American Paris could not help being a fascinating place, but one of the things which impressed me most during my brief stay at this time is not set down in any of the guide-books. That was, when walking up the Champs-Elysées, to see so many people of mature years and belonging manifestly in a large proportion to the educated and mature classes of society, sitting on benches or chairs by the hour without a book, not infrequently without any companion, and with no occupation apparently but looking idly upon what might be passing up and down on that famous driveway. I had been all of my adult life so constantly employed and so accustomed always to have work in prospect demanding my attention or forecast, that I was for some time utterly at a loss to understand the state of mind or theory of life of a man of mature years sitting for hours in any place doing nothing and apparently thinking of nothing. It was a sight which

could never have been seen in New York since I have known it. One might have found our people sitting alone or in groups in cafes drinking and smoking and reading the newspapers, or playing dominoes or games, but never on the street doing none of these things. It was not till I had been in Paris fully three weeks that I began to understand the cause of this difference, and was able to sit on the Boulevard, like Widow Bedott's husband, "a-thinkin' o' nothin'," as long as any Frenchman. The secret was in the climate of Paris, and, I may indeed say, of all France—so much less mercurial and exciting than that of the United States. I have since discovered that the same difference was remarked by Dr. Franklin more than a century before. Whenever I have since visited France, I have uniformly found that for most of the first month of my stay I was languid and indisposed to much physical or intellectual exertion. I felt as I imagine a man to feel who has been deprived suddenly of his customary tipple. Hence it is, I presume, that our physicians so wisely prescribe a few months' exile in Europe for Americans whose nervous system has been overtaxed.

(82)   Two years after his graduation from Dartmouth College in 1862, Edward Tuck became acting vice-consul in Paris, where he married Julia Stell. The young couple returned to New York. Twenty years later having amassed a fortune on Wall Street, Tuck retired and promptly returned to Paris with his family. In 1896 they bought this former mansion on the sunny side of the Champs-Elysées. A few years later they acquired a chateau, which they named Vert-Mont, at Rueil-Malmaison just outside of Paris. Discovering there was no local hospital, they built the Hôpital Stell, but not before sending a French architect and a doctor to study the Massachusetts General Hospital. In 1916 they donated the hospital to the French State. Today, Hôpital Stell enjoys an international reputation for medical applications of laser techniques. Here on the Champs-Elysées the Tucks built a priceless collection of tapestries, early Meissen and Sèvres porcelain, sculpture and paintings. During World War I, they entertained over 10,000 French soldiers. In 1921 they gave their art collection and furnishings to the City of Paris and provided galleries lit by electric lights, the first in a French museum. Today their collection may be seen in the Petit Palais. Both Tucks received the Legion of Honor and a gold medal from the City of Paris. Tuck also provided the funds for the construction of the American University Center on Boulevard Raspail. He died in

France in 1938 at the age of 96. In his honor, the City of Paris named a street running parallel to the Champs-Elysées, from the Place de la Concorde to the Petit Palais, Avenue Edward-Tuck.

120 James Gordon Bennett, the millionaire newspaper owner, moved to France in 1877 and ten years later launched the Paris *Herald*. This newspaper brought American printing methods to Europe: linotype, rotogravure, photo engraving, and the special supplement. But it was Bennett's hobby, an attempt to promote international goodwill, and it lost money. When World War I broke out and the French government and newspapers immediately moved to Bordeaux, Bennett stayed in Paris. His newspaper began to prosper when American troops arrived in 1917. Whenever there was insufficient news to fill the columns, Bennett filled in the empty space with the remark "Deleted by French censor." This drove the French authorities wild. Bennett was eccentric, occasionally gifted, and constantly arrogant. On the walls of the editor's office he kept a list of names which were not allowed to appear in the *Herald*. Included on the list were Theodore Roosevelt and William Randolph Hearst. When Roosevelt ran for President on the Bull Moose ticket in 1912, the *Herald* referred to him as the third-party candidate.

Bennett used this townhouse for receiving visitors and as a head editorial office. It was here that Bennett, ever the sportsman, ordered his coachman to enter the arched entryway at full tilt. In the crash which followed, Bennett hit his head on the keystone and was severely injured, but recovered. He died in Paris in 1918 at 77 and was buried in Passy.

(133) Site of the Hôtel Astoria. Soprano Grace Moore took an apartment in this building in the summer of 1929. Aged 31, she had made her debut at the Metropolitan Opera the previous year as Mimi in *La Bohème*. In Paris, she made her debut at the Opéra Comique in the same role, which she sang in Italian while the rest of the cast sang in French. To improve her French, she took lessons from Georges Thill, leading tenor of the Paris Opera. The lessons were such a success that Monsieur Thill moved in with his lovely American student.

Another guest in the hotel that summer was the 27-year-old Richard Rodgers. He had already teamed up with Larry Hart and had written *A Connecticut Yankee.* That spring in New York, he received an invitation to a party in Paris given by Jules Glaenzer, vice-president of Cartier. Rodgers sailed over on the *Olympic,* thoroughly enjoyed the party, and sailed right back to New York on the same ship. It was the grand life; the Wall Street crash was still a year away.

In 1951, General Dwight D. Eisenhower, Supreme Commander of the Allied Forces in Europe, had headquarters on the top floor. He had asked for a view of his favorite building in Paris, the Arc de Triomphe, and that's what he got. In the 1950s, the ground floor housed the first American drugstore in France. The entire establishment burned down on the night of 27 September 1972 and was replaced by the present building.

Place du Châtelet (4th) Métro: Châtelet

1   Théâtre du Châtelet. The New York Metropolitan Opera Company opened here with *Aïda* on 21 May 1910. The orchestra was conducted by Toscanini, and the cast included Caruso, Antonio Scotti, Olive Fremstad, Geraldine Ferrar, Pasquale Amato, and Louise Homer. The company had crossed on the *Kaiser Wilhelm II,* which Caruso renamed "the High Cs Express." The opening-night performance was a tumultuous success, with an audience which included the French diplomatic corps, Americans such as the Vanderbilts, the Potter Palmers, and the Stotesburys, who had popped over for the evening. Louis Cartier, who was present, estimated that the jewelry worn was worth more than 3 million dollars. The second night was open to the general public, and the French, feeling that the opera company was in reality an "Italian invasion," voiced their displeasure so loudly that the opening curtain had to be delayed. But the voice and beauty of Louise Homer won over a fiercely hostile house, and the second performance also ended in a triumph. Newspaper headlines in New York read, "Homer quells disturbance," and "Contralto stills angry Parisians." The company's repertoire included *Cavalleria Rusticana, Pagliacci, Otello,* and *Falstaff.* Here the company gave its first performance of Puccini's *Manon Lescaut* with the Spanish singer Lucrezia Bori, who

later became a leading soprano at the Metropolitan Opera. To the surprise and delight of the directors of the Met, the company took in some 10,000 dollars per performance.

Raymond Duncan, brother of the dancer Isadora Duncan, gave a performance of *Electra* by Sophocles on a Saturday afternoon in February 1912. The performance, complete with choir, dances, and music "recreated from antiquity," drew polite interest, but no enthusiasm.

2   Théâtre de la Ville de Paris, formerly the Sarah Bernhardt Theater. On Tuesday evening, 22 April 1902, the famous French actress Sarah Bernhardt opened in *Francesca da Rimini,* a five-act play written for her by Francis Marion Crawford. This was a rare instance of an American playwright being asked to write a play for the French stage. Crawford's play, based on a story by Dante, was not very successful, but his historical novels were popular in the United States.

Rue Chauveau-Lagarde (8th) Map F

3   Formerly Victoria Hotel. George Catlin, artist and showman, took a suite in this hotel with his wife and four children in April 1845. Catlin also brought to France fourteen Ioway Indians for his show. In addition, he shipped eight tons of freight, which included Indian costumes and crafts, weapons, and 600 portraits of Indians, many full length. He rented a showroom on Rue du Faubourg St.-Honoré, where the tableaux vivants, it was hoped, would bring in the public to buy the portraits. He hired an open omnibus which toured Paris announcing the show and carrying the fourteen Indians in full dress and costume. Although the French public was amused by the spectacle of real Indians chanting war cries in the Place de la Madeleine, the novelty soon wore off. Sales of paintings declined, and attendance at the daily shows dwindled. Catlin's wife and two Indians died of tuberculosis, and the twelve remaining Indians returned to America that July. Catlin stayed on in Paris, unable to afford the fare home for himself and his children.

King Louis-Philippe, who had received one of the portraits as a present, ordered 15 new ones. Delighted by the result, the king commanded 29 more copies at 100 dollars each. Catlin worked enthusiastically on them for over a year, but in February 1848 Louis-Philippe was forced to abdicate and fled to England. The portraits had not been paid for, and Catlin finally succeeded in rescuing them from the Tuileries Palace and getting them to London.

Catlin had several supporters in Congress, and bill after bill was proposed to purchase his entire collection for the nation. The last bill was defeated by one vote, cast by Jefferson Davis of Kentucky. Catlin returned to America, and in 1871 purchase of his collection of 1,200 full-length portraits and sketches of Indians was again unsuccessfully proposed in Congress. The following year, Catlin died, destitute, at 75. Many years later his paintings were bought by the American Museum of Natural History in New York. Four hundred and seventy full-length portraits of Indians and tribal scenes are in the Catlin Gallery of the National Museum in Washington, D.C.

Rue de Chazelles (17th)

(25)   Grounds of the foundry of Monduit et Béchet, where the Statue of Liberty was constructed. Frédéric-Auguste Bartholdi lived at number 21 while supervising the construction of the statue. On 24 October 1881, American Ambassador Levi P. Morton placed the first rivet into the copper sheeting. The iron framework, upon which hundreds of copper plates were riveted, was designed by the noted French engineer Gustave Eiffel. Within two years, the upheld hand, torch, and head began to tower over the surrounding six-story buildings, and the statue could easily be seen from the Place de l'Etoile. On Sundays, hundreds of Parisians came to admire it and to listen to the impromptu orators who eulogized the land of freedom across the ocean. On 4 July 1884, the statue was officially handed over by the French government to Ambassador Morton.

From Bartholdi's original 9-foot model, the statue stood 152 feet high. The work of dismantling it began that December. The pieces were packed into 49 mammoth wooden cases, and the ironwork was put into 36 others. Special trucks took the crates to the Gare St.-Lazare, where a 70-car train carried them to Rouen. Here they were put aboard the warship *Isère* between 1- 15 May. On 22 May, the ship set sail and dropped anchor in New York Harbor on 17 June. The 150-foot concrete pedestal faced with granite, donated by Americans, was in place and the rebuilding began. The work was supervised by Bartholdi and the chief engineer from Paris, Monsieur Gaget. This gentleman brought with him three suitcases of small statues which were a tremendous success with the American public, who called his models "gadgets." The Statue of Liberty, originally named "Liberty Enlightening the World," was officially inaugurated on 28 October 1886, 21 years after the idea had been proposed by the French historian Edouard Laboulaye. (The workshops here were torn down in 1960.)

Rue de Chevreuse (6th) Map D

4   Reid Hall, formerly the American University Women's Paris Club. Sponsored by Mrs. Whitelaw Reid, wife of the American ambassador to France, it provided a home for American girls studying in Paris. Janet Scudder, the sculptress, left the following description of her stay here in 1894:

> It was a delightful old house in the Rue de Chevreuse, under the direction of a charming French lady who took a personal interest in the young women there and mothered each one of us individually. The students who lived in the house represented every branch of art—painting, sculpture, music and architecture; and just the mere fact of living there, surrounded by so many of them, all working with enthusiasm, was tremendously stimulating. We were made extremely comfortable, had the privilege of using the large library and were often entertained with musical parties and exhibitions got up by the more advanced students; but best of all was the fact that the expense was so little that even I was able to live there until I left Paris.

Today Reid Hall houses several American university programs. The house and garden remain delightful and can be visited.

Rue Christine (6th) Map A

5   Gertrude Stein and Alice B. Toklas moved here in 1938. They had been evicted from 27 Rue de Fleurus by the landlord, who wished to put his son in their flat. But as Gertrude explained to Sherwood Anderson, "we were kind of pleased and now we are very pleased." When war broke out the following year, the two ladies moved south to the hamlet of Bilignin, some twenty miles from Chambéry. With the liberation they moved back immediately,

arriving at Rue Christine at midnight. "Yes it was the same," she wrote, "so much more beautiful but it was the same." Six weeks earlier, however, four members of the Gestapo had visited the apartment holding a photo of Gertrude Stein. All they found were the paintings of Picasso, which they described as "De la saloperie juive, bon à brûler" (Jewish trash, good for burning). Virgil Thomson, who visited her directly after the war, wrote that she was "in love with the GIs." She brought them home, fed them cake and whiskey, and listened to their talk. She was happy to be surrounded by her fellow Americans and wrote, "I could have gone to school with any one of them they were just like the ones I went to school with." She was now at the height of her powers as a writer. Bennett Cerf wrote from New York, telling her of the enormous popularity of her book *Wars I Have Seen,* published in New York in 1945. Although delighted by the end of the war, she was genuinely worried by what she called the "softness" of the GIs. They only liked to eat "soft stuff," soft cheese and soft meat, and "Soft eats makes soft men," concluded Gertrude. On 19 July 1946, she was rushed to the American hospital in Neuilly where she died a few days later. She was buried in Père Lachaise cemetery. Alice B. Toklas, immortalized by her autobiography (written by Stein), lived on Rue Christine until 1964. She died in Paris three years later, and was buried in Père Lachaise cemetery next to Gertrude Stein.

Rue Christophe-Colomb (8th) Map G

16   Henry Adams rented rooms here in 1898. He was busy consulting French medieval manuscripts in preparation for his magisterial study *Mont-Saint-Michel and Chartres.* During his stay the Dreyfus affair flared up again. Four years earlier, Dreyfus, a captain in the French army, had been found guilty of treason by a French military court for having turned over military secrets to the Germans. The military court, permeated by anti-Semitism, had sent him to Devil's Island. The evidence had not only been superficial, but in part fabricated. In 1896, the chief of French army intelligence, Colonel Georges Picquart, had discovered evidence linking a Major Esterhazy, not Dreyfus, with the German consul. Picquart had been silenced by army authorities and sent to Tunis. And now in 1898, Esterhazy had been court-martialed and immediately acquitted.

Adams, former professor of history at Harvard, grandson of

John Quincy Adams, described his own life as being that of a "stable-companion to statesmen." Irony apart, he was the very embodiment of American aristocracy, born to influence and wealth. His attitude toward Dreyfus is important in that it reflects the sentiments of many of the ruling class of Massachusetts and Washington at that time. On hearing the news of Esterhazy's acquittal on 11 January 1898, Adams wrote to John Hay, the American ambassador in England: "You saw how emphatically the Army through the court-martial, set its foot on the Jews and smashed the Dreyfus intrigue into a pancake. . . . The current of opinion is running tremendously strong, now that the whole extent of the Jew scandal is realised. For no one doubts that the whole campaign has been one of money and intrigue; and the French are very furious." Two days later, on 13 January, Emile Zola published "J'accuse" in the newspaper *Aurore.* Tried for libel and sentenced to jail, Zola fled to England. Adams again wrote to Hay on 17 May 1898, commenting: "To my intense regret, Zola has not been sent to the devil or to his island."

In a new court-martial in 1899 Dreyfus was again found guilty. Seven years later, however, he was found innocent by the Supreme Court of Appeals. He was reinstated in the French Army and fought in World War I. In 1930, the publication of private German diaries conclusively proved Dreyfus' innocence in the entire affair.

Boulevard de Clichy (18th) Métro: Pigalle

82   Moulin Rouge. William Faulkner spent an evening here in September 1925 and wrote to his mother:

> Anyone in America will tell you it is the last word in sin and iniquity. It is a music hall, a vaudeville, where ladies come out clothed principally in lip stick. Lots of bare beef, but that is only secondary. Their songs and dances are set to real music—there was one with not a rag on except a coat of gold paint who danced a ballet of Rimsky-Korsakoff's, a Persian thing; and two others, a man stained brown like a faun and a lady who had on at least 20 beads, I'll bet money, performed a short tone poem of the Scandinavian composer Sibelius. It was beautiful.

In 1926, in a major revue, the famous French music-hall artist Mistinguett was to costar with the Dolly Sisters, an American vaudeville act. However, when the Dolly Sisters saw that the French singer's name was billed in massive letters and theirs in small print, they refused to go on. They sued the management and won. Instead, the Dolly Sisters played the Palace Théâtre (8 Faubourg Montmartre), where they headed the bill.

Rue de la Colonie (13th)

(14)   In 1931, Alexander Calder and his wife took the top-floor apartment in a three-story house here. Calder began to make "a number of things that went round and round" and his friend Marcel Duchamp suggested that they be called mobiles (something that moves).

Place de la Concorde (8th) Map F

This impressive square has had many admirers over its long history. Work on the 21-acre site was begun in 1755 and completed twenty years later. The square was originally named in honor of Louis XV, but his equestrian statue (by Gabriel) was pulled down by the mob in 1792 and the name was changed to Place de la Révolution. More than 1,200 people were guillotined here. In 1795, the carnage over, it became Place de la Concorde, symbolizing a hoped-for harmony. But this name did not last and was re-adopted permanently only in 1830.

The square was a showplace from the beginning. On 1 December 1783, Parisians, fascinated by the latest novelty, the hot air balloon, came by the thousands to watch the *montgolfière* ascend. Among the jostling crowd was Benjamin Franklin, who recorded:

> Being a little indisposed, and the air cool and the ground damp, I declined going into the garden of the Tuileries where the balloon was placed, not knowing how long I might be obliged to wait there before it was ready to depart; and chose to stay in my carriage near the statue of Louis XV, from whence I could well see it rise and have an extensive view of the region of air through which, as the wind sat, it was likely to pass. The morning was foggy, but about one o'clock the air became tolerably clear, to the great satisfaction of the spectators, who were infinite; notice having been given of the intended experiment several days before in the papers, so that all Paris was out, either about the Tuileries, on the quays and

bridges, in the fields, the streets, at the windows, or on the tops of houses, besides the inhabitants of all the towns and villages of the environs. Never before was a philosophical experiment so magnificently attended....Between one and two o'clock all eyes were gratified with seeing it rise majestically from among the trees and ascend gradually above the buildings, a most beautiful spectacle. When it was about two hundred feet high the brave adventurers held out and waved a little white pennant, on both sides of their car, to salute the spectators, who returned loud claps of applause. The wind was very little, so that the object, though moving to the northward, continued long in view....I had a pocket-glass with which I followed it till I lost sight first of the men, then of the car, and when I last saw the balloon it appeared no bigger than a walnut.

The balloon rose over 2,000 feet and the two passengers landed safely before sunset at l'Isle Adam, some seven leagues (25 miles) north of Paris. Franklin, who was suffering from "the stone," wondered if balloons might not become the common carriage and save him from jolting pavements. Probably not in his own lifetime, he mused. But could it not convince sovereigns of the folly of war,

since it will be impracticable for the most potent of them to guard his dominions. Five thousand balloons, capable of raising two men each, could not cost more than five ships of the line; and where is the prince who can afford so to cover his country with troops for its defence as that ten thousand men descending from the clouds might not in many places do an infinite deal of mischief before a force could be brought together to repel them?

2   This palatial building was designed by Jacques Gabriel, the most distinguished French architect of the 18th century. Finished in 1775 together with its twin building just to the west, the classical facades, with their purity of form and restraint, provide the architectural splendor for the famous Place de Louis XV. The building had been intended to provide dignified apartments for foreign ambassadors, but it was taken over by the Garde-Meuble, a department of government which looked after and stored furnishings of the royal palaces. Containing furniture, tapestries, and priceless objets d'art, the collection was open on certain days to visitors of rank. Thus on a September day in 1786, Thomas Jefferson, accompanied by the charming and talented painter Maria Cosway, spent an afternoon here and noted in his Account Book: "seeing Gardes meubles 12 f[rancs]." Jefferson was particularly

impressed by Gabriel's facades, which he ranked with the fronts of the Hôtel de Salm and the Galerie du Louvre as being among "the celebrated fronts of modern buildings." In 1791, back in America, he suggested to architect Pierre L'Enfant that the front of the Garde-Meuble be a possible model for the president's house in Washington. Today this building is occupied by the French Navy.

10   Hôtel de Crillon. In October 1918, private James Thurber received his final security clearance in Washington, D.C., by answering one question in the affirmative: "Were your grandparents born in the United States?" After twelve days of desperate seasickness on board the SS *Orizaba,* private Thurber reported for duty as a code clerk with the American Peace Delegation in the Hôtel de Crillon. He did not receive the welcome he had expected. A cable had been sent to Washington in code, asking for twelve code books. It had been decoded to read "twelve code clerks," who duly arrived in Paris to the unhidden horror of Colonel Edward House, the commanding officer. But if Thurber's first weeks in Paris bordered on the farcical, the city itself began to grow on him. He thought of home, Columbus, Ohio, and the conflict of Paris versus Columbus began to loom. As he explained to a friend at the time:

> It's a wonderful place to study in. And you don't have to go to the Sorbonne or the Ecole des Beaux-Arts. Every one is in school. Every museum a college—and the whole of Paris a vast university of Art, Literature and Music. So that it is worth anyone's while to dally here for years. Paris is a seminar, a post-graduate course in Everything.... She is pagan,—with a pagan love of beauty—but with a pagan "love" of women also....One thing is sure sure. I gotta get back pretty soon, and make a few decisions.

One of the many stories about Americans in the Hôtel de Crillon involves Mary Pickford and Douglas Fairbanks, who stayed here in 1920 while honeymooning in Europe. General Pershing was in the suite next door. A large crowd gathered outside the hotel. Pershing thought that the crowd was there to see the two actors, who in turn thought that the crowd was there to see Pershing. As a result, neither party appeared on the balcony and the crowd waited in vain.

*The hot-air balloon ascent from the Tuileries
on 1 December 1783, watched by Benjamin Franklin.
Lithograph. (See page 48.)*

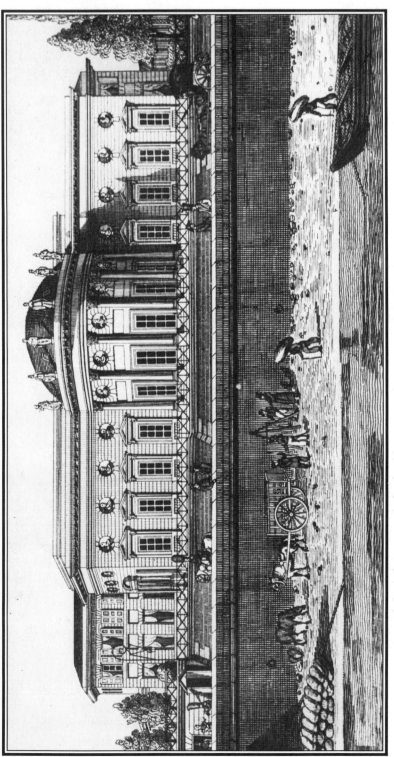

Hôtel de Salm, one of the buildings in Paris which Thomas Jefferson greatly admired. Today the Palais de la Légion d'honneur. (See page 4.)

Engraving, 1820.

Frascati—the famous gaming house, popular with Americans. Lithograph by Debucourt, about 1800. (See page 202.)

The two towers built in 1800 to house Robert Fulton's panoramas— each 46 feet in diameter. The passage between the two is still called Passage des Panoramas. Lithograph by Opitz, 1814. (See page 177.)

Above: "La Belle Limonadière," Café des Mille Colonnes. (See page 172.)
Below: Café Procope, the oldest café in Paris. (See page 5.)
Engravings, 19th century.

Gallery of the Louvre *by Samuel Morse, 1831-33.*
Morse hoped that this massive 73" x 108" conventional
gallery scene would bring him fame in America.

He was to be bitterly disappointed
and by 1840 his career as a painter was over.
(See page 118.)

Details from Gallery of the Louvre.
Above: James Fenimore Cooper, his wife and daughter Susan.
Below: Morse and unidentified student. (See page 118.)

The Galerie Montpensier in the Palais Royal where Aaron Burr
was a frequent client. Exhibited in the Salon of 1804, its painter,
L.L. Boilly, was criticized for such suggestiveness. (See page 172.)

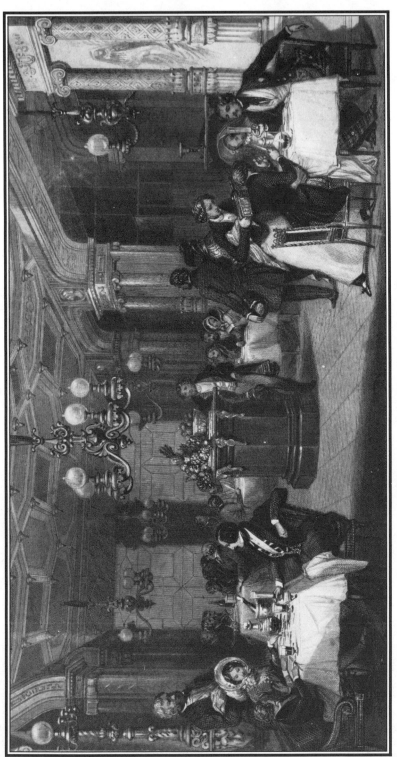

Interior of the restaurant Les Trois Frères Provençaux.
Samuel Morse was honored here by 70 Americans
after the first transoceanic message in 1858. (See page 175.)

Tom Thumb and his carriage, 1844.
Etching.
(See page 203.)

*The Chinese Baths opened on the Boulevard des Italiens in 1792
and were popular with Americans for over 60 years.
The establishment included a beauty salon, a restaurant, and a café. (See page 103.)*

Winslow Homer's drawing Dancing at the Casino *from* Harper's Weekly, *23 November 1867. Wood engraving.*
(See page 137.)

Cells for the insane at the Salpêtrière Hospital, about 1870.
Picture Postcard.
(See page 97.)

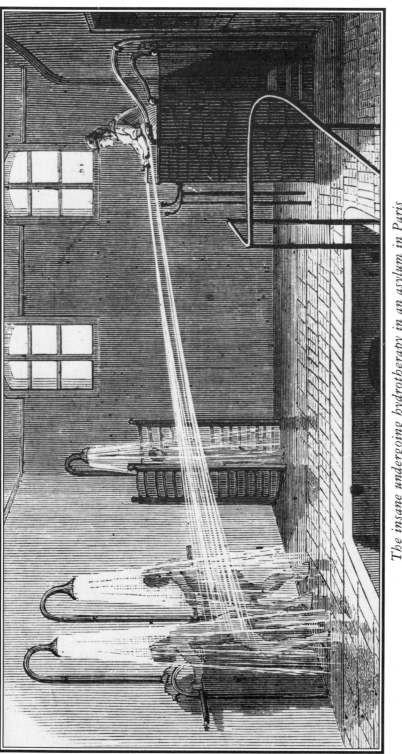

The insane undergoing hydrotherapy in an asylum in Paris in the late 19th century. Wood engraving. (See page 156.)

Examination of a patient in front of medical students
at the Salpêtrière Hospital, 1887.
Engraving in mezzotint. (See page 97.)

Fred and Adele Astaire first visited Paris in January 1924. They had performed in *Stop Flirting* in London for one year, and took a fortnight off in Paris to see Maurice Chevalier, the Dolly Sisters, and Mistinguett perform.

William Randolph Hearst stayed here in September 1928 with his companion, actress Marion Davies. On the 19th, the French foreign minister welcomed both Hearst and Miss Davies to a reception at the French Foreign Office on the Quai d'Orsay. When Hearst returned to America, his newspapers published an exclusive and sensational story. It revealed the existence of a confidential memorandum outlining terms of a proposed Franco-British pact agreeing to a mutual increase in the strength of their two navies. America had not been informed. The Hearst exposé embarrassed both the British and French governments. Two years later, the story apparently forgotten, Hearst returned to this hotel with Miss Davies and eleven of her lady friends from Hollywood. It was a typical Hearst entourage. The party had barely registered when a French official arrived and politely informed Hearst that he was not welcome in France and that he was to leave within four days. Outraged, Hearst left immediately for the Savoy in London, where he wrote the following answer, which appeared two days later in the *New York Times*, 3 September 1930.

> I have no complaint to make. The French officials were extremely polite. They said I was an enemy of France, and a danger in their midst. They made me feel quite important. They said I could stay in France a little while longer if I desired, and they would take a chance on nothing disastrous happening to the Republic.
>
> But I told them I did not want to take the responsibility of endangering the great French nation, that America had saved it once during the war, and I would save it again by leaving it. . . .
>
> The reason for the strained relations—to use the proper diplomatic term—was the publication of the secret Anglo-French Treaty two years ago by the Hearst papers, which upset some international 'apple carts,' but informed the American people. . . .
>
> I think, however, that the general attitude of the French press toward our opposing the United States entrance into the League of Nations, or any protective pact to involve our country in the quarrels of European powers, is mainly responsible. Also

there might have been some slight irritation at the occasional intimations in our papers that France, now being the richest nation in the world, might use some of the German indemnity to pay her honest debts to America, especially because if it had not been for America she would now be paying indemnity instead of receiving it.

But being a competent journalist and a loyal American makes a man persona non grata in France. I think I can endure the situation without loss of sleep.

Quai de Conti (6th) Map A

11 Hôtel des Monnaies, formerly the French Mint. Thomas Jefferson frequently visited La Monnaie, as it is called. Before leaving for France in 1784, he had prepared for Congress *Notes on the Establishment of a Money Unit, and of a Coinage for the United States.* In January 1787, he visited the mint with Ferdinand Grand, the French banker representing United States' interests in Paris. The two men watched a machine strike the two faces and the edge of a coin at one stroke. The inventor, Swiss craftsman Jean-Pierre Droz, had been unable to obtain employment in Paris and had left for London, where he worked for the British Royal Mint. Jefferson tried to get Droz to go to the United States as coiner in the United States Mint, but the plan fell through and Droz was later employed at La Monnaie, where he designed the superb gold pieces known as napoleons.

The medals voted by Congress to commemorate persons and events of the American Revolution were struck here. Jefferson oversaw their execution, consulting the Académie des Inscriptions et Belles Lettres for the inscriptions in Latin, and commissioning artists to execute the designs. Recipients of the medals included Horatio Gates (Saratoga), Anthony Wayne and John Stewart (Stony Point), and John Paul Jones.

Perhaps more important for Jefferson was a salon here where he spent many delightful evenings. The director of the Hôtel des Monnaies, the Marquis de Condorcet, was his good friend and fellow *philosophe.* The director was entitled to an impressive apartment in La Monnaie overlooking the Seine, and his young wife, Sophie de Grouchy, welcomed writers, artists, and scientists to their home. The two men discussed proposals for a French constitution and talked of Condorcet's *Lettre d'un citoyen des Etats-Unis* (Letter from a Citizen of the United States) and his *Réflexions sur l'esclavage des nègres* (Reflections on the Slavery of Negroes). On the eve of his American friend's departure from Paris, Condorcet wrote, "Monsieur Jefferson will always be the friend of the philosophers and of the free men of all countries."

This *hôtel* now houses a museum which contains a number of coins and medals of interest to Americans. Medals struck in honor of Benjamin Franklin, Thomas Jefferson, John Paul Jones, Buffalo Bill, generals Robert E. Lee, Pershing, and Patton, and presidents Wilson, Hoover, Roosevelt, and Kennedy are in the Grande Salle. American writers were also honored: James Fenimore Cooper, Washington Irving, Herman Melville, Edgar Allan Poe, Mark Twain, William Faulkner, Ernest Hemingway, and John Steinbeck. One glass case contains medals by American engraver Victor Brenner, and by James McNeill Whistler.

23   Institut de France. The Institute includes the Académie Française, the Académie des Inscriptions et Belles Lettres, the Académie des Sciences, the Académie des Beaux-Arts, and the Académie des Sciences Morales et Politiques. One of the best descriptions of a French Academy of Science meeting in the early 19th century was provided by the Boston publisher Samuel G. Goodrich.

On 16 February 1824, he visited the French Academy of Sciences, whose membership in those years included many French scientists with international reputations. In his introductory paragraph, Goodrich pointed out how the French Academy proceeded with order and simplicity, in contrast to the pompousness of the London Academy.

> February 16—Went to a meeting of the Institute, held in the Hôtel Mazarin: one hundred and fifty members present. Arago, president; he is tall, broad-shouldered, and imposing in appearance, with a dark, swarthy complexion, and a black, piercing eye. Lamarck, the famous writer on natural history—old, infirm, blind—was led in by another member—a distinguished entomologist, whose name I have forgotten; Fontaine, the architect—tall, homely, and aged: Gay-Lussac, a renowned chemist, under forty, active, fiery in debate: Cuvier, rather a large man, red face, eyes small, very near-sighted; eyes near together and oddly appearing and disappearing; features acute, hair gray, long, and careless; he spoke several times, and with great pertinency and effect: Lacroix, the mathematician, old, and looks like a '76er:

Laplace, the most famous living astronomer, tall, thin, and sharp-featured—reminded me of the portraits of Voltaire; he is about seventy-five, feeble, yet has all his mental faculties.

The principal discussion related to gasometers, the police of Paris having asked the opinion of the Institute as to the safety of certain new kinds, lately introduced. The subject excited great interest, and the debate was quite animated. Thénard, Gay-Lussac, Girard, Laplace, Cuvier, and others, engaged in the debate. Nearly all expressed themselves with great ease and even volubility. They were occasionally vehement, and when excited, several spoke at once, and the president was obliged often to ring his bell to preserve order.

It was strange and striking to see so many old men, just on the borders of the grave, still retaining such ardor for science as to appear at a club like this, and enter with passion into all the questions that came up. Such a spectacle is not to be seen elsewhere, on the earth. The charms of science generally fade to the eye of threescore and ten; few passions except piety and avarice survive threescore. It is evident, in studying this association, that the highest and most ardent exercises of the mind are here stimulated by the desire of glory, which is the reward of success. One thing struck me forcibly in this assembly, and that was the utter absence of all French foppery in dress, among the members. Their attire was plain black, and generally as simple as that of so many New England clergymen.

Goodrich, using a pseudonym, also wrote a successful series of books about America for children, *The Tales of Peter Parley*. He first visited France in 1824 and returned several times, increasingly enamored of French life. He was American consul in Paris from 1852 to 1853.

Thomas Edison was an honored guest here on 19 August 1889. He presented his hosts with a phonograph to record their voices for posterity. In his memoirs, Edison noted that they were surprised—though most discreet—by his lack of scientific training and theoretical knowledge. Edison's formal schooling consisted of three months in Port Huron, Michigan, at the age of 9. His genius lay in the practical application of scientific principles, a genius matched, among those present, perhaps only by Pasteur's.

Rue Corneille (6th) Map B

5   Formerly Hôtel Corneille. Twenty-one-year-old James McNeill Whistler stayed at this hotel upon his arrival in Paris in summer of 1855. He studied in the atelier of Charles Gabriel Gleyre on nearby Rue de Vaugirard. A fellow student, "Taffy" Rowley, later described the young Whistler: "A most amusing and eccentric fellow he was, with his long, black, thick, curly hair, and large felt hat with a broad black ribbon around it. I remember on the wall of the atelier was a representation of him by Du Maurier, a sketch of him... very clever it was and like the original." George Du Maurier achieved fame as an illustrator for *Punch* and as a writer. In his serialized version of *Trilby* (1894), which appeared in *Harper's New Monthly Magazine,* Whistler was satirized as a character called Joe Sibley.

> Then there was Joe Sibley, the idle apprentice, the king of bohemia, *le roi des truands,* to whom everything was forgiven, as to François Villon, "à cause de sa gentillesse." Always in debt... vain, witty, and a most exquisite and original artist; and also eccentric in his attire (though clean), so that people would stare at him as he walked along—which he adored!

When this characterization appeared almost 40 years after their student days, Whistler became furious, threatened a lawsuit, and forced *Harper's* to drop the chapter in the book version of *Trilby.*

Mark Van Doren stayed at the Corneille during the summer of 1919 while working on his study of Dryden at the Bibliothèque Nationale. Van Doren later became one of the most famous teachers at Columbia University.

This hotel was one of the few buildings in Paris to be damaged during World War II. On 24 August 1944, as detachments of SS troops continued to fight in their emplacements in the nearby Luxembourg Gardens, the German troops who occupied the hotel set it on fire before fleeing. Sylvia Beach watched sadly from the top of Rue de l'Odéon as the hotel which had housed Joyce, Yeats, and Synge went up in flames. Today the building is owned by the Banque de France, but in the doorway to your right, you can still see the old reception desk and key racks.

Rue du Croissant (2nd)

(7)   Aaron Burr, former vice-president of the United States, a near penniless exile, moved to this dismal street from Rue de Grenelle in fall 1810. He was reduced to pawning his watch and ring for 1,000 francs to keep alive. His modest room was filled by a "very high bed," an "immense table," and one chair. "I can sit in my chair," he told his daughter, "and reach every and anything that I possess." When winter came, his fireplace, five feet wide and three feet deep, built "on French principles—the principles of stupidity," sent the heat up the chimney and the smoke into the room. In January, a gale blew down the chimney "with such force as to carry ashes and coals over the whole floor. I have been since 4 o'clock in purgatory," he continued, ". . . at length discovered that I could exist by lying flat on the floor; for this purpose I . . . laid a blanket; and reposing on my elbows, with a candle at my side . . . have been reading." Living off bouillon soups, rice, and potatoes, Burr wrote, "I can now conceive why the poor eat so much when they can get it." For entertainment, he did what other poor Parisians did, he walked through the city:

> No sidewalks. The carts, cabrioles, and carriages . . . run up to the very houses. You must save yourself by bracing flat against the wall. . . . Most of the streets are paved as Albany and New York were before the revolution with an open gutter in the middle. Some arched in the middle, and a like gutter to each side. . . . It is fine sport for the hack driver to run a wheel in one of these gutters, always full of filth, and bespatter fifty pedestrians . . . braced against the walls.

Burr obtained work translating a book into English, but his dream of liberating Mexico and making a fortune began to fade before what he perceived as the French government's equivocations. In reality the French were consistent. They were not interested in the adventures of an impecunious American, no matter how close he had come to being president of the United States. Early in the bitter winter of 1811, he confessed to his daughter, "I am just where I was four months ago only with less money."

Rue Daguerre (14th) Map D

22   Alexander Calder took a room in this hotel in winter 1926. "It was a four meter by five meter room, one flight up in the rear, with a skylight. This place was heated by a little gas stove on top of

which was balanced a receptacle of water. It would evaporate, condense on the skylight and dribble down my neck," wrote Calder in his autobiography. "I still considered myself a painter and was happy to be in my own workshop, in Paris." It was during this winter that Calder did one of his first models in wire, Josephine Baker.

Rue Danielle-Casanova (1st & 2nd) Map F

7   Joel Barlow's epic poem "The Vision of Columbus" (1788) made him famous just as he was leaving for Europe to represent the Scioto Land Company. This enterprise had been set up by a group of former army officers headed by General Rufus Putnam. They were joined by William Duer, secretary of the United States Treasury, who expected to make a fortune secretly by using his official position. The Scioto Company held options to buy three and a half million acres of land in Ohio at one dollar an acre. Putnam, unaware that he had been joined by unscrupulous speculators, went to Ohio and founded the city of Marietta, named for Marie Antoinette. Meanwhile, in Paris, Joel Barlow set up shop near the corner of Rue des Petits-Champs (today Rue Danielle-Casanova) and the Place Vendôme. In August 1789, he began to sell land in Ohio to the French. He did not seem to understand that he was not selling a clear title to the land, but simply an option, a distinction he thought was purely academic. (Let us give him the benefit of the doubt.) The outbreak of the French Revolution did not hinder business. To the contrary, the first shipload of French emigrants sailed from Le Havre in January 1790, bound for the banks of the Scioto River. In the first twelve months, Barlow convinced 900 French people to sail to America, where his brochures promised them rich soil, huge crops, fine climate, and a beneficent government. If the French reports back home were favorable, wrote Barlow, he would be able to sell twenty million acres in the next two years. This seems to suggest that he really had no idea what he was selling, for his customers soon discovered upon their arrival in Ohio that they did not possess title to the land and that they were threatened daily by Indian uprisings. To survive, they huddled together and created the pathetic little town of Gallipolis. In the meantime, the entire swindle had become public, thus setting off the Panic of 1792. William Duer went to debtor's prison. When a few French survivors

made it back to Paris, Barlow, fearing for his life, took a room on the top floor of the Hôtel du Palais-Royal overlooking the gardens, where he hid out for most of 1791. But he spent this time composing a *Letter to the National Convention of France on the Defects in the Constitution of 1791,* which promptly earned him French citizenship. He began to feel safer and moved to Rue Jacob on the Left Bank.

Rue Danton (6th) Map A

5   Isadora Duncan took two large apartments at this address in 1909. She lived on the ground floor in the back and used the first floor apartment for her dance school. She subsidized her school by performing at the Gaité Lyrique with the Colonne Orchestra, conducted by violinist Edouard Colonne.

Rue Daunou (2nd) Map F

6   Hôtel Daunou. Oliver Wendell Holmes stayed at this address (formerly Hotel d'Orient) in August 1886, 50 years after finishing his medical studies in this city. He visited only one person in Paris, Louis Pasteur. In his *One Hundred Days in Europe,* Holmes wrote:

> I told him I was an American physician who wished to look in his face and take his hand—nothing more. I looked in his face, which was that of a thoughtful, hard-worked student, a little past the grand climacteric—he was born in 1822. I took his hand, which has performed some of the most delicate and daring experiments ever ventured upon, with results of almost incalculable benefit to human industries, and the promise of triumph in the treatment of human disease which prophecy would not have dared to anticipate.

The previous year, Pasteur had completed his technique of vaccination against anthrax which was then successfully used against rabies.

Rue Delambre (14th) Map D

4   Edward Titus opened a bookshop at this address in 1924. He lived above, in a small but elegant apartment paid for by his wife,

Helena Rubinstein. She stayed on the Right Bank when she came to Paris. This modest but refined bookshop, At the Sign of the Black Manikin, had the air of a cloister, and it became an intellectual sanctuary in a street rarely given to intellectual pursuits. In the following years, Titus began publishing under the name The Black Manikin Press, using the Crete printery just down the street at number 24. In 1929, he agreed to publish *Lady Chatterley's Lover.* D.H. Lawrence had had 1,000 copies of his book printed in Florence in December 1928. For this second edition, which was far too risky for British or American publishers to touch, Titus agreed to run off 3,000 copies at a cost not to exceed twelve francs per copy. (All the copies were sold within two years.) At the same time, Titus published the English version of the memoirs of Kiki, the most famous model and mistress in Montparnasse. The translation was by Samuel Putnam and the introduction by Ernest Hemingway, who warned readers that the original text was so very French that they should learn French and read the original, since a translation was sure to be a "bad job." The memoirs sold well.

In 1929, Titus also took over the review *This Quarter,* which had been launched four years earlier. *This Quarter* had published stories by Ernest Hemingway ("The Undefeated"), Kay Boyle ("Flight"), and Djuna Barnes ("The Little Girl Continues"), and poetry by Carl Sandburg and Ezra Pound. As the new editor, Titus began *This Quarter* with an essay by Marc Blitzstein entitled "Four American Composers." Subsequent issues included works by contemporary Italian authors translated by d'Annunzio and Pirandello. Since the *Little Review* and *Dial* had both expired in 1929, the continuation of *This Quarter* by Titus (and indirectly by Helena Rubinstein, unbeknownst to her) until 1932 was important; it was the only small review to appear in the early years of the Depression. The next-to-last issue of *This Quarter* was devoted entirely to Surrealism and was edited by André Breton. (Essays by Breton, René Crevel, Paul Eluard, Dali, and Max Ernst were translated into English by Samuel Beckett.) Surrealist art was provided by Giorgio de Chirico, Ernst, Breton, Tzara, Man Ray, and Yves Tanguy. The final issue contained works by Beckett, a line drawing by E. E. Cummings, and contributions by Josephine Herbst, James Farrell, and Allen Tate, all of whom achieved literary success later in the United States.

It is only fair that Helena Rubinstein get the last word. She found her husband and his literary friends all to be "wasters."

Hemingway, she recorded, was "a loud-mouth and a show-off"; James Joyce "smelled bad, ... couldn't see ... ate like a bird." Worst of all, wrote Helena, "I always had to pay for their meals."

9   Isadora Duncan moved into this building with its impressive glass front in 1926, the year it was built. Isadora had given and frittered away fortunes in her lifetime. At 48, she was no longer able to command an enormous sum for a single evening's performance, and facing what she termed poverty, lamented that she hardly knew "where the next bottle of champagne was coming from."

10   L'Auberge du Centre, formerly the famous Dingo Bar. It served corn beef and cabbage, real American soup, and thick beefsteaks. Jimmy the barman, an ex-prize fighter from Liverpool, England, enjoyed a faithful clientele. When Jimmy moved to the nearby bar, the Falstaff, in the late 1920s, his customers followed him. His memoirs, *This Must Be the Place* (1934), were edited by American journalist Morrill Cody, with an introduction by his friend Ernest Hemingway. It was in this bar, a favorite hangout, that Hemingway first met Scott Fitzgerald who, three years his senior, had already become the most successful novelist of the era. Robert McAlmon, an habitué of the Dingo bar, described these years in *Being Geniuses Together 1920-1930*.

15   Grand Hôtel des Ecoles. Man Ray lived in this hotel from November 1921 until the following summer. His friend Tristan Tzara, poet and founder of the Dada movement, had a room on the same floor.

39   In 1908, sculptor Jo Davidson took a studio on the ground floor. Like most art students, he was broke. One day he heard that sculptor David Edström was looking for a bust of Wagner which a group of well-to-do American music students wished to present to their teacher. Davidson let it be known that he had such a bust. In the interim, he borrowed twenty francs, dashed out and bought some photos of Wagner, and set to work. That evening, Edström appeared, but the concierge, following instructions, told him that Davidson had gone to the country and would be back the following evening. Davidson kept working. The next evening, Edström reappeared and was delighted by what he saw. "How long have you been working on it?" asked the sculptor. "Oh, for several months," replied Davidson. The price, 1,000 francs (200 dollars), was settled. Davidson had two great qualities: talent and speed. These attributes would enable him in the future to do busts in two-hour sittings of Marshall Foch, General Pershing, Bernard M. Baruch, and John D. Rockefeller.

Place Denfert-Rochereau (14th) Map D

Les Catacombes. These former quarries were used as ossuaries beginning in 1786. Several million bones were brought here from the city cemeteries and today the remains of over six million people lie here. The public was permitted to visit in 1800. Ebenezer Smith Thomas, former editor of the *Charleston Gazette,* visited the Catacombes in 1820 and left the following description:

> There were about twenty ladies and gentlemen in the party, and each carried a wax taper, not simply to afford light for seeing the objects that were arranged there, but to light ourselves back to earth again; for being once caught in the dark, in those subterranean regions, the chance of ever seeing light again, would be rather doubtful. They extend for miles, and the numerous turns and avenues form a labyrinth from which it would be next to impossible to escape, but that a black line is drawn from the entrance, over your head, which, while kept in view, is a safe and sure guide back from whence you came.
>
> The different avenues are very irregular, both in their height and breadth, sometimes compelling you to stoop in a narrow passage, while at others you found yourself beneath a dome of twenty or thirty feet in height, and spread out to as great or greater distance. The first object that strikes the attention, is the skulls, of which there were then about three millions and a half, piled up in rows, to the top, or as far as could be reached; such as were remarkable for any natural defect, or injury, were put by themselves, for more minute observation than the mass required.
>
> The student of anatomy had here an opportunity of perfecting himself, in a knowledge of the human skull, no where else to be met with, and the very first sight of them would put a phrenologist in an ecstasy. Among them we observed several of natural born idiots, of most singular structure; one of them particularly, bore a strong resemblance to a cone with the apex broken off. After these came the bones of the thigh, leg, upper, and then lower joint of the arm, each by themselves, in regular order. Of these, such as were remarkable were selected and placed by themselves. There was a bone of an arm that had been broken

about three inches from the wrist, which, for want of being set, had lapped over upwards of two inches, and grown together perfectly solid. Having completed the subterranean tour, we once more emerged to the light of day.

Rue Descartes (5th) Map E

39 Formerly a hotel. Ernest Hemingway rented a room here on the top floor for 60 francs a month. It was 1922 and though he lived just around the corner on Rue du Cardinal-Lemoine, he took this room in which to write. It had a view to the east over the smoke-stacks and rooftops and a fireplace where he roasted chestnuts. Hemingway described the room in *A Moveable Feast* (1964).

In October 1917, John Dos Passos, aged 21, was living somewhere on Rue Descartes. He wrote to a friend:

> I am in Paris writing in a small chilly room (8 francs a week!) on a certain delightful Rue Descartes.....The reason is that our everblessed Uncle Samuel has decided he will have none of the aid of volunteers, and has replaced all the volunteer ambulance sections with "trained" American army ambulance drivers.... The result is that I am a gentleman of leisure in Paris.

There was more truth to this than Dos Passos perhaps recognized, for he was not only a graduate of Choate and Harvard but possessed a modest income. Dos Passos had originally come to Europe to study architecture before volunteering as an ambulance driver. In Paris he dabbled in painting before settling down to write. He began by immersing himself in the fragile and fragrant beauties of Paris, telling a friend that he was spending

> an atrociously delightful month of wandering through autumn gardens and down grey misty colonaded streets, of poring over bookshops and dining at little tables in back streets, of going to concerts, and riding in squeaky voitures with skeleton horses, of wandering constantly through dimly-seen crowds and peeping in on orgies of drink and women, of vague incomplete adventures— All in a constant sensual drowse at the mellow beauty of the colors & forms of Paris, of old houses overhanging the Seine and damp streets smelling of the dead and old half-forgotten histories.

Rue du Douanier (14th)

In 1933, E.E. Cummings, living on a Guggenheim grant, had an apartment somewhere on this street. He was interviewed for the *Chicago Tribune* (Paris edition) on 30 May 1933, and the reporter was obviously surprised to find the poet painting. "I paint in the afternoons," said Cummings, "and I write poetry in the evenings." Asked what he did in the mornings, he answered that as he had to economize he did the shopping and cooking. Cummings's paintings have been exhibited extensively in the United States.

Rue du Dragon (6th) Map B

E.E. Cummings wrote about the Rue du Dragon:

> myself,walking in Dragon st
> one fine August
> night,i just
> happened to meet
>
> "how do you do" she smiling
> said "thought you
> were earning your living
> or probably dead"
>
> so Jones was murdered by
> a man named Smith and
> we sailed on the
> Leviathan
>
> (1928)

31   For almost a century aspiring American painters have entered this gateway and crossed the charmingly paved courtyard on their way to the ateliers of the Académie Julian. First opened as a school of painting in the Passage des Panoramas in 1868, it moved to larger quarters on Rue du Dragon in 1890. The academy was soon popular among American students anxious to study in Paris but unable to meet the entrance requirements of the Ecole des Beaux-Arts. First, the Beaux-Arts required a language exam of all foreigners. Then each candidate was expected to draw or paint from a live nude model. Americans in the 19th century had no such experience. As a result, the Académie Julian was the principal alternative to the Beaux-Arts. The teaching was conservative, and good to excellent standards were maintained.

The academy had its innovations: In order not to disturb "the Parisian evenings," evening classes were held from 5:00 p.m. to 7:00 p.m., instead of the traditional 8:00 p.m. to 10:00 p.m. But far more original were the classes teaching illustration, design, and layout for publicity, posters, and newspapers. Early in the 20th century, "Monsieur Oznobichine, Lieutenant-Colonel of the Russian Head Quarters and Orderly Staff Officer of His Majesty the Grand Duke George Lichtenbergue," provided prizes for a sketching competition to be held among the students. The first prize was a "motorized three-wheeler with side-car." The next three prizes were money, while the final six contestants received "fifteen bottles of champagne between them." The subject was to be chosen from the following list:

> The Ant and the Grasshopper
> The two Pigeons
> Latona transforming the Shepherds of Lyceum into Frogs
> Hylas and the Nymphs

Elizabeth Nourse from Cincinnati, Ohio, registered at the Académie Julian in 1887, where Gustave Boulanger advised her to work on her own as she was so far ahead of the other students. Her first painting submitted to the Salon of 1888 was accepted and hung "on the line" (i.e., at eye level), an honor for a newcomer. Her painting *Peasant Women of Borst* (1891) was bought by the Cincinnati Art Museum, and *Closed Shutters* (1910) by the Musée du Luxembourg.

Cecilia Beaux, 32, was already an established Philadelphia portrait painter when she arrived in Paris in 1887 and began work at the Académie Julian. Soon she became aware of the importance of Edouard Manet and the Impressionist movement. Her *Sita and Sarita* (1893) was purchased by the Musée du Luxembourg. Beginning in 1895 she became a painter-instructor at the Pennsylvania Academy, a position she held for twenty years.

Maurice B. Prendergast studied here from 1891 to 1893 and also worked at the Académie Colorossi. Prendergast, influenced by Whistler and Manet, became America's first Post-Impressionist. Frederick C. Frieseke, from Owosso, Michigan, studied here in 1898 under Benjamin Constant and Jean-Paul Laurens. Six years later, one of his paintings was bought by the Musée du Luxembourg in Paris. Alfred Maurer also worked at the academy in 1898. Three years later, Edward Steichen, who had come to Paris to study painting, left the Académie Julian after two weeks. Other Americans who studied here included Max Weber (1905), Thomas Hart Benton and his friend Stanton MacDonald-Wright (1909), and Jacques Lipchitz (1910).

George Biddle graduated from Harvard Law School in 1911, was admitted to the Pennsylvania Bar, and promptly sailed for France to study painting. He recorded in his *An American Artist's Story:*

> I registered immediately at Julian's, in the rue du Dragon, off the rue des Saints-Pères. The school was in an enormous hangar, a cold, filthy, uninviting firetrap. The walls were plastered from floor to ceiling with the prize-winning academies, in oil or charcoal, of the past thirty or forty years. The atmosphere of the place had changed little since the days of Delacroix, Ingres or David. Three nude girls were posing downstairs. The acrid smell of their bodies and the smell of the students mingled with that of turpentine and oil paint in the overheated, tobacco-laden air. The students grouped their stools and low easels close about the models' feet. While they worked there was a pandemonium of songs, catcalls, whistling and recitations of a highly salacious and bawdy nature.

John Covert studied at the academy from 1910 to 1912 and Grant Wood from 1923 to 1924.

In 1948, Robert Rauschenberg continued his studies here and met fellow student Susan Weil, who later became his wife. "We agreed that the other was the worst student in the class," he remembered. Later, he wrote that at the time he had been certain that if one wished to become an artist, one had to study in Paris. But in retrospect he concluded, "I think that I was at least fifteen years too late."

꼭

By 1949, thanks to the GI Bill, over 200 Americans were studying painting and sculpture in Paris. In order to receive a monthly allowance (75 dollars in 1949), the school had to be on the American government's approved list, as was the Académie Julian. Thus, the American painter and sculptor Robert Breer, who arrived in Paris in 1949, dropped by the academy once a month to fulfill the attendance requirement and to pick up his check, while actually studying with the sculptor Ossip Zadkine at the Académie Colorossi.

Rue Duphot (1st) Map F

8 Hotel Burgundy. Thomas Wolfe spent July 1928 at this address during a return trip to Europe. Here, he worked on the final pages of *Look Homeward, Angel,* which was published the following year.

Rue Dupuytren (6th) Map B

8 On 19 November 1919, Sylvia Beach opened Shakespeare and Company. In her memoirs Beach recalled how it had been her friend, Adrienne Monnier, who had discovered this shop: "We hurried to the Rue Dupuytren, where, at No. 8 ... [there] was a shop with the shutters up and a sign saying Boutique à louer. It had once been a laundry, said Adrienne, pointing to the words 'gros' and 'fin' on either side of the door, meaning that they did both sheets and fine linen. Adrienne, who was rather plump, placed herself under the 'gros' and told me to stand under the 'fin.' 'That's you and me,' she said."

Within a short while, this lending library became a rendezvous for Americans in Paris. Gertrude Stein was soon a customer, but cancelled her membership after she learned that Sylvia Beach was going to publish *Ulysses.* Other clients included Robert McAlmon, Ezra Pound, Stephen Vincent Benét, William Bird, Ernest Hemingway, Archibald MacLeish, Thornton Wilder, Allen Tate, F. Scott Fitzgerald, and Sherwood Anderson, who was thrilled to find here the only copy of *Winesburg, Ohio* in Paris.

Rue Du Sommerard (5th) Map E

13 Hôtel Marignan. E.E. Cummings shared a room with his friend William Slater Brown in 1921. Appalled by the conservatism of anthologist Louis Untermeyer, Cummings sent off the following note which appeared in the July 1922 issue of *Secession:*

> e.e. cummings. Candidate for the mayoralty of Paris, the present literary capital of America. Indorses *Secession* campaign against Louis Untermeyer, an anthologist best known for the omission of William Carlos Williams and Marianne Moore from his *Modern American Poetry.*

In all fairness, it should be noted that Untermeyer included poems by Williams, Moore, and Cummings in the 1925 edition.

17 Alan Seeger arrived in Paris during the spring of 1912 after graduating from Harvard. His parents had agreed to a modest allowance while their tall, handsome, 24-year-old son pursued his first and only career, poetry. He soon came to love the city: "I have been born anew. Paris is everything splendid." Little by little small literary magazines began publishing his poems, and by July 1914 he put together his first collection, which he rightly called *Juvenalia.* He spent the month showing his manuscript to every publisher in Paris. The reply was always "Nous regrettons." Finally he invited his friends to a public burning of his poems. However they persuaded him to take the poems to England where there was sure to be a market. But Seeger got the same answer in London and returned to Paris in despair. To his surprise, he found his favorite café empty. The owner told him that his American friends had joined the French Foreign Legion and were busy training in the Palais-Royal. By joining the Foreign Legion and not the French army, Americans might lose their lives but not their nationality. An hour later Seeger had joined them and *la légion.* He had frequently thought about war and had written home that war was "a common danger to be shared and overcome, not shunned." At dawn on 25 August 1914 he joined over one hundred American Legionnaires at the Gare St. Lazare enroute to the training camp at Rouen. Two months later they were in the front lines near Epernay in the Champagne countryside. By Christmas, Seeger was one of the few Americans still alive. Despite the fighting he had continued writing, and his scenes of battlefields, artillery attacks, and deserted villages had begun to appear regularly in the New York *Sun*. On 28 April 1915 he described a night patrol:

> The night was warm and windless. There were fruit trees all about this part of the hillside. They were clouded with bloom, reminding one of a Japanese print. But another odor as we advanced mingled with that of the blossoms...the odor of carrion and death. We had not gone fifty steps when they began to appear, these relics of the great battle that terminated here on September 20 last...the dead lie as they fell in the fighting seven months ago. Shapeless, dark masses...Frenchmen and Germans alike, rigid bundles of soaked cloth, filling the thickets, sodden in the muddy beet fields, bare and exposed around the trenches.

His writing had matured. He was thrilled when some of his poems were published in the *Atlantic Monthly* and the editor asked him for more. His most famous poem dates from this period:

> I have a rendez-vous with Death
> At some disputed barricade,
> When Spring comes back with rustling shade
> And apple-blossoms fill the air
> I have a rendez-vous with Death
> When Spring brings back blue days and fair.

Alan Seeger was killed on 4 July 1916.

Rue de l'Echelle (1st) Map F

7   Hotel Normandy. Mark Twain stayed here from April until July 1879. Paris has a reputation for joyous springtimes, but it is subject to rain, as Mark Twain discovered to his sorrow: "May 7th. I wish this terrible winter would come to an end. Have had rain almost without intermission for two months and one week." The first day of June brought "raw, cold rain." Twain sat in the hotel, reread Thomas Carlyle's *History of the French Revolution,* and spent the rest of the day writing. "I sleep like a lamb and I write like a lion. I mean the kind of lion that writes—if any such."

Rue des Ecluses-Saint-Martin (10th)

(41)   This street covers the former Protestant cemetery which lay outside the walls of Paris. In 1905, American Ambassador General Horace Porter began a search for the body of John Paul

Jones, who had been buried here in 1792. Numerous shafts were dug, the bones of the Swiss guards killed defending the Palace of the Tuileries during the Revolution were dug up, and, on 7 April, the lead coffin containing a remarkably well-preserved corpse was discovered in the courtyard, some five feet below the ground. Examined immediately by two eminent professors at the Ecole de Médecine, the corpse's measurements and a peculiar earlobe fully matched the bust of John Paul Jones modeled by Houdon. President Theodore Roosevelt, eager to build up the image of the navy, sent four cruisers to France to bring home the national hero. On 6 July 1905, John Paul Jones's coffin, now encased in mahogany, was taken to a service at the American Cathedral on Avenue George-V. Conveyed to Cherbourg by special train, the body was carried across the ocean on board the SS *Brooklyn*. President Roosevelt headed the commemorative exercise on 24 April 1906 at Annapolis. "America," said the president, "never forgets its heroes."

Rue de l'Ecole-de-Médecine (6th) Map B

12 La Faculté de Médecine de Paris. The medical school opened in 1775, and the original classrooms can still be seen in the inner courtyards of the new school, which was completed in 1900. The school was divided into the school of theory and the school of practice, where the students saw real patients.

Mary Putnam, daughter of New York publisher George P. Putnam, arrived in Paris in 1866 with the intention of studying medicine. France offered the finest medical training in the world at the time. Her recommendations had to be exemplary, since no woman had ever been admitted into the famous Ecole de Médecine. She had already received her medical diploma in New York, and spent her first year in Paris attending lectures and even assisting in wards while waiting to be officially admitted as a degree candidate at the Ecole de Médecine. In a letter to her father, she explained her situation:

> My dear Father,
>   You must know that I have never given up the idea of attempting to enter the Ecole de Médecine. Ever since May I have been occupied with a project for obtaining this permission,

mainly based on the idea of writing a thesis to constitute a sort of title for admission. I have wasted no time over this thesis, because its subject demanded the medical reading and hospital study which I should have given at all events. My thesis was nearly finished when the circumstances of my entering the Ecole Pratique, obliged me to see the Secretary of the Faculty of Medicine who was to give me my card. Now this Secretary had taken a fancy to attend a course that I attended and the professor had said to me, "I will place him beside you in the amphitheatre, and after a week or two, it will be certainly impossible for him to refuse you the right to enter the Ecole." I did not pay much attention to this remark, and when I met the Secretary, had forgotten that I ever had seen him. I happened to say something about the regulations of the Ecole, the terms of admission, etc., and was extremely astonished when he observed, "If you wish yourself to take out inscriptions and graduate with our degree, nothing is easier!" "But, Sir," I exclaimed, almost aghast at anything dropping into my hand like that, "Last year I applied merely for permission to attend the lectures, and the Dean refused me." "Yes, yes, I know, it was I that refused. He consulted me, and I advised him not to allow a lady to enter among the students." "You have then changed your mind?" I said. To this the Secretary returned no definite answer. Suddenly Dr. Feort's prediction flashed across my mind and with apparent irrelevance I inquired if I had had the pleasure of meeting monsieur at such a *cours*. Yes, and I had also been encountered, (and I suppose inspected), at various clinics. The mystery of this sudden graciousness was, however, better explained later, when I learned by means of a mutual friend, that the Minister of Public Instruction, who would give the final formal decision in the matter, is much interested in the question of women physicians, and rather looking around for an opportunity to express his opinion on the subject. There is reason to believe therefore, that the Secretary acted with the distinct idea of pleasing the Minister. At all events, I am told that the word of this official is ample authority for the assurance that my entrance to the Ecole is a settled fact, although the accomplishment of all the necessary formalities will require two or three weeks. I signed yesterday the demand to the Minister that had been prepared by the Secretary, and which is to go with my diplomas and a certificate of citizenship etc., from the American Ambassador. The idea is to enter the Ecole in the title of foreign physician, and share the privilege belonging to this class of individuals, of having my American diploma converted into the title of Bachelor of Sciences, and of passing by certain preliminary examinations, in simply paying for them. This will demand an immediate expense of about 500 francs. The other expenses will come to about 300 dollars, but distributed over two or three years. The honor of being the first woman ever admitted to the famous Paris Ecole, the first in fact at any Metropolitan School, (Miss Garrett graduated at an Apothecary's Hall in Glasgow), is so immense, and will have, I venture to believe, such a practical influence on my future fortunes, that I felt justified in accepting the pecuniary liability, even though I had to borrow it. On the other hand, this official recognition of an American degree is a great thing for the medical education of all women, and I feel singularly honored that the recognition should have been conferred upon them in me. I cannot flatter myself that it is due to any merit of my own, unless the positive virtue of punctuality in being at the hospitals at half past eight every morning for a year, and the negative one of not flirting with the students, have counted in my favor.

On 23 January 1868, Mary Putnam, 24, became the first woman student ever to be admitted to the medical school of Paris. On her first day of attendance, she was given a special chair, close to the lectern and far removed from the male medical students. Although it separated her from the men, it drew their attention to her, and so after a few weeks she was permitted to sit among them. To the surprise of several French faculty, French medical training did not suffer the disaster and collapse which they had so forcefully predicted. Quite the opposite, Mary Putnam graduated second in her class and went back to New York and a distinguished career at the Woman's Medical College of the New York Infirmary.

Rue des Ecoles (5th) Map E

49   Brasserie Balzar. William L. Shirer used to enjoy a choucroute garnie here in the company of James Thurber, Elliot Paul, and other journalists from the *Chicago Tribune*. Shirer believed that this brasserie had, in 1925, the best beer in Paris.

Place Edouard-VII (9th) Map F

8   Théâtre Edouard VII. Orson Welles first saw Eartha Kitt in May 1950 when she was performing in Carroll's, a Parisian nightclub. After a brief audition, he offered her the role of Helen of

Troy in his modernized and clumsy version of Marlowe's *Doctor Faustus*. Hilton Edwards played Mephistopheles and Welles Faustus, with music written by Duke Ellington and sung by Eartha Kitt. After rehearsals, which began in the early afternoon and lasted well into the night, Welles would accompany Eartha Kitt back to her hotel, the Plaza-Athénée. She recalled walking at sunrise up the Champs-Elysées as Welles recited Shakespeare. She learned to appreciate classical French food, she said, thanks to Welles. With opening night delayed four times, the production was a disaster. Few Parisians understood English and the theater was almost empty during several performances. When Eartha Kitt sang, "Now Satan got lonely way down in the pit, so he grabbed Doctor Faustus and put him on the spit," the audience began to wonder if they had not wandered into an insane asylum. The limited run ended on 4 August when the group left for Frankfurt. Upon hearing there was to be a performance of *Faust,* the dutiful German audience appeared with their copies of Goethe. They soon discovered that it was a performance of Welles by Welles.

La Tour Eiffel (7th) Métro: Champs-de-Mars

The 300-meter tower, built for the great Universal Exhibition of 1889, was then the highest structure in the world; it straddled the exhibit grounds. A few days after the inauguration, in the banquet hall on the first landing, the French Society of Engineers gave a dinner in honor of Thomas Edison. At the end of the meal, coffee was taken at the invitation of Alexandre-Gustave Eiffel in his private salon on the top floor. Seventy-five engineers listened to Charles Gounod, who played and sang for them. Afterward Gounod gave Edison an autographed piece of music for his wife, whereupon Eiffel, not to be outdone, sent along a note which said: "This lovely day would have been complete if we had had the pleasure of the company of Madame and Mademoiselle Marion Edison."

Edison, aged 42, was delighted to find himself as honored in France as he was back home, but he could not get used to the continual eating. In his memoirs, he noted:

> I could never get used to so many dinners. At noon I would sit down to what they called *déjeuner.* That would last until nearly three o'clock, and a few hours later would come a big dinner. It was

terrible. I looked down from the Eiffel Tower on the Biggest dinner I ever saw, given to the Mayors of France by the Municipality of Paris. I saw 8,900 people eating at one time.

Edison's outdoor exhibit at the fair was among the largest of the American displays. Its most striking feature was an enormous incandescent lamp, 40 feet high on a 20-foot pedestal. On one side, in red, white, and blue lamps, was the American flag, the French flag on the other.

Some of the exhibits were placed indoors in specially constructed halls. Next to Edison's stand in the Galerie des Machines, situated between the present Avenue Charles-Richer and the Place Joffre, was the exhibit of fellow electrical engineer and inventor, 36-year-old Elihu Thomson. Thomson was a graduate of Central High School in Philadelphia, and had demonstrated the transmission of signals without wires in 1875. He invented the resistance method of electric welding, the repulsion type of induction motor, a three-phase electric dynamo, and a watt meter. Thomson later became acting president of the Massachussetts Institute of Technology (1920-23).

Edison and Thomson were internationally honored for their achievements in electricity, and both lived to the age of 84.

The Eiffel family recently gave their grandfather's papers, experimental models, awards, and gifts to the French nation. Among the gifts was a phonograph from Edison. The original cylinder was carefully cleaned and on it was discovered the clear voice of Alexandre Gustave Eiffel, saved for posterity thanks to Thomas Edison.

Place des Etats-Unis (16th) Map G

This tree-lined square and garden received its present name in 1881. The two bronze statues of Washington and Lafayette were done by Bartholdi after he had completed the Statue of Liberty. They were presented to the city of Paris by Joseph Pulitzer, and unveiled on 4 July 1900 before a large crowd and John Philip Sousa and his 63-member band. Eight years earlier, Sousa had retired as conductor of the U.S. Marine Band and was about to form his own band. His contract with his manager read: "It shall be the aim of the said Sousa ... to make this band equal in executive ability to the band of the Garde Républicaine in Paris." He came to Paris and not only studied French bands, but signed on Europeans to perform for him. Now, on 4 July 1900, the Sousa musicians, world renowned, became the first American band to parade through Paris escorted by mounted units of the Garde Républicaine.

10 Gloria Swanson lived here during October and November 1928 while filming *Madame Sans-Gêne* in Paris. Her lacquered bedroom on the third floor was done in black and had a golden bed in one corner and sunken Roman bath in the other. A visiting movie executive cabled Cecil B. DeMille in Hollywood: "You are right after all! These things actually exist outside of your studio."

11 President Woodrow Wilson stayed here from 14 March until 28 June 1919 while attending the peace conference. He held working sessions here with Georges Clemenceau, Lloyd George, and Vittorio Orlando. The statesmen were referred to as "the big four."

Ned Rorem met the Vicomtesse Marie Laure de Noailles in the fall of 1949. Two years later she gave him a party to celebrate the premiere of his *Six Irish Poems* performed by the Radio Orchestre with soloist Nell Tangeman. "I arrived brash, open-necked and, above all, young," recalls Rorem in his *Paris Diary*. By 3 a.m. he could not remember how many magnums of champagne he had downed. Whereupon, in front of everyone, he approached the vicomtesse and gave her a whack which sent her reeling to the ground. There was an unroar and Rorem was restrained by the *maître d'hôtel*, but the hostess asked that he be released. According to Rorem, she then "rose with a bemused stare of utter satisfaction: she had triumphed before her friends: somebody new *cared*." The 27-year-old American-style wooer moved into this elegant mansion. The vicomtesse, old enough to be his mother, provided him with three pianos, clothed, fed, housed, advised and loved him. More important, she sponsored concerts and introduced him to the Tout Paris. He talked at length with Georges Auric, Francis Poulenc, Darius Milhaud and Philippe Erlanger. He met André Gide, Paul Eluard and Alice B. Toklas. He was sketched by Jean Cocteau and photographed by Man Ray in his studio on Rue Férou. Rorem occasionally stayed in his own room nearby at 75 Rue de Vaugirard.

Rue Fabert (7th) Map C

40 ter   Formerly Hôtel de la Gare des Invalides. In summer 1926, Eugene Jolas and Elliot Paul, editors at the Paris *Tribune,* announced a new literary review, *transition.* They established an editorial office here in a hotel room. The first issue appeared in April 1927 and contained work by Robert Desnos, Philippe Soupault, Archibald MacLeish, Gertrude Stein, and the Austrian expressionist poet Georg Trakl. *transition* was an immediate, albeit controversial success. Twelve issues appeared the first year, but the pace slowed and *transition* became a quarterly with occasional lapses. The editors were interested in exploring a "nightworld hitherto neglected," evoking such Proustian states of mind as dream, hallucination, and half-sleep. "Work in Progress" by James Joyce appeared first in *transition;* later, it was part of *Finnegans Wake.* The third issue of *transition* had an editorial, part of which read:

> "Suggestions for a New Magic"
>
> *transition* will attempt to present the quintessence of the modern spirit in evolution.... We believe in the ideology of revolt against all diluted and synthetic poetry. Against all artistic effects that fail to subvert the existing concepts of beauty.... We need new words, new abstractions, new hieroglyphics, new symbols, new myths.... Perhaps we are seeking God.

Subsequent issues contained the work of Malcolm Cowley, Kay Boyle, Anaïs Nin, Henry Miller, William Carlos Williams, Katherine Anne Porter, Hart Crane, Ernest Hemingway, Franz Kafka, Martin Buber, Carl Jung, H.L. Mencken, Samuel Beckett, James Agee, and Dylan Thomas. Drawings and sketches were contributed by Arp, Picasso, Calder, Miró, Matisse, and Mondrian. The last issue, number 27, appeared in 1939.

(48)   Charles Dana Gibson came to Paris for the second time in 1874. Although only 27, he was famous thanks to his Gibson girl. He took an impressive studio at number 48, decorated with tapestries and armor. At his housewarming party, Loïe Fuller performed her celebrated serpentine dance, and Sybyl Sanderson, the seductive Thaïs of the Opéra Comique, sang.

Gibson had returned to Paris to work. He went backstage, for instance, at the Théâtre du Vaudeville and sketched the stately

Réjane in her famous role in *Madame Sans-Gêne* by Sardou. He joined forces with Richard Harding Davis, who at 26 had been editor of *Harper's Weekly* and now at 30 was the leading American journalist of the day. Strolling through Paris, the two men chronicled the midinettes, the models, the boulevardiers, the can-can, the governess with her charges in navy blue sailor suits, the priest reading his breviary as he strolled the avenue, and the American colony. Gibson's "About Paris" appeared in *Harper's Weekly* and in book form in 1895. He also did illustrations of Paris for *Life*. The year spent in Paris, he later recalled, was the best of his life.

Gibson returned to Paris once again in 1907, financially independent and a family man. However, the Wall Street panic that year forced him back to New York. But Gibson had the golden touch; he was barely off the ship when he was offered 900 dollars per installment to illustrate *The Common Law*, a novel by Robert H. Chambers, which was serialized in *Cosmopolitan*.

Rue du Faubourg-Saint-Honoré (8th) Map G

112   Bristol Hotel. President Ulysses Grant stayed here with his wife and son from 26 October until the middle of November 1887. On Sunday, 30 October, he was invited to share the presidential box at the horse races at Auteuil. He declined on account of the "sacredness of the day." He was on a world tour after eight years in a presidency distinguished by corruption, graft, and scandal.

Sinclair Lewis lived at this hotel in 1925. *Arrowsmith* appeared that year, winning the Pulitzer Prize, which Lewis declined. Here in Paris, he began work on *Elmer Gantry* (1927), a satirical novel dealing with religious hypocrisy in the United States.

On 9 April 1975, a gala party was given here to celebrate Josephine Baker's 50 years in show business. Guests included Princess Grace of Monaco, Sophia Loren, Carlo Ponti, Jeanne Moreau, and Alain Delon. French President Giscard d'Estaing sent a telegram "in the name of a grateful France whose heart so often beat with yours." Josephine Baker died five days later.

233   Villa Wagram Saint-Honoré. In this quiet impasse, at number 3 bis on the first floor, sculptor Augustus St. Gaudens had a studio. Beginning in August 1877, he worked on *The Adoration of the Cross by Angels,* modeled in relief for the chancel of St. Thomas's Church in New York City. Unfortunately, this important commission was destroyed in a fire in 1905, but it was about the time of its execution that St. Gaudens won recognition as a sculptor, and by the end of the year he could afford to move to a larger studio on the increasingly popular Rue Notre-Dame-des-Champs.

240   On Sunday afternoon, 12 December 1875, Henry James, accompanied by Ivan Turgenev, climbed to the fourth floor and knocked at a door. It was opened by the author of *Madame Bovary,* Gustave Flaubert. The two men had come to a Sunday gathering where Flaubert's guests frequently included Zola, Daudet, Maupassant, and the Goncourt brothers. For the 32-year-old James, who had only published in the *Atlantic Monthly* and whose novels *Roderick Hudson* (1876) and *The American* (1877) had yet to appear, it was as if he had entered "the councils of the gods." As he wrote to a friend: "je suis lancé en plein Olympe."

252   Salle Pleyel. On 7 July 1924, Ezra Pound sponsored a private concert here in a small recital hall. The program was entitled "American music (declaration of independence), played by Olga Rudge and George Antheil." Guests included Sylvia Beach, Ernest Hemingway, and James Joyce. Pound felt the declaration necessary because French composers Erik Satie, Arthur Honegger, Georges Auric, Louis Durez, Germaine Tailleferre, Darius Milhaud, and Francis Poulenc dominated musical composition. In June of the following year, selections from Pound's opera *The Testament,* based on the life of François Villon, were played here before a full house. The opera was later broadcast in its entirety by the BBC in Britain.

Duke Ellington performed here in July 1933. After the show, a black singer from Chicago named Bricktop threw a party. Ellington recorded in his memoirs that the most impressive moment of the evening was the carrying in of a huge champagne bottle. Bigger than any member of his band, "it had to be carried by four waiters."

Louis Armstrong played here on the nights of 9 and 10 November 1934. In Louis' own words, the concert was a real gasser: "I had to take so many bows until I wound up taking 'em in my bathrobe." After World War II, he performed here on 2 and 3 March 1948. Thousands of fans were turned away, and after the show Armstrong had to have a police escort to leave the building.

Rue Férou (6th) Map B

2 bis   Man Ray took a studio in this building when he returned to France in 1951. When he first visited this narrow street and entered what had been a sculptor's studio, his wife Juliet, a former dancer with the Martha Graham Company, was appalled. She felt it looked like a garage. Rents were controlled after World War II, so any remaining furniture was sold as "key money," and only an odd chair or two was left to compensate for the low rent. In this case an old sofa remained, which Man Ray took apart and made an object called *Springtime* with the springs. In his *Self-Portrait* (1963), he described the unheated studio as being "a huge whitewashed place flooded with light from skylights and windows on the three sides, twenty feet above." In reality, they were more than 30 feet above. In winter, at breakfast, the temperature was sometimes 42 degrees, but Man Ray was happy to be back in Paris where he concentrated on painting and color photography. He died in Paris on 18 November 1976 at the age of 86. Today the studio contains a rich collection of his postwar works. Between numbers 2 and 4, next to the small gateway, the 2 bis is marked below the bell. You can see his atelier with its skylight above the garage gates.

6   During the summer of 1926, Ernest Hemingway left his wife Hadley and son and moved in with Pauline Pfeiffer, who worked for the Paris edition of *Vogue*. Asked why he had left Hadley, Hemingway answered, "Because I am a bastard." He worked on *A Farewell to Arms* here and then returned to America in March 1928 to complete the novel.

13   James McNeill Whistler dropped in to visit his friend and fellow artist Henri Fantin-Latour one day in 1858. He found him sitting in bed huddled up in his overcoat to keep warm. Whistler sketched him as he found him. The drawing is in the Louvre.

Rue de Fleurus (6th) Map B

27   Gertrude Stein lived in France most of her life. She was born in Pennsylvania and educated in California; an 1897 Radcliffe graduate, she spent two years at Johns Hopkins medical school. She arrived in France in 1902 and took an apartment here the following year with her brother Leo. They were joined by Alice B. Toklas in 1910. At the beginning of World War I, Leo left for Italy and the two women stayed on here until 1937.

Stein began her art collection by buying the early works of Picasso, Matisse, Derain, and other young painters. By the 1920s her salon with walls covered by avant-garde paintings (some of which had become famous) attracted prominent writers and painters. When it came to guests, Gertrude preferred men. Mistresses were preferable to wives, and both were entertained by Alice, who led them off to a corner to talk about food, clothes, and the theater, while Gertrude sat in the living room with the men conversing about literature, art, and music. Convinced of her own excellence as a writer (though it was not until 1933, when her *Autobiography of Alice B. Toklas* appeared, that her work attracted major attention), she offered criticism and encouragement to her fellow writers, influencing Sherwood Anderson and Ernest Hemingway. Her barbs were legendary. Of poet Ezra Pound, she quipped, "a village explainer, excellent if you were a village, but if you were not, not." She coined the expression "the lost generation."

Stein was also interested in composition, and her opera *Four Saints in Three Acts* (1934) was set to music by Virgil Thomson. There are many descriptions of her apartment, and the following is by a young William Shirer, who went to interview her in 1926 for the Paris *Tribune:*

> Miss Stein lived in a pavilion in a courtyard behind 27 Rue de Fleurus. I was ushered by a maid into a large studio salon. Though it was rather dark in the room I could make out the paintings, which already were famous and which occupied every inch of space on the walls. . . . The first things you saw were two canvases of [Picasso], a portrait of Miss Stein done before the Great War and his nude of the girl with the basket of flowers. I thought I also recognized a couple of Matisses and one or two by Juan Gris. . . . Then the author came in.
>
> She was so bulky that, as a note I jotted down reminds me, I thought she looked like a full-blown old Irish washwoman. But this first impression was soon changed. Above her heavyset body

was a face that reminded you of a Roman emperor, masculine and strong and well chiseled, and her eyes were attractive and intelligent. Her hair was closely cropped, like Caesar's. She greeted me in a low, mannish but pleasant voice.

They discussed her recent lectures at Oxford and Cambridge. The failure of American newspapers to report these talks had upset her. Turning to literature, Gertrude Stein continued: "You know the Big Four in literature, don't you?" Before Shirer could answer, she replied, "There is a natural line of descent. Poe to Whitman to Henry James to myself. I am the last. The only living one."

Avenue Foch (16th) Métro: Victor Hugo

23 Henry Adams rented rooms here on and off for several summers in the 1890s. The house was occupied by Elizabeth Cameron, the wife of the Pennsylvania senator. Ever since Adams' own wife had committed suicide, Adams had become increasingly dependent upon the young and beautiful Mrs. Cameron. It was a delicate entanglement. Adams wrote to her: "I am not old enough to be a tame cat...you were right last year in sending me away." But Adams returned and it was here that he began his most important work, *Mont-Saint-Michel and Chartres.* In a letter dated 18 September 1899, he warned his hostess that he was turning her house into a "gay library of twelfth-century architecture." A month later he told her: "Your rooms are becoming a school of romanesque architecture. Last evening Joe Stickney and St. Gaudens dined here, and floundered in architecture on all the chairs." While living, as he noted, like a "twelfth-century monk in a nineteenth-century attic," idealizing the Middle Ages and demonstrating the unity of the 13th century symbolized by these two austere yet wondrous monuments, Adams wrote some of the finest prose in the English language.

41 Dr. Thomas W. Evans, 27, of Philadelphia, came to Paris in 1847 and spent his life here practicing dentistry. He began work as assistant to an already established American dentist. Within a few years, Evans introduced orthodontics and anesthesia and established himself as the foremost dentist in Paris, and later in Europe. As luck would have it, Napoleon III had rotten teeth, bad gums, and innumerable cavities. He also had a princely aversion to suffering. In the intimacy of his private office, Evans became privy to state secrets, thanks to his expertise as a dentist and his discretion as a confessor. Soon the doctor was sent on delicate diplomatic missions under the guise of professional visits. At Windsor Castle a chair and professional equipment always awaited him. In St. Petersburg, he was rewarded for his services with two enormous stallions.

One of his patients was Baron Haussmann, who was busy changing the face of Paris. Thanks to inside information, Evans speculated successfully in real estate and built the first centrally heated mansion here in Paris. Middle-aged and wealthy, Evans tired of his middle-aged American wife, and in French custom took a mistress, Méry Laurent. She introduced him to painters Manet and Whistler, and to poets such as Mallarmé. Evans even wrote an introduction to the English-language edition of poet Heinrich Heine's autobiographical writings. In Evans's autobiography, the chapter entitled "The Beginnings of a Friendship" chronicles the influence Napoleon III had upon him and his fellow practitioners as they moved from what was then considered a trade to what became a profession. Evans described the torture the emperor had endured at the hands of French dentists and the relief which he had provided him:

> His appreciation of such services was something more than personal. It was not limited to me; it reached out and included the whole dental profession. He found the dental art to be of great use to him, and, accordingly, had an excellent opinion of dentists in general, and saw no reason why they should not be as proud of their specialty as the practitioners of any branch of medicine or surgery.
>
> If it was my privilege to render considerable professional services to the Emperor, I was richly repaid in many ways; but more especially by the direct support and encouragement he gave me in the practice of my art, and the social consideration he accorded to me, and, through me, to my profession. Indeed, the immense importance of this can hardly be understood by one not acquainted with the character of the men who practised dentistry when I came to Paris, and the contempt with which they were spoken of and regarded. Those persons who made it their business to treat diseases of the teeth were ranked with barbers, cuppers, and bleeders, just as, a hundred years before, surgeons were, everywhere in Europe. Physicians and surgeons considered the care of the teeth as unworthy of their attention and science; the rectification of those irregularities of dentition that give rise to defects in speech, or disfigure the mouth, they knew nothing

about; and extractions were left to be performed by mountebanks at street corners, or fakirs at fairs, where the howls of the victims were drowned by the beating of drums, the clash of cymbals, and the laughter and applause of the delighted and admiring crowd. This al fresco practice of dentistry was to me one of the most curious and foreign features of street life in the old Paris of 1847.

If the dentist was sent for to attend a patient he was expected to enter the house by the back-stairs, with the tailor and the butcher-boy and the other purveyors to the establishment. The front-stairs were for those only whose social standing gave them the right to use them. Although it was never within my own experience to be invited to go up the *escalier de service,* it is not surprising that the low social standing of dentists in general, at this period, should have been made known to me in ways that sometimes left a sting. But after a while these things ceased to trouble me. In fact, after I had been in Paris a few years, I seldom heard, or overheard, a word in disparagement of my profession. An exception, however, to this experience may be worth mentioning.

At a ball given at the Palace of the Tuileries, in 1857, to which Mrs. Evans and myself had been invited, we overheard a conversation which took place so near to us that very little of it was lost.

"Who is that woman?" said one lady to another—"she is so delicate and ladylike—she looks like an American." "Yes, she is," was the reply; "and only think—she is the wife of a dentist! How dreadful!"

A few minutes later, the Emperor approached us and shook hands with us both.

During the Franco-Prussian War, Paris was under siege, Napoleon III was held captive, and Empress Eugénie was regent of France. On 4 September 1870, the proclamation of the Republic was read at the Palace of the Tuileries. The empress fled the palace with the help of the Italian and Austrian ambassadors. They placed her in a carriage and then quickly abandoned her to her fate. The empress was unable to reach friends in the city, and arrived at Evans's house that evening. Early the following morning, Evans and his country-man Dr. Crane succeeded in smuggling her through the Porte Maillot, which was controlled by the National Guard. The empress arrived in Deauville on the evening of 6 September, where Mrs. Evans arranged immediate passage for her to England on the yacht of Sir N. Burgoyne.

When he died in 1897, Evans bequeathed his *hôtel* on the Avenue Foch to the city of Philadelphia.

Pierpont Morgan Hamilton, great-great-grandson of Alexander Hamilton and nephew of banker J.P. Morgan, lived here with his wife Marie-Louise. When they separated in summer 1926, Hamilton offered use of the apartment, rent-free, to Archibald MacLeish and his family, on condition that they pay for the household staff. The MacLeishes, who had spent the summer on the shore in Normandy at Granville, accepted and arrived in the middle of September. They stayed for eighteen months. It was a twelve-room apartment with a salon 60 feet by 30 feet overlooking the avenue. The staff included a maître d'hôtel, a chef, five maids, and a governess. MacLeish told his mother, "You should see us! Three baths! And a mechanical piano. And me with a valet!!!" A Renault car and a liveried chauffeur, whose salary was 30 dollars a month, came with the apartment. Just paying for the staff kept MacLeish on the verge of bankruptcy.

MacLeish's friends and guests included Ezra Pound, Sherwood Anderson, Sylvia Beach, Allen Tate, John Dos Passos, F. Scott Fitzgerald, Gerald Murphy, and Harry Crosby. His friendship with Ernest Hemingway was complex and not untinged with jealousy. After lunching with Wyndham Lewis, the English writer, he later wrote to him: "As for Ernest—your criticism was just. His stuff has a sensationalist base which I think he would concede & support intellectually. For me he is a true stylist (taught, curiously enough, pretty largely by G. Stein (in conversation) if you will believe his assertion!!)." MacLeish was anxiously awaiting publication of his blank verse poem *The Hamlet of A. MacLeish,* written in Paris, which Houghton Mifflin finally published in October 1928.

Rue Fontaine (9th)

Josephine Baker opened her own club, Chez Josephine, on 14 December 1926. She would perform here after her show at the Folies-Bergère. In an article for *Vogue,* John McMilan wrote:

> I could think of nothing else as I saw her for the first time passing through the room....She had just arrived from the Folies-Bergère, accompanied by her maid, her chauffeur, and a white Eskimo dog. She came in without a wrap, and the length of her

graceful body, which is light sealskin brown, was swathed in a blue tulle frock with a bodice of blue snakeskin worn with slippers to match.... The woman is like a living drawing by Audrey Beardsley or Picasso.

Josephine's admirer and friend, French writer Colette, came to see her perform at this club. (House number unknown.)

Rue François-Ier (8th) Map G

7   Formerly Hôtel du Palais. E.E. Cummings and William Slater Brown sailed for France in April 1917 as part of a detachment of volunteer ambulance drivers. On board ship the two young men became fast friends. Discussing literature each night until the ship docked at Boulogne, they gave the impression of avoiding their fellow volunteers. Later, as the boat train approached Paris, the commanding officer ordered the men to be ready to get off, but Cummings and Brown, busily talking, did not hear the order. The CO, it turned out, had mistaken a suburban station for Paris and the whole detachment had gotten off at the wrong stop. Thus Cummings and Brown were the only two to reach the correct destination, the Hôtel du Palais, headquarters of the Norton Harjes Croix-Rouge Américaine in Paris. It was scarcely the type of success to get them promoted. Separated from their unit, which had somehow reached the front lines, they dallied in military limbo awaiting new orders. Since individuals could not travel to the front alone, they spent a blissful month of May in Paris. Cummings and Brown walked ten to twelve miles a day through the city, and in the evenings attended the theater and saw Stravinsky's *Petrouchka*. Almost 40 years later, in one of his "non-lectures" delivered at Harvard, Cummings recalled those precious days:

> I celebrated an immediate reconciling of spirit and flesh, forever and now, heaven and earth. Paris was for me precisely and complexly this homogeneous duality: this accepting transcendence; this living and dying more than death or life. Whereas—by the very act of becoming its improbably gigantic self—New York had reduced mankind to a tribe of pygmies, Paris (in each shape and gesture and avenue and cranny of her being) was continuously expressing the humanness of humanity. Everywhere I sensed a miraculous presence, not of mere children and women and men, but of living human beings.

When Cummings and Brown finally reached their unit, they

had been branded by the commander, Captain Anderson, as dangerous non-conformists. This was soon confirmed by their insistence on spending their free time with the French rather than with their fellow Americans. That August, both men were arrested by the French military authorities and charged with treasonable correspondence. The charge was as ludicrous as it was pathetic, revealing the growing French fears of military insurrection: After three years of fighting, the allied soldiers still did not hate the enemy. Brown, a graduate of the Columbia School of Journalism, was an intrepid letter writer. Barely 20 years old and shocked by what he saw as senseless carnage, he had written home criticizing the war and pointing out the irony that the ordinary French soldiers disliked the British more than the Germans. His letters, censored by the French, led to the charge "treasonable correspondence." At the instigation of Captain Anderson, Cummings was also arrested as a fellow traveller. In his interrogation, Cummings was asked: "Est-ce que vous détestez les Boches (Do you hate the krauts)?" Cummings replied: "Non, j'aime beaucoup les français (No, I love the French)." Cummings had deliberately refused to answer correctly and was found guilty. Captain Anderson also told the French military court that the repatriation of Cummings and Brown "would be dangerous" to America. The two were therefore confined to a French prison at La Ferté Macé. Here they were held for six months until letters by Cummings' family to the State Department, to senators, and finally to the president of the United States, secured their release. Cummings used the experience in *The Enormous Room* published in 1922.

Avenue Franklin-D.-Roosevelt (8th)

(25)   John Slidell and his family moved here in 1862 and stayed until the end of the Civil War. Slidell, who was Confederate commissioner to France, was personally popular and cordially received, but was unable to get any material aid for the South or official recognition for the Confederacy. After the war, Slidell stayed on in Paris and had an office on nearby Rue de Marigny.

Rue Froidevaux (14th) Map D

69   Ernest Hemingway used Gerald Murphy's apartment on the fifth floor during August 1926, while he corrected the proofs of *The Sun Also Rises*. The building is opposite the Montparnasse

cemetery. In *Hemingway: An Old Friend Remembers,* Jed Kiley wrote:

> He really worked hard. I went round to the cemetery room one day to see him. The concierge told me he was there. So I climbed the five flights and rapped on his door but he wouldn't let me in. The undertaker's assistant who had the room next to him told me that he had been locked in his room for a week correcting proofs. Wouldn't let anybody in. They used to leave coffee and croissants at the door for him.... If genius is really the capacity for taking infinite pains, he is a genius, I thought.

(Note: The author believes that the house number 60, given in a recent edition of Hemingway's letters, is in error.)

Rue de Furstenberg (6th) Map **A**

In April 1930, Henry Miller wrote a description of Furstenberg Square, which appeared in modified form early in the third chapter of *Tropic of Cancer:*

> A deserted spot, bleak, spectral at night, containing in the center four black trees which have not yet begun to blossom. These four bare trees have the poetry of T.S. Eliot. They are intellectual trees, nourished by the stones, swaying with a rhythm cerebral, the lines punctuated by dots and dashes, by asterisks and exclamation points. Here, if Marie Laurencin ever brought her Lesbians out into the open, would be the place for them to commune. It is very, very Lesbienne here, very sterile, hybrid, full of forbidden longings.

Avenue Gabriel (8th) Map **G**

(1)   Les Ambassadeurs nightclub. Following the success of *La Revue Nègre,* American revues became the rage in Paris. In 1926, from the Cotton Club on the corner of 142nd Street and Lenox Avenue in Harlem came the entire 63-member show, including the Blackbirds, "the fifty copper colored girls," comedians, and an orchestra.

42   Miss Henrietta Reubell, 27, a wealthy American expatriate, lived here. "Extremely ugly, but with something very frank, intelligent and agreeable about her," wrote Henry James. "If I wanted to desire to marry an ugly Parisian-American, with money

and *toutes les élégances* [elegant in every way], and a very considerable capacity for development if transported into a favoring medium, Miss R . . . would be a very good objective. But I don't." This somewhat blunt assessment was written by the 32-year-old James to his brother William in April 1876. James and Reubell became good friends and James enjoyed visits with her family over the years.

For James, Miss Reubell was a perfect example of the expatriate American, and he would put her in *The Ambassadors,* complete with rich jewels and laughter, as Miss Barrace, an American sophisticate in Chad Newsome's entourage.

Rue de la Gaité (14th) Map D

4   Isadora Duncan and her brother Raymond lived on this street when they arrived in Paris in 1900. They were delighted to find an inexpensive studio, a mere 50 francs a month. But the first night, as they were going off to sleep, the whole building began to shake. Raymond went out to investigate only to discover that they were directly above an all-night printing press. The concierge provided dinner for one franc each, including wine. Isadora recalled that when the concierge carried in their salad, she would say with a smile: "Il faut tourner la salade, Monsieur et Mesdames, il faut tourner la salade (You must toss the salad, Ladies and Gentlemen, you must toss the salad)."

20   Bobino Music-Hall. On 24 March 1975, Josephine Baker appeared in a show celebrating her 50 years on the stage. On opening night, she received a fifteen-minute standing ovation. She gave fourteen performances before she died on 12 April 1975.

26   Théâtre de la Gaité. On Wednesday evening, 27 January 1909, Isadora Duncan, accompanied by her students, danced to *Iphigénie* by Gluck. The ballet was an outstanding success. A French newspaper critic wrote in *L'Opinion:*

> The stage was adorned with a simple drapery of neutral color lit by a somber and discreet light. Isadora Duncan danced barefoot, dressed in a simple tunic. She draws attention by the harmony of her movements, by the rhythmic subtlety of her body. She dances with exquisite grace, fine elegance, and lightness. Most of all, she gives the illusion of the most perfect naturalness.

Avenue du Général-Lemonnier (1st)

Le Palais des Tuileries. Today, if you stand at the Arc du Carrousel in the Tuileries Gardens, you can look due west across the Place de la Concorde and straight up the Champs-Elysées to the Arc de Triomphe. But before 1871 your view would have been blocked by the Palais des Tuileries, which stretched from the Pavillon de Marsan on the north, to the Pavillon de Flore, close to the Pont-Royal, on the south. The Palais des Tuileries was built in the time of Catherine of Medici and finished about 1610. Louis XIV and Louis XV lived in the palace briefly; Louis XVI was brought here from Versailles in 1789 and then beheaded four years later on the Place de la Concorde. Louis XVIII, Charles X, and Louis-Philippe also lived here. Many Americans were guests at this palace, but the most colorful visitors were George Catlin and his eleven Ioway Indians who performed for King Louis-Philippe in 1845. In his memoirs, Catlin described their arrival:

> On the morning of the day for their reception, the long stem of a beautiful pipe had been painted a bright blue, and ornamented with blue ribbons, emblematical of peace, to be presented by the chief to the King. Every article of dress and ornament had been put in readiness; and, as the hour approached, each one came out from his toilet, in a full blaze of colour of various tints, all with their wampum and medals on, with their necklaces of grizzly bears' claws, their shields, and bows, and quivers, their lances, and war clubs, and tomahawks, and scalping knives. In this way, in full dress, with their painted buffalo robes wrapped around them, they stepped into the several carriages prepared for them, and all were wheeled into the Place Carrousel, and put down at the entrance to the Palace. We were met on the steps by half a dozen huge and splendid looking porters, in flaming scarlet livery and powdered wigs, who conducted us in, and being met by one of the King's aides-de-camp, we were conducted by him into His Majesty's presence, in the reception hall of the Tuileries.

After the performance of dances and war-whoops and the brandishing of tomahawks in front of their tepee, Louis-Philippe chatted with Chief Little Wolf, telling him that he had been in America and enjoyed the hospitality of the Indian tribes. This conversation ended with Little Wolf presenting the king with his tomahawk. In a letter home, one of the Ioway warriors described the king's palace as a "big wigwam."

The palace was burned down during the Commune in 1871.

Rue Geoffroy-Saint-Hilaire (5th) Métro: Jussieu

36 The Intendant's house of the Jardin des Plantes. Thomas Jefferson, a frequent visitor to the botanical gardens, was a dinner guest here on several occasions. He has left us the best description of his host Georges Buffon, the great 18th-century naturalist, who occupied the house from 1772 until his death in 1788:

> It was Buffon's practice to remain in his study until dinner time, and receive no visitors under any pretence; but his house was open and his grounds, and a servant showed them very civilly, and invited all strangers and friends to remain to dine. We saw Buffon in the garden, but carefully avoided him, but we dined with him, and he proved himself then, as he always did, a man of extraordinary powers in conversation. He did not declaim; he was singularly agreeable.

40 Jardin des Plantes. In 1626, Louis XIII decided on the establishment of a Jardin Royal des Plantes Médicinales, modeled on a garden which had opened in Montpellier. The garden was finally opened to the public in 1640 and became known as the Jardin du Roy. The garden was developed as we see it today by Georges Buffon, who was director from 1739 until 1788. It was originally conceived as a practical school for the teaching of botany.

Among the many American visitors none was more frequent, or better informed, than Thomas Jefferson. Long before he arrived in Paris in 1784, he had been familiar with both the garden and Buffon's work. While preparing his *Notes on the State of Virginia,* he had studied Buffon's great *Histoire Universelle,* whose author, "the best informed of any Naturalist who has ever written," had cast "a blaze of light on the field of natural history."

Avenue George-Cinq (8th) Map G

23 American Cathedral. The remains of John Paul Jones lay in state here for three days. At 3:00 p.m. on 6 July 1905, 482 American bluejackets and their 22 officers attended a service at the cathedral. At 5:00 p.m., the coffin, accompanied by French cavalry, infantry, and officials of the French Republic, paraded down the Champs-Elysées to the Gare des Invalides to begin the long voyage to Annapolis. Thus Captain Jones received far greater recognition from the American government one century after his death than he ever received while he was alive.

31   Hôtel George V. Duke Ellington stayed at the George V in July 1933 while playing at the Salle Pleyel. In his memoirs, Ellington wrote that his apartment in the hotel was so vast that he spent five minutes trying to find his way out. Each door he tried either led to another room in the apartment or to a closet.

37   In June 1905, while on their honeymoon, Franklin and Eleanor Roosevelt visited Franklin's aunt Deborah Perry Delano, who owned an apartment here. She took them in her bubble car for a ride in the Bois de Boulogne, where FDR took driving lessons.

Avenue Georges-Mandel (16th) Métro: Pompe

43   Little has changed in this mansion since Winnaretta Singer bought it in 1890. She had a young French architect, Grand'Pierre, remove from the hall the ugly bronze elephants and rhinoceroses spouting water from their mouths and put in a classical 18th-century staircase. He also designed a magnificent music room, complete with mirrors in Versailles fashion.

Helped by the Singer sewing machine fortune, Winnaretta ran what was probably the most important music salon in Paris. Among the first concerts here was the premiere of *Clair de Lune,* poem by Verlaine, music by Gabriel Fauré. On the same program were new pieces by Ernest Chausson and Vincent d'Indy. On 15 December 1893, Winnaretta, 28, married the impoverished aristocrat Prince Edmond de Polignac. The prince, a musician and dilettante with exquisite taste, was a well-known homosexual, which allowed Winnaretta freedom to pursue her own sexual preferences. At the suggestion of her friend John Singer Sargent (no relation), who did her portrait, she began to buy works by Claude Monet, including *La Cathédrale de Rouen, Les Pommiers en fleur, Femme assise sous un arbre, Au Bord de la Seine,* and *La Barque à Giverny.* She also bought *La Lecture* by Manet and paintings by Renoir.

On the evening of 11 April 1907, Parisian society heard the premiere of Raynaldo Hahn's orchestrated suite *Le Bal de Beatrice d'Este,* with the composer conducting from the piano. During the loudest chords, the candlesticks began to totter and seemed about to fall. Marcel Proust was present that evening and reproduced this scene in *A la Recherche du Temps Perdu.* In June 1923, Paul Valéry spoke here on Italian art, and later that summer Winnaretta's guests heard the premiere of Manuel de Falla's *Retable de Maître Pierre*, with Wanda Landowska at the harpsichord, Madame Henri Casadessus at the harp, and orchestra conducted by Vladimir Golschmann. Commissioned works by Stravinsky, Ravel, and Milhaud were also performed. One evening in 1927, two pianists played duets—Stravinsky and Prokofiev. American guests included Henry James, Isadora Duncan, Ezra Pound, and Cole Porter.

Today, this mansion houses the Singer Foundation, which provides scholarships to students of art and music. Concerts are still given here.

Rue Gît-le-Coeur (6th) Map **A**

9   Hôtel du Vieux Paris, formerly Hôtel Gît-le-Coeur. This hotel served as the Paris pad of the Beat Generation of American writers in the 1950s. William Burroughs spent the summer of 1958 here finishing *The Naked Lunch,* published the following year in Paris by the Olympia Press.

It was late one night in July 1923 when John Dos Passos, E.E. Cummings, and Gilbert Seldes, editor of the *Dial,* paused on their way to a club (which Cummings called "the Calvados Joint on the Rue Gît-le-Coeur") while the poet relieved himself. At this point, according to Dos Passos, "a whole phalanx of Gendarmes" set upon Cummings and dragged him off to the Commissariat on Rue des Grands-Augustins. At the police station the following conversation took place:

> "Un Américain qui pisse," said the gendarme.
> "Quoi, encore un pisseur Américain," retorted the desk sergeant.

Although released for the night, Cummings was ordered to report back the following morning. Thanks to the intervention of French writer Paul Morand, the charge against Cummings was dropped. That night he went to a party at Seldes' apartment on the Ile St.-Louis, where posters read "Reprieve pisseur Américain."

Rue de la Grande-Chaumière (6th) Map **D**

9   Hôtel Liberia. Nathanael West moved here from the Hôtel Lutetia shortly after his arrival in Paris in 1926. During the 1920s, it was chic for American writers to talk about their years in Paris, and West was no exception. The dust jacket of *Miss Lonelyhearts* (1933) recounted how he had spent two years in Paris. In reality, he spent twelve weeks there. His most important novel was *The Day of the Locust* (1939), based on the sham of Hollywood, where he had become a scriptwriter.

Robert Breer, painter and sculptor, arrived in Paris in 1949, thanks to the GI Bill, and spent a spring and summer there. He devoted half his time to painting in his hotel room and the rest to studying sculpture with Zadkine at the Académie Colorossi. He became friends with Leo Zimmerman (known as "Monsieur Popcorn" because of his popcorn paintings) and Jack Youngerman, who were also studying in Paris. In 1950, Breer, Zimmerman, and Youngerman exhibited at the Galerie Denise René in Paris.

(10)　　Site of the Académie Colorossi.

14　　Académie de la Grande-Chaumière. Many Americans studied at this academy, especially during the 1920s. Betty Parsons worked here before returning to paint in Santa Barbara, California. In 1946, she opened her gallery on 57th Street in New York and became one of the pioneer dealers in American art.

Alexander Calder studied here upon his arrival in France in 1926. He recorded: "I went to the Grande-Chaumière to draw. Here there were no teachers, just a nude model, and everyone was drawing by himself." Calder had just spent three years at the Art Students League in New York City. He preferred Rue de la Grande-Chaumière, where he found the atmosphere more subdued.

Sculptress Malvina Hoffman arrived in Paris in 1910 at the age of 23 and took a furnished room somewhere on this street. She recalled that "On Monday mornings a long line of models of all colors and nationalities filled the sidewalks leading to these two academies [Académie de la Grande-Chaumière and Colorossi]."

Quai des Grands-Augustins (6th) Map A

This quay, which stretches from the Pont St.-Michel to the Pont Neuf, a distance of some 1,100 feet, was renowned in the 18th century for its bookshops and printers. Thomas Jefferson wrote to his friend Samuel Harrison Smith when offering his own collection to the library committee of Congress: "While residing in Paris, I devoted every afternoon I was disengaged, for a summer or two, in examining all the principal bookstores, turning over every book with my own hands, and putting by everything that was related to America, and indeed whatever was rare and valuable in every science."

(21)   Pissot bookseller. Pissot published the *General Advertiser,* a weekly "English and American Gazette." Thomas Jefferson welcomed the chance to insert American news in the gazette as a corrective to the London newspapers, "those infamous fountains of falsehood," as he called them.

(35)   Froullé bookseller and publisher. Thomas Jefferson negotiated with Froullé for the translation and printing of David Ramsay's two-volume *History of the Revolution of South Carolina,* which was a great success in 1785. It appeared in translation two years later as *Histoire de la Révolution de la Caroline du Sud.* Increasingly bothered by American land agents who were selling titles to Indian-held territories to unsuspecting French immigrants, Jefferson arranged for Froullé to reprint Benjamin Franklin's "Advice to Emigrants" as *Avis à ceux qui voudraient émigrer en Amérique.* When James Monroe was setting out for Paris in 1795, Jefferson advised him that

> speaking of Froullé, libraire, quai des Augustins, I can assure you, that, having run a severe gauntlet under the Paris book-sellers, I rested at last on this old gentleman, whom I found, in a long & intimate course of dealings, to be one of the most conscientiously honest men I ever had dealings with. I recommend him to you strongly should you purchase books.

Froullé was well aware of the knowledge and exacting standards of "Monsieur Chefersone."

37   Galerie Ileana Sonnabend opened in February 1963 with an exhibit of Robert Rauschenberg's work. His "combine-paintings," as he termed them, "made up of painting and sculpture," had already impressed French art critics, and collectors were beginning to buy his works. This show was followed by "Pop'art américain" which grouped the works of John Chamberlain, Oldenburg, Jim Rosenquist, Wesselman, and Andy Warhol with his *Twenty Marilyns,* the first Warhol to be shown in Paris. During the 1960s the Sonnabend Gallery was to become an important display center for young American artists. Rauschenberg exhibited here again in May 1964, Andy Warhol in 1965, and Jim Rosenquist the following year.

Boulevard de Grenelle (15th) Métro: Bir-Hakeim

(8) Site of the Vélodrome d'Hiver which opened in 1910. Ernest Hemingway used to come to this indoor stadium in the 1920s to watch the six-day bicycle races. Hemingway dragged along as many friends as he could, including John Dos Passos. They came with wine, bread, cheese, and blankets for the night. Many confessed later, in their memoirs and journals, that they had no desire to go there, but it was difficult to say no to Hemingway.

Billy Graham preached here in June 1955 while a large French crowd chanted "Beelee, Beelee." Graham supposedly said that "the French just sin and sin, and get weaker." He also preached in a large tent auditorium in a vacant lot in the Flea Market area, where he asked the men in the audience: "Why are you unfaithful to your wives?"

The Vélodrome was torn down in 1959.

Pont de Grenelle (15th) Métro: Javel

L'Allée des Cygnes. On the southwest side of the bridge, in the center of the Seine, lies the extremity of the Allée des Cygnes (Swans' Walk). On 4 July 1887, before a large American and French public, French president Jules Grévy inaugurated a second Statue of Liberty, one-tenth the size of the original. It was designed by Bartholdi, and poured in the foundry of the Thiébaut Brothers on Rue de Villiers on 7 May 1885. This statue was also a gift, but this time to the city of Paris by the local American colony. There was a minor problem before the ceremony: Bartholdi wanted the statue to face downstream, which meant that the French president would have had to unveil the back of the lady, given the bridge and the site of the statue. The problem was solved by having the "grande dame," as the French called her, face upstream for the unveiling ceremony;

afterwards she was turned to face downstream and her sister across the ocean.

Rue de Grenelle (7th) Map C

(7)   Hôtel de Lyon. Aaron Burr arrived in Paris on the evening of Friday, 16 February 1810. Burr's political career had ended after he killed Alexander Hamilton in a duel. He had then become involved in dubious land schemes in the southwest. Arrested, tried for treason, and found innocent, Burr left for Europe in 1808. He spent four years wandering from capital to capital in another scheme to finance the liberation of Mexico from Spain. He tried to secure an interview with Napoleon, but this was countered by Talleyrand, who considered Burr the assassin of the greatest American politician. In addition, the American community in Paris saw Burr as attempting to dismember the United States by urging the western territories to declare independence, and agreed among themselves that anyone who spoke to Burr was to be "shunned as unworthy of society." But Burr persisted. Napoleon's brother Jérome Bonaparte, now king of Westphalia, had been Burr's guest at his New York estate. On 4 April, Burr was received "graciously," his *Journal* recorded, by the new king of Westphalia and "passed half an hour in private with him." But Napoleon was suspicious of Burr and still refused to see him. (The French Archives Nationales contain four of Burr's memoirs outlining his propositions.) Unsuccessful, Burr returned in 1812 to New York City, where he quietly resumed the practice of law.

102   Hôtel de Maillebois. Built in 1660, this mansion was occupied in 1750 by the Duc de Saint-Simon, who worked on his *Mémoires* here until his death five years later at the age of 80. During the French Revolution, the *hôtel* was confiscated by the government and awarded as a prize in the National Lottery. It was won by Edward Church, the American consul in Lisbon, who happened to be on a visit to Paris. He sold it to his fellow American consul, Fulwar Skipwith, in 1796. On 4 July, Skipwith and his companion, la Marquise de la Villette, gave an impressive banquet under a large tent in the garden for their numerous American and French friends. Although these mansions cost little during the revolution, they still required a large staff and massive upkeep. Skipwith sold the house after one year.

105   Madame de Staël lived here, and among her guests on the evening of 15 February 1815 were Lafayette, the financier Le Ray de Chaumont, the Duc de Broglie, and John Quincy Adams. Adams recorded in his diary that there was "some conversation between the lady and a Mr. [Benjamin] Constant"; the hostess "seemed to consider it as a principle to contradict him." Constant had been Madame de Staël's lover.

104-106   Le Temple de Pentemont. During the second half of the 18th century, this well-known convent (the Abbaye Royale de Pentemont) was run by the worldly abbess Madame de Mézières. In the autumn of 1784, Martha ("Patsy") Jefferson, Thomas Jefferson's daughter, became a pensionnaire here. "I was placed in a convent at my arrival," Martha wrote to a friend, "and I ask you to judge of my situation. I did not speak a word of French. ... There are fifty or sixty pensioners in the house, so that speaking as much as I could with them I learnt the language very soon. At present I am charmed with my situation." There was some concern back in Virginia upon learning that Martha had entered a convent. "There are in it as many Protestants as Catholics," Jefferson reassured his sister Mrs. Bolling, "and not a word is ever spoken to them on the subject of religion." Lessons were largely given by visiting "masters" and included reading, arithmetic, geography, history, music, drawing, and dancing. Martha took lessons on the harpsichord from the talented organist of Notre-Dame, Claude Balbastre. The rate for room and board was 175 livres per quarter, exclusive of masters' fees. In the school accounts, the family appears as "Gefferssone," but Martha was always listed as "Mademoiselle de Jefferson." Her fellow pensionnaires called her "Jeff." In 1787, the 15-year-old Martha was joined by her younger sister Mary. Both girls left in the spring of 1789 to join their father at the Hôtel de Langeac before returning to Virginia.

Rue Hamelin (16th) Map **G**

44   Union Hôtel Etoile. Man Ray came to this former apartment building early on Monday morning, 20 November 1922. He had been summoned by Dr. Robert Proust in order to photograph his brother Marcel Proust, who had died two days earlier. It was here that Man Ray made the portraits of the author's folded hands and majestic head. But he was not the only American presence in that stark room. "My room," Proust had written to a friend, "contains in its intentional nudity, only a single reproduction of a work of art, Whistler's *Carlyle,* whose cloak is as serpentine in its folds as the gown of Whistler's *Mother.*" There is a Proust commemorative plaque on the first floor.

Boulevard Haussmann (9th)

On 16 October 1784, after two months in France, Thomas Jefferson signed a nine-year lease for "un hôtel sis à Paris rue et Cul de sac Taitbout Chaussée d'Antin." The house itself, originally at the triangle of Rue Taitbout, Rue Helder, and Place Adrien Oudin, would have been on the north side of Boulevard Haussmann. The rent was set at 4,000 livres per year. From his Account Book, we learn that Jefferson paid 1,500 livres per quarter, so there must have been some private agreement supplementing the official lease. The lease describes the house as having "three main parts *(corps de logis),* a courtyard and two gardens." The mansion had been recently built, but it was relatively small compared to the town houses in the neighborhood. Jefferson himself selected the furniture, linen, blankets, carpets, clocks, silverware, and dishes. The future American minister soon discovered that the "first expences, or Outfit," in spite of being "all plain," exceeded his year's salary. He rented a pianoforte for twelve francs a month and acquired books, paintings, and engravings, most of which would end up in Monticello. The staff consisted of a maître d'hôtel, a valet de chambre, a coachman, and *un frotteur* whose job was to polish floors. During this first year, Jefferson did not have a cook, relying on a local *traiteur* (caterer) for the main dishes. He apprenticed his negro servant James Hemings to the local caterer Combeaux. His guests included William Short, his 26-year-old secretary, who would become chargé d'affaires in 1789 upon Jefferson's departure, and 17-year-old John Quincy Adams. But this was not a happy first year in Paris. In January 1785, Jefferson received the news of the death of the youngest of his three daughters, Lucy Elizabeth, in Virginia.

Boulevard de l'Hôpital (13th) Métro: St.-Marcel

47   Hôpital de la Salpêtrière. Mary Putnam, medical student, worked here in 1867, in a ward devoted to what she described as "hysteria patients." She wrote to her parents: "There are about 400

collected in a most villainously old building," built, she added, "300 or 400 years ago." Actually, the hospital had been built at the orders of Louis XIV and had opened in 1657 to receive women, destitute or ill, while in the basements "mad and incurable women" were chained to the wall in cells which frequently flooded in winter and "where rats roamed at will."

Rue de la Huchette (5th) Map E

28   Hôtel du Mont-Blanc, formerly Hôtel du Caveau. The Hôtel du Caveau is described by Elliot Paul, who lived there in 1925, in his book *The Last Time I Saw Paris*. His friend and fellow journalist William Shirer enjoyed late night parties in the cellar. A few doors away was Madame Mariette's Le Panier Fleuri, a *maison close* (brothel) which opened at 2:00 p.m. and closed punctually at 2:00 a.m. Here Shirer, fresh from a Presbyterian college in Iowa, interviewed the girls to establish the degree to which they were victimized, only to discover "that the girls considered prostitution as a decent means of earning more than an average income." Nor did they feel, he wrote, "that they were being exploited by economics or by men." This street dates from 1284.

Avenue d'Iéna (16th)

(2)   The building was purchased in 1924 by American ambassador Myron T. Herrick. Ambassador Herrick was incensed by the American tradition of not providing suitable houses for ambassadors, but instead appointing millionaires who paid for their own residences. In a letter to the American government, he referred bitterly to "the dollar as the only qualification for appointment to ambassadorial positions." Using his own money, he purchased this house for the sum of 5,400,000 francs (200,000 dollars), the franc having depreciated seriously that year against the dollar. Indeed, at 27 francs to the dollar, the exchange had closed in a panic on 10 March. By pure coincidence, the next morning the ambassador told his bankers to buy 200,000 dollars worth of francs. They asked if they should buy gradually so as to obtain the best rates. No, answered Herrick. Was the purchase of these francs to be considered a secret? Certainly not, answered Herrick. As soon as the Paris Bourse opened and the news spread that the American ambassador was buying up massive quantities of francs, speculators, guessing that the American government had decided to back the French franc, scrambled to buy francs, while those long on dollars raced to sell them. The result was that the plunge of the franc was temporarily stemmed. The secretary of state cabled the ambassador in Paris immediately: "Reports from Berlin...assert that you are speculating in francs. What reply shall I make?"

Three years later, Ambassador Herrick received a famous and unexpected guest, Charles Lindbergh. By early evening on 21 May 1927, rumor swept Paris that *The Spirit of St. Louis* would soon arrive at Le Bourget Airport, fourteen kilometers northeast of Paris. Alexander Calder was seated on the terrace of the Café du Dôme when he heard the news at 7:00 p.m. Calder, along with several fellow Americans, jumped into a cab for Le Bourget. But the road to the airport was blocked by crowds, which Calder and his friends joined as they walked the final kilometers to the airfield. By 10:00 p.m. there were over 100,000 people at the airport watching the evening sky. A few minutes later when *The Spirit of St. Louis* touched down, its 25-year-old pilot barely escaped from the enthusiasm of the French crowd. He eventually reached Ambassador Herrick's residence on the Avenue d'Iéna where he held his first press conference at 3:00 a.m. Lindbergh slept ten hours and awoke the following afternoon to find 25 movie cameramen, 50 newspaper photographers, and 200 reporters in the courtyard of the ambassador's residence. Outside, a vast, enthusiastic crowd blocked the entire avenue. During the night, the ambassador had sent the following telegram to Lindbergh's mother: "Warmest congratulations. Your incomparable son has honored me by becoming my guest. He is in fine condition and sleeping sweetly under Uncle Sam's roof. Myron T. Herrick."

Boulevard des Invalides (7th) Map C

33   Lycée Victor Duruy. At the end of summer 1908, Matisse was forced to move his academy here from Rue de Sèvres. The academy was begun at the suggestion of Michael and Sarah Stein, and although Matisse was little suited to teaching, it drew 120 students between the years 1908 and 1911, when Matisse gave it up. Some fifteen to twenty American students worked here, Patrick Henry Bruce and Max Weber among them. Many other American painters claim to have been here.

In *The Autobiography of Alice B. Toklas* Gertrude Stein described the academy as being disorganized and rife with quarreling, which led at least one American student, Walter Pach, to quit. A few years later, when Pach helped organize the Armory Show in New York, he began to regret his youthful decision, for the reputation of Matisse had started to spread, particularly in the United States.

Bruce, who had his studio next door to Matisse's, was influenced by Renoir and Cézanne while working with Robert Delauney. His painting *Harmony,* exhibited in the Salon des Indépendants, was highly praised by Guillaume Apollinaire. The New York press wrote that Bruce was "the only American painter at all considered by French artists." However, after World War I, he continued working in France in increasing isolation. Just before leaving to return home to New York in 1936, he destroyed all but fifteen of his paintings. His suicide the following year represented a major loss to American art. (*Painting 1930,* Collection Whitney Museum of American Art, New York.)

Esplanade des Invalides (7th) Map C

Hôtel des Invalides. The first stone was laid here on 30 November 1671, and five years later 6,000 homeless French veterans were able to move in, although construction was not finished until 1706. In 1840, the remains of Napoleon were brought back from St. Helena, and his tomb was finished in April 1861.

In 1786, John Trumbull arrived in Paris from London, where he had been studying painting under Benjamin West. Trumbull had had difficulty trying to convince his family to support him while he studied art. In a letter to his father, he dwelt upon the honors paid to artists in the glorious days of Greece and Athens, only to receive the reply from the governor of Connecticut: "You appear to forget, sir, that Connecticut is not Athens." Happily, his father relented and Trumbull went on to become the great historical painter of the War of Independence. Trumbull spoke excellent French and kept a journal while working and studying in Europe. At the Louvre he visited the studio of Jacques-Louis David, saw many of the great private collections thanks to his guide Houdon, and met artist Maria Cosway and her husband. He found David's *Oath of the Horatii* to be "a story well told, drawing pretty good, colouring cold." Houdon's *Diana* was "a very beautiful figure—an honor not only to the artist, but to the country and age in which he lives." It was in Paris, while staying with Jefferson, that Trumbull began the sketches of *The Declaration of Independence* (Yale University Art Gallery, New Haven, Conn.) with his host providing details of the event and a sketch of the room.

Thanks to Trumbull we have the most complete description by an American of many important buildings in Paris in the 18th century. He left fine observations on the Hôtel des Invalides, the Panthéon, the Church of St.-Sulpice, and the Hôtel de Clermont on Rue de Varenne, among others. On Tuesday, 7 August 1786, Trumbull recorded in his *Journal:*

> The Hôtel des Invalides. This is a noble institution; the buildings are extensive and well planned, equal to the accommodation of six thousand men; at present, there are only four thousand seven hundred. The church in which the service is performed is plain; through it you pass to the dome, which is truly one of the most beautiful pieces of architecture in this kind that has hitherto been executed. It is light and airy in its proportions—the sculpture well wrought—the paintings barely tolerable—the whole clean and well kept—the four chapels, in the angles of the dome, are very elegant and rich; but among all the paintings, whether of the chapels or the dome, there is nothing worthy of much attention. The centre of the dome is the best, and in one apartment adjoining the Salle du Conseil there is a small picture, said to be the original design from which this centre was painted, which is very well, much better in truth than the great work. The Salle du Conseil contains a number of portraits of great men, but in general intolerably bad.

On Saturday, 25 April 1789, Gouverneur Morris visited the Hôtel des Invalides. In his diary for that day he recorded:

> A most magnificent piece of architecture. The Chapel and the Dome are sublime. In the Kitchen we are made to observe among other things a little Kettle with 2,500 Pounds of Beef in it for tomorrow's Soup, another with a smaller quantity for Messieurs les Officiers. A Spectacle which excited the greatest effect in my Mind was a Number of mutilated Veterans on their Knees in the Chapel. The most sincere Devotion. Poor Wretches they have no hope on this Side of the Grave.

When the news of George Washington's death on 14 December 1799 reached France the following month, solemn honors were rendered to his memory throughout the country. For ten days the officers of the French army wore mourning and flags were at half-mast. In General Bonaparte's address to his troops, he said, "Washington is dead. This great man fought against tyranny. His memory will be always cherished by the French people as by all free men of the two worlds, and especially by the French soldiers who, like him and the American soldiers, fought for equality and liberty."

American visitors to both the *hôtel* and Napoleon's tomb have been numerous. In June 1840, Elizabeth Cady Stanton was in Europe for a meeting of the World Anti-Slavery Society and wrote:

> We visited the Hôtel des Invalides just as they were preparing the sarcophagus for the reception of the remains of Napoleon. We witnessed the wild excitement of that enthusiastic people, and listened with deep interest to the old soldiers' praises of their great general. The ladies of our party chatted freely with them. They all had interesting anecdotes to relate of their chief. They said he seldom slept over four hours, was an abstemious eater, and rarely changed a servant, as he hated a strange face about him. He was very fond of a game of chess, and snuffled continuously; talked but little, was a light sleeper,—the stirring of a mouse would awaken him,—and always on the watchtower. They said that in his great campaigns, he seemed to be omnipresent. A sentinel asleep at his post would sometimes waken to find Napoleon on duty in his place.

Mark Twain visited the tomb in 1867, and two years later in *The Innocents Abroad* he described it as "that wonder of wonders."

In August 1881, Theodore Roosevelt wrote to his sister, "and what I enjoyed even more [was] the tomb of Napoleon. I do not think that there is a more impressive sepulchre on earth than that tomb; it is grandly simple. I am not very easily awestruck, but it certainly gave me a solemn feeling to look at the plain, red stone bier which contained what had once been the mightiest conqueror the world ever saw."

Boulevard des Italiens (2nd)

(27)   Les Bains Chinois occupied this site from 1792 until 1853. The building, in the form of a giant pagoda, hence the name Chinese Baths, also housed a beauty institute, a restaurant, and a café. Exceedingly popular among Americans, the most glowing description came from the pen of Isaac Appleton Jewett in 1836:

I think the finest bathing rooms I have ever seen, are at Nottingham, Manchester, and at Liverpool, in England. But with their magnificence, their merit ceases. They have not about them any of those hundred little contrivances of ingenuity, whereby an hour passed in a French bath, and under the hands of a French baigneur, is rendered one of the most intensely delicious of any in your foreign life. To lie down in water raised to ninety-six of Fahrenheit; to brush my limbs with laborious toil some thirty minutes; to wipe all moisture, with icy towels, shiveringly away; to dress myself again, and walk homeward,—such were the dreary facts, with which bathing had till now been associated in my memory. My first experience in Paris, convinced me that I had not yet arrived at even the threshold of the bathing art. And still, the most refined system in all this metropolis, advances hardly into the antechamber of the old Roman luxury.

The surest mode for securing all the delight which surrounds a first rate Parisian bath is, to inform the *garçon,* with an amiable smile, that you throw yourself frankly into his hands. Tell him you desire to know the extremity of his talent. Insinuate that you have somehow heard of this establishment, and wish now to test its fame. Surprising, what attachment seems instantly to spring up out of his heart towards you! He places a snowy bed-cloth in the bath. He perfumes the water. He invites you gently to step therein. He presents you a *carte* of his perfumeries, his little wines and refreshments. He places before you, on a convenient stand, the *Journal des Débats.* He shows you the *brevet* whereby he is an authorized "Professor of corn-cutting." He opens his case of professional instruments. He pares and refines your foot, into the delicacy of the noblest lady's hand. He *laves* [washes] you in balmiest *savon* [soap], till your bath-water is mellowed into the whiteness of cream. He pours over you most aromatic cologne, and with his mittened hand, opens wide all doors to perspiration. For forty or fifty minutes, he is continually about your back, and breast, and legs, and feet. His interest in them seems growing into an affection. At length he rings a bell, and soon is conveyed into your presence a huge basket. "Arise, sir," he says, "quick, quick." Ascending up from the soap-foam, as it were, a masculine Venus of the bath, one burning napkin is hurried on your breast, and another over your shoulders; your arms are thrust into the sleeves of a hot peignoir; other napkins replace the moistened ones; an ample robe-de-chambre is wrapped around your body; your legs are enfolded about in tight warm linen; delicate slippers half embrace your nether extremities, and reposing in one cushioned arm chair, with your legs deposited by the baigneur along another, you respond with no describable emotions, to his triumphant question,—"Eh bien, Monsieur, comment trouvez-vous cela?" [Well, Sir, how do you like that?] The *garçon* leaves you now to solitary enjoyment, wherein meditating, you feel your nerves tranquil, and your pulses beating cool; the pleasant of the past is alone remembered, the future is all in light; you feel physically born again, and you declare aloud that the long-sought fountain of rejuvenescence was not altogether a dream. For such skill, and effort, and interest on the part of the *garçon,* and for such satisfaction in yourself, you cheerfully pay seven, eight, and perhaps nine francs.

Rue Jacob (6th) Map **A**

20   Natalie Clifford Barney moved here in 1909 and stayed for over 60 years. Born in Dayton, Ohio, in 1877, she came to Paris as a student and never left. Wealthy, beautiful, and a patroness of the arts, she was portrayed in Radclyffe Hall's *The Well of Loneliness,* in a novel by Colette, and in *Lettres à l'Amazone* by Rémy de Gourmont. Her guests included Virgil Thomson, Sherwood Anderson, Carl Van Vechten, T.S. Eliot, Bernard Berenson, James Joyce, Proust, Apollinaire, and Gide. At Pound's suggestion, in 1926, the premiere of George Antheil's First String Quartet was given here. On a June afternoon in 1934, Edna St. Vincent Millay was present when translations of her poems were read by Rachel Berendt of the Comédie Française. In the garden stands a small Greek temple dating from 1800, once used by the local masonic lodge, with the inscription "A l'amitié." Of Natalie Clifford Barney, Janet Flanner wrote, "she was a perfect example of an enchanted person not to write about."

22   Formerly Hôtel Grande Bretagne. Late in the morning of 28 December 1793, Joel Barlow opened his door to discover his friend Thomas Paine in the hands of two French police commissioners. Paine had been arrested at dawn that morning in the hotel La

Maison de Philadelphie, in the Passage des Petits-Pères. The police, who had orders to arrest him and to confiscate any dangerous manuscripts, wanted to proceed immediately to Paine's house just outside the walls of the city. But Paine's most important manuscript, *The Rights of Man,* lay in the room next door in La Maison de Philadelphie, where it was being read by a friend. In a ploy to gain time, Paine convinced the commissioners and the police escort to have a simple collation at his expense. The meal, served at the hotel, was accompanied by several bottles of excellent wine, and lasted three hours. During this time Paine managed to communicate with his friend, and the two decided that the safest place for the manuscript was in the hands of Barlow. The police detail, headed by Commissioner Doilé, agreed to a brief visit to Paine's "boyhood friend" Joel Barlow before proceeding to Paine's house and then on to prison. Thus Paine was brought here to Rue Jacob where he was able to slip the entire manuscript into a safe hiding place while Joel Barlow chatted amiably with his escort. Shortly after noon, Paine, accompanied by Barlow and the police, journeyed across Paris to his residence at 142 Rue du Faubourg St.-Denis, where they spent the afternoon going through his papers. But the pamphleteer was at ease knowing that his most important work was safe. Late that afternoon, Paine was escorted to the Luxembourg Palace, which was serving as a prison. The jailer Benoît handed over a written receipt in exchange for his American prisoner. In the best tradition of the civil service, Commissioner Doilé devoted many hours to making out a detailed report describing the entire day, from the difficulty of understanding *Peine, Amériquain,* to the need for breakfast due to a *grande fatigue,* followed by the visit to Barlow, *son ami natal* (in reality, the two men had first met in England in 1787). Commissioner Doilé informed his superiors that one of Paine's windows looked onto *le jardin,* while two others opened onto the courtyard. As for incriminating documents, they did not find any, but brought back a number of English and American gazettes which they could not read. (This report remains carefully preserved and may still be consulted in the Archives Nationales, Document F 7 4774 64.)

44   Hôtel d'Angleterre. This hotel is much the same today as when Washington Irving stayed here. Notice the original heavy wooden doors as you enter. Once inside the hotel, look at the first two steps of the staircase to your left. This is the original 18th-century staircase, although some of the higher steps have been repaired or replaced.

Washington Irving moved here from Rue de Richelieu on 4 June 1805. In his journal Irving recorded, "at 60 livres per month room pleasantly situated on the ground floor well furnished with a cabinet etc. looks out on a handsome little garden." The 22-year-old Irving was good friends with the painter John Vanderlyn, who lived nearby. They attended the Porte St.-Martin Theater together, and for 15 June, Irving noted: "Went to a 15 sous ball in Palais Royal with Vanderlyn. Crowded with *filles de joie.*"

Sherwood Anderson stayed at the Angleterre when he arrived in France in 1921, at the age of 45. He rented a large double room for 75 cents a day. Upon his recommendation, Ernest Hemingway and his wife Hadley took a room here that December. Hemingway described the holes in the staircase carpets as "traps for drunken guests." On Christmas Day, Ernest and Hadley walked down Rue Bonaparte and across the Seine to the Avenue de l'Opéra, and had Christmas lunch at the Café de la Paix, having first carefully calculated the cost. After a fine meal came the bill. It was far more than they had anticipated, and Hemingway had to run back to their hotel, leaving Hadley at the table as collateral.

52 Formerly Hôtel de Hambourg. Benjamin Franklin took rooms at this hotel with his two grandsons on 8 January 1777. He stayed until the end of February and then moved to Passy, where he lived for the next eight years. Barely a week after his arrival here from his hotel on nearby Rue de l'Université, Franklin learned good news: Louis XVI had authorized a secret payment of two million livres to be put at his disposal for the purchase of arms and general military supplies.

56 Formerly Hôtel d'York. At 9:00 a.m. on Wednesday, 3 September 1783, Benjamin Franklin, John Jay, and John Adams, representing the United States, and David Hartley and Richard Oswald, representing Great Britain, signed the peace treaty that recognized the independence of the United States. It was customary for heads of state to give presents to the mediators. The British decided, perhaps rightly, that the traditional diamond-encased portrait of George III would scarcely be appropriate for the three

Americans. The sum of 1,000 pounds sterling each was suggested instead, which Hartley qualified as "very handsome and satisfactory." However, none of the American negotiators recorded any such present. Indeed, the final signing after months of negotiations and some intrigue was anticlimactic.

John and Abigail Adams and their children spent a few days here in the beginning of September 1784 before taking a house in Auteuil.

James Baldwin shared an apartment with the painter Lucien Happersberger somewhere on this street in the late 1940s. Baldwin recalled: "We lived in this terrible place on the Rue Jacob, way up on the top floor."

Rue Jacques-Callot (6th) Map **A**

16 The Galerie Surréaliste opened on 26 March 1926 with a show devoted to *Tableaux de Man Ray et objets des îles* (Paintings by Man Ray and objects from the isles). The public was asked to come at midnight.

Rue Jean-Ferrandi (6th) Map **B**

3 bis Sculptor Augustus St. Gaudens returned to Paris from New York in 1897. He was 49 and now famous. His statues of Lincoln in Lincoln Park, Chicago, of Deacon Samuel Chapin (the Puritan) in Springfield, Massachusetts, and the Shaw Memorial on Boston Common had made him the foremost sculptor in America. It was in this narrow street, surrounded by the studios of fellow sculptors, that he spent three years on this, his last visit to Paris. Here he worked on the statue of General Sherman, which was displayed in Paris before going to a permanent home at the 59th Street entrance to Central Park in New York.

On the evening of 10 May 1898, St. Gaudens had as a dinner guest his young cousin Louise Homer. She was on her way to Vichy where she was to make her debut as a contralto. She recalled that the dinner conversation revolved around one subject, the problem of a cloak for Sherman, who sat astride his horse silently in the room next door. Presumably the problem was not easily resolved, for there was a rush in the final days before the exhibit as eleven molders hurried to get Sherman ready for the Paris show. As St. Gaudens told his son:

> Dear Homer:
>
> At last I have a free moment to send you a line. Talk of the insane weather in Cornish, that's nothing to the insane asylum at the above address for the last eleven days. Eleven molders, some of them working all night with the boss lunatic, your illustrious father, at their head! Whew!!! Sometimes I'd cry, then I'd laugh, then I'd do both together, then I'd rush out into the street and howl, and so on. Now it's as peaceful as the ocean in a dead calm. Only I have got a swelled head for the first time in my life, for the "Sherman" really looks bully and is smashingly fine. It's in the place of honor at the Champs-de-Mars, and from a screeching maniac I have become a harmless, drooling, gibbering idiot, sitting all day long looking at the statue. Occasionally I fall on my knees and adore it. And there you are!

These were clearly very happy years. A week later he told a friend:

> This Paris experience, as far as my art goes, has been a great thing for me. I never felt sure of myself before, I groped ahead. All blindness seems to have been washed away. I see my place clearly now; I know, or think I know, just where I stand. A great self-confidence has come over me, and a tremendous desire and will to achieve high things, with a confidence that I shall, has taken possession of me. I exhibited at the Champs-de-Mars and the papers have spoken well, and it seems as if I were having what they call a "success" here. I send you some of the extracts from several of the principal artistic papers here, the *Gazette des Beaux Arts, Art et Décoration,* and from the *Dictionnaire Encyclopédique Larousse;* four of these have asked permission to reproduce my work.

St. Gaudens was made an Officier de la Légion d'honneur and the French government bought his bronze *Amor; Caritas* for the Musée du Luxembourg in Paris.

Avenue Kléber (16th) Map G

19 Centre de Conférences Internationales, formerly Hôtel Majestic, one of the most exclusive hotels in Paris. It was used as general headquarters by the German army during World War II, and then taken over by the French foreign ministry for international conferences. It was here in 1972 that Henry Kissinger represented the United States in the negotiations over the cease-fire with North Vietnam.

On Sunday, 25 March 1928, George Gershwin, accompanied by Ira, Lee, and Frances Gershwin, took a large suite in this hotel, where Gershwin continued working on *An American in Paris*. The work was clearly inspired by the city. In his program notes, Gershwin wrote:

> This new piece, really a rhapsodic ballet, is written very freely and is the most modern music I've yet attempted. The opening part will be developed in typical French style, in the manner of Debussy and the Six, though the themes are all original. My purpose here is to portray the impression of an American visitor in Paris, as he strolls about the city, and listens to various street noises and absorbs the French atmosphere.

One morning, Gershwin, accompanied by composer Alexander Tansman, walked from the Hôtel Majestic up to the Etoile and crossed over to the Avenue de la Grande-Armée. Here they found stores which sold automobile spare parts and they purchased some taxi cab horns. A few days later, a young American piano student, Mario Braggiotti, and his French friend Jacques Frey learned that their hero George Gershwin was in Paris, and they decided to try to meet him. Many years later, Braggiotti recalled:

> So we went to his hotel one morning and boldly knocked on his door. He opened it. He was in his dressing gown, and his hair was all kind of up in what I call the composer's style. I said, "Mr. Gershwin, my name is Mario and this is Jacques. We are music students and we just would like to meet you." "Well, boys, that's fine," he said, "come right in." He was very welcoming. There was a Steinway piano right in the middle of his room and I noticed on the piano a collection of taxi horns—from those old-fashioned taxis they used in the Bataille de la Marne. There were about twenty of them lying there. I hadn't been to New York in a few years, so I thought this was some new American eccentricity or fad. I didn't know what to make of it.
>
> "Oh," he said, "you're looking at these horns. Well, in the opening section of *An American in Paris* I would like to get the traffic sound of the Place de la Concorde during the rush hour, and I'd like to see if it works. I've written the first two pages of the opening. Jacques, you take this horn—this is in A flat. Mario, you

take this—it's in F sharp. Now, I'll sit down and play, and when I go this way with my head, you go 'quack, quack, quack' like that in that rhythm."

So we took the horns, and there we stood, nervous and excited, and for the first time we heard the opening bars of *An American in Paris*—a lanky American walking down the Champs-Elysées. He captured the atmosphere, the feeling, the movement, the rhythm so perfectly.

Well, when we came to the horn parts, he nodded and we came in. That was the first and last time that I ever played French taxi horns with such a distinguished composer.

Gershwin later visited the young men at Frey's apartment and heard them play his songs on two Pleyels. He then asked them if they would like to go to London to open in his new show *Funny Face,* starring Fred Astaire. "Who is Fred Astaire?" they asked. They spent the next year in London with the show and became regular Gershwin recording artists.

Gershwin transformed his hotel suite into a personal recital hall, playing for Darius Milhaud, Francis Poulenc, Georges Auric, Serge Prokofiev, Leopold Stokowski, William Walton, and whoever else dropped in. His brother and lyricist Ira recalled George playing late into the night with Cole Porter.

Rue La Boétie (8th) Map G

19   The Henry James family took an apartment here in September 1856 and stayed until the following spring. Henry, 13, went to school in the nearby Rue Balzac. James recalled in *A Small Boy and Others* (1913) the windows of the family apartment from which he witnessed the life of the *quartier:*

> What faced us was a series of subjects, with the baker, at the corner, for the first—the impeccable dispenser of the so softly-crusty crescent-rolls that we woke up each morning to hunger for afresh.... Then came the small cremerie, white picked out with blue, which, by some secret of its own keeping, afforded, within the compass of a few feet square, prolonged savoury meals to working men, white-frocked or blue-frocked, to uniformed cabmen, stout or spare, but all more or less audibly *bavard* and discernibly critical; and next the compact embrasure of the ecaillere or oyster-lady, she and her paraphernalia fitted into their interstice much as the mollusc itself into its shell; neighboured in

turn by the marchand-de-bois, peeping from as narrow a cage, his neat faggots and chopped logs stacked beside him and above him in his sentry-box quite as the niches of saints, in early Italian pictures.

45 Salle Gaveau. In June 1921, the Harvard Glee Club gave three concerts here. It was the first American glee club to perform in France. It was so enthusiastically received that the French critics urged the formation of similar choruses in French universities. The program included Allegri's Miserere, Lotti's Crucifixus, Handel's Hallelujah! Amen and Adoremus Te, and secular pieces. The singing group was received at the Elysée by French President Millerand. Satie, Milhaud, and Poulenc offered to write music for the club.

An entire concert devoted to young American composers was given on 5 May 1926 by the Société Musicale Indépendante. It was sponsored by Nadia Boulanger and Walter Damrosch, who taught at the American Academy of Music at Fontainebleau. The program included Virgil Thomson's Sonata da Chiesa for five instruments, two pieces for violin and piano by Aaron Copland, a piano sonata by Walter Piston, piano pieces by Herbert Elwell, a violin-piano sonata by Theodore Chanler, and a string quartet by George Antheil. Virgil Thomson wrote of the concert:

> All these pieces were characteristic of the newest in American talent, as well as of postwar Parisian ways, which is to say that they applied old-master layouts to contemporary melodic inspirations and harmonic concepts. My way of doing this, also Antheil's, was derived from the latest works of Igor Stravinsky; the others had theirs more in Boulanger, who was both an organist conditioned to Bach and a pupil of Gabriel Fauré. A certain unity of musical method, nevertheless, underlay personal variations and gave to the concert a recognizable impact, just as fine executions gave it brilliance.

52 John Singer Sargent and his parents lived at number 52 in 1874. Born in Florence, Italy, to American parents, aristocratic, cultured, and urbane, Sargent was the very image of Henry James's American expatriate. At 18, Sargent had already studied painting for two years in Italy, but had not yet visited the United States.

Rue de La Condamine (17th) Métro: La Fourche

22 Man Ray arrived in Paris on 14 July 1921 at the age of 31. It was his first visit to Paris, and he was met by Marcel Duchamp, whom he had known in New York. Duchamp's painting *Nude Descending a Staircase* had been a sensation in the New York Armory Show. Man Ray took a room here on the top floor and stayed for four months. He was soon friends with Dadaists Tristan Tzara, André Breton, Louis Aragon, and Francis Picabia, and eventually was the only American to be considered a member of the French Dada group.

Rue Lamartine (9th) Métro: Cadet

5 Offices of the *Chicago Tribune*. William Shirer was interviewed on 20 August 1925 for a job as a beginning copywriter. His credentials consisted of two years as editor of his college newspaper in Iowa. Reminiscing half a century later, Shirer felt that he had gotten the job because he had told them he came from Chicago. In Paris, they wanted someone from back home. What he neglected to tell his interviewer, the night editor, was that he had left Chicago when he was nine and didn't much like what little he recalled. He began work that very evening. At the desk next to him was "a lanky, owl-eyed man with thick glasses" named Jim Thurber. Shirer soon discovered that to fill eight pages each evening required primarily imagination. They would get a skimpy 100-word cable from New York and would set to work. If the boxing news was that the favorite had won by a KO in the fourteenth round, they would then describe the fight in detail, round by round. The same held true for baseball. Thurber's specialty was reproducing the inane homilies of President Coolidge. When Coolidge did not give speeches, Thurber wrote them anyway. He once had Coolidge address a convention of Protestant church leaders, where he had him declare "a man who does not pray is not a praying man." Shirer was hired at 1,200 francs (60 dollars) per month. In his *20th Century Journey*, "Growing up in Paris, 1925-1927," he wrote that to be fresh out of Iowa, young, free, and to have a job with a newspaper in Paris "was getting as near to paradise on this earth as any man could ever get." He was promoted to foreign correspondent after two years and his friend Thurber went to work for the *New Yorker*.

In fall 1931, Henry Miller got a job at the *Tribune* as a proofreader, thanks to his friend Alfred Perlès who worked there. Miller enjoyed the work, the atmosphere, the noise of the machinery, the French typesetters working at night. It was genuine and it reminded him of Brooklyn. Miller submitted articles for the newspaper under the name of Perlès, since only the editorial staff were permitted to publish in the paper. In his book *My Friend, Henry Miller,* Perlès reproduces Miller's article, "Rue Lourmel in Fog."

Rue Las-Cases (7th) Map C

23   Archibald MacLeish arrived in Paris with his wife, 6-year-old son, and infant daughter in September 1923. He had just committed what most reasonable men regarded as an act of sheer folly: he had declined a partnership in the prestigious law firm of Choate, Hall and Stewart and had come to Paris to write poetry. It should be added that he continued to receive an allowance from his father and was well aware that in 1923 it was cheaper to live in France than in New England, and infinitely more pleasant. For the next five years, the MacLeishes lived in Europe, mainly in France, and frequently in Paris. To his mother, he wrote:

> I am simply delighted to be here at long last. "Here" is the little apartment on the rive gauche.... It has a little salon adequate for about four people at one time, a dining room only slightly larger than the ordinary stomach, one decent sized bed-room, two small ones, a tiny bath-room, a cell-like "horror" and a bit of a hall.

The best part of all, wrote MacLeish, was that it lay under the very walls of the Church of Sainte-Clothilde. "Here in the center of the world, here in the midst of Paris, all is peace and sweet quietude. The bell of St. Clothilde rings its patient quarter hours and tolls at dawn and at dusk for mass." Like most Americans in Paris, the MacLeishes walked extensively. One late winter afternoon they crossed the Place de la Concorde "in time to see the winter sun going down over the water," wrote MacLeish, "in a cold rose sky the reflection of which in the stream was mauve and opalescent and changeable as the throat of a pigeon." Their six-year-old son attended the famous Ecole Alsacienne on Rue d'Assas, and his wife Ada took singing lessons. MacLeish continued working on his poem

"Biography of Mr. Beck the Suicide," which was later retitled and published as "Einstein" in *Streets in the Moon* (1926). The MacLeishes lived here until summer 1924, when they moved to Granville on the shore in Normandy.

Rue Leconte-de-L'Isle (16th)

(6)   Jo Davidson purchased the house in the 1920s and added a studio in the garden. He had become so successful as a sculptor that he needed more space than his studio on Avenue du Maine could provide. But success has its price, and in his autobiography *Between Sittings* Davidson noted that it felt like going to live in the country; he had been "at home in Montparnasse." Davidson's clients included H.G. Wells, George Bernard Shaw, Sir James Barrie, Arthur Conan Doyle, D.H. Lawrence, W. Averell Harriman, Vincent Auriol, Nicholas Murray Butler, Sinclair Lewis, and Luigi Pirandello.

Rue Léon-Jouhaux (10th)

Le Diorama. The site of the Diorama is covered by the southwest corner of the *caserne* (military barracks) Vérines, at the intersection of Rue Léon-Jouhaux and the northwest corner of the Place de la République.

The Diorama was opened in 1822 by inventor and chemist Louis Daguerre, and contained a series of illusionistic painted stage sets and vast pictorials viewed with changing lights. It was similar to Robert Fulton's Panorama, but much more advanced and impressive. Housed in a rectangular building, its screen was 70 feet long by 45 feet high. The whole affair burned down in 1839 but was quickly reopened on the Boulevard Bonne-Nouvelle.

On Saturday, 10 June 1837, Dr. Willard Parker recorded in his *Journal:*

> We went to the Diorama. 1st. We saw the dedication of Solomon's Temple. 2d—the Valley Goldau of Switzerland. 3rd. Mass at midnight in the Church of St. Stephen—the light was good & the scene beyond conception. Solomon's Temple, you see the stars. You see the Bridges lighted up in the distance. It gradually becomes light & you see myriads of people worshiping in the court. You hear the Organ. You see the great temple lighted up.

Gradually it darkens—then becomes somewhat light & all are gone. 2d. La Vallee de Goldau-Suisse. You see this beautiful vallee by day. The Lac de Zoug. La Montaigne at the Right 5676 high. Night gradually approaches, the scene is hidden in Darkness. You see the lightening afar—the Moon light breaks in & you see the Eboulments or avalanche which happened in 1806—2d. of Sept. and overwhelmed & buried that little village. You see crowds of people with hands uplifted & imploring. The scene changes & the vale returns. 3 church of St. Stephen & mass at midnight. I have seen nothing in Paris that surpasses this exhibition.

Rue de Lille (7th) Map **A**

9   Richard Wright lived in a friend's apartment at number 9 after he moved permanently to France in 1947. He rented a small hotel room directly across the street in which to write.

19   Harry and Caresse Crosby, proprietors of the Black Sun Press on Rue Cardinale, owned a very large apartment here during the 1920s. Archibald MacLeish wrote to them on 13 August 1927 from Ashfield, Massachusetts: "Are you going to stand vacant at 19 rue de Lille or are you filling yourself all three floors and lovely cellashoop [sic] with Boston relatives? (Boston relatives to what?) Because if not we know two nice youngish though not so young as once Americans of mildly lit'ry tastes named MacLeish who would be so careful of your hearth and pay large rentals and add tone to the neighborhood." The MacLeishes had returned to Massachusetts after five years in Europe and although they dreamed of returning to Paris, Archibald MacLeish had begun to find a new voice and he remained in his native land.

(59)   All American residents in Paris in 1929 agreed on one thing: the behavior of the American Legionnaires at their tenth anniversary celebration held in the city that summer was characterized by boorishness, bad taste, and rowdyism.

Playwright Elmer Rice pointed out that the antics of these middle-aged adolescents could be endured in America because everyone knew that they would return home at the end of the day. Overseas they were representatives of their country and were a major embarrassment to the ordinary American tourist and resident. Rice recorded in his autobiography, *Minority Report:*

An uproar in the Rue de Lille informed me that the Legionnaires were in town. Drawn to the window of my hotel room, I saw one of the visiting merrymakers on the balcony outside his room at the Hôtel Palais d'Orsay, across the street. Stripped down to his underwear, he was brandishing a bottle to which he had frequent recourse. To the passing women in the street below he addressed pointed invitations; to the men he shouted, "What you make in francs I make in dollars." For almost the only time in my life, I wished that I were anything but an American. This opening note was repeated over and over, with variations. Everywhere one saw blowzy men in fatigue caps, drunk, boisterous, quarrelsome, trying to bargain with shop-keepers, drinking champagne at little bistros at eleven in the morning, lining up in the stifling heat and the stench of frying fat to buy doughnuts in the barracks which the Salvation Army had erected in the citadel of French cookery.

On the final day of the convention, the day of the big parade, there was an incident that was both hilarious and grim. We posted ourselves in the Place de la Concorde to get a good view of the proceedings. The Parisians who packed the huge square stared in amazement as the paraders, state by state, marched by, the trim drum majorettes cavorting, the men arrayed like members of the chorus in an operetta with a Ruritanian setting. In due course the Massachusetts delegation appeared, resplendent in scarlet or green or purple. Suddenly someone shouted, "Où est la chaise électrique?" [Where is the electric chair?] The memory of the Sacco-Vanzetti execution was fresh; the crowd took up the cry with savage delight. Soon it filled the whole square. The men from Massachusetts, interpreting it as some special tribute, beamed and waved in grateful acknowledgment.

Rue de Longchamp (16th)

(36)   Stephen Vincent Benét had been living at 89 Avenue de Neuilly (today Avenue Charles de Gaulle) before he moved here in summer 1927. He was spending the year working on his poem "John Brown's Body." Earlier that spring, he had written home:

> The Poem is getting along—I am typing the 3rd installment—sometimes I think that it is good & sometimes wonder who will read it but the typesetters—but I shall finish it or explode in loud fragments of Battles and Leaders of the Civil War all over my quaint little room on the 5th floor which has two quaint little porthole windows that let out all the heat of the quaint stove on one of the quaint winter days.

By November, he had almost completed the poem, and told a friend, "I was sweating at John Brown's damn body whenever I had a minute trying to get it off." The poem was awarded the Pulitzer Prize in 1929.

Rue du Louvre (1st) Métro: Louvre

On 29 April 1778, Benjamin Franklin and Voltaire met at the Académie des Sciences, then located in the Louvre. The Frenchman, aged 84, had been permitted to return to Paris after long years of exile in Ferney on the Swiss border. John Adams, that dry New Englander, recorded the meeting in his diary:

> Voltaire and Franklin were both present, and there presently arose a general cry that M. Voltaire and M. Franklin should be introduced to each other. This was done, and they bowed and spoke to each other. This was no satisfaction; there must be something more. Neither of our philosophers seemed to divine what was wished or expected; they however took each other by the hand. But this was not enough. The clamour continued until the explanation came out: *Il faut s'embrasser à la française.* [You must kiss French style.] The two aged actors upon this great theatre of philosophy and frivolity then embraced each other by hugging one another in their arms and kissing each other's cheeks, and then the tumult subsided. And the cry immediately spread throughout the kingdom, and I suppose all over Europe: *Qu'il est charmant de voir embrasser Solon et Sophocle.* [How charming it is to see Solon and Sophocles embrace.]

In 1820, Ebenezer Smith Thomas visited the Louvre and noted in his *Reminiscences:*

> The attention of the French to foreigners, (to be met with in no other country,) was here conspicuous—they were freely admitted at all times, while the mass of their own citizens were only admitted on Sundays.... At one of my visits, there were four chimney sweeps among the crowd, lounging very leisurely through the immense gallery, and making their observations to each other. It was, to me, truly gratifying to see them; there were none who appeared to enjoy the sight more. What a contrast to the state of things before the first revolution, when no man was allowed to walk in the gardens of the chateau, except in full dress, bag wig, and sword.

✦

During the 19th century many American and European painters eked out a living by copying masterpieces for wealthy patrons back home, or for their fellow citizens in Europe. Thurlow Weed, New York state senator and owner of the *Albany Evening Journal,* visited the Louvre in 1834 and recorded seeing six artists copying the Madonna by Murillo.

Samuel Morse frequently copied in the Louvre. As a young man of 23, Morse first went to England, where he studied under Benjamin West and Washington Allston. He wrote to his father, who was doubtful that he could earn his living in America other than by doing portraits:

> Had I no higher thoughts than being a first-rate portrait painter, I would have chosen a far different profession. My ambition is to be among those who shall rival the splendor of the fifteenth century: to rival the genius of a Raphael, a Michael Angelo, or a Titian; my ambition is to be enlisted in the constellation of genius now rising in this country; I wish to shine, not by a light borrowed from them, but to strive to shine the brightest.

This was a letter written by a young man, and it was ironic that when Morse returned to America in 1815 he achieved success as a portrait painter. When he announced his intention of returning to Europe, he was able to finance the trip by accepting orders for copies of pictures in the Louvre and in galleries in Florence and Rome. Back in France in 1829, his order book contained 21 requests amounting to over 3,000 dollars. One such order read:

> Philip Hone, $100—to be disposed of in such way as may be most agreeable to Mr. Morse. A picture not larger than Newton's or Leslie's—say twenty-five by thirty. [Hone was a politician and the mayor of New York City in 1825.]

Frederick Sheldon wanted for his $100 "say a landscape of Claude or Poussin." Stephen Van Rensselaer of Albany, New York, wanted two or more pictures. He had just founded his Technical Institute in Troy.

In Paris, Morse became a friend of James Fenimore Cooper, who used to like to take a stroll to the Louvre and watch Morse paint after he had finished writing for the day. The future inventor of the Morse Code was busy on a massive six-foot by nine-foot tableau called *Gallery of the Louvre.* It showed several Americans looking at paintings in the museum's Salon Carré, while in the foreground was

Morse himself as teacher leaning over a student's shoulder. In the left-hand corner was Cooper, his wife, and his daughter, who was a student of Morse's. Surrounding them were miniature reproductions of paintings by Rembrandt, Leonardo, Rubens, Raphael, and Titian. The painting was conceived as an exhibition piece and Morse hoped that the public would pay to look at it, but the painting failed to attract public interest. On 16 March 1832, Cooper wrote to his friend William Dunlap, a painter and playwright whom he had watched paint, to tell him of Morse's project:

> He is painting an Exhibition picture that I feel certain must take. He copies admirably and this is a (picture) drawing of the Louvre with copies of some fifty of its best pictures. I get up at eight, read the papers, breakfast at ten, sit down to the quill at 1/2 past ten—work till one—throw off my morning gown—draw on my boots and gloves, take a cane that Horace Greenough gave me, and go to the Louvre, where I find Morse stuck up on a high working stand, perch myself astraddle of one of the seats, and bore him just as I used to bore you when you made the memorable likeness of St. Peter. "Lay it on here, Samuel—more yellow—the nose is too short—the eye too small—damn it if I had been a painter what a picture I should have painted."—and all this stuff over again and which Samuel takes just as goodnaturedly as good old William. Well there I sit and have sat so often and so long that my face is just as well known as any Vandyke on the walls. Crowds get round the picture, for Samuel has quite made a hit in the Louvre, and I believe that people think that half the merit is mine. So much from keeping company with ones betters.

In a letter to Peter Jay, son of John Jay of New York, Cooper wrote: "I shall send out, by some early packet, a copy of a Rembrandt made by Mr. Morse for me. It is capitally done, though one of the most difficult pictures in the Louvre to be done. I know no artist that has improved as much as Mr. Morse. He really has created a sensation in the Louvre, having a little school of his own, who endeavor to catch his manner." Although Cooper thought "that the picture must take," it did not, at least not in Morse's time. *Gallery of the Louvre* was given as a gift to Syracuse University in 1884. In 1982 it was purchased by Daniel J. Terra for 3,250,000 dollars, the highest sum ever paid for a work by an American artist. Today it is on display in the Terra Museum of American Art in Evanston, Illinois.

Avenue de Lowendal (7th) Map C

5   Formerly Librairie Six. Man Ray had his first Paris exhibition in December 1921 in this small bookshop owned by Philippe Soupault. The exhibition catalog announced: "It is no longer known where Man Ray was born. He had been a coal salesman, a millionnaire several times and chairman of the Chewing Gum Trust." Included in the catalog were texts by Dadaists such as Louis Aragon, Paul Eluard, Max Ernst, Tristan Tzara, and Soupault. Erik Satie, who came to the opening, would befriend Man Ray. To his host Soupault the artist gave a present of a flatiron with a row of small nails down the middle. Together with *Object to Be Destroyed*, a metronome with an eye attached to the moving arm, the two objets d'art became universally known. Although the display of Man Ray's 35 objects, such as *Export Commodity* (an olive jar filled with ball bearings in oil) attracted many visitors to this new gallery on the Avenue Lowendal, it drew no sales, and Man Ray took up photography to earn a living. Within three years, he became one of the most sought-after photographers in Paris.

Rue Lulli (2nd) Map F

1   Formerly Hôtel Louvois. Journalist A.J. Liebling, 35, arrived here in November 1939 to cover the war for the *New Yorker*. His room and bath on the second floor cost eleven dollars per week. From his balcony, which overlooked the small park below and the Bibliothèque Nationale beyond, he counted 23 trees, four buxom female statues, one fountain, and a *pissoir* and a *chalet de nécessité*. His first visit was to the Paris branch of the Morgan Guaranty Trust, where he learned the most frightful news: the war, it was said at the Bourse, "was going to be called off." Fortunately for Liebling on his first overseas assignment, this tip, like most stockmarket tips, was incorrect. After spending Christmas in a fort on the invincible Maginot Line, he spent the next six months in Paris listening to encouraging reports from the French Ministry of Information. At 6:00 p.m. on Sunday, 10 June 1940, seated at an Anglo-American press conference at the Hôtel Continental, Liebling heard the French minister assure them that "from a military standpoint" the situation was "improving steadily." As to the rumor that the French government was about to leave for the south of France, the press was advised to disregard such tattle. "We shall have many more chats in this room," the minister assured them. The French

government left the following morning at dawn. Back at the Hôtel Louvois, there remained but six guests in the 180 rooms, and seven staff, including the bookkeeper Mademoiselle Yvonne. Liebling left on Tuesday, 12 June, with Waverly Root and John Elliott of the *Herald Tribune.* Four years, two months, and sixteen days later, Liebling, still a war correspondent, returned to Paris. His jeep was temporarily stalled by thousands of excited Parisians (and Parisiennes) at the Place d'Orléans, but after entering Paris, Liebling abandoned his fellow correspondents at the Hôtel Scribe and returned to the Square Louvois on foot. Here he discovered only fourteen trees, all four statues, and no pigeons. As he recalled in *Normandy Revisited,* he entered the hotel feeling highly emotional. Mademoiselle Yvonne was still seated behind the same desk going over her accounts: "'Bonjour, Monsieur Liebling,' she said, barely looking up. It was as if I had just stepped out for a walk around the fountain.'"

Jardin du Luxembourg (6th) Map B

These gardens have long been admired and enjoyed by American visitors. On 23 July 1826, Henry Wadsworth Longfellow sent the following description to his brother:

> After five weeks' residence in Paris I have settled down in something half-way between a Frenchman and a New Englander:—within,—all Jonathan—but outwardly a little of the *Parlez-vous.* That is to say, I have good home-feelings at heart—but have decorated my outward man with a long-waisted thin coat—claret-coloured—and a pair of linen pantaloons:—and on Sundays and other fete days—I appear in all the glory of a little hard French hat—glossy—and brushed—and rolled up at the sides—it makes my head ache to think of it. In this garb I jostle along amongst the crowds of the Luxembourg, which is the favorite promenade in St. Germain.
>
> From what my own thoughts were, before I saw the Public Gardens of Paris, I imagine that you have no very correct idea of them: at least, I think that I can give you a more perfect conception of them by a short description of any one—say—for instance—the Luxembourg. This is a very extensive and beautiful garden—with long, shady gravel walks over which the tall old trees, which are all regularly planted, form perfect arches—and directly in the center, a valley or lower level of the ground in which are little plats of flowers—rows of orange trees, and a little

pond with two beautiful white swans. You descend from the higher grounds to this little vale, which is an amphitheatre, open towards the palace—by flights of stone steps, which here and there interrupt the stone balustrade around the brink. On the higher grounds, and in an oval,—parallel to this balustrade, are placed the marble statues of the garden, each upon a high pedestal in a niche cut from the boughs of the trees. This part of the garden is the general lounge and promenade:—and is full of rush-bottomed chairs! Not to an absolute plenum,—but a row or two on each side of the walk, where the ladies sit to be looked at—and the gentlemen to look at them, whilst a crowd of both sexes run the gauntlet between them. Here the people gather every evening at about six o'clock and laugh and talk 'till the gates are closed—at 10. It is very pleasant, I assure you to take a high seat in the synagogue here, and review the multitude passing and repassing, in all the ridiculous peculiarity of French dress, and with all the ridiculous variety of French countenance. This must answer for the Luxembourg.

Sculptress Malvina Hoffman was privileged to have her work *Russian Bacchanale* put on permanent display in the garden in 1917. But in 1941 the Germans took away her statue, cast in bronze, to melt it down for shells.

Isadora Duncan, 22, arrived in France in 1900. She records that she used to dance in the gardens in the summer when they opened at 5:00 a.m.

In his early years in Paris, immediately after World War I, Ernest Hemingway, like so many other aspiring American writers, was frequently hungry. To supplement dinner he would wait near the Medici Fountain until closing time when the *gardiens* (watchmen) were busy, seize a pigeon, strangle it, and hide it under the blankets of the baby carriage which contained his son Bumby.

Palais du Luxembourg (6th) Map B

In 1793, the Palais was used as a prison to hold some 1,000 suspects. Citizen "thomas peine" was brought here on 28 December 1793, the third American to be imprisoned by the Committee of Public Security. Thomas Griffiths of Baltimore had already spent nine weeks in jail here, and William Haskins of Boston, five weeks. Paine was assigned to a damp room on the ground floor, "level with the earth in the garden and floored with brick." The jailor, a considerate gentleman named Benoît, did his best to provide a pleasant atmosphere. Paine was free to write, to walk in the common room and visit with other prisoners, and to exercise in the courtyard. Prisoners paid for their own food and Paine, in the early days, ate well. He had assumed that his stay would be brief. As an American citizen he felt that there was no legal ground for his arrest. However, the conservative American minister Gouverneur Morris disliked Paine and everything he stood for. According to Morris, by serving in the French National Assembly Paine had given up whatever claims he had to American citizenship. But others among Paine's fellow Americans did not feel this way, and on 20 January 1794, twenty Americans were permitted to address the Convention on his behalf and plead for his release. Their plea was refused. Paine met with Danton, who said to him: "What you have done for the happiness and liberty of your country, I have in vain tried to do for mine." Danton was taken away and executed on 3 April 1794. Paine fell ill with a fever which lasted five weeks. During this time, orders arrived for the execution of 150 prisoners, including Paine. The condemned had an "X" marked on their doors, but as Paine's door was open when the guards passed, the "X" was put on the inside of the door. Thus, he was saved. Thanks to the efforts of the new American minister James Monroe, on 5 November 1794 Paine left the Palais a free man. He was one of the last prisoners to be rescued.

Rue Madame (6th) Map B

58 Michael Stein, Gertrude's older brother, moved here with his wife Sarah and son Allan at the end of 1903. The apartment was in a building used by the Protestant Church and consisted of a large converted loft with a pot-bellied, cast-iron stove in the living-dining room. Another brother, Leo Stein, had taken an atelier at 27 Rue de Fleurus. The Stein years in Paris were about to begin. Sarah Stein was a serious student of painting, and she and her husband became close friends of Matisse. The chronology is important, for it was in the 1905 Salon d'automne that Matisse's work, along with that of Derain, Vlaminck, Dufy, and others, was condemned as Fauvisme (from the French word *fauve,* meaning wild animal). At this Salon the Steins bought Matisse's *La Femme au chapeau.* The following year, when the Steins returned to see their family in San Francisco after the earthquake, they took with them Matisse's *Portrait à la raie verte* and *Nu devant un paravent*. While in America, Sarah Stein promised to buy a Matisse for the painter George Of. She chose the *Nu dans les bois* (Brooklyn Museum, New York). The Steins' living room was large and soon looked like a Matisse museum. Visitors could see several studies for *Le Bonheur de vivre*, *Les Oignons roses*, *L'Autoportrait*, *Nature morte bleue*, *Le Madras rouge*, *L'Intérieur aux aubergines*, and after World War I, such masterpieces as *Le Thé*. The Steins also bought Matisse's sculptures, including *La Femme appuyée sur ses mains*, and *Nu couché*. In 1916, Matisse did a portrait of Michael Stein (Museum of Modern Art, New York). Harriet Lane Levy, a friend of Alice B. Toklas, recalled that Sarah Stein would sit on a divan in a corner of the living room and explain to everyone what made Matisse a genius. Two friends from Baltimore, Claribel and Etta Cone, were persuaded by Sarah to purchase 43 paintings by Matisse, a purchase considered pure folly back in Baltimore, but which today constitutes part of the richness of the Baltimore Museum of Art. The Stein living room on Rue de Fleurus had the richest collection of Matisses, Picassos, Renoirs, and Gauguins in Paris in the early part of the century. In 1927, Michael and Sarah Stein moved their collection to a villa designed for them by Le Corbusier in Garches.

Place de la Madeleine (8th) Map F

L'Eglise de la Madeleine. Of all the monuments in Paris, this church has been the most admired by Americans. In 1837, Dr. Willard Parker of Boston found the church to be "the most magnificent building that I have seen in the Old World." William Dana, Presbyterian minister from Boston, on his first evening out in Paris, found the church to be a "perfect Greek Temple," as he admired the whiteness of its columns against the setting sun. It remained for John Saunderson, journalist and teacher from Philadelphia, to observe that there was nothing Christian about the design of the building, so much so, noted Saunderson, "that in the event of another revolution, it could serve as a stock exchange, a bank or a temple of some pagan divinity, or a mosque without the alteration costing anything." Saunderson was right, for the Church of the Madeleine had been originally planned as part of Gabriel's layout for the Place de la Concorde to complete the vista of the Rue Royale.

Construction was begun in 1764, but was halted by the revolution 25 years later. Since churches were turned into theaters and other public buildings, various uses for the Madeleine were suggested, including a chamber of commerce, the stock exchange, the Bank of France, a theater, and a reception hall for official banquets and the bestowal of the Légion d'honneur. On 2 December 1806, Napoleon ordered that it become a Temple of Glory dedicated to his Grande Armée. With the return of Louis XVIII in 1815 it became a church again, and its construction was finally completed in 1842, 78 years after Louis XV had laid the first stone.

On 15 April 1975, Josephine Baker was accorded the grandest funeral for an American ever witnessed in Paris. She was the only American woman ever to receive a 21-gun salute. She had received the Légion d'honneur and the Médaille de la Résistance. The hundreds of floral arrangements were later distributed throughout Paris and placed on the monuments to those who died in World War II.

Avenue du Maine (15th) Map D

14 Jo Davidson took a studio here in 1919. It consisted of two rooms and a large balcony with a southern exposure. He also rented an atelier for stonecutting on nearby Rue Antoine-Bourdelle. The following ten years were busy and successful for Davidson. He worked quickly, three or four hours of sitting for a bust, and as he said in his memoirs, *Between Sittings,* during those hours he had the person to himself. To this studio came James Joyce, Clarence Darrow, Arnold Bennett, Andrew Mellon, Bernard Baruch, and as always, Gertrude Stein. Davidson was astonished to hear Stein incessantly intoning "a rose is a rose is a rose." She did a verbal portrait of him which was published in *Vanity Fair,* along with his portrait of her. In 1924, Davidson went back to New York to model John D. Rockefeller, then returned to his Paris studio to finish the head in stone. The bust is placed in the Standard Oil Building at 26 Broadway in New York City.

Boulevard Malesherbes (8th) Map G

83 In 1861 Isaac Singer of sewing-machine fame fled America to escape the Civil War and a bevy of mistresses. Six years later, remarried and accompanied by his 2-year-old daughter Winnaretta and his 1-year-old son, the inventor moved into a large apartment on this new boulevard created by the Baron Haussmann. Winnaretta, who turned into a remarkably beautiful and talented young woman, became famous in Paris as the lesbian wife of Prince Edmond de Polignac.

Rue Mansart (9th) Métro: Blanche

11 May Alcott lived here for one year. She was a friend of Mary Cassatt and had one painting accepted in the Salon of 1877. Her stay in Paris was paid for by her sister Louisa May Alcott (*Little Women*, 1868). The two Alcott sisters had stayed in Paris together several years before (no address available).

Rue de Marignan (8th) Map **G**

10 Mary Cassatt lived on the fifth floor here from 1887 until her death in 1926. During her early years in Paris she was at the height of her fame. In 1890, she and Degas went to see a Japanese print exhibition, an event which profoundly influenced her. However, it was the theme of mother and child which began to dominate her work. *The Bath* (Art Institute of Chicago) and *The Boating Party* (National Gallery of Arts, Washington, D.C.) reflect the influence of the Post-Impressionists, particularly Gauguin.

Avenue de Marigny (8th) Map **G**

1 John Steinbeck and his family took this house for the summer of 1954. His wife Elaine discovered it, and in a letter to friends Steinbeck wrote:

> she found a pretty little house right in the center of Paris ... if you want Paris—there you got Paris. It is very French and I think we will love it. Besides it has a courtyard you can drive a car into—a covered courtyard. The kids could even play basketball there in the rainy weather.

The author of *Cannery Row* continued:

> The Marigny house has a terrace on the roof with lots of flower boxes so we can have geraniums and morning glories and all such things. Oh! I hope we get it. It even has a little study where I can

work. What joy. And right beside it is a park with ponies and a carousel and balloon men and millions of children play and the whole thing shaded with chestnut trees.

He ended the letter later that day announcing that the house was theirs. He signed the letter "Jean." In a note to Richard Rodgers and Oscar Hammerstein, he described the house as "next to the Rothschilds and across the street from the President of France. How's that for an address for a Salinas kid?"

Rue des Mathurins (9th)

(9)   In the fall of 1838, Samuel Morse shared a parlor and bedchamber with an intervening hallway in a hotel at this address with a Reverend Dr. Kirk. Morse placed his galvanic battery on a table in the bedroom and extended the wires through to the parlor where the receiver was set up. French scientists were invited to witness Morse sending his code. Twenty years later, when Dr. Kirk wrote his *Recollections,* he had not forgotten the amazement shown by the visitors:

> When the model telegraph had been set up in our rooms, Mr. Morse desired to exhibit it to the savants of Paris. But, as he had less of the talking propensity than myself, I was made the grand exhibitor. Our levee-day was Tuesday, and for weeks we received the visits of distinguished citizens and strangers, to whom I explained the principles and operation of the telegraph. The visitors would agree upon a word among themselves, which I was not to hear. Then the Professor would receive it at the writing end of the wires; while it devolved upon me to interpret the characters which recorded it at the other end. As I explained the hiero-glyphics, the announcement of the word, which they saw could have come to me only through the wire, would often create a deep sensation of delighted wonder.

Rue Mazarine (6th) Map A

62   L'Alcazar. In 1970, Duke Ellington's 71st birthday was celebrated in this nightclub. Guests included Baron Edmond de Rothschild, Salvador Dali, and Maurice Chevalier, who gave the Duke the straw hat he was wearing. An enormous cake in the shape of a camembert was lowered from the ceiling and out stepped three nude dancers, "to everybody's intense satisfaction," noted Ellington in his memoirs, *Music is My Mistress* (1973).

Rue Médéric (17th) Métro: Courcelles

9   The Swedish and Norwegian Lutheran Church. In 1921, Virgil Thomson used to practice the organ here daily while studying with Nadia Boulanger.

Rue de Miromesnil (8th) Map **G**

8   Formerly Galerie Daniel Cordier. In May 1961, the first Rauschenberg exhibition in Paris was held at this gallery. Individual paintings such as the *Bed* had already been shown in Paris, but this was his first one-man show, and the reviews were excellent.

Rue de Mogador (9th) Métro: Trinité

25   Théâtre Mogador. On 31 March 1928, George and Ira Gershwin heard *Rhapsody in Blue* performed by the Pasdeloup Orchestra, conducted by Rhené-Baton with pianists Wiener and Doucet. The two pianists divided the solo part, to the utter dismay of George who went to hide in the bar, unable to continue listening. The Parisian audience, however, was delighted, and at the end the composer took a bow on stage. For an encore, the two pianists played "Do! Do! Do!" from *Oh! Kay!*

Isadora Duncan danced at this theater for the last time in Paris in 1927. The theater was packed, but Isadora was 49 and alcohol had begun to take its toll. Her dancing, more static than in earlier years, was nevertheless imposing. She returned to Nice where she was killed when her scarf caught in the wheel of her open sports car.

Rue de Monceau (8th)

(28)   President Woodrow Wilson and his wife were guests of the French government in the Murat mansion from 14 December 1918 until 14 February 1919 while attending the peace conference. The interior design was a marriage of exquisite taste, practicality, and comfort. Indeed, the peace and quiet of the grounds behind its great wall and the opulence of the house was in stark contrast to the horrors of trench warfare which had just ceased. It was a privileged world, as Edith Bolling Wilson recognized in *My Memoir*:

> The property was one of the finest in the city and so private, with its great wall in front, broken by two large entrances, double doors looking solid and massive enough to defy an army.
>
> On our approach the great street doors were thrown wide, and we swept up a semicircular drive to the steps of the palace. Extricating ourselves from the flowers, we entered the house. I found it charming in every way. On the lower floor were three formal drawing rooms, a lovely ballroom with a gleaming polished floor, tall mirrors between long French windows hung with flame-coloured brocade curtains, gilt benches and chairs. There was also a formal dining room, and a grand sweeping stairway that had a small entresol halfway up on which was located a sort of *cabinet de travail,* or secretary's room.
>
> The second floor had a broad central hall, with suites of rooms on either side and a very comfortable library opposite an informal dining room, which we preferred to the big one below. On opposite sides of the hall were two enchanting suites for the President and me. On his side, one entered first a large square room. The walls were hung in crimson damask and the same material curtained four large windows opening on the garden. There were a few choice pictures with lights to bring out their rich tints and leather-bound books in wall cases of carved cedar. An open fire and low comfortable chairs formed a background for an exceedingly handsome Napoleonic writing table fitted in tooled leather.
>
> From this cheerful workroom opened the door into a rather austere bedchamber. The walls were dark green, with bees embroidered thereon in gold, and the bed covering and curtains the same. The bed itself, a single one with high head and footboard, was placed with the side against the wall. By this stood a bed-stand which, like the dressing table and large flat desk, was ornamented with fire-gilt Napoleonic eagles. There were heavy velvet carpets, so not a sound could be heard at any time. This room communicated with a dressing room and bathroom.
>
> My own quarters opposite followed a different plan except the first big sitting room which duplicated the one opposite in size and crimson hangings. It was furnished in more affluent fashion, however—cabinets filled with *objets d'art,* low sofas, smaller chairs and so forth. Beyond was the bedroom with a complete set of ivory-tinted furniture; the bed regal with a canopy of delicate blue, and an elaborate lace covering over blue; a chaise longue of blue, a bed table with gold and crystal decanter of orange flower

water. An open fireplace afforded the only heat in this room, though the rest of the house was furnished with central heating.

Next was a dressing room, panelled in soft grey wood. Behind these panels were cupboards for every possible use—one for hats, one for shoes, another for lingerie, one for stockings, one for gloves, and, of course, one for gowns. Each was lined with quilted blue satin, with hat rests, shoe trees or slipper pads, coat and dress hangers—everything complete and so dainty. There was a toilet table in front of a great mirror, and a small telephone table near by with a low armchair.

The bathroom beyond had a tremendous built-in stationary double washstand with two basins, one equipped with a shower for shampooing hair. The entire toilet set was gold with the Murat crest on each piece.

52　Columnist Art Buchwald and his wife moved here in September 1956 with their three young children. One day a representative of the French social security office called to inform them that they were to receive 50 dollars a month for child maintenance. (It was French government policy to encourage and support the birthrate after World War II.) The Buchwalds pointed out that other French families surely needed the money more than they did and declined the offer. But with implacable logic the French agent replied that it would cost far more in accounting costs and readjustments to refuse the money than to simply accept it, which they did. The Buchwalds returned to America in 1962.

Rue Monsieur (7th) Map C

13　Shortly after World War I, Cole Porter and his wife bought an apartment here. He had married the former Linda Lee Thomas in December 1919 at the Mairie of the 18th arrondissement. Porter was fluent in French, and although he came from a wealthy family, he proceeded to make his own fortune. Some of that fortune was lavished on his apartment, which became the talk of the town—walls covered in zebra hide, red chairs lined with white kid, one room done up in platinum wallpaper. *Within the Quota,* written in 1923, was an immediate success at the Théâtre des Champs-Elysées, but the New York production failed. The following year, Porter's *Greenwich Village Follies* was a smash hit and his career was launched. When the Charleston came to Paris in 1924, the black singer and dancer Bricktop, from the Dingo Bar on Rue Delambre, taught the dance in Porter's apartment to friends, who included Elsa Maxwell and Aga Khan. Porter left Rue Monsieur and Paris in 1939. His song "C'est magnifique," written upon his return after the war in homage to the city he loved, was an instant hit.

Rue Monsieur-le-Prince (7th) Map B

14   In May 1948 Richard Wright took a five-room apartment on the third floor with his family. He lived here for over eleven years and wrote his autobiography and two novels, *The Outsider* (1953) and *The Long Dream* (1958), in this apartment. Martin Luther King was a guest in March 1959.

22   It was in a studio at number 22 on the second floor that James McNeill Whistler completed the portrait of Count Robert de Montesquiou (Frick Museum, New York) in 1892. Montesquiou, considered the archetype of decadence, inspired the character Baron de Charlus in Proust's *A la Recherche du Temps Perdu*. Being a friend, Montesquiou paid a modest fee for the portrait and ten years later sold it for 75,000 francs. Whistler was deeply hurt.

39   Mary Putnam was 24 when she arrived in France in summer of 1866 and took a room on the fifth floor at this address. On 18 September, she wrote to her mother, "There has been a full moon and in the evening when I go to bed, the towers of Notre Dame loom up grandly through the slight silvery mist like a dream." In December of that year, the editor of the *New York Evening Post,* Parke Godwin, proposed that for ten dollars a week she write a weekly article from Paris. But Mary Putnam had come to Paris with the intention of entering the Ecole de Médecine. She was permitted to attend lectures at the city clinics and to work as a student with the city hospital teaching staff. On the basis of their personal recommendations she hoped to gain admittance to the Ecole de Médecine. As the following letter indicates, within a few months she was beginning to be noticed by the French faculty:

> My Dear Mother,
>
>   I think you are rather naive to ask me if "I meet many educated French ladies who are physicians." Such a thing was never heard of. Mme. Boivin and Madame La Chapelle, who lived

in the early part of this century, were celebrated midwives, and wrote treatises that have long been regarded as standard works, but their sphere of study or action never extended beyond the Maternity.

You speak of English prejudices. You must know that French prejudices rest upon an entirely different ground from those that obtain in England or America. An Englishman would say that it was indelicate to admit women to study medicine, a Frenchman, that it was dangerous. The French disbelief in women is so rooted, and their whole social system is constructed so entirely on the principle of keeping young men and women as far apart as flame and gunpowder, that they would consider as a perfect absurdity any attempt on the part of their own countrywomen to study medicine. They believe, (and with reason), in the greater coldness of temperament and reliability of character among our people, and consequently they are much more ready to admit Americans. I suppose that I am considered very much of an anomaly, but the peculiarity is attributed to the influence of Americanism. It was upon my appreciation of this kind of prejudice that I based my calculations in coming to Paris instead of to London. I knew well enough I was not "dangerous," and that Frenchmen would instantly perceive that I was not, and when once that first difficulty was overcome, that I could be much more at my ease here, than where the "other days" ideas were liable to be suggested. Of course I have met with opposition to going to some places—the lectures, and certain clinics at the largest hospitals. But wherever I have been received it has always been on the most agreeable footing. I receive a certain special treatment, composed of the frankness with which a physician generally treats his students, the deference and politeness due to a woman, and the consideration accorded to a rather small person in a very large place where she has to encounter many difficulties. I find this composite reception exceedingly charming. I now attend three different clinics and two sets of clinical lectures, given in an amphitheatre, besides the anatomical class of which I have spoken to you. Dr. Herard proposed yesterday to introduce me to a fourth clinic for diseases of the larynx, which introduction I shall certainly avail myself of. The third clinic I have mentioned is a surgical one, that I have just commenced. I attended the first lecture last week, the first time I had been at a surgical lecture or in an amphitheatre containing a hundred students, or have met a professor of the Faculty of Medicine. The lecture was most brilliant, and my uniform experience in regard to the politeness of the students, was confirmed as usual. I heard dreadful stories of what the students might say, (I do not mean apropos of this special thing, but language in general), but I have never had the slightest difficulty. You must know that the two medical clinics constitute a practical class for diagnosis. At Lariboissière, the patients are examined in the presence of the students, either by one of them, or the chief, and each student is called upon to express his opinion, I among the rest. At Beaujon, the students examine the patients before the visit, and make a report of the case. M. Montard procured for me the special privilege of visiting the hospital in the afternoon, so that I see the new patients before any one else, and have far more leisure for their examination. It is exactly like working a sum in miscellaneous examples. I generally have a report ready on all the patients, sometimes ten or twelve, so as to be prepared whenever M. Montard calls upon me, which he always does at least once or twice. The other students only study such cases as they expect to report. All this is really exciting, and when you talk about my "working too hard" etc., I feel quite ashamed to think of your getting up such kind solicitude on my behalf, when I really am only enjoying myself. You see it is not as if I were chained so many hours to a desk or a library, although I spend from three to five hours a day in the hospitals, besides the two or three hours a day lectures, and generally manage to have three or four hours a day besides for reading etc. All these things are separated by so much walking and talking, the hospitals present so much that is stimulating, (and do not be shocked if I add amusing) that I am never conscious of the slightest head strain. When bed time comes I am generally exceedingly sleepy, but you know that is nothing new. No, I assure you, my only trouble is a chronic perplexity as to why I should nearly always have what I want, when hardly anybody else has. I certainly do nothing to deserve superior prosperity, and if anything should happen suddenly to cut me off or cripple me, or make me an invalid for the rest of my days, (a thing that will not occur through carelessness, *sois tranquille* [rest assured]) I should feel that it was only fair balance for the uninterrupted happiness that has been granted me for the first twenty-four years of my life.

Mary Putnam spent the next five years studying medicine in Paris.

49   On 20 June 1826, Henry Wadsworth Longfellow, 19, took a room *chez Madame Potet,* for 36 dollars plus 50 cents per week for washing. Longfellow set out to learn French and soon reported to his father:

I know of but one objection to my residing here whilst at Paris, and that is that there are seven of us boarders—"Sons," as Madame calls us—all Americans. Perhaps you will think there is danger of speaking too much english—and there would be indeed, if we were much together—but we seldom assemble except at meals at which all english is forbidden—and he who speaks a word of it is fined one sou. Moreover three of the boarders have resided some time in Paris and speak French well. My chamber is small but very beautifully furnished—tho' you seldom see a carpet in Paris, the floors of the houses being made of oak finely polished and waxed or of little tiles painted red. Indeed I think I could not be so well situated elsewhere, nor could I obtain a place where I should enjoy so great advantages for acquiring a knowledge of the French language. If I had my chambers at a Hotel I should have a thousand solitary hours, because I cannot speak french well enough to go into French society—but now if I wish to be alone I can shut myself up in my chamber—if I wish for society I can go at any hour into Madam's parlour—and talk my kind of French with her and her daughters,—besides the pleasure of hearing most delicious music.

(55)   Oliver Wendell Holmes lived here from 1833 until 1835 while studying medicine. In the middle of the 19th century, Paris was an important medical training center for Americans, as Edinburgh had been earlier and as Berlin and Vienna would become later. Holmes worked at the Hôpital de la Pitié and spent his free time at the Café Procope.

Rue Monsigny (2nd) Map F

4   Théâtre des Bouffes-Parisiens. In February 1862, Sophie Bricard, a singer from New Orleans, made her debut in *Florian,* a new opera by Offenbach. The guest of honor at the performance was to be Napoleon III. John Slidell, the Confederate representative to France, and his wife took their seats in the front of the orchestra. Slidell, a tall distinguished-looking man with long, iron-grey hair, was quickly recognized, and supporters of the South began to applaud so loudly that he was obliged to rise and bow. A few minutes later, William L. Dayton, the representative to France from the North, entered the theater and was immediately hissed. The management was fearful that when the emperor arrived there might be an incident. It was well known that Napoleon III wished to avoid taking sides in the Civil War. Gendarmes were summoned,

and the public was warned to remain quiet, which they did. However, during the reception which took place between the second and third acts, just as Sophie Bricard was being presented to the emperor, she caught sight of Slidell and exclaimed: "Voilà, Sire, voilà le representant de mon pays souffrant. [Here, Sire, here is the representative of my suffering country.] The South is fighting for freedom. I supplicate your Majesty to give us the friendship of France." Everyone was startled, and the emperor stepped back astonished, quickly turned to Slidell, whom he had not met before, shook his hand, and without another word left the theater. Offenbach was livid. Rumor soon reached the Unionists among the American colony in Paris that Bricard had introduced Slidell to the emperor, who had avowed his sympathy for the Secessionist cause. The next evening, a group of Unionists packed the theater and booed Bricard when she appeared on the stage. Meanwhile, Dayton complained to the French foreign minister. The prefect of police warned Mlle Bricard to stop wearing a small Confederate flag in her bosom and to refrain from making any remarks which could have political overtones. Sophie Bricard's career in Paris soon came to an end.

Avenue Montaigne (8th) Map G

2   Formerly Hôtel Elysée-Bellevue. Sinclair Lewis spent the winter of 1924-25 here finishing *Arrowsmith*. But Paris did not provide him the pleasures he had imagined. He felt himself faced by hostile American writers in cafés such as the Dôme. This hostility he attributed to the commercial success of *Main Street* and *Babbitt*.

13-15   Théâtre des Champs-Elysées. When this theater was built in 1913, the figure of Isadora Duncan was carved in the bas-relief of Antoine Bourdelle and in the murals by Maurice Denis. Loïe Fuller danced here in *Les Nuages* and *La Mer* by Debussy in 1913.

On 2 October 1925, *La Revue Nègre* opened. Local American talent had helped with the production, including a youthful John Dos Passos, who lent a hand painting the set. At 9:30 p.m. the curtain went up to reveal a bare stage and a backdrop with an awe-inspiring view of Manhattan, as Sidney Bechet trundled a gaily colored vegetable cart across the stage before taking up his clarinet. He was joined by Josephine Baker, who danced the Charleston to "Yes, Sir, That's My Baby." The French audience, which included painters Picabia and Fernand Léger and poets Blaise Cendrars and Robert Desnos, was stunned. Josephine had arrived.

On 19 June 1926, a big event in the musical world took place. George Antheil's *Ballet Mécanique* was performed here to a full and riotous house. Sylvia Beach recalled the struggle to get into her seat and then the anxious wait:

> There was plenty of time ... because George Antheil couldn't put on his tails until his friend Alan Tanner had darned the moth hole in the front, and the concert couldn't begin without the chief pianist. There were the Joyces in a box. There was our rarely seen T.S. Eliot, so handsome and so elegantly attired, and with him was Princess Bassiano. Up in the top gallery, at the centre of a group of Montparnassians, was Ezra Pound to see that George Antheil got a fair deal. In the orchestra, a distinguished looking lady in black was bowing to everyone graciously. Royalty, it was whispered. "It's your concierge," Adrienne [Monnier] explained.

The orchestra was conducted by Vladimir Golschmann. The work was scored for sixteen electric player pianos, synchronized and linked up to the master piano with George Antheil at the keyboard, six electrically driven airplane propellers, a dozen smaller fans, numerous xylophones, car horns, gongs, and other devices to recreate the noise of modernity. The propellers produced a major draft, blowing off, according to William Shirer, the wig of one elderly gentleman. There was soon bedlam in the hall. Sylvia Beach continued: "Objectors on the floor were answered by defenders above; Ezra's voice was heard above the others, and someone said they saw him hanging head downward from the top gallery." The following morning, Elliot Paul reported in the Paris *Tribune:* "The combatants filed out peacefully at the end of the concert, while Antheil was greeted with 'uproarious applause'. . . . There was an atmosphere about the theater most wholesome for the art of music, ... Everyone knew that they had been somewhere." In her letter of 24 October 1926 in the *New Yorker,* Janet Flanner wrote of the *Ballet Mécanique:* "It is really very wonderful. It sounds like three people: one pounding an old boiler, one grinding a model 1890 coffee grinder, and one blowing the usual seven o'clock factory whistle and ringing the bell that starts the New York Fire Department going in the morning. It's good but awful." A performance of the work two years later in New York caused equal controversy among critics and concertgoers.

Two years later, on 16 April 1928, the Gershwins attended a new ballet, "La Rhapsodie en Bleu," performed by the Ballet Russe. Anton Dolin, the choreographer and principal dancer, had heard Gershwin play *Rhapsody in Blue* at a party three weeks earlier. Dolin's ballet depicted the struggle between jazz and classical music, jazz succumbing at first, but triumphant in the end.

In May 1927, Charles Lindbergh's autograph was auctioned off here for charity and fetched 1,500 dollars. Perhaps one reason for the veneration which the young American aroused in France was that the name of his plane, *The Spirit of St. Louis,* was not associated with Missouri, but with the long line of French kings. However, all the political goodwill which Lindbergh had won single-handedly was swept away three months later with the execution of Sacco and Vanzetti, which produced the worst anti-American rioting of post-World War I France.

25 Hôtel Plaza-Athénée. Captain George Patton lived here in December 1918. It was from a window in this hotel that Patton watched President Woodrow Wilson pass by in an official car to the enormous acclaim of the French population. Four years after graduating from West Point in 1909, he had visited Normandy and Brittany and taken fencing lessons at the French military academy in Saumur. During World War I he was wounded while commanding a tank brigade. While staying at the Plaza-Athénée, Patton, now 33, gave a series of talks stressing "the employment of tanks as supporting weapons for the infantry." Such novel ideas were dismissed by the French and British high commands, but one 28-year-old French officer listened. His name was Charles de Gaulle.

(49-53) The site of the Bal Mabille. Winslow Homer was 30 when he sailed for France. His illustrations of the Civil War, published in *Harper's Weekly,* had won him fame. The war was over, and on the high seas for the first time, Homer found the experience a source of wonder. The power and majesty of the ocean stirred him and would be expressed in his paintings years later.

France, where he was to spend ten months, proved to be a delightful interlude. He had come to visit the great Universal Exhibition of 1867 in which he displayed two paintings, *Prisoners from the Front* (Metropolitan Museum of Art, New York) and the *Bright Side.* Paul Mantz wrote in the *Gazette des Beaux-Arts* that Homer's work was "firm and precise, like that of Gérôme but with less dryness." When the international jury made its awards for American artists, Homer received four votes, but the medal went to Frederick E. Church for his huge canvas *Niagara Falls* (The Corcoran Gallery of Art, Washington, D.C.). In the Louvre, Homer sketched aspiring students seated on stools in the galleries, studiously copying the masterpieces. In Montmartre he shared an atelier with a friend, Albert Kelsey. Together they visited the Casino de Paris where he sketched a lady's skirt whirling up above her knees during a waltz. Here on Avenue Montaigne the two friends visited the Bal Mabille. Begun as a simple *buvette* (popular bar) in 1813, by the middle of the 19th century it had become one of the largest and most popular dance halls in Paris, with an orchestra of 50 musicians and a chorus line. While watching the girls dance the can-can—heady stuff for two bachelors from Belmont, Massachusetts—Homer noticed a rose fall to the floor from a dancer's dress. This provided just the touch of abandon he needed for his sketches. *Harper's* published the two sketches, but with a pious word of warning: "We shall not venture to look into the abyss on the brink of which these frenzied men and women are dancing....This is work for the severe and steady eye of the preacher and moralist."

Rue Montalembert (7th) Map A

7   Hôtel Pont Royal. During the winter of 1949, one of Truman Capote's favorite haunts was the bar of the Hôtel Pont Royal. Basking in the recent success of his novel *Other Voices, Other Rooms,* the 25-year-old author successfully resisted a *Time* magazine interviewer. "Now there's Orson Welles at the bar," Capote said loudly, "looking exactly like Julius Ceasar. You do know," Truman told the unhappy reporter, "that Julius Ceasar was a homosexual, don't you?" Capote burbled on happily, and absolutely unquotably. When two smartly dressed French women got up from a table, several men turned to watch them leave. Capote promptly quipped to his interviewer, "Don't they know that women are passée?"

John Paul Jones's coffin on its way to the American Cathedral on Avenue George-Cinq on the morning of 6 July 1905. (See page 89.)

The booths of Thomas Edison and Elihu Thomson
in the American section of the Paris Universal Exhibition of 1889.
(See page 73.)

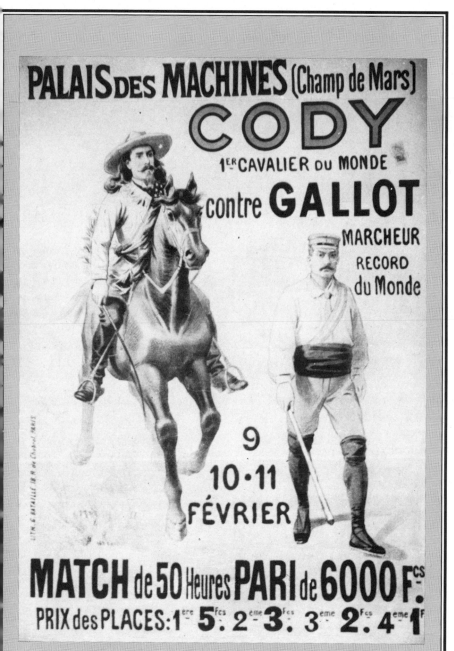

Buffalo Bill challenging French walking champion Monsieur Gallot to see who could go the farthest in 50 hours—the winner to receive 6,000 francs. Poster, 19th century. (See page 236.)

*President and Mrs. Woodrow Wilson arriving in Paris
at the Gare du Bois de Boulogne, 14 December 1918.
President Poincaré is behind President Wilson. (See page 128.)*

*General John Pershing about to decorate French officers
with American medals in the courtyard of the Hôtel des Invalides, 1920.
(See page 100.)*

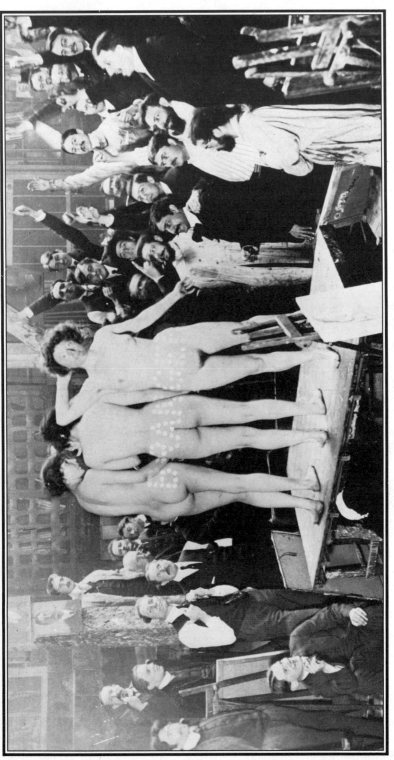

Students celebrating the end of a day's work at the Académie Julian, 1910.
(See page 63.)

*Michael and Sarah Stein, Henri Matisse, Allan Stein,
and Hans Purrmann in the Steins' apartment, 1907.
(See page 123.)*

Above: Gertrude Stein, 1925. (See page 79.)
Below: Alice B. Toklas in the living room at 5 Rue Christine, 1951.
(See page 45.)

Above: Gertrude Stein's living room at 27 Rue de Fleurus, 1909.
(See page 79.)
Below: a Gertrude Stein collage. (See page 45.)

Sylvia Beach with unidentified friend
in Rue Dupuytren, 1920.
(See page 66.)

*George Antheil climbing up to his apartment
at 12 Rue de l'Odéon under the admiring eye of Sylvia Beach.
(See page 160.)*

Above: Sylvia Beach and James Joyce reading reviews of Ulysses, *1922.*
Below: Myrsine and Hélène Moschos, Sylvia Beach, Ernest Hemingway
at Sylvia Beach's birthday party, March 1928. (See page 159.)

Left: Ezra Pound, about 1920. (See page 229.)
Right: A young Ernest Hemingway, about 1922. (See page 36.)
Both men photographed in Shakespeare and Company by Sylvia Beach.

Alexander Calder and his circus.
Photo by André Kertész, 1929.
(See page 37.)

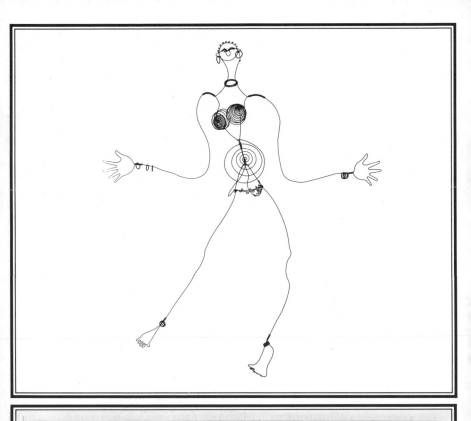

Above: Josephine Baker by Alexander Calder, 1926. (See page 56.)
Below: George Gershwin stayed here in 1928 while working
on An American in Paris. *(See page 109.)*

Virgil Thomson, Walter Piston, Herbert Elwell, and Aaron Copland in Nadia Boulanger's apartment. The occasion was a concert of their works on 5 May 1926 by the Société Musicale Indépendante. (See page 111.)

Boulevard du Montparnasse (6th & 14th) Map **D**

60 Formerly Hôtel de Versailles. Alexander Calder arrived in France in July 1926 at the age of 28. He had worked his way over from New York on a rusty British freighter. The ship was so ancient, wrote Calder, that he was assigned to paint it in the hope that this would prevent it from breaking up at sea. He spent four months in this hotel in a modest room on the top floor before moving to nearby Rue Daguerre.

(81) Situated on the corner of the Impasse Robiquet, at the end of the courtyard, the sign read "Atelier des élèves de Monsieur Carolus-Duran." Sculptors occupied the ground floor, while painters worked on the floors above. It was here in 1872 that Carolus, who had achieved fame with his painting *La Dame au Gant* in the Salon of 1869, began teaching.

One morning in May 1874, John Singer Sargent, 18, accompanied by his father, sought admission. When the two men appeared, Carolus was busy commenting on the week's work of his 24 students. The young Sargent, much to his consternation, was asked to lay out his sample drawings and paintings before the entire class. An American student, J. Carroll Beckwith, present that morning, recorded Carolus as saying that, while Sargent had much to "unlearn," his work contained "promise above the ordinary." He was accepted on the spot. Carolus' new atelier was considered the most avant-garde in Paris. He did not have the patience to teach drawing. He taught "painting." Carolus did not believe that the painter had to understand the organic nature of the objects he painted. One painted what one saw. The advantage was that the student avoided the painstaking discipline of drawing and learning human anatomy imposed by the traditional schools in Paris. This was all very well; however, it assumed that the student was already a draftsman and this was rarely the case. But Sargent was an exception, and soon became the leading student in the atelier. Work began at eight o'clock every morning and finished at noon. Carolus came twice a week.

In January, the students gave the annual dinner for the master. Sargent wrote to a friend: "We cleared the studio of easels and canvasses, illuminated it with venetian or coloured paper lanterns, hired a piano and had what is called 'a devil of a spree.' Dancing, toasts and songs lasted until 4." During the evening, Carolus himself sang and played guitar.

In 1877, Sargent was invited by Carolus to help him complete a ceiling decoration for the Luxembourg Palace. The next year Sargent's entry at the Salon, an outdoor painting of *The Oyster-Gatherers at Cancale* (Museum of Fine Arts, Boston), received an "honorable mention." It clearly showed the influence of Monet. After 1878, his student days over, Sargent occasionally dropped in at the Carolus atelier, but he preferred working on his own on the nearby street, Notre-Dame-des-Champs.

99 Café Le Sélect. During the summer of 1927, the pending execution of Sacco and Vanzetti touched off a series of demonstrations in Europe, and particularly in Paris. Most of the American community in Paris was against the execution. Isadora Duncan got into a fight on the Sélect terrace with newspaperman Floyd Gibbons, who felt that the two men were guilty.

105 Site of the original Café de la Rotonde. The café opened in 1911 and took over, in 1924, the Café du Parnasse at number 103. The clientele included Apollinaire, Picasso, Derain, Vlaminck, Max Jacob, and Modigliani. Its café, grill room, artists' gallery, and nightclub were most popular with Americans. In May 1922, Edna St. Vincent Millay dined here almost daily with her mother. She wrote to her sister, Norma Millay:

> Mummie & I about live in this here kafe. We feed on *choucroute garnie,* which is fried sauerkraut trimmed with boiled potatoes, a large slice of ham & a fat hot dog,—yum, yum, werry excillint. That's about all they serve here in the cafe—that and onion soup & sandwiches. And mummie & I come every day & eat the stinkin' stuff, & all our friends hold their noses & pass us by till we've finished.

Several of her letters bore the address "Café de la Rotonde," and were penned during the meal. Another letter to her sister written on 25 April 1922 began: "Here are your mother and sister sitting with Margot Schuyler at the famous sink of corruption (see above) of the Latin Quarter." She continued: "Later.—Have et my soup,—am using the wine list, spread open before me as a writing desk," and concluded, "Margot now says I must eat my *noix de veau braisé aux endives* while it is hot." The postscript read, "Griffin & Curtis Moffet who have just come in say that I must eat my *tarte aux cerises* while it is cold!"

108   Café du Dôme. Opened in 1897, its pre-World War I clientele included Lenin and Trotsky. In the 1920s it became one of the most popular cafés for American artists, writers, journalists, students, and tourists. Together with the cafés La Coupole, Le Sélect, and La Rotonde, the Dôme provided Americans who lived in small hotel rooms with a place to meet and talk. After the daily stroll to American Express to pick up mail, and hopefully a check from home, the café was the place to go, where writer or artist, ensconced on the terrace, watched the world go by; time had lost its fearful American urgency. In London Englishmen had their clubs; in Paris, Americans had their cafés where everyone was welcome and they could even meet the French, who rarely invited strangers to their homes. But not every American discovered happiness in cafés. Sinclair Lewis spent the year 1924–25 living on the Right Bank writing *Arrowsmith* (Pulitzer Prize, 1926). Hailed as the author of *Main Street* and *Babbitt,* he was somewhat drunk one evening at the Dôme, when he apparently boasted of the number of copies sold and even compared his writing to that of Flaubert. From a nearby table came a very audible remark: "Sit down, you're just a best seller." In the October 1925 issue of the *American Mercury,* Lewis took his revenge. He singled out the Café du Dôme, rich with American expatriates and would-be writers, in a particularly ungenerous article:

> Nowhere in America itself is this duty-ridden earnestness of the artist and his disciples so well shown as at that Brevoort and cathedral of American sophistication, the Café Dôme in Paris.
>
> Among the other advantages of the Dôme, it is on a corner charmingly resembling Sixth avenue at Eighth street, and all the waiters understand Americanese, so that it is possible for the patrons to be highly expatriate without benefit of Berlitz. It is, in fact, the perfectly standardized place to which standardized rebels flee from the crushing standardization of America.
>
> On view at the Dôme is the great though surprisingly young author, who by his description of vomiting and the progress of cancer, in a volume of sixty-seven pages issued in a limited edition of three hundred copies, has entirely transformed American fiction. There is the lady who has demolished Thomas Hardy, Arnold Bennett, and Goethe. And king of kings, Osimandias of Osimandiases, supremest of Yankee critics, ex cathedra authority on literature, painting, music, economics, and living without laboring, very father and seer of the Dôme, is that Young Intellectual who, if he ever finishes the assassinatory book of

which we have heard these last three years, will tear the world up by the roots. He is going to deliver unto scorn all the false idols of the intelligentsia, particularly such false idols as have become tired of lending him—as the phrase is—money.

Sinclair Lewis's "king of kings" was Harold Stearns, who in 1921, at the age of 30, published *America and the Young Intellectual*. It immediately became a veritable credo of the postwar generation, which disliked, Stearns said, "almost to the point of hatred and certainly to the point of contempt, the type of people who dominate in our present civilization." Civilization had gone wrong. Life in America was uncreative, vulgar, and tawdry. It was a race after money. In an article in the January 1921 issue of the *Atlantic Monthly,* Stearns defended the "moral idealism" of the young in America and wrote, "We of the younger generation make our plans for leaving the country of our birth and early affection." On 4 July 1921, he boarded an ocean liner and told the dozen reporters who had come to see him off that he would probably never return. His arrival in London was less dramatic. He called on Sinclair Lewis, who loaned him sufficient money to live a year in Paris, a loan which he never repaid. When Lewis came to Paris, he discovered that the former prophet of so many young Americans had become a pathetic figure drifting from café to café, mooching drinks, and borrowing money. Journalist William Shirer was as surprised as he was disillusioned to discover his former hero writing a daily column on horse racing for the *Chicago Tribune.*

On 23 December 1921, immediately upon arriving in Paris, Ernest Hemingway wrote to Sherwood Anderson and his wife. They had met in Chicago that spring and Anderson had provided Hemingway with letters of introduction to Sylvia Beach, Gertrude Stein, and Ezra Pound. Hemingway and his wife stayed at the Hôtel d'Angleterre on Rue Jacob, at Anderson's suggestion.

Dear Sherwood and Tennessee:
  Well here we are. And we sit outside the Dôme Café, opposite the Rotunde that's being redecorated, warmed up against one of those charcoal brazziers and it's so damned cold outside and the brazzier makes it so warm and we drink rum punch, hot, and the rhum enters into us like the Holy Spirit.
  And when it's a cold night in the streets of Paris and we're walking home down the Rue Bonaparte we think of the way the

wolves used to slink into the city and François Villon and the gallows at Montfaucon. What a town.

135 Formerly Hôtel des Etats-Unis. John Singer Sargent moved to this address in 1875 so that he could be closer to the atelier of Carolus-Duran at 81 Boulevard du Montparnasse.

Art Buchwald lived here in 1948 while writing the "Paris after Dark" column for the *Herald Tribune*. He was supposedly studying French at the Alliance Française on the Boulevard Raspail. In *Seems Like Yesterday,* he joyously recalled these days, adding that to receive the 75 dollars allowance a veteran had to have proof of actual attendance. Happily this problem was overcome by giving two dollars a month to the lady at the Alliance who took attendance. A fellow boarder was ex-bomber pilot Gary Davis, who gave up his U.S. passport and became a Citizen of the World. When Davis announced that he wished to make the hotel the World Head-quarters of the Citizen Movement, he was invited to leave immediately.

137 Harry Leon Wilson, the editor of the humorous weekly *Puck* from 1896 to 1902, gave up the arduous task of constant editing and moved to Paris to become a novelist. His works include *The Splendors* (1902) and *The Lions of the Lord* (1903), the story of the great Mormon trek to Utah under the leadership of Brigham Young. Wilson collaborated with Booth Tarkington on several plays: *Your Humble Servant, Foreign Exchange,* and, the most successful, *The Man from Home.* Wilson shared his apartment here with Julian Street, who wrote a popular guide to restaurants called *Paris à la Carte.*

159 Formerly Hôtel Venetia. Edna St. Vincent Millay passed the months of April and May 1922 here with her mother. The 30-year-old poet had spent sixteen months in Europe, writing poetry for pleasure and prose for pay. Under the pen name of Nancy Boyd she published "Diary of an American Art Student in Paris. Showing How She Succeeded in Going to the Louvre Every Day" in the November 1922 issue of *Vanity Fair.* In spite of her cheerful letters home, she had been intensely lonely and finally convinced her mother to join her. She told her sister that their mother "has seen more of Paris in the five weeks she has been here than I saw in five months... the only thing that has saved me from an early grave, is the fact that she has just acquired a small blister on her heel, & is content with doing not more than twelve miles an afternoon." In the mornings, the young writer worked on a series of sonnets inspired in part by her love for her fellow American poet Arthur Ficke. To him she wrote one of her most touching sonnets: "I know I am but summer to your heart."

Much to her surprise, Arthur Ficke turned up in Paris, but accompanied by a young painter, Gladys Brown, with whom he had fallen in love. He invited Edna Millay and her mother to meet his newly beloved at the very fashionable Prunier's restaurant, imagining perhaps that the setting would be appropriate. As soon as Edna Millay walked in the door she recognized her rival, and said: "I just knew when I saw you across the room as we were coming in that you were Gladys Brown! I said to myself, 'There's the girl who took my fellow away!'" The future Mrs. Ficke could not help but admire such a greeting.

166　Katherine Anne Porter married Eugene Pressly at the Mairie of the 6th arrondissement on 11 March 1933. The couple moved here where Porter reworked her story "Hacienda," published the previous year in the *Virginia Quarterly Review*. She was, as the expression goes, "a writer's writer," and during her four years in Paris she experienced financial hardship. Her early stories, published as *Flowering Judas* (1930), won her critical acclaim and a Guggenheim. The grant also paid for her voyage from Mexico to Germany on the German passenger freighter *Vera,* a trip which took 27 days in 1931. This voyage was later described in *Ship of Fools* (1962), which brought her public recognition and, at 72, financial security. Porter summed up her own feelings about Paris in the words of Mary Treadwell in *Ship of Fools:*

> I want to live in that dark alley named l'Impasse des Deux Anges, and have those little pointed jeweled blue velvet shoes at the Cluny copied, and get my perfumes from Molinard's and go to Schiaparelli's spring show to watch her ugly mannequins jerking about as if they were run with push buttons, hitching their belts down in back every time they turn, giving each other hard theatrical Lesbian stares. I want to light a foot-high candle to Our Lady of Paris for bringing me back and go out to Chantilly to see if they've turned another page in the Duke's Book of Hours. I'd like

to dance again in that little guinguette in rue d'Enfert-Rochereau with the good-looking young Marquis—what's his name? descended from Joan of Arc's brother. I want to go again to la Bagatelle and help the moss roses open....I'll go again to Rambouillet through those woods that really do look just as Watteau and Fragonard saw them. And to St. Denis to see again the lovely white marble feet of kings and queens, lying naked together on the roof above their formal figures on the bier, delicate toes turned up side by side....I'm going again to St. Cloud next May to see the first lilies of the valley....Oh God, I'm homesick. I'll never leave Paris again, I promise, if you'll let me just get there this once more. If every soul left it one day and grass grew in the pavements, it would still be Paris to me, I'd want to live there.

171   La Closerie des Lilas. Ernest Hemingway's favorite café-restaurant. He and his friend John Dos Passos had been studying the Old Testament and would sit here to read aloud from the Song of Deborah, Chronicles, and Kings. Dos Passos recorded in *The Best Times:* "My story was that basing his wiry short sentences on cablese and the King James Bible, Hem would become the first great American stylist."

It was at this café that F. Scott Fitzgerald asked Hemingway to read his latest manuscript, *The Great Gatsby* (1925), and in the fall of 1925 that Hemingway read to Dos Passos from the manuscript of *The Torrents of Spring,* his ungenerous parody of Sherwood Anderson's novel *Dark Laughter.* Dos Passos found parts of the parody amusing, the rest sentimental and silly, and he urged Hemingway not to publish it. He advised Hemingway instead to follow *In Our Time* (1925) with something of equal quality. Hemingway, however, was tired of being compared to Anderson and sought a break with him. *The Torrents of Spring* appeared in 1926. It was also on this terrace that Hemingway wrote most of *The Sun Also Rises,* which he finished in six weeks. Much of the story is set here.

Rue du Montparnasse (14th) Map D

42   Café Falstaff. Toward the end of the 1920s, the Falstaff became very popular with Americans in Montparnasse. "Jimmy the Barman," as he was known, a former British prize fighter, moved here from the Dingo Bar with a waiter from Brooklyn, Joe

Hildesheim, known as "Joe the Bum." They ran the bar in an easygoing, haphazard manner with ready advice for the horse race of the day. The bar's oak panelling and padded seats gave it a certain charm. It was quieter than the Dôme, and became a refuge for serious drinkers.

Morley Callaghan, a Canadian author, describes in *That Summer in Paris* walking in here with F. Scott Fitzgerald and Ernest Hemingway: "I laughed and said that by tomorrow word would go around the café that I, shamefully, was letting Fitzgerald and Hemingway tell me what to do about a book. Ernest said, 'What do you care? We're professionals. We only care whether the thing is as good as it should be.'" The summer in question was 1929; Hemingway was reading the proofs of *A Farewell to Arms* and Fitzgerald was working on *Tender Is the Night*.

Rue de Montpensier (1st) Map F

30   Harrison of Paris Press. Barbara Harrison and Monroe Wheeler sent out a prospectus in 1930 announcing that their new press intended to publish limited editions in English. These were to be illustrated by "brilliant draughtsmen," executed by the "chief European presses," and printed on "durable and in some instances precious papers, variously cased or bound." The prospectus promised the French system of printing "a few copies on China or Japan Vellum...Holland or Madagascar or hand-made Auvergne." Harrison provided the money, Wheeler the technical expertise. One of their first endeavors, *The Wild West,* was a collection of seven tales by Bret Harte, including "The Luck of Roaring Camp" and "The Outcasts of Poker Flat." They felt that Harte, "spokesman and laureate" of the Old West, deserved better than cheap popular editions printed on "muddy looking paper." Harrison promised to print a volume worthy of that "good and handsome Californian." The edition was illustrated with eight watercolor drawings by Pierre Falke. This was followed by Thomas Mann's "A Sketch of My Life," which had just been published in German, and Glenway Wescott's *The Babe's Bed.* Wescott, who hailed from Wisconsin, had just written his best novel, *The Grandmothers* (1927), and *The Babe's Bed,* which Random House rejected, was immediately accepted by Harrison. In 1931, the Harrison Press put out *The Fables of Aesop* (the Sir Roger L'Estrange translation), illustrated with 50 drawings by Alexander Calder. One of the fables, "A Man with Two Wives," pictures the unfortunate husband standing naked in a state of obvious shock as his two wives, in similar lack of attire, gleefully pluck the two remaining hairs from his head. The Fables was printed on Auvergne paper, made "just as in 1326," wrote Wheeler—the same paper that later served for the first editions of Molière. In 1933 Katherine Anne Porter's *French Song Book* appeared, followed the next year by her final version of "Hacienda." This was the twelfth and last publication of Harrison of Paris.

Rue du Mont-Thabor (1st) Map F

4   Washington Irving moved to Paris from London in late summer 1820. In this quiet street, which faced the back entrance to the Hôtel Meurice, the ever sociable Irving joined friend John Jacob Astor for lunch. Although he enjoyed basking in the recent triumph of *Rip Van Winkle* and *The Legend of Sleepy Hollow,* he had unaccountably become older, 39, and in a letter to his brother William he confessed: "Either Paris or myself has changed very much since I was here before. It is by no means so gay as formerly; that is to say the populace have a more grave and triste appearance."

Furthermore, fame was one thing, fortune was another. Although Irving had succeeded in getting away from the family bankruptcy and had resumed writing, he was distracted by a new idea. Travelling from London to Paris with his brother Peter, the two men had disembarked at Le Havre and had come by boat to Rouen. What France needed, they decided, was a steamboat service (Had not Robert Fulton achieved fame and fortune on the Hudson?) between those two ports. Irving wrote to his brother William and asked him to put up 5,000 dollars which, added to the royalties invested from *The Sketch Book,* would launch brother Peter on a splendid career. But William had seen fortunes evaporate in the steamboat business and wisely declined involvement, leaving Peter Irving in Le Havre—when he was not interrupting his brother Washington on Rue du Mont-Thabor. Suffice it to say that at the end of his stay here, Irving's writing had little advanced, while his fortune had seriously declined.

If you stand across the street and look at the entrance to number 4, you will notice, just above the doorway on both sides, the *flambeau* (torch) holders which provided light during the winter evenings in the 19th century.

Rue Morgue

This street came into being thanks to Edgar Allan Poe. "The Murders in the Rue Morgue" (1841) was the first modern detective story. The narrator of the story lived in Paris with his friend C. Auguste Dupin, a genius of extraordinary analytic power. They learned of the murders of Madame L'Espanaye and her daughter Camille in their fourth-floor apartment in the Rue Morgue. The police were baffled by the lack of motive, the obvious superhuman strength of the killer, and his grotesque and unintelligible voice. Dupin visited the scene of the murder, discovered new clues, and deduced that the murderer was an ape. An advertisement brought a sailor to Dupin's apartment who confessed that he had brought an orangutan to Paris to sell, and the ape had escaped and committed the murder. The culprit was recaptured and sold to the Jardin des Plantes. Edgar Allan Poe never set foot in France and this is the only nonexistent street in this guide.

Avenue de New York (16th) Métro: Alma-Marceau

On the evening of 7 August 1803, a crowd gathered on the Right Bank of the Seine between the Barrière des Bons Hommes (roughly where the foot bridge, the Passerelle Debilly, crosses the river) and the Perier steam pump at Chaillot (opposite 2 Avenue de New York). They had gathered to watch the latest folly of the Paris season, Robert Fulton's steamboat. Seventy feet long, eight feet wide, and three feet deep, with paddle wheels twelve feet in diameter, the boat was propelled by an eight-horsepower steam engine leased from the engineering firm of Perier.

The French newspapers reported Fulton's experiment at length. *Le Journal des Débats* wrote:

> At six o'clock in the evening assisted by only three persons, he put the boat in motion with two other boats in tow and for one and a half hours he provided the odd spectacle of a boat moved by wheels like those on a cart, the wheels containing paddles or flat plates, moved by a fire engine. As we followed it along the quay, upstream the speed appeared to be that of a swift pedestrian, that is about 2,400 toises [2.9 miles] per hour; downstream, it was more rapid. It went up and down the river four times from the Barrière des Bons Hommes as far as the Chaillot engine. It manoeuvered with ease, turned to the right and to the left, dropped anchor and started again.

During this trip the steamboat passed one of the three floating swimming pools moored in the Seine. The newspaper went on to inform its readers that several representatives of the Institut des Sciences had taken a trip on the boat. It stressed the advantages that such an invention could bring to commerce on the Rhône, Seine, and Loire. "The towing of barges which now takes four months to come from Nantes to Paris would take but ten to fifteen days," reported *Le Journal des Débats*. "The author of this invention is M. Fulton, an American and celebrated engineer." But Fulton was unhappy with the demonstration. He had calculated that the speed of the steamboat would be sixteen miles per hour, while it was but three or four. A more powerful engine was required and this meant more money. Napoleon, who had financed Fulton's work on his submarine, was definitely not interested in the steamboat.

Fulton returned to America in 1806 after an absence of twenty years. The following year his steamship the *Clermont,* would paddle from New York to Albany, a distance of 150 miles upstream, in 32 hours. Fulton's reputation and fortune were assured.

On the upstream side of the Passerelle Debilly there is a plaque commemorating Fulton's demonstration.

Rue Nollet (17th) Métro: La Fourche

15   Langston Hughes, the black poet, took a room here in April 1924. Aged 22, he worked first as a dishwasher and then as a waiter at the famous Grand Duc nightclub in Pigalle. At the time, top black musicians such as Cricket Smith and Buddy Gilmore were playing the blues there. At the end of the year, Hughes left for Italy.

Place du Parvis Notre-Dame (4th) Map E

> The cathedral of Notre Dame does not budge an inch for all the idiocies of this world.
>
> e.e. cummings

1   Hôpital Hôtel-Dieu. By the beginning of the 19th century, Paris had become an important medical training center for Americans. In his book *The Hospitals and Surgeons of Paris* (1843), Dr. Campbell Stewart wrote:

> All the public hospitals in Paris are so admirably conducted and so abundantly supplied with every convenience and comfort for the sick, that respectable individuals from the middle classes of

society are frequently induced to resort to them in cases of sickness, both with a view to economy and for the advantage of being well and properly attended during the continuance of their illness. No stigma whatever attaches to those who seek hospital relief; hence all classes of citizens who could not be properly attended at home, may with perfect propriety do so, and they are often induced to avail themselves of the rare advantages which they possess in having access to such noble and liberally provided institutions.

Addressing himself to the American student, the author stressed that "as no difficulty exists in gaining a free and easy access" to the great medical facilities of Paris, "it may be asserted that in no part of the world can the same practical experience be acquired by the attentive student as in the French capital."

Samuel Goodrich of Boston visited this hospital in February 1824 and saw the famed French surgeon Guillaume Dupuytren on rounds with medical students. Dupuytren had been a professor here since 1812 and was noted as a diagnostician and lecturer. He wrote frequently on surgery and described a fracture of the fibula and a contraction of the hand that bear his name. He founded the chair of pathological anatomy at the University of Paris.

As in all hospitals, stories abounded, and Goodrich recorded:

...went to the Hôtel Dieu, a medical and surgical hospital. Saw Dupuytren and his pupils, visiting the patients. He is a rather large man, of a fine Bonapartean head, but sour, contumelious looks. He holds the very first rank as a surgeon. His operations are surprisingly bold and skillful. Edward C..., of Philadelphia, who is here studying medicine, told me a good anecdote of him. He has a notion that he can instantly detect hydrocephalus in a patient, from the manner in which he carries his head. One day, while he was in the midst of his scholars at the hospital, he saw a common sort of man standing at a distance, among several persons who had come for medical advice. Dupuytren's eye fell upon him, and he said to his pupils—"Do you see yonder, that fellow that has his hand to his face, and carries his head almost on this shoulder? Now, take notice: that man has hydrocephalus. Come here, my good fellow!"

The man thus called, came up. "Well," said Dupuytren—"I know what ails you; but come, tell us about it yourself. What is the matter with you?"

"I've got the toothache!" was the reply.

"Take that"—said Dupuytren, giving him a box on the ear—
"and go to the proper department and have it pulled out."

Dr. Willard Parker, who later became professor of surgery at the New York College of Physicians and Surgeons, visited the Hôtel-Dieu on Wednesday morning, 12 April 1837. In his *Journal* he noted its accommodations for 1,500 patients. He saw Chomel and Blondin, and watched Roux operate for "hydocile injection." He returned the following week to hear Roux lecture and watched him remove tumors from the scalp and operate "for fistula in Ano and the removal of the breast in encephaloid state." Parker felt that Roux lectured well, but "in operation, treatment and lecturing I think we Yankees can beat."

Rue Notre-Dame-des-Champs (6th) Map D

(49)   In 1878, Augustus St. Gaudens rented a large studio to work on the statue of Admiral Farragut. Three years later, the finished work was shipped to America and placed in Madison Square in New York, where it set new standards for public monuments.

70 bis   Ezra Pound, 36, took a ground-floor apartment here with his wife Dorothy at the end of 1921. He had been in Paris since spring 1920 and had spent the previous fourteen years in London, where he had won recognition as a major poet. It was here, in the quiet of Rue Notre-Dame-des-Champs, that Pound worked on the *Cantos.* His apartment in the back of the building looked onto a courtyard and a garden. He had made the furniture himself, a low tea table from rough boards, and two large armchairs from boards and canvas. Hemingway described the apartment as being "as poor as Gertrude Stein's was rich." But Pound's parties were renowned. In *Paris Salons, Cafés, Studios,* Sisley Huddleston recalled that "whoever has not seen Ezra Pound, ignoring all the rules of tango and of fox-trot, kicking up fantastic heels in a highly personal Charleston, closing his eyes as his toes nimbly scattered right and left, has missed one of the spectacles which reconcile us to life."

One day, Wyndham Lewis, having knocked at Pound's door without success, simply walked in to discover a splendidly built young man, stript to the waist, and with a torso of dazzling white standing not far from me. He was tall, handsome and serene, and was repelling with his boxing gloves— I thought without undue exertion—a hectic assault of Ezra's. After a final swing at the dazzling solar plexus (parried effortlessly by the trousered statue) Pound fell back upon his settee. The young man was Hemingway.

Hemingway later claimed that he had taught Ezra Pound how to box and, in exchange, Pound had taught him how to write.

Katherine Anne Porter took over Pound's former apartment from 1934 until she returned to Texas two years later.

72 Up two flights of squeaking stairs was the first "north light studio" of sculptress Malvina Hoffman. (You can still see the skylights from the street.) It was, she wrote, "a stage setting worthy of a scene in *La Bohème*." Her first commission in 1910 was to sculpt the American ambassador to France, Robert Bacon.

73 bis In winter 1877, John Singer Sargent shared a studio with Carroll Beckwith. Both young men had been students at the atelier of Carolus-Duran a few blocks away on the Boulevard du Mont-parnasse. Sargent had made the acquaintance of Augustus St. Gaudens and would walk up the street to watch the progress of the statue of Farragut. It was here that Sargent did his first important commission, that of the prosperous French playwright Edouard Pailleron. (The portrait is in the Musée National de Versailles.) You can see the studio down the alleyway, above the Académie Charpentier.

86 James McNeill Whistler took a large studio on the top floor, with a superb view, at the time, over the Luxembourg Gardens. The narrow, twisting staircase leading to the seventh floor has not changed since his day. He worked here from 1892 until he left Paris for the last time ten years later. In this studio, in 1894, he did the portrait of the well-known Chicago lawyer and amateur art critic Arthur J. Eddy (Chicago Art Institute), and three years later, the portrait of George W. Vanderbilt (National Gallery of Art, Washington, D.C.). It was here on Rue Notre-Dame-des-Champs that Whistler worked at his latest passion, lithography, in which he excelled.

109   Ecole Alsacienne. Christian Herter attended the school as
a young man, from 1906 to 1912. Later he joined the State
Department where he helped develop the Marshall Plan. He served
as U.S. secretary of state from 1959 until 1961.

(113)   On 10 February 1924, Ernest Hemingway wrote to Ezra
Pound:

> Dear Prometheus
>
> We have trouved [found] an appt at 113 Notre Dame des Champs
> semi furnished over a saw mill on a 3 mos to 3 mos to 3 mos etc.
> basis.

Hemingway had just returned from Canada where he had abandoned
journalism in order to devote himself fully to fiction. Until the
success of *The Sun Also Rises,* his finances were most precarious,
which accounts for living above the sawmill. On 15 August, he told
Gertrude Stein: "It is quiet today. The Sawmill isn't running on
account of Assumption."

Rue Notre-Dame-des-Victoires (2nd)

(1-5)   Site of Les Messageries Royales, the "bus terminal" of
Paris during the 18th and 19th centuries. All public conveyances
arrived and left from here. It bustled with customs and passport
controls, porters barking the superiority of their hotels, hospitable
ladies, guides, interpreters, and vendors of all sorts accosting
bewildered travellers as they descended from carriages.

Nathaniel P. Willis, 25, from Boston, arrived here in 1831. A
Yale graduate, he had founded and edited the *American Monthly
Magazine* in 1829, and had already been hailed as a leading
American poet. He kept an amusing journal of his six-month stay in
Paris, which he later published under the title *Pencillings by the
Way.* Willis had come from Rouen and had entered Paris via the
Porte St.-Denis:

> I entered Paris on Sunday at eleven o'clock. I never should have
> recognised the day. The shops were all open, the artificers all at
> work, the unintelligible criers vociferating their wares, and the
> people in their working-day dresses. We wound through street
> after street, narrow and dark and dirty, and with my mind full of
> the splendid views of squares, and columns, and bridges, as I had
> seen them in the prints, I could scarce believe I was in Paris. A

turn brought us into a large court, that of the Messagerie, the place at which all travellers are set down on arrival. Here my baggage was once more inspected, and, after a half-hour's delay, I was permitted to get into a *fiacre* [horse-carriage], and drive to a hotel.

Willis took rooms at the Hôtel des Etrangers on Rue Vivienne.

(16)   In May 1848, Ralph Waldo Emerson recorded that "we now dine daily at a table d'hôte at No. 16 Rue de Notre Dame des Victoires, where five hundred French habitués usually dine at 1 fr. 60 centimes. Of course, it is an excellent place for French grammar. Nouns, verbs, adverbs and interjections furnished gratuitously."

Avenue de l'Observatoire (14th) Map D

61   L'Observatoire. Constructed on a hill outside Paris in 1672 on the orders of Louis XIV, the building in stone was completed without the use of metal in order not to disturb the magnetic compass, and without wood in order to avoid a fire. Three centuries later the observatory remains in excellent condition. As a center of research it has had several distinguished directors, including Laplace who established beyond a doubt Newton's hypothesis of gravitation. In the 19th century, American researchers included Charles Sanders Peirce, physicist, astronomer, and logician. His experiments with the pendulum in 1875 were watched by Henry James.

Place de l'Odéon (6th) Map B

Théâtre National de l'Odéon, formerly Théâtre Français. In 1782, the Comédie Française opened the doors of the largest theater in Paris with 1,913 seats. To Parisians, the theater seemed to be far away from the city, and they complained that the hackneys overcharged. Thomas Jefferson was an enthusiastic theatergoer and saw *Les Plaideurs* by Racine, and *Amphitryon* by Molière among others. On 4 August 1786, he saw the Comédie's newest and most successful comedy, *Le Mariage de Figaro* by Beaumarchais.

During the Revolution the actors split into opposing factions; the name of the theater was changed to the Théâtre de l'Egalité and the theater was completely destroyed by a fire in 1799. The Comédie Française found a new home on the Right Bank, and the Théâtre de l'Odéon as it exists today dates from 1819. It has enjoyed mixed fortunes, presenting comedy, tragedy, drama, vaudeville, comic opera, Italian opera, dance, and ballet.

On 29 May 1805, Washington Irving attended a performance of *Les Templiers* by François Raynouard with the leading actors of the day. Talma played the role of Marigny fils and Mlle Georges that of Jeanne de Navarre. Irving, who later became Talma's friend, noted in his journal: "Talma fine figure— great powers—I do not admire french style of acting."

6 Hôtel Michelet-Odéon, formerly Hôtel de la Place de l'Odéon. Dr. Pliny Earle and his friend Dr. Usher Parsons of Providence, Rhode Island, arrived in Paris in fall 1837 to spend the year studying in French hospitals. Earle had been advised to go to Europe by his cousin, Dr. Elisha Bartlett, who had just returned from a year's stay. He had written to Earle at the medical school in Philadelphia to tell him of the costs:

> First, as to the cost of twelve or fourteen months' absence on a trip to Europe, staying eight or nine months in Paris and travelling as far as Rome or Naples, —I suppose $1,000 or $1,200 will do very well. It cost me about $1,100 including everything, clothes, books, etc.

Earle soon felt that the reputation of Paris as the leading center for medical research and training was justified. In a letter to a colleague written in spring 1838, six months after his arrival, he noted:

> Although the most volatile of Europeans, the French furnish a very large number of the most learned men. No nation has produced more profound students in the abstract sciences, and their professional men are paragons of industry. To visit in the hospitals from fifty to one hundred patients, and prescribe for them by candlelight in the morning; then to give a lecture of an hour before breakfast; between breakfast and dinner to visit an extensive circle of patients in private practice, and perhaps attend the meeting of a medical society; after dinner (at 6 P.M.) to pass the evening in poring over professional books or in writing some original essay,—such is the life of any one of the more eminent physicians of Paris. The honors and emoluments of the profession scarcely will recompense this unremitting toil.

Treatment of the insane in France was considered advanced by world standards. Dr. Philippe Pinel had been appointed director of the Bicêtre Hospital for the Insane in 1793 and had obtained permission to remove the chains from the demented. He insisted upon humane treatment, established the custom of keeping well-documented case histories, and stressed the role of passions in mental disease. But if France was progressive in the care of the mentally ill compared to the rest of the world, the conditions remained harsh and the treatment based on discipline appears barbaric by modern standards. While Dr. Earle did not condemn what he saw at Bicêtre, he obviously disagreed with some of the methods used to cure the unfortunate patients:

The insane department of the Bicêtre contains seven hundred and sixty men, besides about two hundred idiots. We found them under the medical care of Pinel the younger, Ferrus and Leuret. The latter accompanied us on our tour of inspection. Dr. Pinel, the son of him who first unchained the maniacs here, has written for the Academy of Sciences an account, no doubt correct, of that famous deed of his father, Philippe Pinel, early in the year 1793, when Couthon, the friend of Robespierre, finally consented that the chains should be removed from about fifty of the madmen then at the Bicêtre. . . . Dr. Leuret, showed us the bathing-room, and explained his manner of using the douche for purposes of mental and moral discipline, which appeared to me injurious. The scene of this treatment contained about a dozen bath-tubs, over each of which was a douche-pipe with a capacity for a three-quarter-inch stream. In two tubs we saw patients, each kept from leaving the tub by a board fitted to his neck where he sat, as a man stands in the pillory. One was a robust man, subject to varying hallucinations, who now thought himself the husband of the widowed Duchess of Berri, and had been permitted the day before to have writing materials on condition that he would not write such vagaries as that he was a favorite of the exiled Bourbons and of Louis Philippe. He had written, however, his usual absurdities about the Duke of Bordeaux, Charles X., etc. Dr. Leuret, with this letter in his hand, reminded the patient of his promise, read him the nonsense he had written, and asked him if he still believed that. "Oui, Monsieur." "Give him the douche," said Dr. Leuret to the attendant, who at once turned the cock and discharged the stream on the madman's head. He screamed and writhed, and begged to have it stopped. It was checked; and he was asked, "Do you still believe you are the intimate friend of Charles X?" "I think I do." "Let him have the douche." He again floundered, shouted, and begged for mercy. "Well, are you the chum of Charles X and the Duke of Bordeaux?" "I . . . I presume so." "Give him the douche once more." In this way, sometimes with argument and sometimes with the cold stream, the doctor labored for half an hour to break up his fantastic notions. At last the patient gave in, and his tormentor gave him a lesson to be learned for the next day.

Turning to the other man in his tub, Dr. Leuret said he had yesterday refused to do a task assigned to him, leaving the work untouched. He then asked the man why he had neglected to work. "To tell the truth, Monsieur, I did not feel any special desire to work." This was said with a jocose leer which almost made us laugh. "Well, will you work hereafter when you are told?" Reflecting an instant, with the same comic air he said, "*Parole d'honneur* [word of honor], I will not work." "Give him the douche," said Dr. L. The effect of the stream was now instantaneous. Like a child who is whipped, he cried, "I will, I will!" The douche was then stopped, and orders given that he should do the task before night.

Allen Tate, writer and poet, stayed at this hotel from September to December 1929, when he and his wife returned to New York. He was introduced to Ernest Hemingway by Sylvia Beach. The two men walked up the Rue de l'Odéon from her shop to the Place de l'Odéon, where they sat down at the Café Voltaire. Tate recalled in *Memoirs and Opinions* that they had barely sat down when Hemingway mentioned two reviews which Tate had written about his work in the *Nation,* implying in them that Hemingway had studied the British sea captain turned author, Frederick Marryat. "You're wrong about that," said Hemingway, "Never heard of Marryat." Tate later talked to John Bishop who assured him that Hemingway kept a copy of *Peter Simple* by Marryat on his night table in 1923. Tate concluded: "Ernest Hemingway was handsome and even his malice had a certain charm; I couldn't have known then that he was the complete son of a bitch who would later write about certain friends, all of them defenselessly dead, in *A Moveable Feast.*"

Rue de l'Odéon (6th) Map B

2   Thomas Paine lived at number 2 from April 1797 until he returned to the United States in October 1802. He lodged at the house of Nicolas Bonneville, his printer and friend. His friends Robert Fulton and Joel Barlow called on him here. Sixty years old, embittered by his imprisonment during the Terror and impoverished, his creative years were over. During his residence here the street was called Rue du Théâtre-François. (Paine's address number 4 corresponds to number 2 today.)

8   Contact Editions. During summer 1921, 26-year-old Robert McAlmon appeared on the doorstep of Shakespeare and Company. Sylvia Beach recalled being quickly charmed by his "Irish sea-blue eyes and nasal drawl." Convinced that Paris needed another small publisher for American and British writers, McAlmon launched Contact Editions, using Shakespeare and Company as a business address before moving here in 1922. Ezra Pound and James Joyce believed that McAlmon had talent as a writer. Soon, however, McAlmon began to dissipate his energies in the bars and cafés of Montparnasse until he had deteriorated into what his former admirer Sylvia Beach called "a malicious gossip." McAlmon had one stroke of fortune; he had married the daughter of Sir John Ellerman, "the heaviest taxpayer in England." He received 70,000 dollars in 1923 from Sir John, a fortune at the time, which enabled him to help writers such as Joyce and to publish books which commercial presses could not afford to handle. Robert McAlmon later became embittered by the lack of public interest in his own writing, which was mediocre. Contact Editions published William Carlos Williams's *Spring and All* (1922), Ernest Hemingway's first work *Three Stories and Ten Poems* (1923), Gertrude Stein's *The Making of Americans* (1925), and *The Ladies Almanack Written & Illustrated by a Lady of Fashion* (1926), written anonymously by Djuna Barnes. In 1926, McAlmon paid a brief visit to America before returning to run Contact Editions on the Rue d'Anjou.

12   Shakespeare and Company. Perhaps the best-known American address in Paris between 1921 and 1940. Sylvia Beach moved her lending library and bookshop here in July 1921 from the nearby Rue Dupuytren. She handled only English-language books, while her friend across the street, Adrienne Monnier, handled only French. American books were expensive in France in the 1920s, and at this shop customers could borrow a book with payment of a weekly fee. Each customer had a library card kept by Beach. Today among her papers at Princeton University, one can discover that Paul Valéry read poems by Robert Frost and essays by Ralph Waldo Emerson, while a young Simone de Beauvoir read Faulkner and Hemingway, who in turn read Turgenev.

On 11 July 1920, Sylvia Beach met James Joyce at a party. Joyce became intrigued by the name Shakespeare and Company and paid a visit to her shop. The result was an agreement to publish *Ulysses* in France. An order for 1,000 copies was placed with Monnier's printer, Maurice Darantière in Dijon. The first two copies were delivered on the eve of Joyce's 40th birthday, 2 February 1922. It was thanks to Beach's belief in Joyce's genius that she permitted him to add phrases, entire lists of names, and whole paragraphs which enriched the final text and nearly doubled the cost of publication.

During the 1920s, every American writer in Paris frequented this bookstore to borrow books (Hemingway to borrow money), pick up mail, cash checks, and meet other writers. Other American visitors, in addition to tourists, included Paul Robeson, Aaron Copland, George Gershwin, Allen Tate, Thomas Wolfe, and Elizabeth Bishop.

An important Walt Whitman exhibition was held here from 21 April to 20 June 1926. *Leaves of Grass* was Beach's most consistent seller after *Ulysses*. Joyce, who later quoted Whitman in *Finnegans Wake* (1939), came to the opening of the exhibition, declaring to a friend that he was going to "Stratford-on-Odéon." The following year Beach published Joyce's *Pomes Penyeach* and agreed to publish *Finnegans Wake*. Reactions, however, to portions of *Finnegans Wake* published in *transition* were so negative that even Ezra Pound and Harriet Weaver, strong admirers of Joyce, withdrew their support.

Joyce, faced with such hostile criticism, ill and discouraged, even considered abandoning the book. His need for money far exceeded his royalties: he was burdened with glaucoma attacks, a series of operations, and a mentally ill daughter. Sylvia Beach went into debt to advance Joyce money, but in 1932, just as the twelfth edition of *Ulysses* was to go to the printers, she discovered that the author was negotiating with Bennett Cerf of Random House to publish an American edition. Surprised and deeply hurt, she cancelled the printing. The novel was published in America in February 1934. Sylvia Beach received nothing for her rights as publisher of *Ulysses*. But Shakespeare and Company's financial problems did not begin or end with Joyce. The Depression sent American expatriates home, subsidies from Mom or Dad to struggling artists and writers ceased, and tourists became rare. In an attempt to keep the bookshop alive, a number of writers, mainly French, gave readings to which an entry fee was charged. Gide and Valéry read here in February 1936, Jean Paulhan in May, T.S. Eliot in June. Later, Hemingway and Stephen Spender gave a joint reading, but these soirées did little to increase business. Shakespeare and Company was kept alive from the mid-thirties on by the generosity of Bryher, former wife of Robert McAlmon and daughter of Sir John Ellerman. When the Germans occupied Paris in 1940, Sylvia Beach kept her shop open, although business was almost nonexistent. One day in 1941, a German officer asked to buy her personal copy of *Finnegans Wake,* which was on display in the window. When she refused, he threatened to have her entire stock confiscated. She closed the shop, and with the aid of friends promptly moved every book to a safe place. She was later interned for six months at Vittel. She returned to Paris and hid until the Liberation, but she visited Adrienne Monnier's bookstore regularly. On 26 August 1944, one of her favorite American authors reappeared. His return is recounted in the final paragraph of Sylvia Beach's own book *Shakespeare and Company:*

> There was still a lot of shooting going on in the rue de l'Odéon, and we were getting tired of it, when one day a string of jeeps came up the street and stopped in front of my house. I heard a deep voice calling: "Sylvia!" And everybody in the street took up the cry of "Sylvia!" "It's Hemingway! It's Hemingway!" cried Adrienne. I flew downstairs; we met with a crash; he picked me up and swung me around and kissed me while people on the street and in the windows cheered. We went up to Adrienne's apartment and sat Hemingway down. He was in battle dress, grimy and bloody. A machine gun clanked on the floor. He asked Adrienne for a piece of soap, and she gave him her last cake. He wanted to know if there was anything he could do for us. We asked him if he could do something about the Nazi snipers on the roof tops in our street, particularly on Adrienne's roof top. He got his company out of the jeeps and took them up to the roof. We heard firing for the last time in the rue de l'Odéon. Hemingway and his men came down again and rode off in their jeeps—"to liberate," according to Hemingway, "the cellar at the Ritz."

George Antheil, 22, arrived in Paris on 13 June 1923. He took a room on the first floor directly above Sylvia Beach's Shakespeare and Company. As he wrote later, "to have Sylvia Beach, American ex-ambulance driver and present publisher of *Ulysses* as a landlady seemed so enormously attractive." It was here that he would compose his Quintet, two violin sonatas for Olga Rudge, First String

Quartet, Second Symphony, and *Ballet Mécanique*. He became a friend of Virgil Thomson. Antheil and Sylvia Beach provided tea and music in his flat at 4:30 every day. One afternoon he played for James Joyce, T.S. Eliot, Ford Madox Ford, Wyndham Lewis, Ezra Pound, and Ernest Hemingway. Antheil had spent the two previous years in Berlin, where he had achieved considerable success.

18   Sylvia Beach shared an apartment at number 18 with her lover and mentor Adrienne Monnier from 1921 until 1937. Adrienne Monnier ran a bookstore called La Maison des Amis des Livres at 7 Rue de l'Odéon. During the 1920s, it was a meeting place for the élite of French writers—André Gide, Paul Valéry, Paul Claudel, Louis Aragon, Pierre Reverdy, André Breton, and Valéry Larbaud among others. Sylvia Beach had started frequenting the bookstore in 1917. It was Adrienne Monnier who discovered a vacant shop for Shakespeare and Company on Rue Dupuytren before welcoming this flourishing American lending library and bookstore to the Rue de l'Odéon.

(25)   Charles Sumner took "neat and comfortable quarters" here on 20 January 1838. This 28-year-old lawyer would, as a U.S. senator, give "The Crime against Kansas" speech on 20 May 1856 in the Senate and be grievously assaulted by a relative of Senator Butler of South Carolina. Young Sumner was fascinated by Paris and was determined to learn French. "Think of me coming by childlike progression to the use of my tongue," he wrote, "hearing sounds which convey no idea, and thus in a degree, barred from society and scenes of this great metropolis." Sumner took lessons, went to lectures, and attended the theater, following with the printed text. By the end of April 1838, he tells us he was able to serve as an interpreter before a French magistrate on examination of a fellow countryman.

Avenue de l'Opéra (2nd) Map F

39   Hôtel Edouard VII, formerly Hôtel Bellevue. Bret Harte lived here in July 1880 before making his way to Glasgow, where he took up the post of American consul. He had become famous with his short stories "The Luck of Roaring Camp," "The Outcasts of Poker Flat," and "Tennessee's Partner." His popularity in America had peaked, but his short stories continued to find a public in Great Britain, where he died in 1902.

49   *New York Herald* office. There was a large reading room here open free to the public. In 1896 it displayed 120 American newspapers and periodicals, including the *Detroit Free Press,* the *Philadelphia Evening Telegram,* the *St. Louis Globe Democrat,* and the *Yonkers Gazette.*

Place de l'Opéra (9th) Map F

L'Opéra. The present opera house opened on 5 January 1875. At the time it was the largest theater in the world, with 2,156 seats and a stage 85 feet wide, 170 feet deep, and 200 feet high. Its construction cost 35,400,000 francs.

On 25 April 1876, a special program was given to help finance the Statue of Liberty. Five hundred choristers and an orchestra were directed by Charles Gounod. The program included a hymn written by the composer entitled "Body of Bronze... Soul of Fire." The performance was followed by a banquet given in the opera house.

In 1889, while visiting the Universal Exhibition, Thomas Edison was given the use of French president Sadi Carnot's private box. Edison was asked to come early so that the manager could show him the underground labyrinth containing the wires and dynamos for his incandescent lamps which lit the theater. When Edison entered the royal box, to his intense embarrassment the orchestra struck up the "Star Spangled Banner," and the audience stood.

In June 1910, the Metropolitan Opera Company, after a triumphant run at the Théâtre du Châtelet, gave a benefit performance here for the survivors of the French submarine *Pluviose.* Just before dawn on the morning of 26 May, the submarine was surfacing outside the harbor of Calais when it was struck by a ferry boat. The submarine sank and 27 officers and men were trapped inside and slowly suffocated. This was one of the first such accidents in France.

The program included scenes from the second act of *Tristam,* with Louise Homer as Brangane and Olive Fremstad as Isolde. It was the first time since the Franco-Prussian War of 1870-71 that a work in German had been sung in the Paris Opera House.

❦

On 29 May 1928, the European premiere of Gershwin's Piano Concerto in F took place here. The soloist was Dimitri Tiomkin, and the orchestra was conducted by Vladimir Golschmann. This was the first opportunity that Gershwin had had to hear another artist play this music. The Gershwin concerto delighted both the audience and the critics. Arthur Hoeree noted its "inexhaustible verve," the "fascination of its flowing melodies," and the composer's "keen feeling for the orchestra." Emile Vuillermoz wrote: "This very characteristic work made even the most distrustful musicians realize that...jazz might perfectly well exert a deep and beneficent influence in the most exalted spheres."

Quai d'Orléans (4th) Map E

10　James Jones, the author of *From Here to Eternity* (1951), lived here with his family from 1958 until 1975. He bought three floors in this house as they became available with the income from writing part of the film script of *The Longest Day*.

Ensconced behind the French windows on the first floor overlooking the Seine, Jones wrote *The Thin Red Line* (1962), *A Touch of Danger* (1973), and *Viet Journal* (1974), an account of his trip to Vietnam. Jones kept open house with an apparently inexhaustible supply of liquor. Friends included Romain Gary, who had been a collaborator on *The Longest Day,* Mary McCarthy, who lived in Paris, William Styron, James Baldwin, Sylvia Beach, Henry Miller, Man Ray, Alexander Calder, Max Ernst, and Alice B. Toklas. The list of visitors on the Quai d'Orléans reads like a who's who of the 1960s: Eunice and Sargent Shriver, William Burroughs, Allen Ginsberg, Gregory Corso, Samuel Beckett, James T. Farrell, Kenneth Tynan, Louis Malle, John Frankenheimer, Gene Kelly, Gore Vidal, Pat Lawford, Abraham Ribicoff, Frank and Eleanor Perry, Art Buchwald, Arthur Miller, Thornton Wilder, and Cyrus Sulzberger.

Although Jones lived in France for seventeen years, he never felt at home there, and had difficulty making himself understood in French. Like some of his fellow countrymen, he liked France but disliked the French. Jones's novel *The Merry Month of May,* based on the uprisings or *les événements du mois de mai* in Paris in May 1968, was a failure, although Jones had been present during the turmoil. The book's failure reflected his inability to understand

French society. In 1975, fearing that he was losing touch with his native language, Jones returned home. (The house is on the corner, entry at 2 Rue Budé.)

18-20   Walter Lippmann lived here briefly in 1938 with his second wife. There is a picturesque interior courtyard.

Quai d'Orsay (7th) Map C

37   Le Ministère des Affaires Etrangères. This ministry is commonly called "le Quai d'Orsay." President and Mrs. John F. Kennedy were guests here from 31 May to 3 June 1961. The president was on his way to face Krushchev in Vienna. It was his first meeting with General de Gaulle, who greeted the young couple at Orly Airport and escorted them to the ministry. Upon arrival Kennedy took a hot bath to help relieve a backache, and one hour later, at 11:00 a.m., began talks with his host. He listed the American alternatives in the face of Russian threats over West Berlin. De Gaulle told him that Krushchev had been laying down six-month deadlines on Berlin for over two-and-a-half years, adding that if Krushchev really wanted war he would have already declared it. The two presidents held a total of six meetings dealing with East-West relations, Laos, tensions between Peking and Moscow, the Congo, Angola, and possible French withdrawal from NATO. The talks went well and both men were impressed with each other. De Gaulle offered Kennedy some advice, permitted, he said, by the prerogative of age. He suggested that Kennedy not pay too much respect to policies he had inherited, nor pay too much attention to his advisors. What mattered was a man's own judgment, concluded the general. The fiasco six weeks earlier at the Bay of Pigs, surely must have caused Kennedy to consider this piece of Gaullist philosophy.

Jacqueline Kennedy enjoyed great success with the Parisian public. Her charm, style, fluent French, and knowledge of France had won her many admirers, beginning with André Malraux, then the French minister of culture. In his press conference on the final day, Kennedy said, "I am the man who accompanied Jacqueline Kennedy to Paris, and I have enjoyed it."

65   The American Church in Paris. Reverend Sylvester Wood-bridge Beach served as associate pastor of the church from 1902 to 1905. His two daughters, Sylvia and Cyprian, pursued their studies and fell in love with Paris. Cyprian went on to a successful career in the French cinema, and Sylvia achieved fame in the world of letters.

The present church was built in 1931. Martin Luther King preached here in 1964 after receiving the Nobel Peace Prize.

83   Art Buchwald and his wife lived in a ground-floor apartment here from 1952 to 1956. Buchwald continued to write for the *Herald Tribune* and his column was carried in an increasing number of American newspapers.

Rue de l'Ouest (14th)

(64)   Thomas Eakins took a studio here in 1867. The following summer his father and sister Fanny visited. She recorded:

> Yesterday morning we went to his studio. He had not yet finished any of his paintings (that is lady's work, he says) and of course they are rough looking, but they are very strong and all the positions are fine and the drawing good. He thinks he understands something of color now, but says it was very discouraging at first, it was so hard to grasp.

The family spent the summer travelling, and in fall 1868, Eakins resumed his studies with Gérôme at the Ecole des Beaux-Arts. He moved to an apartment on Rue d'Assas, but kept his studio here.

Rue de la Paix (2nd) Map F

(10)   Site of the Hôtel de la Paix. In spring 1857, Charles Sumner had an apartment on the top floor from which he could see "all the monuments of Paris." He met with de Tocqueville and discussed prison reform. The following summer he returned to this hotel and visited Turgenev at his home at Rueil.

13   Hotel Westminster. This hotel was popular with Americans during the 19th century. Guests included Theodore Parker, minister of the Congregational Society of Boston, Hamilton Fish, secretary of state under Grant, and John Bigelow, author, editor, and diplomat.

The James family, including 12-year-old Henry, took rooms

here in June 1856 while looking for an apartment to live in for the year. The following March, Senator Charles Sumner took rooms here, but moved across the street after two days.

20   This building still retains the original reception hall of the once elegant Hôtel de Hollande. Henry James took a room here on 24 October 1889, and stayed until early December. During his stay he spent an evening with Alphonse Daudet and agreed to translate his latest Tartarin novel. James visited the Universal Exhibition and devoted evenings to finishing the last chapters of *The Tragic Muse*.

Boulevard du Palais (1st) Map E

Le Palais de Justice (the Law Courts). The Ile de la Cité, beginning with the Roman governors, has housed the administrative offices of the City of Paris for 2,000 years. During the 13th century, St. Louis lived in the Upper Chambers (today the First Civil Court) and dispensed justice in the courtyard. Later, French kings preferred to live in the Louvre or outside of Paris, leaving the palace to house Parliament, which was the kingdom's supreme court. During the revolution the name was changed from the King's Palace to the Palace of Justice, and many lesser courts were added.

In addition to the bustle of robed judges, lawyers, clerks, plaintiffs, police, and prisoners, there were newspaper vendors, public scribes, booths for renting robes, and cafés for everyone. By far the best description of this intimate French world was recorded in 1836 by Isaac Appleton Jewett.

Jewett began his visit with the Great Hall called La Salle des Pas-Perdus (Waiting room, literally Hall of the Wasted Footsteps).

> Entering the court, I ascended, by a flight of many steps, through one of three portals surmounted by statues of Justice, Prudence, Abundance and Strength, into a large and dimly-lighted hall. It was a hall of the Palais de Justice. I was in the great centre of the administration of French law. I was where daily congregate the judges, the clients and the advocates of Paris.
>
> The first object that particularly attracted my notice was a little red-visaged woman, located near the door in a sort of glass bureau, upon which were largely painted these words—*Lecture et abonnement de journaux* [Reading and newspaper subscriptions]. Around her were ranged some fifteen or twenty newspapers, among whose titles I recognised the following:—La Loi—

Le Droit—Gazette des Tribunaux—Journal Général des Tribunaux. Every now and then a person would advance to the bureau, touch his hat, take a journal, walk off a few paces, read it intently for a few moments, then return it with a sous, receive the smile and the merci of the dame, touch once more his hat, and profoundly bowing, walk away again. Nearly adjacent was a little room warmed by a central stove, and around whose sides ran a tier of benches. These were occupied by silent Frenchmen, the eyes of each fixed fiercely upon the loaned gazette before him, some of them in elegant apparel, and some in those shattered habiliments, which here as well as elsewhere reveal, alas! the patron and the victim of the law.

Walking onwards, my attention was next arrested by these words over the entrance to some small cabinets:—*Bosc; Costumier des Cours et Tribunaux* [Dispenser of Judicial Robes]. Over these cabinets likewise presided a female. Their walls were hung about with black vestments, while upon their two or three shelves were ranged several small bandboxes. The mystery which at first surrounded them was soon dispelled. A gay-looking gentleman, with an immense bundle of manuscripts—not a green bag,—briskly advanced, and entering one of them, twitched off his coat and hat, thrust his arms into a *manteau* [robe], which the damsel held wide-extended for their reception, suspended a white band beneath his chin, clapped a black unrimmed toque, or cap, upon his head, and seizing again the huge mass of papers, rushed away. Two minutes had sufficed to work an extraordinary metamorphosis. He who had entered the wardrobe, a brilliant Parisian smacking of the Boulevard des Italiens, or the garden of the Tuileries, came out therefrom a costumed *avocat* [lawyer], much resembling those funereal portraits we sometimes see of the judges of the Inquisition, or the antique doctors of the Sorbonne.

In different quarters of the hall were some dozen Ecrivains. An *écrivain* is a little dried up man—sometimes a woman—who holds himself ready to do any sort of writing. He is in great favor with the grisettes and all the common people. They seem to place unbounded confidence in whatever he says or does. There he sits behind his desk in a comfortable arm chair, itself flanked by two others for the convenience of his customers. His black woollen cap is stuck significantly upon his head; his nose is pinched within a pair of huge green glasses; and as he listens to a dame or damsel, stating in her diabolical patois what she wishes to have written down in a petition, his mouth and eyes take an expression of important gravity which is quite irresistible. Before him upon his desk are, among other things, a seal, a calendar, a snuff-box, a bunch of used-up pens, a roll of bread, whereof every now and then he takes a crumb, and a little volume whose title you perceive to be *Les Six Codes* [The Six Law Codes]. Having listened to a case, he hems two or three times, adjusts his green glasses, takes snuff, looks for a moment into *Les Six Codes,* and finally takes pen and paper to commence operations. He can afford to be important and at his ease, for he is in great demand. His desk is almost always surrounded by half a dozen white caps, whose wearers, quite unacquainted with the law and the quill, are patiently waiting to entrust some little commission to his ability.

When Jewett left the Great Hall, described by Balzac as "the cathedral of chicanery," he threaded his way through the unlit corridors to the Sixième Chambre. Here five judges presided, sitting in a semicircle, dressed in black silk robes and velvet caps encircled with silver braid.

Entering, I perceived three or four of the municipal guards of Paris, armed with swords and muskets, stationed at the door and in different parts of the court room. A trial was going on. A middle-sized one-eyed woman was on the prisoners' bench. She was accused of having in a wrathful moment seized one of her neighbors by the throat, of having then and there held firmly on, wrenching the same, and thereby working much discomfort unto said neighbor. "Un témoin [a witness]," shouted the huissier [bailiff]. "Jean Battiste," exclaimed a man with a paper in his hand, at the other end of the room, at the same instant opening the door of the witnesses' apartment. The witness advanced. The president judge addressed him, and received answers as follows: "Votre nom et prénom?" "Jean Battiste." "Votre âge?" "Fifty years." "Votre profession?" "Grocer." "Votre demeure?" "Rue Clichy, No. 58." "Levez votre main. You swear to tell the truth, and nothing but the truth?" "Oui, monsieur," replied the witness. "Faites votre déclaration," said the judge. This was all despatched with a rapidity and nonchalance which surprised me.

As soon as the French judge before me had said, "faites votre déclaration," the witness began. He was going on with vociferations, and multitudinous shrugs and inexplicable gestures, when he was interrupted by the prisoner screaming out in her highest key. "Faux, faux, faux, faux." The wrath of her lost optic was concentrated in, and flashing forth from, the single one which remained. "Silence," said the huissier,—"Chut,"—said the president judge,—"Paix," said a gendarme, and then the deputy-judge interposed his speech, and two *avoués* [lawyers] interjected their voices, and the assembled spectators burst into a roar, and still the cry of the prisoner was audible above them all. Peace was at length restored, and the prisoner sat down with a threatening wag of the head at the witness, which seemed to say, "I'll fix ye when the trial is over." Alas! the result was against her, and in a few moments she was conducted out, her arm locked affectionately within that of a gendarme, while her head and tongue still wagged, as much to the annoyance of the court, as to the amusement of divers curious spectators that thronged the apartment.

Then, Jewett entered the Cour Royale:

The judges of the chamber into which I now passed, were costumed black and mysteriously, like those of the inferior court I had just visited. The case before them was not uninteresting. Jean Jacques Pillot had, without proper authority, established a church *unitaire et réformatrice* [reformed unitarian]; and had moreover, himself usurped the sacerdotal robe. For these offences he had by an inferior tribunal been sentenced to six months' imprisonment. From that sentence he had appealed to the Cour Royale. Ferdinand Barrot, brother of the celebrated orator of the Chamber of Deputies, was his defender. The throng in the court room indicated that the case had awakened some popular interest. It seemed to be one involving liberty of conscience. The speech of the *procureur-général* [prosecutor] was full of warmth, and here and there burst forth strains which, judging from their effect upon the audience, must have been good specimens of French eloquence. . . . When I say that the speaker before me was fluent in the extreme, I only say that he was a Frenchman. To me his volubility seemed next to marvellous. Words chased words from his lips with speed incredible. When he had concluded, Ferdinand Barrot arose, and with energy uttered a good deal of French law and much good common sense. I was somewhat amused, upon his citing the authority of a learned judge of the Cour de Cassation, to hear the president interrupt him with the remark that living judges were continually changing their opinions, beseeching him at the same time to cite the authority of those who were deceased, "of whom," said he, "there is quite a sufficiency." With him, the death of their author was indispensable to confer validity upon his opinions. The power to change them having ceased, their value was no longer a question. Barrot smiled at the judge's superstition or his waggery, and continued his well-digested argument. The way was wide open for him to make a large and moving speech on freedom of conscience. He did no such thing. He walked within the narrow sphere prescribed by the facts of his case. It was not until the very last moment that he grew vivid and eloquent, while congratulating the court and country on the re-awakening of a purer religion in France, and the gradual decline of infidelity, of the école Voltairienne, as he was pleased to call it. This was done in a style which apparently went through every man in the room. The movement was universal. He did not succeed, however, in getting reversed the sentence of the inferior tribunal. Sieur Jean Jacques Pillot had indeed a right to the benefit of the fifth article of the charter which provides: "Chacun professe sa religion avec une égale liberté, et obtient pour son culte une égale protection." [Every man is free to exercise his religion and every religion is equally protected before the law.] But he must enjoy that right in conformity with certain legislative enactments. Jean Jacques had not so done; a huissier waited upon him to prison.

Jewett concluded the day with a visit to the Cour d'Assises, which dealt with serious crimes. A verdict was rendered by the jury, which in France is assisted in its deliberations by the judge who does not vote. A popular American myth has it that in France a person is guilty until proven innocent. This is untrue, and Jewett did not suffer from this misconception. French judges are freer than their American counterparts to interrupt, question, comment, and draw conclusions. This renders a French trial more personal, less procedural, and sometimes casts light where facts and motives might remain hidden, as Jewett acknowledges:

At the time I entered, a man was on the prisoners' bench, accused of the murder of his wife. The witnesses were all questioned by the judge. Their examination was not in the presence of each other. One feature in this part of the proceedings I was pleased with. After each witness had made his declaration, the judge asked the prisoner if he had anything to say respecting that testimony. Whereupon the accused, if he pleased, arose, and either contradicted, or confirmed, or explained it. The judge listened patiently, pointing out familiarly any contradictions, and sometimes even argued the matter with the prisoner. I am sure, that in several instances explanations of the accused threw an illumination over passages, that otherwise would have remained dark and inexplicable. The testimony having been heard, the jury were, by the officer of the government and the prisoner's counsel, addressed. These are the only courts of the kingdom in which juries are known. Their number is twelve, of whom seven are sufficient to convict an offender. In this case their verdict was Guilty, "mais, avec des circonstances atténuantes." Now, under this *mais* is contained a very important qualification. When a jury find an accused guilty, "but with extenuating circumstances," the court has no right to deliver the culprit over to the penalty which the law has made a consequence of his act; they are bound to sentence him to some punishment less severe. How much less severe, lies within the discretion of the judge.

Place du Palais-Bourbon (7th) Map C

L'Assemblée Nationale. John Adams visited this former palace on Thursday, 26 November 1778. He had been in Paris six months and shared quarters at the imposing Hôtel de Valentinois at Passy with Franklin. Adams felt ill at ease in Parisian society. He admired the architecture, theater, opera, and art, yet he distrusted the French:

> Went to see the Palace of Bourbon, belonging to the Prince of Condé. It is a City. The Apartements of the Prince, are very rich, and elegant. The Gallery has many fine Paintings. But I have no Taste for ringing the Changes of Mirrors, Gold, Silver, Marble, Glass, and Alabaster.—For myself I had rather live in this Room at Passy than in that Palace, and in my Cottage at Braintree than in this Hotel at Passy.

This palace was converted to its present function for the Assemblée Nationale in 1827.

Twenty years later, Margaret Fuller sat in the visitors' gallery at a meeting of the Chamber of Deputies to hear a spirited debate on the Spanish royal marriage. It had been proposed that the youngest son of King Louis-Philippe marry the 14-year-old sister of the queen of Spain. Fuller was amused to see the audience loudly criticize a dull speaker. She visited the library of the Chamber where she excitedly touched the yellow, fading papers of Jean-Jacques Rousseau. Later she wrote, "He was the precursor of all we most prize."

Place du Palais-Royal (1st) Map F

The gardens of the Palais-Royal, as they are today, were enclosed between 1776 and 1780 on three sides by elegant apartment houses and ground-level shopping arcades trimmed with a magnificent uniform facade. The basements and the first floors (i.e., above the ground floor) housed cafés, restaurants, and gaming houses.

Designed by well-known architect Victor Louis, who also designed the present Théâtre Français, they were owned by the Duc d'Orléans. The three new streets which resulted were named after the younger Orléans brothers, Valois, Montpensier, and Beaujolais. The duke forbade the police to enter these gardens and imposed his own rules. The arcades were closed off at 1:00 a.m. in summer and 11:00 p.m. in winter; ordinary soldiers, delivery boys, and women in aprons were not permitted. The popularity of the gardens was immediate. It became fashionable to stroll in the arcades during the evening, admiring the military uniforms, the beauty of the ladies of easy virtue, and the richness of the gaming houses. Americans, from Thomas Jefferson to Washington Irving, commented upon their pleasure at walking here. When gambling was stopped in Paris at midnight, 31 December 1837, the gardens lost their appeal and took on the air of sadness they have had ever since.

During his stay in Paris in 1820, Ebenezer Smith Thomas recorded his visit to the Palais-Royal in his *Reminiscences:*

It was the world in miniature, in which was to be found almost every thing desirable and useful to man, except an apothecary's shop; that would remind us of sickness, and mortality, and consequently had no place within its walls. This vast building formed a hollow square, in the centre of which was a beautiful *jet d'eau* [water jet]. The number of shops, coffee houses, etc., contained in it, was then about five hundred. It was the resort of all ranks and conditions. There were shops in it where you could have a suit of clothes made, while you sat and read the newspapers! Among the coffee houses, was one called the Mille Colonnes, from its having rows of pillars set with looking-glass, which multiplied them to a thousand. This room was of great size, and while you drank your wine, or sipped your brandy and water, you were gratuitously entertained with rope and wire dancing, and balancing, by the best masters in Europe. It was customary, in Paris, to have the handsomest young female that could be found, to sit in the bar, and receive the money from customers. The lady who officiated in that capacity, at the Mille Colonnes, was extremely beautiful, and that her seat might correspond with her beauty, the proprietor had purchased in Naples, at an expense of five thousand francs, the identical throne on which Murat was seated, as King of Naples, by Napoleon. Thus seated, she received not only the money, but the homage of the visitors—every one who entered the room, from the highest to the lowest paying her the most profound respect. She was very affable, and conversed well in English. There were frequently from one to two hundred persons congregated at this coffee-house, of an evening, and yet there was as perfect order and decorum, as in any private drawing-room. Here, the arts, sciences, literature, and politics, were all subjects of conversation. I could not help drawing comparisons, and truth compels me to say, that the result was against us.

The Café des Mille Colonnes (actually some 30 columns, but covered in mirrors) was on the first floor at number 36. It opened in 1807, and the lovely cashier was Madame Romain *la belle limonadière* (the beautiful barmaid), who, in 1815, was judged to be the most beautiful woman in Paris.

Nathaniel Parker Willis arrived in Paris in 1831. Travelling as a correspondent for the *New-York Mirror,* he took rooms on nearby Rue Vivienne and began his six-month stay in Paris with a stroll to the Palais-Royal:

It still rained at noon, and finding that the usual dinner hour was five I took my umbrella for a walk. In a strange city I prefer always to stroll about at hazard, coming unawares upon what is fine or curious. The hackneyed descriptions in the guidebooks profane the spirit of a place, I never look at them till after I have found the object, and then only for dates. The Rue Vivienne was crowded with people, as I emerged from the dark archway of the hotel to pursue my wanderings.

A walk of this kind, by the way, shows one a great deal of novelty. In France there are no shop-men. No matter what the article of trade—hats, boots, pictures, books, jewellery, anything and everything that gentlemen buy—you are waited upon by girls, always handsome, and always dressed in the height of the mode. They sit on damask-covered settees, behind the counters; and when you enter, bow and rise to serve you, with a grace and a smile of courtesy that would become a drawing-room. And this is universal.

I strolled on until I entered a narrow passage, penetrating a long line of buildings. It was thronged with people, and passing in with the rest, I found myself unexpectedly in a scene that equally surprised and delighted me. It was a spacious square enclosed by one entire building. The area was laid out as a garden, planted with long avenues of trees and beds of flowers, and in the centre a fountain was playing in the shape of a fleur-de-lis, with a jet about forty feet in height. A superb colonnade ran round the whole square, making a covered gallery of the lower story, which was occupied by shops of the most splendid appearance, and thronged through its long sheltered pavés by thousands of gay promenaders. It was the far-famed Palais Royal. I remembered the description I had heard of its gambling-houses, and facilities for every vice, and looked with a new surprise on its Aladdin-like magnificence. The hundreds of beautiful pillars, stretching away from the eye in long and distant perspective, the crowd of citizens, and women, and officers in full uniform, passing and repassing with French liveliness and politeness, the long windows of plated glass glittering with jewellery, and bright with everything to tempt the fancy, the tall sentinels pacing between the columns, and the fountain turning over its clear waters with a fall audible above the tread and voices of the thousands who walked around it—who could look upon such a scene and believe it what it is, the most corrupt spot, probably, on the face of the civilized world.

Some of the finest restaurants in Paris were in the Palais-Royal. Ebenezer Smith Thomas ate at the Véry, the first major restaurant to introduce *le prix fixe*. Located at number 83, the Véry became part of the Grand Véfour, which was next door in 1859. The Grand Véfour is open today after two centuries at the same spot. Thomas recalled:

> Verree's eating rooms, (I know no other name for them,) are the best in Paris. His daily bill of fare is larger than the largest newspaper in the city, and contains every luxury that Europe affords, which are daily served at his tables. It was common for ladies to dine there, and at other coffee houses in Paris, with their husbands, brothers, or friends. The French are fond of society, and hence it is that many of those in affluence, or easy circumstances, spend a large part of their time at coffee houses; not in dissipation, but in rational conversation, or innocent amusements—such as dominoes, drafts, and chess.

Isaac Appleton Jewett, who lived in Paris in 1836, left us the best description of the French ritual of drinking coffee:

> Coffee is to the Frenchman, what tea is to the Englishman, beer to the German, eau-de-vie to the Russian, opium to the Turk, chocolate to the Spaniard, and, I dare not say what, to the

American. Men, women and children, of all grades and professions, drink coffee in Paris. In the morning it is served up under the aromatic name of *café au lait*. In the evening, it is universally taken as *café noir*. After one of Véfour's magnificent repasts, it enters your stomach in the character of a settler. It leaves you volatile, nimble and quick; and over it might be justly poured those pleasant compliments which Falstaff bestowed on Sherris sack. The garçon at your call for a demi-tasse, has placed before you a snowy cup and saucer, three lumps of sugar, and a *petit verre*. He ventured the *petit verre*, inferring from your red English face that you liked liqueur. Another garçon now appears. In his right hand is a huge silver pot covered, and in his left another, of the same material, uncovered. The former contains coffee, the latter cream. You reject cream, and thereupon the garçon outpours of the former in strange abundance, until your cup, ay, and saucer too, actually overflow. There is hardly space for the three lumps; and yet you must contrive somehow to insert them, or that *café noir*,—black it may indeed be called,—will in its concentrated strength, be quite unmanageable. But when thus sweetly tempered, it becomes the finest beverage in the whole world. It agreeably affects several senses. Its liquid pleases all the gustatory nerves; its savor ascends to rejoice the olfactory, and even your eye is delighted with those dark, transparent and sparkling hues, through which perpetually shines your silver spoon. You pronounce French coffee, the only coffee. In a few moments, its miracles begin to be wrought. You feel spiritual, and amiable and conversational.

Mrs. Caroline Kirkland, accompanied by two lady friends, set out for Europe in April 1848, and later described her experiences in *Holidays Abroad*. Her observations and advice were directed at "the lady traveller," which distinguished them from countless other "reminiscences" of the 19th century. Her accounts were first serialized in American newspapers. Mrs. Kirkland, wife of a professor from Hamilton College in Clinton, New York, had already published books for use in public schools. The three lady travellers stayed at the Hôtel Meurice on Rue de Rivoli; here, in the Palais-Royal, they dined at one of the best restaurants in Paris at the time, Les Trois Frères Provençaux. Run by three men who were neither brothers nor from Provence (they came from Marseille), their restaurant opened in 1786 and closed in 1877.

Dining at a restaurant is one of the novelties of the lady-traveller in Paris. Taking a sandwich or a plate of oysters at Thompson and Weller's is a considerable feat, and some of our ladies at home roll up their eyes at the boldness which can venture thus far. But to sit down in a public room, to a regular dinner of an hour's length, or more, is quite another affair, and it really requires some practice before one can refrain from casting sly glances around during the process, to see whether anybody is looking. But these restaurant dinners are very pleasant things when you are once used to them. At the Trois Frères Provençaux, for instance, which is one of the best, you are seated at a table covered with damask fine enough for royalty, with napkins to match, all of an extreme purity and whiteness. You have silver forks and spoons to as many plates as you can contrive to use in succession; your food is all served in silver dishes, quite hot, and the cuisine is of the greatest delicacy, as well as variety. All about you are immense mirrors, statuary, flowers; fruits in elegant baskets of china or ormolu, and whatever luxury can devise to enhance the pleasure of dining; and, withal, though there may be twenty other parties dining at as many tables within sight, yet nobody looks at you, or seems to know that you are there. One waiter takes you under his special care, and the different courses are served with the precision of clockwork, everything being as neat and elegant as possible. One feels at first as if it was a transgression; but after a while this subsides into a feeling of agreeable abandon, unalloyed by any sense of naughtiness; and a dinner at a restaurant becomes one of the natural events of a Paris day.

On 17 August 1858, seventy Americans sat down to a dinner in Les Trois Frères Provençaux in honor of Samuel Morse. The previous day the first transoceanic message had crossed the Atlantic. In his speech after the "rich repast," Morse said that the telegraph was no Minerva sprung full grown from Jove's head, but the work of many—Galvani, Volta, Ampère, and Arago. He had learned the essentials of electromagnetism 30 years earlier from Professor James Freeman Dana at the Athenaeum in New York. He closed his speech with hope that the Atlantic cable would help serve the cause of peace among the peoples of the world. Yet there was an irony in this celebration. Morse had first come to France as a promising painter, and now that he was at last being applauded in Paris it was not for his talent as an artist but for his ingenuity as an inventor. On this triumphant trip he did not even visit the Louvre, where he had

spent so many hours. He had already written to his longtime Paris companion, James Fenimore Cooper: "Alas, my dear Sir, the very name of pictures produces a sadness of heart I cannot describe. Painting has been a smiling mistress to many, but a cruel mistress to me."

103 Formerly Café des Aveugles (on the corner of 1 Rue Beaujolais). This café was opened in the basement in 1792. It had an inscription which read: "Ici on s'honore du titre de citoyen, on se tutoie et l'on fume." (Here one is addressed as Citizen, one uses the "tu" form, and one smokes). The café was known for its orchestra of four blind musicians playing flute, violin, clarinet, and bass. It had a reputation as a haven for prostitutes, which is certainly what drew Aaron Burr to this café on 18 February 1810. Barely two days after his arrival in Paris, Burr recorded in his *Journal:* "... a cellar vaulted 80 or 100 sq. feet. Well furnished. Music, an orchestra of blind performers. Entry gratis. We were four and took beer and biscuits. 3 sous each. Ladies of all sorts. Will talk with you, sit, eat, drink but no further solicitations unless you make overtures."

156 Galerie de Valois. John Howard Payne lived at this address in 1823, above the Café de Valois. Here he wrote the opera *Clari, the Maid of Milan* with its famous song, "Home Sweet Home":

> Mid pleasures and palaces, though
> we may roam . . .

Passage des Panoramas (2nd) Map F

On 26 April 1799, a ten-year patent for a *tableau circulaire* (circular painting or panorama) was awarded by the French government to Robert Fulton, "painter and inventor."

Fulton had seen the first panorama in Leicester Square, London, and took note of the crowds lined up to marvel at seemingly endless and thrilling scenes. In Paris, Fulton took a partner, James Thayer, from Charleston, South Carolina, who handled the construction and daily management problems. On 27 May 1800, Thayer purchased part of the large garden of the Grand Hôtel de Montmorency on the south side of the Boulevard Montmartre and built two towers, each 46 feet in diameter, to house the panoramas, thus framing the alley which became and remains today Le Passage des Panoramas. Fulton himself supervised the "endless painting," which was done by Pierre Prévost, well known for his dramatic reproduction of historical scenes. He painted a total of eighteen panoramas over the years, beginning with the port of Toulon, which the British had evacuated in 1793; the burning of Moscow, a subject which had been popular for over a century in France, and which was reenacted in 1812; and a view of all of Paris as seen from the top of the Tuileries. The venture was an enormous success from the start. Open every day, Parisians paid one franc fifty centimes and stood in wonder, if not in silence, before the entire city of Moscow in flames.

Panoramas remained very popular for twenty years and led to the diorama, and all manner of "orama" shows, songs about panoramas and, of course, Le Café des Panoramas. The money which Fulton made helped subsidize his submarine and steamboat ventures. The two towers were taken down in 1831.

Above the entrance to the Passage des Panoramas, at the corner of Rue Vivienne, was a pension which was very popular with Americans. Ralph Waldo Emerson took a room in June 1832. During that winter in Paris he attended lectures at the Sorbonne, the Institut de France, and the Jardin des Plantes. He went to the theater regularly, noting in his *Journal,* "More than twenty theatres are blazing with light and echoing with fine music every night."

Académie Julian. Rodolphe Julian opened his academy in this passageway in 1868 to teach painting and sculpture. It was an immediate success and a women's atelier, run by his wife, was opened in 1880 at 51 Rue Vivienne.

The first American student of note to study at the academy was 25-year-old Thomas Wilmer Dewing from Boston. Dewing worked here for two years (1876-78) under Gustave Boulanger and Jules-Joseph Lefebvre, both specialists in the nude and draped figure, and Jean-Léon Gérôme, Charles Gleyre, and Jean-Louis Hamon. In 1880, Dewing settled in New York, where he taught at the Art Students League. (Many of his paintings are in the National Museum of American Art, Smithsonian, Washington, D.C.)

Henry Fitch Taylor came to work here in 1881, under the direction of Gustave Boulanger and Jules-Joseph Lefebvre. Taylor was a close friend of Wyatt Eaton, who was studying at Barbizon. Willard Leroy Metcalf arrived in Paris in 1883 at the age of 25. Like

Dewing, Metcalf had financed his own trip to Paris by selling paintings and working; it was this kind of maturity which frequently distinguished American students from their European counterparts. Metcalf worked under the same teachers as Dewing, but soon discovered Giverny, the cradle of Impressionism, where he went to work with fellow Americans Theodore Wendel and Theodore Robinson. They all hoped to receive guidance from the master, Monet. Needless to say, Impressionism was considered a horror by the teachers at the Académie Julian, the Ecole des Beaux-Arts, and the committee for the yearly Salon. But not all young Americans were drawn to Impressionism. One student after visiting the Third Impressionist Exhibit in 1877 wrote to his parents that it resembled "a chamber of horrors.... They do not take into account design or form, but only give the impression of what they call nature."

Thirty-year-old John Henry Twachtman from Cincinnati, Ohio, also arrived at Julian's in 1883. During his three years in France, he became an Impressionist along with his fellow American students Frank Benson, Robert Reid, and Edmund Tarbell. (Twachtman's *End of Winter* hangs in the National Museum of American Art, Smithsonian, Washington, D.C.)

In 1885, Theodore Wendel arrived in Paris having studied in Munich and painted in Venice. He spent a winter at the academy before going to work for the summer at Giverny. (*Ruisseau, Giverny,* 1889, hangs in the Vose Galleries, Boston.)

Childe Hassam studied here from 1886 until 1889. He was particularly attracted to Monet, Pissarro, and Sisley, and worked under Gustave Boulanger and Jules-Joseph Lefebvre. (Hassam's *Union Square in Springtime,* Smith College Museum of Art, Northampton, Massachusetts; *Washington Square in Springtime,* The Phillips Collection, Washington, D.C.; and *Rain, Rue Bonaparte,* Hirschl and Adler Galleries, New York.) *Rain* was done in 1887 while Hassam was still a student at the Académie Julian, and it made him one of the foremost American Impressionists.

Charles Dana Gibson arrived in Paris in September 1889, and spent two months studying and working here. At 21, Gibson had paid for his trip to France by working as an illustrator in New York. He returned to New York after two months of courses.

The following year, 1890, the Académie Julian moved to more spacious quarters on the Left Bank, on Rue du Dragon, where it is today.

Place du Panthéon (5th) Map E

Le Panthéon. It took the French over 100 years to decide what they wanted this building to be. In 1744, Louis XV fell dangerously ill at Metz. When he recovered, he vowed to have a new church built on this spot. Construction was begun in 1755, and the Church of Sainte Geneviève was finished in 1790. This accounts for John Trumbull's description of the church, near completion, when he visited it on two occasions in 1786. In his *Journal* for Monday, 6 August, he recorded:

> From the Palais Royal we went to the new church of St. Geneviève; it is unfinished, but the entrance at the grand portico is really in a fine style of architecture, and to judge from that part of the interior from which the scaffolding is removed, and which is nearly finished, the whole will be one of the most elegant works in Europe.... All the ornaments are intended to be of sculpture only, in white stone; no paintings are to be admitted in the church. The exterior has much novelty and elegance.

Four days later, Trumbull returned for a more thorough visit.

> Went again to the church of St. Geneviève.... The view of Paris from this highest scaffolding is magnificent and vast; it was a very fine day, so that the eye, without interruption, wandered over the immense extent of buildings, which lay beneath it. The Tuilleries, the Louvre, with the church of Notre Dame, St. Sulpice, the dome of the Invalides, the Bastille, the Salpêtrière, Val de Grace, and a vast number of inferior buildings, towering above the dwelling houses. The extent of the city; the vast and opulent country, terminating partly in rough and broken hills, partly in fine champaign, ornamented with the palaces of Meudon and St. Cloud; the aqueduct of Marly, the convent of Mount Calvaire, and a number of other splendid buildings, form altogether a *coup d'oeil* [view] entirely superior to any thing I have heretofore seen.

In 1791, the Assemblée Nationale voted to turn the church into a Pantheon where distinguished men would be buried. Thus Mirabeau, Voltaire, and Rousseau were laid to rest here. The pediment bas-relief of cross and angels was replaced by France crowning Virtue, destroying Despotism, etc. In 1806, Napoleon restored the building to its original purpose. Down came France, Virtue, and Despotism; up went cross and angels. In 1830, Louis-Philippe changed the church to the Panthéon. Mirabeau's casket had been removed in 1794, when documents were discovered suggesting that he had corresponded with the British, and was later returned in a state of grace and reburied here. In 1851, under Napoleon III, the Panthéon became a church again. In 1885, for Victor Hugo's burial, the Third Republic changed it from church back to the Panthéon, which it has remained, complete with the cross on the top of the cupola.

In 1886, Dr. Oliver Wendell Holmes visited the Panthéon. He did not think of it as a "sacred edifice," or as a resting place for the "grands hommes." He wrote:

> I was thinking much more of Foucault's grand experiment, one of the most sublime visible demonstrations of a great physical fact in the records of science. The reader may not happen to remember it, and will like, perhaps, to be reminded of it. Foucault took advantage of the height of the dome, nearly three hundred feet, and had a heavy weight suspended by a wire from its loftiest point, forming an immense pendulum—the longest, I suppose, ever constructed. Now a moving body tends to keep its original plane of movement, and so the great pendulum, being set swinging north and south, tended to keep on in the same direction. But the earth was moving under it, and as it rolled from west to east the plane running through the north and south poles was every instant changing. Thus the pendulum appeared to change its direction, and its deviation was shown on a graduated arc, or by the marks it left in a little heap of sand which it touched as it swung. This experiment on the great scale has since been repeated on the small scale by the aid of other contrivances.

Holmes was referring to Jean-Bernard Foucault (1819-1868), the French physicist who determined the speed of light in air and water. In 1852 he invented the gyroscope. The Foucault pendulum demonstrated the earth's rotation.

In 1952, Helen Keller attended the centenary of the death of Louis Braille. She was made a Chevalier de la Légion d'honneur and gave her acceptance speech in French.

Rue de Perceval (14th)

14   The *Paris Review* was born in Peter Matthiessen's apartment on Rue de Perceval in Montparnasse one sunny afternoon in spring 1952. William Styron recalls that George

Plimpton, who was chief editor, arrived at the third-floor apartment bearing two bottles of absinthe. Styron added that, according to the *Britannica,* absinthe "acts powerfully upon the nerve centers, and causes delirium and hallucinations, followed in some cases by idiocy." In any event, Thomas Guinzburg, Harold Humes, William Pène du Bois, John Train, Plimpton, and Styron remained clear-headed enough that afternoon to choose a name for the review and, more important, to decide upon a policy. The review would publish genuinely creative work of young writers and not stale literary essays. They also decided to do interviews of famous writers. Unable to pay for big names, they felt writers would be more accessible if they were flattered by an interview. With the theme, "How Writers Write," the *Paris Review* interviewed the most prestigious contemporary writers on the international scene: E.M. Forster, Joyce Cary, François Mauriac, James Thurber, Thornton Wilder, Frank O'Connor, Alberto Moravia, Angus Wilson, Truman Capote, Françoise Sagan, Harold Pinter, Jorge Luis Borges, Pablo Neruda, and Isaac Bashevis Singer. By using two interviewers at one time, they could maintain the pace of a natural conversation. These interviews, published as dialogues, resulted in a creative form of their own. The *Paris Review* moved to New York in 1972.

Le cimetière du Père-Lachaise (20th) Métro: Père-Lachaise

These grounds belonged at one time to the Jesuits and were named for the confessor of Louis XIV. The site was transformed into a cemetery in 1803. A number of Americans are buried here, including Benjamin Franklin's grandson William Temple Franklin, Isadora Duncan and her two children, Gertrude Stein, Alice B. Toklas, and Richard Wright.

In 1831, Nathaniel P. Willis recorded impressions of the cemetery, which were later published in *Pencillings by the Way:*

> This beautiful cemetery is built upon the broad ascent of a hill, commanding the whole of Paris at a glance. It is a wood of small trees, laid out in alleys, and crowded with tombs and monuments of every possible description. You will scarce get through it without being surprised into a tear; but if affectation and fantasticalness in such a place do not more grieve than amuse you, you will much oftener smile. The whole thing is a melancholy mock of life. Its distinctions are all kept up. There are the fashionable avenues, lined with costly chapels and monuments,

with the names of the exclusive tenants in golden letters upon the doors, iron railings set forbiddingly about the shrubs, and the blessing-scrap writ ambitiously in Latin. The tablets record the long family titles, and the offices and honors, perhaps the numberless virtues of the dead. They read like chapters of heraldry more than like epitaphs. It is a relief to get into the outer alleys, and see how poverty and simple feeling express what should be the same thing. It is usually some brief sentence, common enough, but often exquisitely beautiful in this prettiest of languages, and expressing always the kind of sorrow felt by the mourner. You can tell, for instance, by the sentiment simply, without looking at the record below, whether the deceased was young, or much loved, or mourned by husband, or parent, or brother, or a circle of all. I noticed one, however, the humblest and simplest monument perhaps in the whole cemetery, which left the story beautifully untold; it was a slab of common marl, inscribed "Pauvre Marie!" nothing more. I have thought of it, and speculated upon it, a great deal since. What was she? and who wrote her epitaph? why was she *pauvre Marie?*

Before almost all the poorer monuments is a miniature garden with a low wooden fence, and either the initials of the dead sown in flowers, or rose-trees, carefully cultivated, trained to hang over the stone. I was surprised to find a public cemetery, in December, roses in full bloom and valuable exotics at almost every grave. It speaks both for the sentiment and delicate principle of the people. Few of the more costly monuments were either interesting or pretty. One struck my fancy—a small open chapel, large enough to contain four chairs, with the slab facing the door, and a crucifix encircled with fresh flowers on a simple shrine above. It is a place where the survivors in a family might come and sit any time, nowhere more pleasantly. From the chapel I speak of, you may look out and see all Paris; and I can imagine how it would lessen the feeling of desertion and forgetfulness that makes the anticipation of death so dreadful, to be certain that your friends would come, as they may here, and talk cheerfully and enjoy themselves near you, so to speak. The cemetery in summer must be one of the sweetest places in the world. It would be a sufficient inducement of itself to bring me to Paris from almost any distance in another season.

Rue Pergolèse (16th) Métro: Argentine

10 Scott and Zelda Fitzgerald took an apartment at this address on 1 November 1929 and stayed until the following July. They had travelled from America to Genoa that summer, a crossing marked by violent storms. Fitzgerald settled down and produced a fine short story entitled "The Rough Crossing." He was having problems with *Tender is the Night,* on which he worked sporadically. His return to Paris was marred by the presence of Ernest Hemingway. Fitzgerald insisted on seeing a typescript of *A Farewell to Arms,* and as with *The Sun Also Rises,* he gave Hemingway detailed suggestions for revisions. The younger Hemingway, whose reputation was well on the rise, did not take kindly to this gratuitous advice. But he strengthened the famous closing passage of the novel, which Fitzgerald had found overwritten and lame, and later denied that the author of *The Great Gatsby* had ever given him any help.

Zelda, who had been trying to establish her own identity as a writer and dancer, believed, or rather hoped, that she was about to receive a professional offer as a dancer with the Ballet Russe. Her friends had all told her how good she was, but Diaghilev's emissary never called, and on 23 April 1930 she suffered a total breakdown. She spent the following year in a clinic near Montreux in Switzerland, diagnosed as schizophrenic.

Rue de Picpus (12th) Métro: Picpus

35 Le cimetière de Picpus. Lafayette died on 20 May 1834 in his house on the Rue d'Anjou and was buried in this cemetery two days later. Lafayette had come to America in 1777 at the age of 20, was wounded at the battle of Brandywine, shared the hardships of Valley Forge, and performed brilliantly at Yorktown. In 1824, he returned to the United States and received a tumultuous welcome. He enjoyed honorary American citizenship, which is still possessed by his descendants. General Pershing placed roses on the tomb here on 15 June 1917, as did President Wilson on 15 December 1918.

Rue Pierre-Demours (17th) Métro: Ternes

6 Hotel Regent's Garden. Cornelia Otis Skinner lived in this delightful former pension in summer 1921. She took elocution lessons from the famous French actor Jean Hervé and joined her father's acting company. In her autobiographical *Family Circle,* she recalled how the good-looking Hervé listened to wealthy young American would-be actresses reciting Phèdre while he wrote letters, learned his own roles, and even spoke on the latest gadget, the telephone.

Rue Pierre-Lescot (1st) Métro: Etienne Marcel

16 Au Père Tranquille. Arthur Rascoe, critic, editor, and columnist, recounted in his autobiographical *We Were Interrupted* (1947) that a long night out with Morris Bishop, writer and teacher, Lewis Galantière, businessman and critic, E.E. Cummings, and others, ended in this popular all-night restaurant in Les Halles. This later became the setting for Act III of *Him,* a play by Cummings.

Rue Pigalle (9th)

(3) William Morris Hunt, of Brattleboro, Vermont, arrived in Paris in 1846 at the age of 22 to study sculpture. But when he saw a painting by Thomas Couture in a gallery, he decided to take up painting. He spent the following year studying with Couture and sharing his studio. He met Jean-François Millet in about 1850 and moved to Barbizon, where he worked with the Frenchman. After almost ten years in France, Hunt returned to Boston, where he introduced the ideals and methods of the Barbizon school to his students. These techniques were to influence American art. It was at Hunt's urging that Bostonians purchased Millet's paintings, which accounts for the richness of the Barbizon collection at the Museum of Fine Arts in Boston. Hunt's pictures include *Girl at a Fountain* and *The Bathers* (Metropolitan Museum of Art, New York). His brother was the architect Richard Morris Hunt.

Boulevard Poissonnière (2nd) Map F

29 Café La Porte Montmartre. In *Of Time and the River,* Thomas Wolfe revealed himself as a night person haunting the alleys, the streets, and boulevards of Paris, as most of her citizens slumbered.

> The way things go: At 6:10 A.M. the street lights of Paris go off. I sit at a little all-night café in Grand Boulevard opposite Rue Faubourg de Montmartre and watch light widen across the sky behind Montmartre. At first a wide strip of blue-grey—a strip of violet light. You see the line of the two clear and sharp. The paper truck of Hachette, *Le Petit Parisien,* etc., go by.
> In the bar a rattling of leaden, hole-y coins—the five, ten and twenty-five centime pieces. Taxi-drivers drinking café rhum, debating loudly in hoarse sanguinary voices. A whore, the blonde all-night antiquity of the quarter streets, drinking rich hot

chocolate, crunching crusty croissants at the bar. The veteran of a million loves, well known and benevolently misprized, hoarse with iniquity and wisdom. A pox upon you Marianne: You have made Monsieur Le Président très triste; the third leg of the Foreign Legion wears a sling because of you!

A swart-eyed fellow, oiled and amorous, sweetly licks with nozzle tongue his whore's rouge-varnished face: with choking secret laughter and with kissy, wetty talkie he cajoles her; she answers in swart choked whisperings with her sudden shrill whore's scream of merriment.

A morning rattle of cans and ashes on the pavements. With rich jingle-jangle and hollow clitter-clatter a Paris milk wagon passes. Suddenly, a screak of brakes: all over the world the moaning screak of brakes, and racing, starting motors.

Across the street in faint grey-bluish light the news kiosque is opening up.

"Est-ce que vous avez *Le New York 'Erald?*"

"Non, monsieur. Ce n'est pas encore arrivé."

"Et *Le Tchicago Treebune?*"

"Ça pas plus, monsieur. C'est aussi en retard ce matin."

"Merci. Alors: *Le Matin.*"

"Bien, monsieur."

Passage of leaden sous: the smell of ink-worn paper, dear to morning throughout the world. A big Hachette truck swerves up, an instant halt, the flat heavy smack of fresh-corded ink-warm paper on the pavement, a hoarse cry and instant loud departure.

Rue de la Pompe (16th)

(99)   Isadora Duncan bought a house here in 1919. It was the former Salle Beethoven located at 9 Avenue de Montespan, a quiet, private cul-de-sac on the corner of 99 Rue de la Pompe. She lived with the pianist Walter Rummel, whom she calls "Archangel" in her memoir *My Life;* he introduced her to the music of Franz Liszt. Isadora decided to rebuild her school of dance, which quickly filled with American students. She accepted an invitation from the king of Greece to perform with her school in Athens, and the entire group sailed for the glorious Mediterranean. But amidst the ruins of Kopanus, with the sun setting over the Acropolis diffusing rich purple and golden rays across the sea, Isadora, 43, noticed that Archangel was no longer playing his rapturous Liszt for her, but for one of her students, half her age. She returned to her house on the Rue de la Pompe alone. The following year, 1921, she accepted an invitation from the Russian government to open a school and left for Moscow.

Pont Royal (7th)

Site of Les Bains Publics. Galignani's *New Paris Guide* for 1824 advised its readers:

> In the year 1760, M. Poitevin established on the river warm baths, constructed on boats, and the speculation proved successful. Of this kind four are now kept by Vigier. They are stationed near the Pont Marie, the Pont Neuf, and above and below the Pont Royal. That above the Pont Royal, opposite the palace of the Tuileries, is the most spacious and elegant. It was constructed by Bellanger in 40 days in 1801, on a boat as long as the largest vessel. It is two stories high, and the galleries are adorned with pillars, pilasters, and handsome ceilings. It contains one hundred and sixty baths, which in summer are generally occupied from day-break till eleven at night. In winter the establishment closes at 10 p.m.

John Adams, rarely one to praise the French, was a frequent client, and after his visit on Sunday, 27 October 1782, he commented on the privacy and excellent service: "You are shewn into a little Room, which has a large Window looking over the River into the Tuileries. There is a Table, a Glass and two Chairs, and you are furnished with hot linen, Towels, etc. There is a Bell which you ring when you want any Thing."

In May 1805, having taken a bath here, Washington Irving commented on how fond the French were of the bath and noted that "french women very attentive to the cleanliness of their persons."

Boulevard de Port-Royal (13th) Métro: Port-Royal

85 William L. Shirer, aged 21, stayed in a pension upon his arrival in Paris in 1925. The pension, Shirer wrote, "[was] presided over by an elderly white-haired lady invariably in black who treated us from the beginning as though we were members of the family." Shirer had just graduated from a small Presbyterian college in Iowa, where he had been editor of the college newspaper. With this rich background, he applied for a job with the two American newspapers in town, the *New York Herald* and the *Chicago Tribune*. In both offices they showed him the stacks of applications from young Americans in Paris. His chances were nil. But on the last day in Paris, with a ticket in his pocket to Le Havre, he returned to find a *pneumatique* under his door. It read: "Dear Mr. Shirer, If you still want a job would you be kind enough to come in to see me some evening about nine? David Darrah." This letter from the *Chicago Tribune* launched Shirer's career as a journalist.

Avenue Rachel (18th) Métro: Blanche

Le cimetière de Montmartre. On Thursday, 15 June 1837, Dr. Willard Parker and a friend visited the abattoir of Montmartre, and then proceeded up the hill to the cemetery. Parker was particularly observant of the way the French handled their dead. The ritual in the church, the journey to the cemetery, and the cost were carefully recorded by Parker in his *Journal:*

> Next we visited Mont. Martre. Here is the 2d great necropolis of Paris. In splendor it stands next to Père Lachaise—yet is far inferior—the natural beauties surpass Père Lachaise—some fine monuments of taste & splendor. the principal is that of the Duchesse of Montmorency & a smaller one of Prince Ernest of Saxe Coburg who died at Paris in 1832—This was once a Gypsum quarry, well known to every geologist—is where the great Cuvier figured & made his splendid observations—first called the *champs de repos.* Now Mont.Martre—from Mons. Mars—a name which the old Romans gave it from a Temple there to that God—Leaving the cemetery we mounted the higher part of the Hill—where we saw the place. Paris the country North & West—beautiful—beautiful. On this summit are 6 wind mills for grinding Plaster. We visited a fine little church in this place—saw in it ordinary garniture. Paintings, crucifixes etc. by it are the relics of an old convent of the Benedictine Nuns. Upon the Tower of it is still a Telegraph which held communication with Bordeaux, Brest & Spain—from this place is seen Mont Calvaire—the highest elevation about Paris. N.W. from the city—2 Leagues—upon it are 3 Crosses. As we descended & even while in the cemetery the city began to pour forth its dead. We met droves of the undertakers with their black cocked hats—horses & carriages seeming to shew forth in all the habiliments of death. Some with much & some with little display. On one of the carriages—the coffin was covered with a white pall & passing

from the sides of the coffin were 4 white Ribbons—which were trailing each a young Miss or Lady dressed in white & over the head of each was a large white veil—no bonnet—after these were 75 or 100 following in the same attire. They do not, as with us, walk 2 & 2. Females. I have never seen before going to the grave. This was a Virgin!! Yes, so said in Paris—After this we met a member of the Legion of honneur, his trappings were born after him. The French seem to give but very very little of that manifestation of feeling which is so common among us. Why is it so—is it the religion or because they have less affection? All seems to be done when the dead is hid and a Chaplet of life Everlasting is placed over the grave— The dead of Paris are a source of great revenue—the whole business is let out to contractors & such, a percentage is paid to government, 67 percent, the dead rest but 5 years & then are dug up to make room for others—and in Paris about 30,000 die annually. From thence I went to my Banker & settled up.

Rue Racine (6th) Map B

5   Early in the 19th century the Sorbonne began to attract an increasing number of foreign students. The *pension de famille* (family boarding house) was generally their first home, but the advantages of speaking French at the dinner table with "Madame" (they were generally run by women) were frequently outweighed by the restrictions—home by midnight, breakfast at 7:30 a.m., etc. Because many students wanted greater freedom, a series of large boarding houses opened in the area around the Sorbonne. They offered private rooms with or without meals, and students were free to come and go as they chose. Guests were allowed in the afternoon, evening, or even later, providing the rent was paid up. These houses used the name *pension,* which had a reassuring ring to the folks back in Kalamazoo or Oshkosh, where the term "hotel" might have conjured up ominous images.

If you walk into the entranceway of number 5, a former pension, you will notice the large hallway and the central staircase discreetly placed by the main desk, both of which Henry Wadsworth Longfellow knew well. On 19 October 1826, during his fourth month in Paris, the poet wrote home recounting his efforts to find suitable lodgings in a strange city:

My dear Mother,

    I write this from "Winter Quarters:"—Rue de Racine Fauxbourg St. Germain. If ever a man deserved a comfortable dwelling-place, I do—for no man ever toiled harder to find one. But at length I believe I am suited. I have found a little nook in this quiet part of the city, where I shall stay the Autumn out, and from which I hope to give you in due season a few sketches of "Winter in Paris." I am within a few steps of the house where I resided when I first came to the city.

Longfellow, like any student, had grown tired of the restrictions of the pension de famille (in his case with Madame Potet in nearby Rue Monsieur-le-Prince). In a letter to his mother he took obvious pains to justify his decision to move:

This has determined me to hire my chamber separately, and to dine at a Restaurateur's or at a "Table d'hôte"—that is to say at a table where a certain number meet daily, and pay so much each. This is very convenient, I can assure you, for in whatever part of this great city you may happen to be, you are sure of not losing your dinner. You have only to step into a "restaurateur's"—and immediately a bill of fare is handed you, with the price of each dish marked: so that your dinner costs what you please or rather what your appetite pleases. But the price of the "Table d'hôte" is fixed, and all sit at one table,—whereas at a Restaurateur's the rooms are fitted with small tables of two,—four,—or six plates each.

    The general breakfast hour is ten o'clock; and all the French take at this hour their "Déjeuner à la fourchette"—a breakfast eaten with a fork—very much like one of our dinners—hot cutlets—beefstakes— poultry—and vegetables. The Dinner hour is 5:—and I am sure you would wonder at a French dinner:—such an endless variety—nobody but a Frenchman can "endure unto the end." For my own part I generally hold out more than half way through—but never quite through the affair—dessert and all. And now that I am free from the dangerous temptation of eating too much at a family table, I shall seldom visit a "table d'hôte," but dine cheaply and simply at a Restaurateur's. It strikes a person very singular at first—and he can hardly bring himself to sit down at a little table by himself, and eat before ten thousand strangers— but it is the custom of the place—and though before coming to France I thought I should never be able to eat in such a multitude—yet at present I find no difficulty—and can cry "garçon" to the servant as loud and bold as anybody.

When he returned to Paris after the summer holidays, he was

surprised to learn that classes at the Sorbonne did not begin till 1 November. He had come to Europe to prepare himself for a professorship of Modern Languages at his alma mater, Bowdoin College. In his letters to his father he reported his progress in French:

> It is now exactly eight months since my arrival in Paris—and setting all boasting aside—I must say that I am well satisfied with the knowledge I have acquired of the french language. My friends all tell me that I have a good pronunciation—and altho' I do not pretend to anything like perfection—but in comparison with what others have done—I am confident that I have done well. I cannot imagine who told you that six months was enough for the French—he would have been more correct if he had said six years—that is—speaking of perfection in the language.

Longfellow's letters to his sisters dealt with less academic concerns. Here he stresses the proverbial light side of French life—holidays and social etiquette:

> New Year's day in France is always a day of great gaiety and rejoicing—a holiday for all classes of people. The streets are filled with people—and every passage—lane—and blind alley pours forth its turbulent tide of men—women and children. It is a day of glory for pastry-cooks and confectioners. Their windows are decorated with all that is sublime in pie and sugar plumb: and the wistful eye and watery mouth of many a sweep and pennyless urchin bears witness to the complete victory of matter over mind.
>
> Frivolity and lightheartedness are proverbial characteristics of the French. The holiday customs of the New Year's Day afford an excellent proof and illustration of their peculiar levity. Here, as in some parts of our own country, those who are in society, expect a visit from each of their friends. Of course a gallant man—who would sin against a point of etiquette, and thereby bring death into the little world of his pretensions—if he omitted a duty of such regular standing as are the morning calls of his day—has little to do but run round with his visiting cards from morning till night. This may be well enough for ought I know—but the French make light of the business by expecting in addition to the visit a pocket full of sugar-plumbs. This custom of giving pepper-mints—and lozenges—
>
> Lollipops and bull's-eyes
> With sugar-plums of full size—

prevails through all classes—and a lady in the first circles would think herself not a little slighted if a gentleman should call on New Year's morning without the customary offering of a paper of "Bonbons." Thus fashion rules us—and gives to frivolity the name and sanction of a wise and venerable custom.

Longfellow's observations on French life did not confine themselves, however, to modes of habitation. After four months in France, he was able to warn a friend that "all French women are naughty women...as a general rule."

Boulevard Raspail (6th & 14th) Map **B**

43-45 Hôtel Lutetia. William Carlos Williams, poet and physician from Rutherford, New Jersey, stayed here in January 1924. In Paris he met with James Joyce, Harold Loeb, George Antheil, Marcel Duchamp, Man Ray, Mina Loy, Sylvia Beach, Louis Aragon, and Ezra Pound.

Nathanael West arrived in Paris in 1926 at the age of 23, two years after graduating from Brown University. He spent but a few days here before moving to more modest quarters on Rue de la Grande-Chaumière.

207 Hôtel du Carlton-Palace. Aaron Copland took rooms here with a friend for the winter of 1921–22. He later recorded how he used to see James Joyce going into Shakespeare and Company around six o'clock in the evening with page proofs. During the winter he became a friend of George Antheil, who introduced him to Virgil Thomson.

On 1 December 1921, Copland's *Old Poem, Pastorale* was performed at the Salle Pleyel by M. Hubbard and Nadia Boulanger.

216 In 1929, Edward Titus announced that he was going to build an apartment house at this address, which besides tenants would house a "little American theater" with 300 seats. He told reporters that he intended to produce only avant-garde plays. Financed by his wife Helena Rubinstein, the theater put on plays in French, English, and Italian, and although performances were only for private audiences, the theater was closed on orders of the French authorities, on the ground that the plays attacked the French government.

Rue Raymond-Losserand (14th)

(60)   Site of the Hôtel Alba. Henry Miller lived in the Alba briefly during winter 1930. He offered English lessons à prix modeste. He had no pupils, and therefore no money, and so moved to the office of the cinema manager in nearby Vanves, where he spent nights.

Rue Raynouard (16th)

(62-70)) Site of the Hôtel de Valentinois. Benjamin Franklin, minister to Versailles, accompanied by his two grandsons (Temple, 16, and Benjamin Franklin Bache, 7) moved into this hôtel in March 1777. At the time, Passy was "a neat village" wrote Franklin, "half a mile from Paris with a large garden to walk in." This spacious estate was owned by a wealthy merchant, Le Ray de Chaumont, who traded extensively with America and provided Franklin accommodations rent-free. The grounds were laid out in formal gardens, with alleys of clipped lindens. The mansion stood on the crest of the bluff and had terraces leading down to the Seine, with views overlooking Paris. Franklin was comfortably installed in a pavilion on the grounds, complete with a lightning rod on the roof and a printing press in the basement. It seems, however, that he changed quarters occasionally and occupied the main house at the end of his stay. Young Temple served as secretary to his grandfather, while Benjamin Bache, after several years in the local school at Passy, was placed with François Didot, the eminent Parisian printer, to learn the trade.

The accounts show that Franklin and his frequent guests lived well, catered to by a staff of six to nine servants. Breakfast of bread, butter, honey, and coffee, chocolate, and tea was served at eight on weekdays and nine or ten on Sundays. For dinner, a joint of beef, veal, or mutton was followed by fowl or game, two sweets, two vegetables, pickles, radishes, fruits, two compotes, cheese biscuits, bonbons, and ices twice a week in summer. The cellar was well stocked: the inventory for February 1779 recorded 1,040 bottles, made up of red and white Bordeaux, Burgundies, some champagne, numerous sparkling white wines, and 48 bottles of rum.

John Adams, who had arrived the previous year, found the mode of living extravagant and wasteful. He felt that Franklin lived rather like the French aristocracy and was also appalled by

Franklin's failure to keep clear accounts. Franklin admitted, but not to Adams, that frugality was "a virtue I could never acquire in myself." But to the French public Franklin was another man. Without wig, in his sober and unembroidered brown coat topped with a fur collar in winter, he played the role of the simple Republican.

Adams was forced to admit that "Franklin's reputation was more universal than that of Leibnitz or Newton, Frederick or Voltaire; and his character more beloved and esteemed than any or all of them." But recognition was one thing, friendship was another, and both men were happy when Adams moved out after unsuccessfully trying to pay Le Ray de Chaumont his portion of the rent. Adams would not be in debt to any man.

During his eight-year tenure here, Franklin received every American of importance in Paris. One of his most colorful guests was the dashing, good-looking American sea captain John Paul Jones, who visited from 1778 on. Sailing from French seaports such as Nantes, Lorient, and St.-Malo, Jones was in constant need of supplies, money, men, and occasionally ships. He also needed an agent to dispose of his prizes, ships which he had captured from the British. Championed by Franklin, he was recommended to Le Ray de Chaumont, who owned a fleet of merchant ships and made money procuring supplies for the French navy. But his warmest support came from the young Madame de Chaumont, who taught the 31-year-old Jones to speak French. Franklin had advised him that to learn French he should find a "sleeping dictionary." Thus Madame and Jones were soon lovers, and all of Jones's needs in Paris and at French seaports were soon met. As Franklin could have told him, however, it was one thing to acquire a mistress, and another to abandon her. One year later, on 13 June 1779, from the safety of his cabin on board the *Bonhomme Richard* moored at Lorient, Jones wrote to his former French teacher to say farewell, adding: "My Soul's Supreme Ambition is to merit the praises of my Friends which I know I have not yet done by my Services. I can only add that whatever my future fortune may be, I shall carry with me thro life the most Constant and Lively sense of your polite Attentions and of your delicate and Unreserved Friendship." It was an 18th-century farewell. When Jones returned to Paris after his summer cruise and naval triumph, he stayed with John Adams on Rue d'Auteuil.

Franklin had come to France to obtain money, arms, and munitions. He sought official French recognition of the United

States, and most importantly, he had come to France to get that nation involved in a war with England. He succeeded in all these aims. When he left Passy, on 11 July 1785, at the age of 79, he was probably the most respected foreigner in France.

Rue Régis (6th) Map B

4   In January 1960 Richard Wright took a three-room apartment here on the ground floor. He died the following November and was buried at Père Lachaise cemetery.

Place de la République (11th)

During the 19th century, circuses were popular throughout Europe, and American entertainers, particularly sharpshooters and bareback riders, performed frequently in Paris. In 1875 J.W. Myers obtained permission to erect a tent here for his American-style circus. The big tent was placed on the site previously used for the Salon des Refusés (for the works of painters refused by the official annual salon). This square was used for all types of exhibits and it was only on 14 July 1884 that the Statue de la République was inaugurated.

Rue de Richelieu (1st & 2nd) Map F

In the 18th century, this was one of the most elegant and important streets in Paris. One thousand yards long, it stretched from the Place du Théâtre Français (the Comédie Française) to the Boulevard des Italiens. It was lined with a series of magnificent *hôtels particuliers* built between 1660 and 1680. By 1776, the aristocracy had begun to move away, and the *hôtels particuliers* became hotels and luxurious rooming houses, flanked by restaurants, theaters, gaming rooms, and other places of pleasure. The street was especially popular with Americans until the middle of the 19th century and is often mentioned in early American memoirs.

During the turbulent years 1789 to 1815, French hotel names changed frequently, reflecting the hazards and fortunes of the times and the dangers of allegiance to the past. Hôtel du Roi was quickly renamed Hôtel des Patriotes; the Hôtel de Grande Bretagne became La Maison de Bretagne. Nowhere were these shifting alliances more evident than in the Rue de Richelieu, where, for instance, the name Hôtel de Richelieu reoccurs at different street numbers in different years. This may have led to errors on our part in the identification of some hotels.

2   Théâtre Français, home of the Comédie Française. The first theater to be built on this site was begun in 1786 and completed four years later. However, the Comédie Française had scarcely begun performing here when, in 1790, it divided politically, separated, and performed in two groups. Reunited in 1799, it opened at this theater with *Le Cid* by Corneille and *L'Ecole des Maris* by Molière. In his *Journal* Gouverneur Morris recalls that he often came to see the actor Bréville. Early in the 19th century, John Howard Payne and Washington Irving used to come to see Talma perform.

Mrs. Caroline Kirkland attended the theater in May 1848, a few months after the overthrow of King Louis-Philippe. It was a time of political agitation. As she noted in *Holidays Abroad:* "The French are a nation of sentiments. Words are things to them. The number of inscriptions of Liberté, Egalité, Fraternité, in the city, already, when the king's traces are hardly cold, is truly wonderful." But what she found even more impressive was the singing of the "Marseillaise" by Mlle Rachel, the leading tragedienne of the Comédie Française:

> She appears . . . in the simplest possible tragic drapery, majestic in simplicity; the voice is nothing, as a voice, but her declamation of the hymn is sublime. Her eye, her tones, her gestures, are passionate in the extreme; and at each refrain she becomes a Pythoness, and her audience is spell-bound until the last word, when they burst forth in acclamations that rend the skies. For the last stanza she grasps the tri-color; she kneels before it; she clasps it to her bosom; she waves it with a frantic eagerness; and she carries her hearers with her throughout. It is a perfectly unique exhibition, and one which only a Rachel could make sublime, instead of ridiculous.

Rachel, whose real name was Elisa Feliz, was born in Switzerland in 1821; she joined the Comédie Française at 17, playing in Corneille's *Horace.* She was soon recognized as the greatest tragedienne in Europe. She played in London in 1841–42, and came to America in 1853, where her lack of English limited her appeal. She died of tuberculosis in 1858.

꙳

Ralph Waldo Emerson also saw Rachel in May 1848, playing her best-known role, Phèdre by Racine. The New Englander noted:

> The best part of her performance is the terror and energy she can throw into passages of defiance or denunciation. Her manners and carriage are throughout pleasing by their highly intellectual cast. And her expression of the character is not lost by your losing some word or look, but is continuous and is sure to be conveyed. She is extremely youthful and innocent in her appearance, and when she appeared after the curtain fell to acknowledge the acclamations of the house and the heaps of flowers that were flung to her, her smile had a perfect good nature and a kind of universal intelligence.

The interior of the Théâtre Français was destroyed by fire in March 1900, and the theater reopened that December. During the summer of 1905, Franklin and Eleanor Roosevelt saw Beaumarchais's *Le Barbier de Séville*. FDR recorded that the comedy was "wonderfully given and so distinct that even I could understand it."

(17)   Site of the Hôtel de Valois. John Adams' diary reads:

> April 8th. Wednesday 1778. We rode through Orléans and arrived at Paris about nine O Clock. For thirty miles from Paris the Road was paved and the Scaenes were delightfull.
>
> On our Arrival at a certain Barrier We were stopped and searched and paid the Duties for about twenty five Bottles, of Wine which were left, of the generous present of Mr. Delap at Bordeaux. We passed the Bridge over the River Seine, and went through the Louvre. The Streets crouded with Carriages with a multitude of Servants in Liveries.
>
> At Paris We went to several Hotells which were full; particularly the Hôtel D'Artois, and the Hôtel Bayonne. We were then advised to the Hôtel de Valois, Rue de Richelieu, where We found Entertainment, but We could not have it, without taking all Chambers upon the Floor, which were four in number, very elegant and richly furnished, at the small price of two Crowns and an half a day without any thing to eat or drink. I took the Apartments only for two or three days, and sent for Provisions to the Cooks. Immediately on our Arrival We were called upon for our Names, as We had been at Mrs. Rives's at Bourdeaux. My little Son had sustained this long Journey of nearly five hundred miles, at the rate of an hundred miles a day, with the utmost firmness, as he did our fatiguing and dangerous Voyage.
>
> April 9. Thursday. 1778. Though the City was very silent and

> still in the latter part of the night, the Bells, Carriages and Cries in the Street, were noisy enough in the morning.

That morning Adams went by coach to see Franklin in Passy, and it seems from his diary that he moved in with Franklin that evening.

Three years later, in October 1782, John Adams returned to Paris from Holland to assist Franklin in the peace negotiations. He again stayed at the Hôtel de Valois. After his sojourn in hardworking, Protestant Holland, he was quick to record his reservations about the French.

> The first Thing to be done, in Paris, is always to send for a Taylor, Peruke maker and Shoemaker, for this nation has established such a domination over the Fashion, that neither Cloaths, Wigs nor Shoes made in any other Place will do in Paris. This is one of the Ways, in which France taxes all Europe, and will tax America. It is a great Branch of the Policy of the Court, to preserve and increase this national Influence over the Mode, because it occasions an immense Commerce between France and all the other Parts of Europe. Paris furnishes the Materials and the manner, both to Men and Women, every where else.

30 Formerly Hôtel d'Orléans. Thomas Jefferson, his 11-year-old daughter Martha, and his negro servant James Hemings, arrived in Paris on 6 August 1784 and put up at this hotel. It was opposite the gardens of the Palais Royal, which the popular French novelist Sébastien Mercier described as "the Capital of Paris," where "you can see everything, hear everything, learn everything." In his meticulously kept Account Book, Jefferson noted 72 livres for "house rent for six days in the Hôtel d'Orléans, rue Richelieu." During these first days in Paris, he bought clothes for himself and his daughter, including lace ruffles, a sword and belt, "shaving apparatus," and a map of Paris for three livres. At the end of the week, he moved to a hotel of similar name on Rue Bonaparte.

58 La Bibliothèque Nationale. Edmund Wilson had first tried to carry out research in this great library in 1921. Forty years later he returned to seek information about the French caricaturist Sem, only to discover that nothing had changed. His experience has been shared by many scholars.

> You have to get a pass, in the first place, to be admitted to the building at all. But this was the least of my difficulties. Inside, I asked one of the snippy old ladies by whom the place seemed

largely to be staffed where I could find Sem's albums and information about him. "Il faut choisir," [You must choose] she enjoined. Couldn't I see them both? "Pas à la même fois." [Not at the same time.] I consulted the catalogue and discovered, to my astonishment, that the entries had never been typed but were still being written out in an old-fashioned early-nineteenth-century hand, to keep up the tradition of which, I reflected, they must now have to train special scribes. And these entries have not been arranged all in one alphabetical catalogue but are divided up into sections, each of which is supposed to cover books published between certain dates, and I was informed by a frequenter of the library that titles were often assigned to the wrong years. I found only one entry for Sem. I was told to make out two slips. When I handed them in at the desk, the old frustrator presiding there snapped at me with "Comment voulez-vous que j'accepte des fiches au crayon?" [How do you expect me to accept slips filled out in pencil?] so I had to borrow a pen and make out another pair. I was then given information which must have been intentionally misleading, for I was told to go up to the third floor. This involved climbing a high marble staircase, getting sidetracked in an exhibition of the manuscripts and portraits of Alfred de Vigny, for which I had to pay two francs, and making my way through long marble corridors till I finally discovered an elevator, by which I ascended to more marble corridors, and found myself at last confronted by the door of the print department. I inquired of a young man, who told me to go down to the ground floor. I explained that I had been told to come up there. He called up the reading room to check, then said yes, I must go below. There I handed in my slips and was directed to a numbered seat, to which presently my single item was brought by a very old man. It was an article of about five pages, written by a friend of Sem's at the time of the latter's death. The albums, I was now told, were kept in the print department, from which I had just come. I went above again, and the helpful young man got them out, but there were only four or five of them—whereas I had myself a great many. He could throw no light on the dates; he explained that there was no bibliography of Sem.

63   Grand Hôtel de Malte, formerly Hôtel Richelieu. Gouverneur Morris took rooms at the Richelieu on 3 February 1789. He had left Philadelphia on 17 December and after "a tempestuous crossing" of 40 days arrived at Le Havre on 27 January 1789. He had come to France to replace Jefferson as the American minister. After the relative calm of Philadelphia, Morris noted in his *Journal* that

"A man in Paris lives in a sort of whirlwind." Armed with letters of introduction from George Washington, and his own charm and wit, all doors were open to him. On 5 June 1789, Morris agreed to the requests of Houdon and Jefferson that he "stand for the figure of George Washington," but not without commenting that this was surely an example of doing "all things for all men." Although the storming of the Bastille was not to take place until the following month, Paris had become the scene of daily disturbances. Morris noted in his *Journal:*

> it is impossible to do business this day...dress and wait for my carriage...walk to the Louvre and order my carriage to follow; later I go to Mr. Jeffersons and am stopped near the Pont Royal and obliged to turn in the Rue St. Honoré. Stopped again at the Church St. Roch, and a number of foolish questions asked. Colonel Gardner came to see me; is very happy to be in Paris. So am I.

(69)   Site of the Hôtel de Richelieu. Washington Irving arrived in Paris on 24 May 1805. Aged 22, he had been sent on a tour of Italy and France by his parents. As soon as he and his travelling companion, Joseph C. Cabell, had found rooms, they went for a stroll in that most fashionable area, the Palais Royal. Irving noted in his *Journal:* "The garden was thronged with frail nymphs that wander about it. One of them joined us & we had a long walk and talk with her. A very pretty little girl with a peculiar archness of countenance; her conversation was lively even witty and her manners easy and exceedingly polite—what singular beings these French women are!" The following evening, the two gentlemen attended the Théâtre Montpensier, also in the Palais Royal. Irving continued: "This is a little theatre much frequented by the frail ones—Acting humorous & rather gross—Scenery tolerable house crowded." Asked by a fellow American why they had gone first to "the most disreputable theatre in the city," Irving replied that he "had caught Paris by the Tail."

In 1805, when Napoleon was at the height of his popularity, those who governed under him had been chosen upon the basis of ability rather than of birth. In conversation with fellow Americans, Irving noted: "France owes her power to years of elective government in which time the men of abilities rose to the top & managed affairs...crowned heads make a contemptible appearance—at present Bonaparte is the most brilliant and the most intelligent next to him is the Emperor of Prussia."

(89)   Site of the Hôtel York. Washington Irving joined his friend, dramatist John Howard Payne, in the Hôtel York on 3 October 1823. Irving had gone back to America from Paris in 1806. Ten years later he returned to England to take over the ailing family business but was unable to save it from bankruptcy. Encouraged by Walter Scott, Irving took up writing again. *The Sketch Book,* published in 1820, contained stories such as "The Legend of Sleepy Hollow" and "Rip Van Winkle," which rapidly made their author famous. Payne introduced Irving to Talma, and the two men became friends.

95   Hôtel Cusset, formerly Hôtel des Patriotes Etrangers. Gouverneur Morris lived here and noted in his diary: "The art of living consists, I think, in some considerable degree in knowing how to be cheated."

James Monroe, who had been sent to France to replace Gouverneur Morris as American minister, arrived with his family at Le Havre on board the *Cincinnatus* at the end of July 1794. The Monroes took rooms at number 95 on their arrival in Paris on 2 August, five days after the execution of Robespierre. In November, Monroe succeeded in freeing Thomas Paine from imprisonment at the Palais du Luxembourg. He invited the writer to stay with him here on the Rue de Richelieu for a few days in order to recuperate from his ordeal. But Paine was ill and penniless and to the embarrassment of Monroe stayed on for two years. It was here that Paine completed the second part of *The Age of Reason.*

(97)   Site of the Hôtel du Nord. John Quincy Adams stayed here from 4 February until 2 May 1815. On 7 February, he was presented to Louis XVIII. A month later, he noted in his *Journal* that Napoleon had escaped from Elba and had landed near Cannes with "twelve hundred men and four canon." The king promptly issued a proclamation declaring Bonaparte a rebel and a traitor. Two weeks later, with Napoleon nearing Paris, Louis XVIII spoke to the two legislative chambers of "dying in defence of the country," noted a caustic Adams. Three days later, the royal family fled, and Napoleon reinstalled himself in the Palais des Tuileries. Adams added that the troops which had been sent to oppose him had joined him, that they were enthusiastic, and that the people were seemingly content.

(108)   Site of the Hôtel Frascati. Galignani's *New Paris Guide* (1824) describes the hotel as follows: "This was originally a public garden and is now a gaming-house, which may be considered the second in Paris in point of respectability, as the company is select, and the persons frequenting it generally venture high stakes. Ladies are admitted here, and balls and suppers are occasionally given." In 1837 the French government closed all gaming houses in Paris. Charles Sumner, 27, future U.S. senator, arrived in Paris on the very evening that the gaming houses were to close. He dropped his trunk at his hotel and rushed to Frascati's to enjoy the last two hours. He was fascinated with the roulette and card tables, where gold and silver were "spread on the table to a vast amount." Young Sumner did not bet one franc, but he did notice young women moving from table to table who possessed, he noted, "considerable personal attractions."

Rue Richer (9th) Métro: Cadet

32   Théâtre des Folies-Bergère. Many American artists performed at this theater, which opened in 1869. Leona Dare, a tall, good-looking trapeze artist, slid down a steep rope brandishing two American flags. After this spectacular entry, she appeared on the high trapeze carrying a man suspended "at the tip of her teeth" from her "steel jaw." She frequently starred in French circuses.

In 1897, Loïe Fuller appeared here and became the sensation of Paris. Possessing neither an attractive figure nor any particular choreographic talent, she introduced the dazzling lighting effects of the modern stage show. She wore huge veils which fluttered in the wind from electric fans offstage, and illumination was provided by multicolored light beams. This great American showwoman brought the technology of Thomas Edison to the French theater. She created the serpentine dance, the fire dance, the dance of the flowers, the butterfly, and the dance of the mirrors. Within a year she was earning 24,000 francs a month, a fabulous salary at the time. The director of the Folies-Bergère was so afraid that she might leave for another theater that he rented an apartment for her next to the theater and had a wall pierced so that after performances she would not risk catching cold from going outside in the damp winter evenings.

American sharpshooters were always popular with the French public. Charley Austin and "The Evil Spirit of the Plains," accompanied by "Doc" William Carver, performed impressive feats of marksmanship at this theater. Toward the end of the 19th century, Ira Paine, the "Famous American Marksman" as he was billed, carried out the "William Tell Trick," shooting an orange from his wife's head.

In 1926, after her success in *La Revue Nègre,* Josephine Baker triumphed at the Folies-Bergère in her banana belt costume for the first time in "Folie du Jour."

Rue de Rivoli (1st & 4th) Map F

24 Formerly Hotel Bedford. In 1844 the great American showman Phineas Taylor Barnum, 34, arrived in Paris with General Tom Thumb, who would be seen by over 20 million people on both sides of the Atlantic. (Barnum did not join his competitor Bailey until 1881.) According to Barnum, Tom Thumb was two feet tall, weighed less than sixteen pounds, and was "a perfectly formed, bright-eyed little fellow, with light hair and ruddy cheeks." Tom Thumb captured the imagination of Paris. The two-month season, wrote Barnum, "was more than a success: it was a triumph." On their first day in Paris, Barnum and his midget were received by King Louis-Philippe and his court at the Tuileries. Special permission was given for General Tom Thumb to join the parade at Longchamp. There, among the splendid equipages carrying ambassadors to the Court of France, none attracted greater attention than a superb small carriage, drawn by four ponies attended by liveried coachmen and footmen. *Le Figaro* printed a cartoon showing a mastiff running off with the general's carriage and with horses between his teeth. Statuettes of *Tom Pouce* in plaster, sugar, and chocolate appeared in the windows; songs were written about him; hotels, bars, and restaurants were named for him; and his lithograph appeared everywhere.

164 Le Louvre des Antiquaires, formerly Grand Hôtel du Louvre. Opened in 1855 in time for the Universal Exhibition of that year, this massive luxury hotel stretched a full block from Rue de Rivoli to Rue St.-Honoré, and from Rue Marengo to the Place du Palais Royal, where its front door was located. It was taken over by Les Magasins du Louvre, a department store, and later transformed to house antique dealers, as it still does today. If you stand on the Place du Palais Royal, you may see the name Grand Hôtel du Louvre carved in stone above the doors.

In the second half of the 19th century, wealthy American tourists frequently stayed at the Grand Hôtel. Nathaniel Hawthorne took a suite of rooms on 6 January 1858. He had arrived from England, where he had served as American consul in Liverpool for four years. Accompanied by his wife, the former Sophia Peabody, one of three remarkable Peabody sisters from Salem, Massachusetts, the couple took dinner in their rooms, and Hawthorne noted:

> All the dishes were very delicate, and a vast change from the simple English system, with its joints, shoulders, beefsteaks and chops; but I doubt whether the English cookery for the very reason that it is so simple, is not better for men's moral and spiritual nature than French. In the former case, you know that you are gratifying your animal needs and propensities, and are duly ashamed of it; but, in dealing with these French delicacies, you delude yourself into the idea that you are cultivating your taste while satisfying your appetite. This last, however, it requires a good deal of perseverance to accomplish.

William Dean Howells, novelist, editor, and critic, stayed here in December 1862 and married Elinor Gertrude Mead at the American Legation on Christmas eve. He had written a campaign biography of Lincoln and had been rewarded with the post of American consul in Venice, which resulted in *Venetian Life* (1866), the first of his many travel books.

Mark Twain was here from 8 to 11 July 1867, before taking the train from the new Gare de Lyon to Marseille. Twain noted his "grand room" with its "sumptuous bed." Armed with Galignani's *New Paris Guide* for 1867, and accompanied by friends, Twain set out to see the sights. At the front desk the travellers asked for a guide. The first guide looked like a pirate. The second began in a simpering voice: "If ze zhentlemans will to me make ze grande honneur to me rattain in hees serveece, I shall show to him every sing zat is magnifique to look upon in ze beautiful Paree. I speaky ze Angleesh pairfaitemaw." He was immediately dismissed. The final applicant's opening speech was perfect. "It was perfect in construction, in phraseology, in grammar, in emphasis, in pronunciation—everything," noted Mark Twain. The sightseers were delighted, only to learn that his name, presented upon "a snowy little card," was A. Billfinger. They had expected Henri de Montmorency or

Armand de la Chartreuse, Alexis du Caulaincourt or Alphonse Henri Gustave de Hauteville. They could not travel with "Billfinger" and renamed him Ferguson. Thus it was that Monsieur Ferguson proved himself for the next three days to be one of the biggest rogues ever to enrich the travels and grace the pages of *The Innocents Abroad* (1869).

George Palmer Putnam, the New York publisher, stayed here in March 1869 while visiting his daughter Mary, who was enrolled at the Ecole de Médecine in Paris.

202   Hôtel St.-James et d'Albany. Sinclair Lewis stayed at this hotel with his wife and son in October 1921. At 36, he had just achieved recognition with *Main Street* and was working on *Babbitt*. He found, however, that he was not able to work in Paris, and returned home.

206-208   Formerly Hôtel du Jardin des Tuileries. Henry Adams moved into this hotel on 20 December 1879 and stayed for six weeks. In a letter to his friend Henry Cabot Lodge, dated 22 February 1880, he wrote: "At the best of times, Paris is to me a fraud and a snare; I dislike it, protest against it, despise its stage, condemn its literature and have only a temperate respect for its cooking." He spent these wintry weeks working on French manuscripts among French state papers. His fine study *Mont-Saint-Michel and Chartres* covered the Middle Ages and had nothing to do with the France of the late 19th century, which he pretended to dislike.

218   Hotel Brighton. Mark Twain was a frequent guest here.

228   Hôtel Meurice. This hotel has long been popular with Americans. Galignani's *New Paris Guide* for 1824 described the hotel as follows:

> It is situated in a fine and agreeable spot near the palace and garden of the Tuileries. Apartments may be had by the day, breakfasts are served in the coffee room or in private apartments, and visitors may dine at the table d'hôte or in their own rooms. A list is presented to every stranger, which contains the charge for every article, servants, etc. The bill is sent in every week; the linen is washed three miles from Paris with soap, and not beaten or

brushed as is the custom generally in France. The greatest regularity prevails in forwarding and delivering letters, and information of every kind is furnished. From the first of November until the end of May, Mr. Meurice makes arrangements with single persons or families, as boarders by the day or by the month, either at the table d'hôte, or in their apartments, wine and every thing included, except wood, which they are at liberty to purchase. He also lets lodgings without board by the day, week, or month. In this hotel there is an office for changing money; and confidential couriers, interpreters, return carriages for Calais, Boulogne, and all parts of the Continent, etc. may be obtained.

During the early part of the 19th century, American travellers recorded that the Hôtel Meurice was the only hotel in France to provide soap for its guests.

Ebenezer Smith Thomas stayed here from 17 to 20 August 1820. During his three-day stay, he was assigned an English-speaking valet, who, recorded Thomas, was "an intelligent man... he attended me in all my rambles, so that I had no difficulty in getting the most correct information." Thomas was particularly impressed by the hotel and is the only American traveller to have described his departure from the Meurice for Calais, a journey which would have taken five days. Thomas notes that Louis XVIII furnished a post horse, meaning that all post horses in France were run by the French government. The system was exceedingly efficient and the cost was clearly established in advance. The distance from Paris to Calais, via Amiens, was some 185 miles with 34 posts or changes of horses. Every post had to be run in one hour or less. Thomas undoubtedly stayed in the Hôtel Meurice in Calais, which was run by the same family.

The latter end of August, it was the 20th, I quitted Paris, having hired a carriage of Mr. Meurice, to take me down to Calais. His majesty, Louis the Eighteenth, furnished post horses, and the drivers wore the royal livery, blue and red. As I entered the carriage, Mr. Meurice came out, and handed me eight open letters, to the keepers of the hotels where I would dine, lodge, and breakfast, on my route, observing, "as you do not speak our language, I thought these might be of use to you, as you will find the English language spoken in all those hotels."

The many acts of kindness I received from this gentleman, independent of his being my host, endeared him to me, and I shall ever remember him with the most friendly recollections. As I took the last shake of his hand, my postillion came out to the side of the carriage, which was drawn up in the court yard; he was a dapper little fellow, rather under the middle size, and dressed in his blue round-about, with red facing, etc., and blue pants, tied close around the ankle, and shoes, with a glazed hat, whilst he had a pair of jack boots hanging over his shoulder, that could not have weighed less than twelve or fifteen pounds! I had long before read of such articles (I think Sterne mentions them in his journey,) but I had no idea their use had descended to the nineteenth century, and had I been going to embark from France for the United States, I would certainly have procured a pair of them, to present to some one of our museums, as a curiosity, equal to at least a large majority of those exhibited in them. With no small exertion, he raised his feet high enough to enter the tops of them; no exertion whatever was necessary to reach the bottom; this being accomplished, an ostler, of Herculean form, caught him up, jack boots and all, and placed him in his seat; he cracked his whip, and I was off.

Henry Wadsworth Longfellow returned to France in summer 1836 before taking up his new position of professor of Modern Languages at Harvard. He stayed here from 3 September until 4 October and called on his former landlady on Rue Monsieur-le-Prince, where he had lived in a modest room ten years earlier.

Mrs. Caroline Kirkland and two lady friends stopped here in May 1848, just too late to witness the overthrow of King Louis-Philippe. Mrs. Kirkland's observations were serialized in an American newspaper. "These sketches," she wrote, "are written for Americans and in particular for 'the lady traveller'":

> We were made very comfortable at the Hôtel Meurice, the customs of which are somewhat accommodated to the habits of American and English travellers. But what a different thing is a French hotel from an English or American one! To begin with the broad porte cochère through which you drive into a paved court on which look numerous windows and doors of the house and offices. A pair or two of stairways present themselves, and at the foot of one of them you alight, meeting the concierge and his wife and also the maître d'hôtel or head waiter, who ushers you up stairs. At Meurice's, we encountered, besides these, the lady of the house, Madame C., a portly dame in silk and ringlets, and her husband, a person of gentlemanly and obliging manners: after looking at several suites of apartments, we chose one in the

entresol, not liking the continental fashion of living near the sky. Here we had bare floors, but much upholstery in gold-colored damask; a French clock in every room, not one of which went; and narrow French beds, hung with very showy curtains—but all very comfortable and quite clean.

The tired traveller's first cry is for tea, the next for hot water. "De l'eau chaude!" [Hot water.] "Oh! un bampier? oui, madame, certainement." [Oh! a *bampier?* yes, Madam, certainly.] "Apportez de l'eau chaude!" [Bring hot water.] "O! certainement, madame; un bampier." [Oh! certainly, Madam, a *bampier.*] We were weary and meek, and so waited quietly for the mystery to solve itself. By and by appeared some great tubs of hot water, and we found our good fille-de-chambre had all the time meant *bains-de-pieds,* or foot-baths, but in her curious patois had given the word or sound which was as Chaldee to our unaccustomed ears.

Herman Melville arrived in Paris on 28 November 1849. He stayed here the first night and crossed the river the following morning, taking a room on the fifth floor of a boarding house at 12 and 14 Rue de Buci, the "Rue de Bussy," as he noted in his *Journal.* It was bitterly cold and with a blue nose he visited Notre Dame, "a fine old pile." He dropped by Galignani's, read the latest news about the California gold rush and finally dined in the Rue Vivienne for two francs before returning home. "It is the first night I have taken possession, & the 'Bonne' or chambermaid has lighted a fire of wood, and lit a candle. I am struck by the apparition of a bottle containing a dark fluid, a glass, a decanter of water.... But though if I use these things they will doubtless be charged to me, yet let us be charitable,—so I ascribe all this to the benevolence of Madame Chapelle, my most polite, pleasant, and Frenchified landlady below. I shall try the brandy before writing more." The following morning, accompanied by his friend George Adler, the German philologist, the two travelers visited the Hôtel de Cluny. "The house is just the house I should like to live in," Melville noted. "Glorious old cabinets— ebony, ivory carving. Beautiful chapel. Tapesty, old keys. Descended into the vaults of the old Roman palace of Thermes. Baths." (This scene soon found its way into *Moby Dick:* "Ahab's larger, darker, deeper part remains unhinted. But vain to popularize profundities, and all truth is profound. Winding far down from within the very heart of this spiked Hotel de Cluny where we all here stand—now quit it and take your way, ye nobler, sadder souls, to those vast Roman halls of Thermes.")

Henry James stayed here from 8 March until 23 March 1899. He spent the fortnight correcting proofs of his novel *The Awkward Age* and entertaining his two young cousins. "I breakfasted, dined, theatr'd, museumed, walked and talked them," he wrote. The Dreyfus affair had broken out again, and James found Zola's "J'accuse" to be "one of the most courageous things ever done." James was on his way to the south of France to stay at the estate of the French writer Paul Bourget, near Hyères. Bourget was violently anti-Dreyfus, as were many Frenchmen at the time. James, who believed firmly in the innocence of Dreyfus, was apprehensive about the trip, but the visit went off without incident. Four years later, in *The Ambassadors,* the following description of a room in a hotel on Rue de Rivoli appeared:

> Hotel in the Rue de Rivoli. The glazed and gilded room—all red damask, ormolu, mirrors, clocks—looked south, and the shutters were bowed upon the summer morning; but the Tuileries gardens and what was beyond it, over which the whole place hung, were things visible through gaps; so that the far-reaching spreading presence of Paris came up in coolness, dimness and invitation, in the twinkle of gilt-tipped palings, the crunch of gravel, the click of hoofs, the crack of whips that suggested some parade of the circus.

In 1907, Wilbur Wright came to Europe hoping to sell airplanes. In May, he moved into the Hôtel Meurice and was joined by his brother Orville in August. Their plane, shipped from Dayton, Ohio, to Le Havre, was held up by French customs officials who pointed out that since it didn't fit into any of the categories of machines previously imported into France, they would have to wait for instructions from Paris. The Wrights finally flew their plane at the racetrack at Le Mans. In negotiations with the French Ministry of War, the Wright brothers argued that the destructive potential of the airplane was so great that its adoption would prevent wars. Such reasoning, of course, did not interest the military, and the negotiations led nowhere. However, the French public was fascinated by the plane, and France was flooded with postcards of the two brothers and their plane. A monument to the Wrights was dedicated at Le Mans in 1920.

Walter Lippmann, successful journalist and reporter, was less successful when it came to his summer retirement years, which he envisioned spending in France. He purchased a picturesque old mill near Fontainebleau. In July 1967, he moved with his wife into the mill only to move out again six days later. Renovation of an 18th-century mill, being done by what Lippmann felt were grasping local workmen, was more than he had bargained for. He put the mill up for sale and spent the remainder of July in the Hôtel Meurice.

Boulevard de Rochechouart (9th)

(63)   Site of the Cirque Médrano, named after the famous clown Médrano Boum-Boum, illusionist, acrobat, and dancer. During the 1920s Josephine Baker had one serious American rival in Paris—a trapeze and high-wire artist named Barbette. For her finale at the Cirque Médrano she wore a costume of ostrich feathers, and at the final bow tore off her blonde wig to reveal a man's head. Barbette's real name was Vander Clyde and he hailed from Texas. He was the rage of Parisian society and frequently appeared at the Casino de Paris. He was particularly admired by Jean Cocteau, who also championed another American performer, the black boxer Panama Al Brown. In 1938, Panama performed song and dance acts, and Cocteau wrote the program notes describing him as "a phantom, a shadow, more terrible than lightning and the cobra." Luckily, the world bantamweight champion was a far better fighter than dancer and easily won his bout that summer.

Buster Keaton appeared regularly at the Médrano between 1947 and 1954. His routine included "putting the girl to bed," which he had performed with Dorothy Sebastien in *Spite Marriage,* and a comic dueling sequence he had perfected with Gilbert Roland in *The Passionate Plumber.* Edmund Wilson watched him do the presser's delivery-boy act here in February 1954. Keaton wore a flat porkpie hat, string tie, baggy clothes, and flap shoes. Morose and detached, he wandered about the ring trying to deliver a clean dress suit on a hanger while the circus was going on. After fifteen minutes, the suit was a wreck on the arena floor, and the French audience was in hysterics. Wilson concluded: "Hollywood has not made the best of him. He is a pantomime clown of the first order."

Cité Rougemont (9th) Métro: Rue Montmartre

4   Writer and lecturer Margaret Fuller spent some months on this private street in the Hôtel de la Cité, beginning in December 1846. She was single, 36, and the epitome of Boston's intellectual and literary society. A friend to Hawthorne, Emerson, and Lowell, her first published work was a translation of Johann Eckermann's *Conversations with Goethe*. She was an ardent feminist, and her *Woman in the Nineteenth Century* (1845) dealt with the political, economic, intellectual, and sexual aspects of feminism. In 1846, Fuller became the first literary critic of the *New York Herald Tribune*. She continued to write for this prominent newspaper while in Europe, and some of her articles on American literature were published in Paris in *La Revue Indépendante*.

Fuller met the French Roman Catholic apologist and liberal Lamennais, who had been excommunicated by the Pope some years earlier. Both were interested in social reform, and in 1848 she wrote to him from Rome on popular movements. She also met the great lyric poet and republican Béranger. But most important of all, she spent several hours with George Sand. Although they were close philosophically, Fuller could not help but remark upon Sand's "series of lovers." Thanks to a mutual friend, she was introduced to Chopin, and found him "as frail as a snowdrop, but an exquisite genius." He played for her, but she had as much pleasure from his conversation as from his music. She left France for Italy, where she participated in the Revolution of 1848. Pregnant, she married the father of her child, Marchese Ossoli, a follower of Mazzini. The ship which brought her back to America in 1850 was wrecked off Fire Island, and she, her husband, and infant son were drowned.

Rue Saint-André-des-Arts (6th) Map A

28   La Gentilhommière, a bar, today a pizzeria. In June 1962, Jack Kerouac spent five days in Paris sightseeing and looking up the origins of the family name in the Bibliothèque Nationale before leaving for Brittany in an attempt to track down relatives. He was unsuccessful in both searches but did enjoy this bar, where he spent several evenings and which he described in *Satori in Paris* (1966).

46   E.E. Cummings lived here in a single room in 1923. He had just painted his first self-portrait, which a friend, Stewart Mitchell, promptly bought.

Rue Saint-Benoît (6th) Map A

24 Hôtel Crystal. James Thurber had worked in Paris for the *Chicago Tribune* in the early 1920s. In 1937, he visited Paris with his wife. The following anecdote from his misadventures catches the French scene as Thurber saw it and loved it. His letter is dated 6 October 1937:

> Helen has been in bed in our red room (everything in the room is red) for three days, and I have established a remarkable relationship with a waiter at the Café de Flore on the corner. This café is one of the few places in France which makes orange juice the way Helen wants it: pressed out of fresh oranges, strained, served with ice. Last night I went there to explain in my unusual French that I wanted a glass of orange juice to take to my sick wife in the Hôtel Crystal just around the corner. The waiter wanted to sell me orange juice that comes in a bottle, but I said I had to have it in a glass. So everybody in the café got in on it and finally the patronne of the café said all right, if I paid a deposit of three francs on the glass. So I did that. Then next time I borrowed a glass from the hotel, and taking the café's glass back, explained that now they could keep their glass and give me the three francs and put the fresh orange juice in this, my own glass. Helen said I would never be able to work that, and she was right.
>
> There was a discussion in French, English, American, and gestures, about this, and although I got my idea over, it was flatly rejected. All the waiters got in on it, as well as the patronne, the gérant, the patron, his sister, a dishwasher, and two Frenchmen who were sitting in a corner. It was decided that the orange juice should again be put in the café glass which I had brought back and that the hotel glass should be returned to me, which it was. I have made several trips since then, taking the café glass back and having it filled up again. I'm going to try to work in the hotel glass again in a few days when things quiet down, and although I don't expect to get away with it, it is all very good practice in speaking French and in understanding the French people.... It is things like this, small, intense, unimportant, crucial, that make life in France a rich experience.

Rue Saint-Dominique (7th) Map C

59 Formerly Hôtel Ste-Suzanne. James Fenimore Cooper and his family moved here in April 1831. Except for trips to England and Europe, this was to be their home until they returned to America in 1833. In a letter to a friend, Mrs. Cooper described both the environs and their new home:

Any one versed in the mysteries of Paris will tell You it is a very pleasant, and a very distingué part of the Town—we have two floors . . ., and the Dining Room which is on the lower one, opens into a very pretty Garden—the Parlour is upstairs—and adjoining it is Mr. Cooper's library, and my Bedroom—the four Girls have two Rooms between them . . . We are very comfortable, and very quiet, and overlook half a dozen Gardens, besides our own, which besides being very agreeable, gives us good air.

Upon his return to America, Cooper published *A Residence in France,* part of his four-volume series *Gleanings in Europe,* where he described the Hôtel Ste-Suzanne:

The salon is near thirty feet in length, and seventeen high. It is panelled in wood, and above all the doors, of which, real and false, there are six, are allegories painted on canvass, and enclosed in wrought gilded frames. Four large mirrors are fixtures, and the windows are vast and descend to the floor. The dining-room, which opens on a garden, is of the same size, but even loftier. This hotel formerly had much interior gilding, but it has chiefly been painted over. It was built by the physician of the Duc d'Orléans, who married Madame de Montesson, and from this fact you may form some idea of the style maintained by the nobles of the period; a physician, at that time, being but a very inferior personage in Europe.

The rent was 3,000 francs per month unfurnished, a considerable sum at the time. Cooper anticipated earnings of some 20,000 dollars in 1831. Here on Rue St.-Dominique Cooper finished *The Bravo,* which with *The Heidenmauer* and *The Headsman* completed a trilogy intended to destroy the glamor of feudalism and to herald the rise of democratic liberalism. His day-to-day preoccupations were political.

In November 1830, the Poles had risen up against their Russian occupiers. Successful at first, the revolt was ultimately crushed and the Polish army defeated. Thousands of Poles emigrated to Paris. Sympathy for them was particularly strong among the Americans, who saw a parallel between their own revolution and that attempted by the Poles. A meeting of prominent American residents in Paris was held on Rue de Richelieu on Saturday, 9 July 1831, to form an American-Polish Committee. Cooper was elected chairman. Cooper was particularly struck by the obstinate refusal of the ruling classes in Europe to accept any political or social changes which seemed to him, as an American, inevitable. According to

Nathaniel P. Willis, Cooper made his home "the nucleus of republican sympathies in the great capital." The American-Polish Committee held its weekly meetings here. Lafayette was rarely absent. Willis recalled that Cooper's,

> daily breakfast table [was] open to all friends and comers-in (and supplied, we remember, for hour after hour of every day with hot buckwheat cakes, which were probably eaten nowhere else on that side of the water), many a distinguished, but impoverished, Polish refugee ate his only meal of the day, and, to the same hospitable house, came all who were interested in the great principle of that struggle, distinguished men of many nations among them.

The original garden walls of number 59, described by Mrs. Cooper, may be seen by looking at the entrance of number 57.

Rue Saint-Florentin (1st & 8th) Map F

2 Hôtel Saint-Florentin. This magnificent mansion overlooking the Place de la Concorde was built in 1767 and bought by Talleyrand in 1813. The foreign minister died here in 1838 at 84. Shortly after World War II, it housed the American administrators of the Marshall Plan. The staff was headed by Averell Harriman, and his aides included David Bruce of OSS fame, Milton Katz, on leave from Harvard Law School, and a young Harvard graduate, Kingman Brewster, future president of Yale. Theodore White, who was working in Paris as a reporter at the time, described them as the brightest group of administrators he had ever met.

13 James Fenimore Cooper and his family took rooms at this address in December 1830. During the five months which they spent here, Cooper began *The Bravo.* He had decided to stay on another year in France and began to look for larger quarters, which he found on Rue St.-Dominique. His five children "rattled off French like the natives," he told a friend, and he did not want them to lose this ability. But more important, Cooper had discovered that he was able to write while living in Paris.

Boulevard Saint-Germain (6th) Map B

151 Brasserie Lipp. During the summer of 1928, a most incongruous pair of friends, about to start out on a walking tour of France, dropped in at the Lipp for a drink. Thornton Wilder, 31, was accompanied by Gene Tunney, one year his junior. Wilder had just won recognition with *The Bridge of San Luis Rey* (Pulitzer Prize, 1927), while Tunney had just retired as undefeated world heavy-weight champion, having beaten Jack Dempsey. Tunney had been in France in the U.S. Marines during World War I, where he had won the light heavyweight championship in Paris in 1919. Intellectually inclined, Tunney was interested in writing, and during their two weeks in Paris, Wilder introduced him to the literary life of the capital. Their visit to the Brasserie Lipp was reported by Janet Flanner in her "Letter from Paris" in the *New Yorker.*

170   Café des Deux Magots. In *Exiles from Paradise,* Sarah Mayfield recalled that she seldom passed St.-Germain-des-Prés without seeing Hemingway either at the Café de Flore or the Café des Deux Magots. "Usually he was alone, bent over his notebook, writing slowly as if he weighed every word, cutting his sentences sharply, as he chiseled his gem-hard prose.... Now and then Robert McAlmon, one of the most active of the expatriate editors..., would be at table with him or Ford Madox Ford."

James Baldwin came to the Deux Magots directly upon his arrival in Paris on 12 November 1948. One of the first Americans he saw was Richard Wright talking with the editors of *Zero* magazine. Wright had already met Baldwin in Brooklyn, read his work, and had encouraged him. Now at the Deux Magots they talked briefly and Wright helped Baldwin find a hotel. Six months later, Baldwin published an article, "Everybody's Protest Novel," in *Zero,* in which he denounced Richard Wright and Harriet Beecher Stowe for robbing blacks of their humanity. Bigger Thomas in *Native Son,* like Uncle Tom, was a stereotype, Baldwin argued, and Wright was perpetuating the very myth which he had been bent on destroying. Wright never forgave Baldwin.

Rue Saint-Honoré (1st) Map **F**

145   L'Eglise de l'Oratoire, or Temple de l'Oratoire. In 1811, Napoleon permitted this church to be used by the Protestants. Many Americans, including James Fenimore Cooper, used to attend Sunday services here.

229-235   Thomas Jefferson visited the well-known French writer Abbé Morellet, who lived in this house. Morellet translated Jefferson's *Notes on the State of Virginia* (1786).

239   Hôtel de France et Choiseul. Franklin D. Roosevelt was 23 when he and Eleanor stayed here on their honeymoon in 1905. He received news that he had failed the Harvard Law School entrance exam and promptly broke out in hives. (He later graduated from Columbia Law School.) He visited Madame de Noël, the famous clairvoyant, and commented afterwards: "I am to be president of the United States or of the Equitable [Life Insurance Company], I couldn't make out which!" The young couple continued on to Venice.

༄

During the summers of 1920 and 1921, the well-known actor Otis Skinner and his family, including his daughter Cornelia, stayed here.

༄

Carson McCullers and her husband Reeves arrived in Paris early in December 1946. They took a three-room attic apartment in this charming former convent, with windows looking out over Paris. The rooms had been reserved for them by Kay Boyle, who also lived here. Carson and Reeves were ecstatic with the period French furniture, open fireplace, and cabbage rose wallpaper. McCullers' award-winning novels, *The Heart Is a Lonely Hunter* (1940) and *Reflections in a Golden Eye* (1941), had just been published in French. Janet Flanner said that "Carson bursts like a tiny bottle of glass on Paris—melodramatic, a genius."

McCullers, aged 30, met Colette, André Gide, Jean-Paul Sartre and Simone de Beauvoir, André Malraux, and Albert Camus, but her inability to speak or understand French limited her contacts. McCullers claimed that she listened well in French, nodding "oui, oui" from time to time. This she felt went down better than saying "non." One day a well-dressed, earnest young Frenchman called on her. He spoke enthusiastically and McCullers nodded "oui, oui." They shook hands and the young man left, obviously happy. She thought no more of it until a few days later Kay Boyle dropped in with an announcement which she translated for McCullers. It read: "The Sorbonne is honored to announce that Carson McCullers, American novelist, will speak on American and French literature in the Salle Richelieu" three days hence. Carson panicked. She knew nothing about French literature and could not speak French anyway. Kay Boyle suggested that she do the can-can, but McCullers replied that her dancing was even worse than her French. She was finally rescued by a friend, John Brown, a professor of comparative literature, who suggested that the two of them appear with the well-known French professor René Lalou. The two men would deliver her lecture while McCullers would sit between them and look as intelligent as possible. At the end of the lecture, McCullers recited one of her poems. The appearance was deemed a great success.

McCullers, however, was to discover, like many other American writers, that she could not discipline herself to work while in Paris. Daily life consisted of a round of parties, cafés, restaurants, and nightclubs. There was wine with lunch and dinner, and a bottle of cognac as a nightcap. The spring of 1947 was the couple's last season of moderate health. Arguments festered, friends abandoned them. Reeves stormed out one night, returning the following morning to find his wife unconscious on the floor. At the American hospital, partially paralyzed from a stroke, she was told that she could not drink again and survive. She agreed to take over Richard Wright's apartment for six months and settle down to write seriously. But soon both she and Reeves were re-hospitalized. They were flown home on 1 December 1947.

(249)   Site of the Salle Valentino. In June 1845, George Catlin opened his gallery of Indian portraits and fourteen Ioway Indians performed in tableaux vivants in this showroom. The French press described the Indians, Les Sauvages, as the most extraordinary sight ever seen in Paris. Although visitors included Victor Hugo, George Sand, and Baron Von Humboldt, few bought paintings, and within two months the show closed, leaving Catlin holding an expensive and lengthy lease.

Place Saint-Jacques (14th)

It was on this spot, named la barrière St.-Jacques, on the corner of Rue du Faubourg St.-Jacques and Boulevard St.-Jacques, that executions took place from 1832 until the end of the 19th century. Executions, although public until 1939, were carried out at dawn to prevent crowds. From 1830 to 1848 there were 558 such executions in Paris. The executioner and his aides gathered at Le Cabaret du

Bourreau on the corner of Rue de la Tombe-Issoire and Boulevard St.-Jacques. Occasionally special guests were invited to watch the slice of the guillotine. Early in the 19th century, Theodore B. Witmer made such a request and was delighted when several weeks later a special messenger appeared at his lodgings in the Hôtel Meurice begging his presence at an execution scheduled for the following morning:

Last night I received a very polite invitation from Monsieur Henri to be present this morning whilst he performed his duty upon some unfortunate victim, whose organ of destructiveness had led him to knock out the brains of one of his fellow creatures with a hammer.

Executions in Paris, considering the population, are quite rare, and always take place early in the morning, without any previous announcement. The criminal himself is only informed of the hour the night before. All this precaution is intended to prevent a crowd, and also to avoid whetting the appetite of the people with the sight of the Guillotine in play. It is generally erected after midnight, so that few, except those in the immediate neighborhood, can have time to congregate between daylight and the moment of execution.

Eight o'clock was the hour appointed, and we were advised to be there in season, as the government is very punctual in its performances. It was hardly daylight when we reached the Barrier of the Rue St. Jacques. We found but few persons there. A small body of mounted municipal guards formed the inner circle round the spot; immediately behind these were stationed some grenadiers; three or four paces apart. The majority of lookers-on appeared to be soldiers off duty, and the ubiquitous "gamins" of the Faubourg. We, as invited guests of the executioner, were conducted into the smaller circle, and placed only a few yards from the instrument of death. The platform of the guillotine had a railing, and was rather higher than I had expected, there being some eight or ten steps to mount, so that the execution may be seen some distance off. The guillotine itself is a very simple contrivance—nothing but two perpendicular shafts about eighteen inches apart, and some 15 or 20 feet high. Between them, near the top, the axe, or knife, is held suspended by a spring, which being touched, it descends rapidly along the grooves in the sides of the shafts. The axe is triangularly shaped, and leaded at the top, so as to run swiftly and forcibly. At the lower part of these shafts is a wooden collar to fit the neck. The victim stands erect, a short distance off, on a foot-board, which reaches up to his breast.

This board has straps attached for binding the party, in case he should prove unruly, and turns upon a pivot in the centre, so that the executioner merely raises up the lower end of the board—it immediately brings the man into a horizontal position, with his neck in the collar—the spring is at the same time touched and the knife falls—a box receives the head, and a log basket, which runs parallel with the victim, receives the trunk.

While we were awaiting the arrival of the principal personage in the drama, we overheard one of the guards giving an account of the execution of Fiesche, of "infernal machine" memory. I asked him how many executions he had witnessed. He did not recollect; but he said that he had seen eleven persons executed in fourteen minutes. At the time I could not credit this assertion, but I soon had evidence of the possibility of the fact. Early as it was, the crowd began to increase rapidly. They laughed and joked together as though it was a farce instead of a tragedy they were about to witness. There was quite a ludicrous dispute kept up for some time between the occupants of sundry trees, near the scene of action, and the "gens d'arms," who insisted on their vacating this leafy eminence. Plenty of witticisms were bandied about as these ragged climbers scrambled away from the points of the bayonets. Nothing can dampen a Frenchman's animal spirits.

The prisoner came in a close carriage with the executioner. He alighted, and paused a moment at the foot of the steps to speak to his confessor. He was a young man, stout, but small sized, and dressed in the blue "blouse" of a laborer. His face was pale as death, and his step somewhat unsteady. He had probably never seen the guillotine, for his eye ran over the instrument, and at last settled with a stare upon the glittering knife, which had just caught the first rays of the morning sun. There must have been one dreadful concentration of agony as that poor fellow's imagination shaped the fatal process. The mere sliver of the knife is nothing; but who can paint that one instant of consciousness as the first noise of its descent strikes his ear—before its cold edge passes with the crushing weight of eternity to its fearful goal. He had scarcely mounted the scaffold, and placed himself upon the foot-board, before the executioner had stripped him to the waist, and pushed him gently forward. His feet rose with the motion of the board, and there he lay, perfectly horizontal, with his face downwards and his neck in the collar. The knife came with a whizzing sound—the head jumped forward—the trunk quivered convulsively, but was instantly rolled into the basket, and every trace of that unfortunate man disappeared from sight, save the "gouts" of blood upon the knife!

I could scarcely believe my own eyes! Was it possible that life had been taken? But a moment since, I had seen that man step out of the carriage: and now he was gone—vanished—dead! It was the quickness of thought—hardly time for an emotion. His rapid transit from the carriage to his wicker coffin forbade even sympathy. He passed away like a shadow—almost too quick for the exercise of vision. No evidence of violence—no struggle—no torture—no apparent agony—no lifeless body—no distorted features, to brand their hideous impression upon the spectator. With the exception of a cold shiver as the heavy jar of the knife broke the painful silence, there was no other feeling produced in me during the execution, and that, too, was momentary. I had nerved myself for horror, and there was not enough to shock the most sensitive.

The guillotine—that name of terror, which had sounded the shame of France in every quarter of the globe—appeared to me the most humane of instruments. We all looked at each other as if there ought to be more: there was an unsated something, which almost amounted to a desire for another victim, as "if the appetite increased by what it fed upon." We could partly account for the calm indifference with which man after man was sent to the embrace of this infernal machine during the period of the first Revolution. There is a neatness—a despatch—a cold-blooded apathy about the whole affair—that deceives a man into the belief that all is mere machinery. It only wants the aid of steam to make it perfect. There is no realizing sense of violence—and one almost doubts whether the victim be a man of straw, or real flesh and blood. It would have sounded very natural to hear the crowd cry out—"Give us another! and let it be done slower so that we may see." I am by no means bloodthirsty, and yet I fear I should have joined in.

The executioner was a very benevolent looking individual, with a soft, sleepy eye, and a certain quiet, gentlemanly manner, that was quite insinuating. He handed the criminal up the platform with the polished grace of the ancient regime, and no doubt begged his pardon as he removed the poor fellow's cap.

After the execution, water was thrown upon the instrument. The head was thrown into the same basket with the trunk, and both handed over to the dissecting knife. I noticed two drummers stationed near the scaffold—intended, perhaps, to drown the voice of the party in case he should address the crowd. It was thus Henriot stopped Louis XVI, when he attempted to speak.

I afterward went to the Ecole Pratique to see the remains. The neck had been very smoothly severed, about the third vertebra. The expression of the face was remarkable: not the least trace of pain—not the slightest distortion of feature; but there was a settled sorrow—an intense sadness—about every line of that pallid visage. It had more the appearance of deep sleep than death—the sleep that follows mental exhaustion. We were satisfied that no muscular action could have taken place after the blow.

Rue Saint-Jacques (5th) Map E

171 At the end of this dismal alleyway there is a small courtyard, where little has changed since November 1858 when James McNeill Whistler stood next to the printer Delâtre to watch his first set of etchings run off. There were twelve prints in the series, which became known as the "French Set," some done in London, some in Paris, and the rest during a hiking trip along the Rhine.

269 Schola Cantorum. Cole Porter stayed on to study music here with the French composer Vincent d'Indy after serving with the American forces in France in World War I.

Rue Saint-Lazare (9th) Métro: St.-Lazare

108 La Gare St.-Lazare. For Americans arriving in Paris from the seaports of Cherbourg or Le Havre, this vast, gray, soot-laden, steam-filled railway station provided a sad gateway to the city of light. But for many this arrival was the realization of a long-awaited dream—to live in Paris.

One such dreamer was sculptor Jo Davidson. Aged 24, he arrived here in 1907 with 40 dollars in his pocket and a bundle of blankets on his back. (His mother had come to America as a refugee from Russia and never travelled without blankets.) Davidson was met by a friend and they sat down at a café just outside the station. It was 5:00 a.m. and Paris was not yet awake. The air was cold and filled with a pungent perfume from the rain falling on the tar and cedar-wood pavements peculiar to Paris in those days. But as Davidson recalled some 40 years later, during those first few moments, as he sipped a *vin blanc citron,* he felt that he was already "firmly installed in heaven."

It was here, in 1838, on the line from Saint-Germain-en-Laye, that Samuel Morse carried out his first telegraph experiments in France. Morse had originally come to Paris in 1829 as a painter. When he returned to America three years later on the French ship *Sully,* he watched messages being relayed by the semaphore and decided that it was too slow for Americans. Apparently it was at this time that he first had the idea for the telegraph. He discussed his idea with a fellow passenger, Dr. Charles Thomas Jackson, a physician and scientist from Boston who had been studying magnetism and electricity in Paris. Jackson later claimed to have first suggested the idea to Morse and a bitter lawsuit followed, which Morse won. Upon his return to France in 1838, Morse presented his system of telegraphy on 29 September to the Académie des Sciences, whose members included Gay-Lussac, Arago, and Baron Humboldt.

The first experiment in France with an Alexander Graham Bell telephone took place in 1878 at this station.

Rue Saint-Louis-en-l'Ile (4th) Map E

5   William Aspenwall Bradley, a writer and editor from New York, served in France in World War I, married a French woman, and settled down to translate leading French writers. Thanks to his experience in New York, he began to work as a literary agent and negotiated the sale of Gertrude Stein's *Autobiography of Alice B. Toklas* (1933) to Harcourt, Brace, while persuading the *Atlantic Monthly* to accept excerpts for serial publication. He recognized the importance of Henry Miller's *Tropic of Cancer* and advised Miller to see Jack Kahane at the Obelisk Press. He represented at various times Natalie Barney, Stephen Vincent Benét, Louis Bromfield, John Dos Passos, Katherine Anne Porter, Ezra Pound, Samuel Putnam, William L. Shirer, Edith Wharton, and Thornton Wilder. In her "Letter from Paris" in the *New Yorker* for 9 February 1929, Janet Flanner called Bradley the "leading agent and prophet here on transatlantic affairs."

31   Formerly Hôtel de Bourgogne. Ellsworth Kelly, 25, arrived in Paris in 1948. He was accepted in the Ecole des Beaux-Arts and lived off his GI Bill. The following year he took a large room at the

hotel "on a high floor" and made it his studio. He worked and lived here on and off until his return to America in July 1954. Kelly was a serious student, but was described as a loner and ill at ease in French. Thanks to Jack Youngerman, a fellow American in the Ecole des Beaux-Arts, he examined the works of the 74-year-old Brancusi in the Impasse Ronsin and saw some of Picasso's paintings and collages on Rue Christine. Kelly also met with Picabia, Alexander Calder, and Hans Arp. It was the reliefs of Arp and of the late Sophie Taeuber-Arp which encouraged Kelly to move away from the easel and into the making of objects. But it was primarily Picasso's outline paintings, such as *The Kitchen,* which led Kelly into abstraction and then relief. This influence may be seen in works such as *Window, Museum of Modern Art, and Paris* (1949). Kelly had slowly moved from narrative figurations known as Boston Expressionism (he had trained at the School of the Museum of Fine Arts in Boston) to the geometric abstractions of post-World War II France. When the GI Bill expired, Kelly needed money to survive and took a job teaching art at the American School in Paris. Here he tried to teach the sons and daughters of wealthy American executives living in Paris, none of them interested in painting. In the spring of 1951, he had his first one-man show at the Galerie Arnaud in Paris. News that he was an avant-garde artist reached the school and he was promptly fired. But that fall, four of his paintings were chosen for display in the Galerie Maeght. Kelly heard that one of the visitors—Georges Braque—had greatly admired his work. Kelly is one of few who was successful as a painter and sculptor, and in retrospect is the foremost figure in the last generation of American artists to have studied in Paris.

Rue Saint-Martin (3rd) Métro: Arts et Métiers

292 Le Conservatoire National des Arts et Métiers. This museum houses Robert Fulton's drawings and plans for his steamboat, submarine, and canal system. His treatise *Improvement of Canal Navigation* was translated into French and published in Paris in 1799. The French edition of his *Letters on Submarine Navigation* appeared in 1811, seven years after Fulton had returned to New York.

The museum has a superb collection of 19th-century American harvesting machines, which were displayed by the Deering Harvester Company of Chicago at the Universal Exhibition of 1900 in Paris. In addition, there is a model of the locomotive designed by

William Norris and presented to King Louis-Philippe in 1841. The locomotive ran on a model railroad in the gardens of the Tuileries. Americans have always been attracted to this collection because it appealed to their sense of practicality. As early as 1820, Ebenezer Smith Thomas was fascinated by the technical aspects of the conservatory and by the richness of the collection:

> The conservatory of the Arts was an immense building, filled with one of the most valuable museums in Europe. On the ground floor, the first objects that met my view, was the models of all the ploughs, from the days of the patriarchs, down to the time in which I saw them. Conspicuous in the front row, were Thomas' and Freeborne's American patents; they deserved to be there, for they far surpassed all others, in the immense collection, both in form and finish. There were also every kind of agricultural implements in great variety, together with a vast variety of mechanisms; among them a model of the machine of Marley, by which the water of the Seine was forced up seven hundred feet, through pipes of eight or nine inches diameter, laying on the surface of the ground. It was there received into a reservoir, from whence, by an aqueduct, it was taken to Versailles, for the use of the water works in the splendid gardens of the palace at that place; of which more hereafter. The workmanship as well as the mechanism of this machine, which was of brass and steel, attracted my particular attention, as being unsurpassed in finish and beauty, so very unlike some brass locks I had noticed a day or two before, on the inner doors of the palace of Condé, which would have got a boy a whipping, who had not been twelve months at the business, in Birmingham. In the second story, on a table some two or three hundred feet in length, was exhibited the models of all the vessels from Noah's Ark, to the then present time; or, at all events, from a Roman galley to a New York packet ship. In this immense collection were also displayed a sample of every kind of manufacture carried on in France. There were looms with webs of cloth of gold, of silver, of steel, and of brass; besides numerous specimens of manufacture in wool, cotton, flax, and hemp. To be brief, I consider this collection of the productions of the mechanical arts, from ancient down to modern times, as incomparably more useful than all the others I ever saw.

Boulevard Saint-Michel (5th) Maps D & E

38   Richard Wright rented a furnished apartment here in 1946. He sat and wrote "among the stuffed crocodiles" of a French professor who had gone to Australia for the year.

Café du Dôme, 1925.
Photo by André Kertész.
(See page 141.)

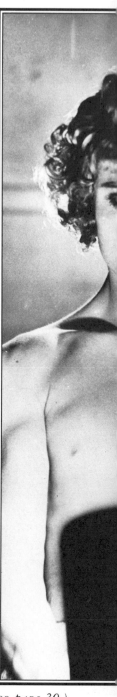

Left: Janet Flanner in the late 1920s. (See page 30.)
Center: Barbette by Man Ray, in the 1920s.
(See page 210.)

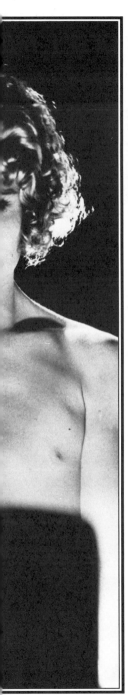
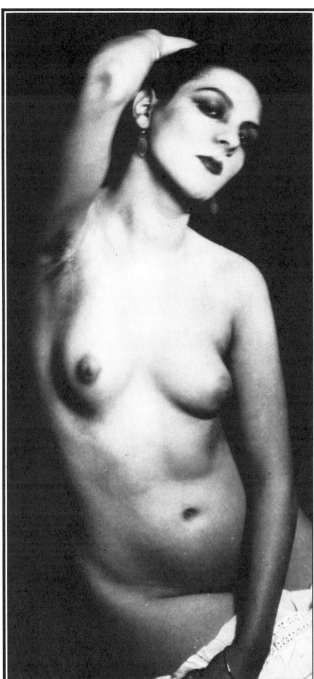

Right: Kiki of Montparnasse.
Photo by Man Ray, about 1922.
(See page 35.)

*Charles Lindbergh touched down at Le Bourget Airport
at 10:21 p.m. on 21 May 1927 after his nonstop flight from New Yor*
Here The Spirit of St. Louis *is being protected from the crowd.*

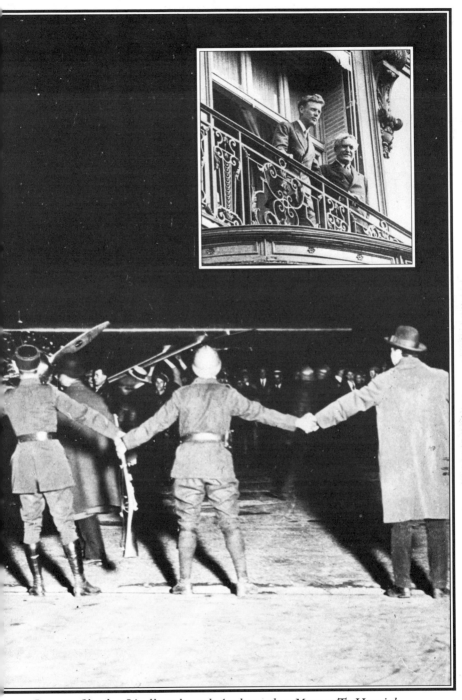

Insert: Charles Lindbergh and Ambassador Myron T. Herrick at the ambassador's residence on Avenue d'Iéna. Lindbergh is facing a sea of newspaper reporters and radio broadcasters. (See page 99.)

The French demonstrated their disapproval
of the planned execution of Sacco and Vanzetti
by protesting in the streets, summer 1927.

*Most of the American community in Paris
believed the men innocent.
(See page 140.)*

Armistice Day, 11 November 1944, on the Avenue des Champs-Elysées
Insert: General Dwight D. Eisenhower in Paris
immediately after the liberation, 1944.

Insert: Eisenhower and de Gaulle on the Champs-Elysées, 14 June 1945.
Overleaf: American troops
parading down the Champs-Elysées, spring 1945.

Buster Keaton in Paris,
about 1950.
(See page 210.)

Above: Sidney Bechet playing the saxophone in Club du Vieux-Colombier.
Claude Luter, in the center, is beating time. (See page 267.)
Below: Duke Ellington and Louis Armstrong, Paris 1960. (See page 77.)

President John F. Kennedy laying a wreath before the eternal flame under the Arc de Triomphe, June 1961.
(See page 164.)

President Charles de Gaulle greets
President and Mrs. John F. Kennedy at the Elysée Palace,
June 1961. (See page 164.)

John Steinbeck in Paris in 1962
after receiving the Nobel Prize.
(See page 126.)

93   Foyer International des Etudiantes. Sylvia Beach spent the years 1942–44 in a small kitchen on the top floor hiding from the Germans.

Place Saint-Sulpice (6th) Map **B**

L'Eglise St.-Sulpice. This church was begun in 1646 and was only partially finished in 1788 with the help of a lottery. Servandoni's design for the towers was judged inappropriate for his own facade, and the architect Maclaurin was commissioned to build two different towers. Both were in place by 1749. Few people were happy with this result, and the architect Chalgrin was commissioned to produce two new towers. He worked on the northern tower from 1777 to 1788 but was unable to begin work on the second tower. The result is scarcely harmonious.

John Trumbull, who visited this church in 1786, was an excellent critic of architecture. However, he made no comment on the two towers, imagining that under Chalgrin the church would finally be finished. In his *Journal* of Wednesday, 8 August, he recorded:

> Grecian architecture, but heavy, clumsy, and unpleasing; some pictures, but none of a high class; St. Jerome, in the first chapel on your right, as you enter the church, is a finely colored picture, but incorrect in the drawing, and there is a Nativity in a chapel near the choir, still on the right hand, which I could not approach near enough to see well, but it appeared to be a sweet thing, and over it was another small picture of three half figures; the Creator and two Angels adoring, which, at the distance from which I saw it, had a very good effect, and beautiful color.

During the Revolution the St. Jerome painting disappeared and the altar was destroyed except for the Chapel of the Virgin.

Charles Widor was organist at the church from 1869 until his retirement in 1934. He wrote a total of ten symphonies for organ. In 1891, he succeeded César Franck as professor of organ at the Paris Conservatory. Many Americans came to hear him, among them Consuelo Vanderbilt, the granddaughter of William H. Vanderbilt, who recalled as a young lady having listened to Widor play his Mass for Two Organs. She married a colonel in the French army and spent most of her life in France.

Rue Saint-Sulpice (6th) Map **B**

13 Hôtel de l'Odéon. In spring 1837, Dr. Willard Parker spent three months studying the latest surgical techniques in Paris. Thirty-seven, with a medical degree from Harvard, Parker had trained at Massachusetts General Hospital and had taught surgery. He watched operations in the Hôtel-Dieu, Hôpital de la Charité, Hôpital de la Pitié, and Hôpital Necker and met the leading French surgeons. He encountered no difficulties in visiting wards and sitting in on lectures at the Ecole de Médecine. From his *Journal,* we see that he visited the Paris sights, studied French, and worked hard.

People walked a lot in 19th-century France, and on Monday, 5 June 1837, setting out from the Place de l'Odéon, Parker must have easily covered twelve miles before getting back for his usual dinner with other American doctors and friends at 5:00 p.m. We can follow him by reading his *Journal* entry for that day:

> Monday—I rose at six—made my toilette and started for Charenton. It is about 2 leagues from Paris. The walk was very pleasant—up the Seine. Charenton is a village that in the time of Henry 4, Louis 13 & 14 was celebrated for its religious controversies. Now for its large Insane Establishment at the head of which is the old & distinguished Esquirol. The Hospital is in magnificent order and in an admirable situation— contains 500 inmates. This place is designed for the reception of hopeful cases only. The treatment is moral & a steady unrestrained occupation—On my return I passed over to Alfort to visit the veterinary school where are some 200 or 300 pupils. The establishment is spacious permanent and in a most perfect state of preservation.

Parker was a handsome man, over six feet tall, an admirer of the French medical system, and with time he became more tolerant of the French. He decided God had substituted gaiety for their "lack of virtue."

Rue des Saints-Pères (6th & 7th) Maps **A** & **B**

(39-45) Site of the Hôpital de la Charité, founded in 1606. The hospital was run by five brothers of the Order St.-Jean-de-Dieu, brought to Paris from Florence by Marie de Medici. The brothers had to be surgeons and apothecaries to work here. The hospital expanded over the years until a new entrance to the grounds was created at 45 Rue Jacob. By 1786 there were 208 beds, with but one patient allowed to a bed. Only men were treated and those suffering from incurable or venereal diseases were excluded. The hospital was considered the best run in Paris, with ample space in the wards between the beds, and gardens to walk in.

By 1824, when Samuel Goodrich visited the wards, women were admitted, and there were 426 beds and a clinical school. Goodrich was fortunate to see Laennec, the inventor of the stethoscope, making rounds. On 21 February 1824, Goodrich recorded in his *Journal:*

> Went to the Hospital of La Charité. Saw Laennec, with his pupils, visiting the patients. He makes great use of the stethoscope, which is a wooden tube applied to the body, and put to the ear: by the sound, the state of the lungs and the vital organs is ascertained. It is like a telescope, by which the interior of the body is perceived, only that the ear is used instead of the eye. It is deemed a great improvement. Laennec is the inventor, and has high reputation in the treatment of diseases of the chest. He has learned to ascertain the condition of the lungs by thumping on the breast and back of the patient, and putting the ear to the body at the same time. He is a little man, five feet three inches high, and thin as a shadow. However, he has acute features, and a manner which bespeaks energy and consciousness of power.
>
> The whole hospital was neat and clean; bedsteads of iron. French medical practice very light; few medicines given; nursing is a great part of the treatment. Laennec's pupils follow him from patient to patient. He conversed with them in Latin. One of the patients was a handsome, black-eyed girl, not very sick. All the young men must apply the stethoscope to her chest; she smiled, and seemed to think it all right.

On Tuesday, 11 April 1837, Dr. Willard Parker, who had arrived in Paris the previous day, walked down from his hotel on Rue St.-Sulpice to begin his observation of French medical practices. In his *Journal* he recorded:

> Went to the Hospital de la Charité. One of the mighty concentrations of disease. I saw Bouillaud, famous for his investigations of the heart; Fauquier, famous for diseases of the Kidneys. Saw Velpeau in the ward & then cut out a breast. He is a man of great learning, not otherwise remarkable. Came home at 11, breakfasted. Engaged French instructor. At 2 P.M. visited the great occulist, Sichel, German, saw very many cases.

Jean-Baptiste Bouillard was a famous diagnostician and known for the practice of bloodletting. He pointed out the connection between aphasia and a lesion in the anterior lobes of the brain and called attention to the relation between heart disease and rheumatism. Alfred Armand Louis Marie Velpeau was a professor of clinical surgery. He wrote a three-volume work on operative surgery in 1832, which was edited in translation by the well-known American surgeon Valentine Mott.

By the end of his first week in Paris, Dr. Willard Parker confided in his *Journal:* "These French are strange people, light, frivolous, gay, under the full influence of the Catholic Religion." By the end of April, Parker was beginning to discern a few French qualities. His *Journal* noted:

> Sunday. This makes another day I have spent of the Lord in this city. No one can conceive of the habits & peculiarities of the French People. They are economical, never drunk and not quarrelsome but for the light and gay amusements they cannot be surpassed and probably are not equalled. This morning visited the La Charité. On my return from that I visited a Church, induced to do it from seeing a coffin carried to it. Strange what ideas these people have.
>
> 1. The coffin is covered by a black pall, lights burning upon coffin & a cross with Christ. The coffin was exposed at the Door of the House. Every one that passes the dead must raise his hat as he passes. "The Drivers" are men of Function with a chapeau bras & trimmings. After this the coffin was carried to the church. It was exorcised then was brought in another of young woman unmarried, hence white pall & a chaplet of white roses upon it. We came home. Breakfasted *(café au lait)* we then, Friend St. John & Myself, concluded we would go out that we might see these people on Sunday. We passed to the Bank of the Seine and passed down the River by the Palais du Roi Romain, the Chamber of Deputies. Palais de Bourbon, Hotel des Invalids & the Champs de Mars. This is a grand open field where military Parades are now held, here Louis 16th held the great fete in 1790, here Napoleon held his Review previous to the Battle of Waterloo. It is a Parallelogram—4 rows of Trees on East & West side. North is the Ecole Military, the Field is for Mil'y. Here this day were horse races, several Thousand people were assembled. Everything arranged in ample order. Many of the Nobility were present, their carriages in Royal equipage. Saw 3 Races, the 2nd was foil'd, the Horse Fell, threw the Rider & injured him some. From this place we crossed the River by the Bridge of Iena, ascended a mound & had a

magnificent view of the City. We visited the Triumphal Arch of Napoleon 150 ft. high, marble, much good sculpturing upon it (vid. Galignani). From this spot we came through the Champs Elysees & of all the sights for Sunday. Hosts of people. Theatrical exhibitions of all kinds mostly however low. Flying horses ships, Wheel swings, shooting Billiards, all kinds of games. Booths etc. etc. Music & a girl say 20 in Peasant's dress upon the back of Jill. Astride. She had a basket in her hand and was holding forth to the multitudes! Every other man is a soldier or an officer and in this way is order kept. I am inclined to believe that the Roman Catholic Religion is no Religion.

Dr. Parker returned to New York City in summer 1837 and was appointed professor of surgery at the College of Physicians and Surgeons, a position he held until 1859. The Willard Parker Hospital for Infectious Diseases was named for him.

52 Hôtel de Cavoie. This *hôtel particulier,* built in 1640, was first occupied by Jean de Groots, the Swedish minister to France. Duchesse de Villers-Brancas bought the *hôtel* in 1658 and later it was owned by the Marquis de Cavoie, who had shared tutors with the future Louis XIV. After a series of owners, it was virtually abandoned at the beginning of this century.

From 1920 to 1929, when the French franc was weak against the dollar, wealthy Americans purchased French *hôtels particuliers* and lovingly renovated them. Mrs. Henry Symes Lehr (née Elizabeth Drexel) bought this property in 1923 and meticulously restored it. The Hôtel de Cavoie passed from the Drexel family in 1980 to French owners, who are continuing the restoration.

59 Hôtel du Pas-de-Calais. Ezra Pound moved to this hotel in May 1921. He called it his "roost" and spent the summer here before moving to an apartment with his wife on Rue Notre-Dame-des-Champs. Scofield Thayer, coowner and editor of the *Dial,* described the 36-year-old poet as having "a pointed yellow beard and an elliptical pince-nez and open Byronic collar and an omelette-yellow bath robe." Pound had been a contributing editor to the *Dial* and to the *Little Review.* But the hard times which he had known in London somehow followed him to Paris. As he explained to his good friend Ford Madox Ford:

Deer Foord:

In viewwww of the fffffacts that: the *Dial* has finally sacked me; and the *Little Review* has been most noble in getting

suppressed for Joyce, even unto the nth time; we are making the
L.R. a quarterly, and I am bringing out a special summer number.

The quarterly was to contain twenty photos of "Brancusi's stuff,"
Cocteau's "Cap de Bonne Espérance," and contributions by Picabia,
Wyndham Lewis, and Picasso. But Pound went on to assure Ford
that the *Little Review* was to remain "American." Pound enjoyed
Paris. "Bloody fools," he wrote, were "less in one's way" than in
London. His new interests were modern sculpture and modern
music. He was busy blue-pencilling Eliot's poems and urging him to
come to Paris. In August, he asked Ford: "Will any bleeding son of a
whore's behind publish a book by me on Brancusi (the beautiful
genius)?"

64   Formerly Hôtel du Bon Lafontaine. While staying here in
1892, James McNeill Whistler did a lithograph of Mallarmé which
appeared as a frontispiece in his *Vers et Prose* the following year.
The two corresponded over the years.

65   Hôtel des Saints-Pères. Edna St. Vincent Millay was 29
when she stayed here upon her arrival in Paris in January 1921. A
Vassar graduate, she had won recognition with her first book
Renascence and Other Poems. She had a contract with *Vanity Fair*
for two articles a month, but she refused to sign them with her real
name, as she wished to be known as a serious poet. She had been
anxious to leave New York, as her many suitors, including Edmund
Wilson (who wanted to marry her), left her little time to be alone
and write poetry, or so she imagined. She felt at home in Paris,
telling her sister, "I go out nearly every afternoon & walk miles &
miles. It is so fascinating, when I once get started, that I can't stop."
As she commented at the end of her letter: "It is beautiful here even
now. What will the spring be?" Most of her energy went into
completing a five-act verse play, *The Lamp and the Bell,* for Vassar
College. She lived here for some three months before moving to Rue
de l'Université.

Rue de la Santé (14th) Métro: St.-Jacques

La Prison de la Santé. It was a warm summer evening in July 1929
when the author of *White Buildings,* 30-year-old poet Hart Crane,
left a group of friends at the Closerie des Lilas, strolled along
Boulevard du Montparnasse, and took a seat at the terrace of the

Café Sélect. He was in the throes of writing a major poem in which the Brooklyn Bridge served as a mystical and unifying symbol of civilization's evolution. Columbus, Pocahontas, Rip Van Winkle, Poe, Whitman, and the subway were a part of this great American experience. Crane, alone, sat and drank. When it came time to pay the bill, he announced that he had no money. The manager, Madame Sélect as she was called by Americans, told a waiter to throw him out. Crane resisted, and when the gendarmes arrived, he promptly floored the first one, to the great admiration of his fellow drinkers. Beaten to the ground, he was dragged away feet first and taken to the Prison de la Santé. He was held incommunicado for one week until writers on the Paris *Herald Tribune* forced the French authorities to try him. He was fined 800 francs and given an eight-day suspended sentence. Discharged from the prison at 8:00 p.m., he was handed over to Harry Crosby and Whit Burnett of the *Herald Tribune*. Crane was unshaven, ravenously hungry, and as an alcoholic, anxious for a drink. His two friends took him across the street to the bar "à la Bonne Santé" before going on to the Chicago Inn for a meal of cornbread and poached eggs on toast. A few weeks later, Crane left for New York, where he finished *The Bridge* (1930).

Villa Santos-Dumont (15th) Métro: Convention

25   At the end of this charming, unpaved, 19th-century alleyway in the middle of 20th-century Paris stands the three-story house of sculptress Malvina Hoffman. She bought a vacant plot of land here in 1927 and designed her own house, which was completed the following summer. On the third floor you can see her studio with the windows in the roof. For ten years Hoffman worked hard, frequently modeling the neighbors—including *Bill Working* (Musée du Jeu de Paume, Paris). She left for America just before World War II, and when she returned in 1948, after an absence of ten years, she found the garden overgrown, but the house, which had stood empty, in perfect condition. One of her first visitors was Father Teilhard de Chardin, whose bust she modelled. It was purchased by the French Ministry of Beaux-Arts and is in the Musée d'Art Contemporain in Paris. She also did the War Memorial for the large American military cemetery in Epinal, in the Vosges. She sold the house in 1961, after almost a half-century of association with France.

Rue Scribe (9th) Map F

1   Hôtel Scribe. This hotel served as press headquarters for the Allied Forces from August 1944 until late fall of the following year. An elaborate overseas cable system was installed for reporting Allied victories. Censorship officers worked on the second floor. Those newspaper correspondents who could not find a room came by the hotel to take the only hot bath available in Paris that winter. One correspondent who did get a room at the Scribe was 49-year-old John Dos Passos. The enthusiasm for the early years he'd spent in Paris at the close of World War I was gone. On 12 October 1945 he wrote:

> Here in people's faces, in the papers, in the advertising of plays and concerts you get the feeling that it's just *plus ça change plus c'est la même chose* only drearier and deadlier.... Just saw a rather bad film about François Villon—but at least it had none of the Hollywood moral turpitude. It was gotten up by people who had some notion of human decency.... Went to a press conference to see what De Gaulle looks like. He's not quite so tall as his pictures show...he talks remarkably well in a rather professorial manner—he has two voices the Sorbonne voice and the *père de famille* Henry Quatre—bonne soupe kind of voice—There's more to him than we had been led to believe I think.

2   Le Grand Hôtel. The Grand Hôtel opened in 1860. Its luxury ushered in a new era in international travel. In July 1866, Reverend Phillips Brooks, who would become famous as the minister of Trinity Church, Boston, stayed here. He wrote the not very immortal phrase, "to see this epitome of all Europe and of all the world, the cosmopolitan city, sparkling, beautiful Paris."

Henry James spent November and December 1882 at this hotel. After travelling through France and taking notes for *A Little Tour in France* (1885), he was delighted to discover as fellow guests two American friends, John Hay and Clarence King. Hay, a journalist and author and former assistant to Abraham Lincoln, was the American ambassador to Great Britain under presidents McKinley and Roosevelt. King also published a series of popular sketches entitled *Mountaining in the Sierra Nevada*. Henry James wrote of King: "He is a delightful creature and is selling silver mines and buying water colours." James spent an hour with his friend

Turgenev, who had moved from Paris to Bougival. The Russian author was ill with an undiagnosed cancer from which he would die a few months later.

Rue de Seine (6th) Map **A**

31   Akademia Raymond Duncan. Raymond Duncan, brother of Isadora Duncan, taught Greek philosophy, lectured on ancient Greece, showed his disciples how to make sandals, weave rugs, print pamphlets, and paint posters. Shod in sandals, covered with a toga, and crowned in laurels, this self-appointed prophet, poet, and vegetarian ran a series of commercial enterprises in Paris and Nice.

52   Hôtel de Seine. Lawrence Ferlinghetti, poet and owner of the City Lights Bookshop in San Francisco, stayed here in June 1963 and revisited his old haunts.

Rue Servandoni (6th) Map **B**

26   Grand Hôtel des Principautés Unies. William Faulkner arrived in France in summer of 1925. At 28 he had already published *The Marble Faun,* a collection of poems. On 18 August, he took a room on the top floor. He wrote to his mother: "I have a nice room just around the corner from the Luxembourg gardens, where I can sit and write and watch the children. Everything in the garden is for children—its beautiful the way the French love their babies." He was working on *Mosquitoes* (1927), a satirical novel set in New Orleans. He made no attempt to join the American literary group, never called on Gertrude Stein, and never met Sylvia Beach, although he visited Shakespeare and Company. He returned to America in December 1925. Four years later, *The Sound and the Fury* was published, followed by *As I Lay Dying.*

Rue de Sèvres (7th)

(84-88)   At the suggestion of Michael and Sarah Stein, it was here in an atelier of the Couvent des Oiseaux that Matisse opened his academy early in 1908. His American students included Sarah Stein, Max Weber, Patrick Henry Bruce, Morgan Russell, and Arthur B. Frost. There was no program. Matisse came on Saturday mornings and commented on the week's work. According to American painter Maurice Sterne, who was not a student here but who accompanied Matisse on his first Saturday morning visit, they found a series of large paintings with tormented forms splashed with loud colors. Matisse was appalled. He left the atelier and returned after a few moments with a plaster model of a Greek head. He set it on a stand and told his students that they should begin with antiquity. He then took them to the Louvre to see Poussin and Chardin. He insisted that they start with the conventional, master the traditional form, and then they could perhaps hope to begin experimenting with the bold distortion of form and exuberant colors which characterized Fauvism. The convent was closed in summer 1908, and the Matisse Academy moved to the Boulevard des Invalides.

Place de la Sorbonne (5th) Map E

La Sorbonne. John Trumbull came to Paris in 1786 at the invitation of Thomas Jefferson. He kept a careful *Journal,* and, on Friday, 10 August, he visited the Church of the Sorbonne. The church had been rebuilt by Jacques Lemercier in the middle of the 17th century for Cardinal Richelieu.

> Friday, August 10th. Went to the Sorbonne. The church is very good architecture; no paintings worthy of much notice. The monument of Cardinal Richelieu is finely conceived and executed; the figure of Science weeping at his feet, is, of all the marble I ever saw, the most expressive; it is the only thing of this kind which ever forced an involuntary tear from my eye—such dignity of sorrow, yet so simple and unaffected, so directly addressed to all the tender feelings, that the heart which does not melt before it, must be harder and more cold than the marble. In one of the halls for disputation is a whole length portrait of the Cardinal, very finely painted, and worthy of Vandyck; this hall contains many other pictures, unworthy to be remembered. Here, two learned young men were carrying on a most edifying theological dispute in Latin, upon the merits of Judas and the degree of his sins, before two grave doctors, who sat wisely nodding over their theses, and a most attentive audience, consisting of one young man.

On Wednesday, 26 May 1909, Andrew Carnegie was guest of honor at a luncheon given by the rector Dr. Liard. Carnegie had already given an annual subsidy for research in radioactivity. On this occasion he announced a gift of one million dollars for a fund to reward "authors of heroic acts."

The arctic explorer and discoverer of the North Pole Robert Edwin Peary gave a talk about his travels in the polar regions on Friday evening, 6 June 1913.

1   Hôtel Sélect. Eric Sevareid took a room here in fall 1937 for 50 cents a day, which included breakfast. Sevareid, 25, went to work for the Paris *Herald,* but the carefree life was overshadowed by the rumblings from Nazi Germany. Sevareid interviewed Gertrude Stein in her apartment on Rue de Fleurus. She assured her young listener: "Hitler will never really go to war. He is not the dangerous one. You see, he is the German romanticist. He wants the illusion of victory and power, the glory and glamour of it, but he could not stand the blood and fighting involved in getting it. No, Mussolini— there's the dangerous man."

Rue Stanislas (6th) Map D

6   Known as the Passage Stanislas. It was in these two small houses that the Académie Whistler opened in 1898, under the guidance of Madame Carmen Rossi. When James McNeill Whistler first visited the academy which he had financed, he was shocked to discover men and women students together painting a nude model. The students were then separated. Whistler came by once a week to give guidance, but quickly tired of his new school, which closed three years later.

Rue Taitbout (9th)   Métro: Chaussée d'Antin

(24)   In 1823, Samuel Welles and family moved to this mansion, which had belonged to Talleyrand. Welles headed the Paris branch of the Boston banking firm Welles & Co., the most prominent international banking firm of the day. Washington Irving was frequently a guest here, and Americans such as James Fenimore Cooper used the Welles bank as a Paris mailing address.

The American financial panic of 1837, brought on by irresponsible financial operations in western lands and by President Andrew

Jackson's suppression of the Bank of the United States, took but four or five weeks to reach Europe. Many Americans would have been stranded but for the immediate intervention of the Banque de France, which saved Welles & Co. from going under. Fears of Americans abroad were reflected in Dr. Willard Parker's *Journal* for 10 June 1837:

> Vendredi. I have heard again that my Banker has failed. If so, what is to be done? In a Foreign Land and no funds.

The next day's entry read:

> Samedi. This morning I was in much trepidation from learning last evening that Welles & Co. has stopped payments. If so I was "done up." Early I called upon him and found all well. The Bank of France has aided him and his.

Although Dr. Willard Parker never hesitated to comment on the frivolity of the French, nowhere in his *Journal* does he bother to show the slightest degree of gratitude for the promptness of the French intervention. That the French acted to protect their own interests is obvious, but the first beneficiaries were the Americans in Paris.

74   William Saroyan lived at number 74 from November 1960 until the following summer. In his autobiographical *Here Comes, There Goes, You Know Who,* he describes his apartment here on the fifth floor at length.

Porte des Ternes (17th)

One of the most popular Americans in France during the 19th century was the Honorable William Frederick Cody, known as Buffalo Bill. Buffalo Bill's Wild West Show camped here for seven months during the great Universal Exhibition of 1889. The site was 30 acres just outside the city walls and fortifications, crossed today by the Boulevard Pershing. Huge canvas backdrops depicting the wilds of Wyoming and Montana were hung from the fortifications, which also served as a fort and a last outpost.

The advertisements announced that new incandescent lamps by one Thomas Edison made "night as light as day" for evening performances. The show opened on the evening of 18 May, before French president Sadi Carnot and his ministers, Isabella II, the former queen of Spain, Gustave-Alexandre Eiffel, and a public of

20,000. Other guests included Thomas Edison himself, who filmed the show, and the Prince of Wales, who rode in the Deadwood coach. On this special occasion the American master of ceremonies (from Arizona) spoke in French, which the newspaper *Le Temps* (20 May) described as "incomprehensible." But everyone understood the show with the rough riders, calf roping, gun spinning, bareback riding, scouts, covered wagons, Indian warriors, squaws, stage coaches, outriders, cowboys, buffaloes, and horses. The French thrilled to General Custer's Last Stand, the Great Train Holdup, the Bronco Buster's Busy Day, and the attack on the lone Pioneer house. The most popular star of all was Annie Oakley, "little sure shot" or "dead-shot Annie," as she was called. No Frenchman had ever imagined that a woman could handle a gun, let alone shoot accurately.

That summer western style became the rage in Paris: Indian dresses, cowboy hats, boots, western shirts, saddles. No respectable Frenchman could ride in the Bois de Boulogne without his lasso. French aristocracy competed for the honor of sitting on a log next to Buffalo Bill at breakfast.

Thomas Edison, thoroughly tired of endless French banquets, joined Chauncey Depew, president of the New York Central Railroad, Whitelaw Reid, the American ambassador to France, and Buffalo Bill for a dinner of "things American." There was apple pie, Boston baked beans, peanuts, and, of course, a massive rib roast, washed down by American coffee and a swig from a hip flask—as the sun set in the golden west over Normandy.

A French anthropologist spent the summer here observing the Indians, their mores, the texture of their hair, the color of their skin. Crowds of French boys stood around all day, all summer, in hope of seeing a real cowboy or a real Indian. French painter Rosa Bonheur did a series of portraits of Indians, horses, and buffaloes (*The Horse Fair*, Metropolitan Museum of Art, New York). Her oil painting of Buffalo Bill on his favorite horse is in the Buffalo Bill Museum in Cody, Wyoming.

When the American hero died in Denver in 1911, French newspapers devoted entire pages to his life story.

Place du Tertre (18th) Métro: Anvers

In August 1918, at the tender age of 24, John Dos Passos recorded: "I shall send my heart to be preserved in a pichet of Vin de Beaujolais in the restaurant in the place du Tertre on the summit of Montmartre."

Rue de Tilsitt (8th) Map G

12 Francis Jacques (Harvard 1903) arrived in Paris early in March 1915 to work with the American Distribution Service, which aided the families of French servicemen. In a letter to his family, he described a German air raid on Paris:

> Paris, March 22, 1915
>
> Saturday night, or rather early Sunday morning, the Germans treated us to the long-expected spectacle of a Zeppelin raid on Paris. They hoped without doubt to strike terror to the hearts of the population of Paris.... They only succeeded in treating the city to a most interesting spectacle, and in making everyone feel that one had not been waked for nothing.
>
> Four Zeppelins started for Paris; two were headed off, and two flew over the northwestern part of the city. I was sleeping peacefully in my small apartment near the Etoile, when I was awakened by the firing of cannon, about 2 a.m. I stumbled out of bed, trying to make out whether I was in Dunkerque, or Calais; and finally waked up enough to realize that I was in Paris, and that the Zeppelins must be coming at last. I went out on my balcony, which commands a view over the house-tops in every direction, except the southeast, and saw the shells from the French guns describing great arcs across the sky, passing over my house. I could see nothing in the way of Zeppelins, and so went in again and dressed, and then took up my position at the corner of my balcony, where I could see the whole sky. It was a wonderful, starry, cold, clear night. Search-lights were playing about the heavens in every direction searching the skies, and below in the streets I could hear the *pompiers* [firemen] in their automobiles, rushing through the city, warning people by their "honk-honk," and their bugle calls of *garde à vous* [alert] to seek refuge in the cellars. It was good advice; but Paris was out to see a Zeppelin, and the balconies had as many people as the cellars.
>
> As I was watching a great beam of light to the northwest playing up and down, I suddenly saw something bright, like a white moth, shine out in the path of light; the search-light swept up again, and there it was like a long, white cigar in the sky. At last I was looking at a Zeppelin—Paris had not been waked up in vain. I could not have been better placed to see it. On it came towards the Etoile, always followed by the great search-light. It looked like

a white Japanese lantern, lighted up inside, with the light shining through the paper. Of course it carried no lights; but the search-light gave it that effect. The light seemed to play along its sides in ripples as on the water. When about one thousand yards from where I was, it gradually swung round broadside and started off to the east over the northern part of the city.

In the meantime the French cannon were firing away at it. Some shells were coming from my left near the Bois, others passing over my head from behind, and others from the Arc de Triomphe to my right. It was a wonderful sight, as the shells—like great round red balls of fire—described their arcs against the starry sky. I could follow each shell, and involuntarily, I found myself saying "Pas assez loin." [Not far enough.] "Trop à gauche." [Too far to the left.] As though I were at some kind of a tremendous big game-hunt. At all the balconies, I could hear the same remarks, as each one followed the course of each shell with passionate interest. I could distinctly see the two passenger-baskets under the balloon part of the Zeppelin. Suddenly, just as the shells began to fall near the Zeppelin, it disappeared out of the beam of light, and that was the last I saw of it, while over the city we could distinctly hear the roar of the motors, like a train of cars in the distance.

About 5 a.m. the *pompiers* went about to let people know that all the Zeppelins had gone off. I am sorry that they did not bring at least one of them down to earth to put with the other trophies at the Invalides. Of course, the shots fired at them while there over the city were more to drive them off, than to bring them down, as it would have been dangerous to have brought down a "160 metres" Zeppelin on the roofs.

14   Scott and Zelda Fitzgerald lived in an apartment here on the fifth floor from 22 April 1925 until the end of the year. The previous year they had come to France, where Zelda felt that they could "live on practically nothing a year." However, a year in the south of France had been expensive, and upon their arrival in Paris Fitzgerald owed 6,200 dollars to Scribner's. His royalties from 1920 to 1924 totalled 113,000 dollars, and this did not include income from what he called his "trash" articles for magazines. *The Great Gatsby* received excellent reviews and by October had sold over 20,000 copies. The sales neither matched Fitzgerald's expectations nor his expenditures. He was at the height of his fame and had already produced his best work. Later, he described the summer of 1925 as one of "1,000 parties and no work." He was now drunk for

periods of a week or more. Toward midnight, he would show up at the offices of the *Chicago Tribune* on Rue Lamartine. Staggering into the newsroom, he would shout out: "Come on, boys. Let's get out the goddam paper." William L. Shirer recorded how difficult it was to get Fitzgerald out of the office and back home to the Rue de Tilsitt. After he was guided into the street, Fitzgerald would insist on visiting a few bars until he passed out. Shirer and James Thurber shoved Fitzgerald into a taxi and sat on him while they drove to 14 Rue de Tilsitt. Half a century later, Shirer would record: "From an upper story a woman appeared at a window and shouted, 'Scott, you bastard! You're drunk again!'" Her husband replied: "'Zelda, darling... Yuh... Yuh... re... wrong... dead wrong... I... I'm as sober, darling... really... I am... as... as... a... polar bear.'"

Rue de la Tombe-Issoire (14th) Métro: St.-Jacques

100   Villa Seurat is a private cul-de-sac some 100 yards long, which joins Rue de la Tombe-Issoire on the east side of the street near number 100. The houses along this short street, which was opened in 1926, were built for sculptors and artists. Number 7 bis was designed by Auguste Perret, who also designed the Théâtre des Champs-Elysées. Numbers 1, 3, 4, 8, 9, and 11 were designed by André Lursat. Soutine and Georges Seurat lived and worked here.

House number 18 of Villa Seurat was owned by Michael Fraenkel. As a young man he had arrived in New York from Russia, and by 1926 had made enough money selling books so that at 30 he was able to retire to Paris, where he hoped to become a writer. In 1931, he met Henry Miller, who was penniless, and Fraenkel allowed him to live here for a few months rent-free. Miller cast him as Boris in *Tropic of Cancer.* Villa Seurat was sufficiently removed from the hubbub of Montparnasse to give Miller the peace he needed to write. Miller felt at home at the villa, which symbolized for him the richness of Paris:

> The whole street is given up to quiet, joyous work. Every house contains a writer, painter, musician, sculptor, dancer, or actor. It is such a quiet street and yet there is such activity going on, silently, becomingly, should I not say reverently too? This is how it is on my street, but there are hundreds of such streets in Paris. There is a constant army of artists at work, the largest of any city in the world. This is what makes Paris, this vast group of men and women devoted to the things of the spirit. This is what animates the city, makes it the magnet of the cultural world.

On 1 September 1934, the day that *Tropic of Cancer* appeared, well-to-do writer Anaïs Nin rented the top-floor apartment at number 18 for Miller. "Interesting conjuncture," wrote Miller later, "when one knows the importance of this book and of the Villa Seurat in my life." In December, well-known French writer Blaise Cendrars began his review of Miller's book with the statement "Unto us is born an American writer." In 1925, Miller started a correspondence with Lawrence Durrell, who would soon be a frequent visitor here. At the end of 1937 Miller became editor of the Villa Seurat series, an adjunct of the Obelisk Press run by Jack Kahane. During the next two years, three books appeared: Miller's *Max and the White Phagocytes, The Black Book* by Lawrence Durrell, and *Winter of Artifice* by Anaïs Nin. Miller left the Villa Seurat to visit Durrell in Greece in July 1939. With the coming of war, he returned to America. Many years later he wrote that his years in Paris were the happiest, and those in the Villa Seurat, the most serene.

Quai de la Tournelle (5th) Map E

45   In spring 1919 John Dos Passos took over the apartment of a friend, playwright John Howard Lawson. Dos Passos had served in the American Ambulance Corps and was taking his discharge in France, thus waiving his right to transportation back home. He was about to begin work on what was to be his first successful novel, *Three Soldiers* (1921). As the following letter shows, the war was over, and the prospect of demobilization, combined with spring-time, was almost too much for 23-year-old Dos Passos:

> Frankly—I, though I may seem a rather solemn serious bespectacled person, though I am a registered and accepted candidate for a doctorat at the University of Paris, though I am head and shoulders deep in dusty tomes on dry dead dusty divinities, I—am going crazy, spring-struck, moon-struck...I feel like an entire pompeian frieze of little red naked people dancing, I feel like a room full of orgiastic and rather indecent Greek vases. I feel like an election parade that's forgotten the names of the candidates. I feel as a horse chestnut tree in bloom would feel if everyone of the little mouths that form the tiers of the white pagodas of the flowers should start singing the Internationale in falsetto voices.
>
> I feel like standing on my head on top of a taxi-cab, like making a proposal of marriage to eighteen elderly spinsters, like

jumping into the Seine. I probably have suddenly and accidentally become an incarnation of Dionysus by some crossing of the celestial wires of fate. This morning I sat down in a barber chair to have my hair cut and the chair fell to pieces under the mightiness of my sitting. At any moment I expect the fourteen volumes in dark green cloth of Mr. Frazer to turn into maenads, arms stained to the elbows with wine, or the chair to start singing like a lark, or the roof of the house to open like the corolla of a flower, or the gutters of the Quai de la Tournelle to run ~~amythest~~ amethysts— How d'you spell them?

And all this caused by six fine days and the prospect of demobilization.

In spring 1921, after hiking through the Pyrenees with E.E. Cummings, Dos Passos again took over Lawson's rooms to work on the last chapters of *Rosinante to the Road Again,* which was published the following year.

Rue de Tournon (6th) Map **B**

19   John Paul Jones took a room here on the second floor in May 1790 and died here almost penniless on 18 July 1792. After the War of Independence, he had been sent back to France to collect prize money due the United States. With the coming of the French Revolution, this became impossible, and Jones, frequently ill, lonely, and bitter over his treatment by Congress, remained in Paris, where at least he was recognized as a hero. But as Emerson once observed, "Every hero becomes a bore at last." The American minister in Paris, the conservative Gouverneur Morris, observed on 14 November 1790: "Paul Jones calls on me. He has nothing to say but is so kind as to bestow on me all the Hours which hang heavy in his Hands." Morris saw Jones in his final hours and recorded his will. The American minister gave instructions that Jones be buried as cheaply as possible. When the French National Assembly learned of this economy, it was outraged that a hero of the American Revolution, a man who symbolized the cooperation between the two countries, should be treated so shabbily. It ordered a national funeral with full honors. The cortège assembled here in the late afternoon of 20 July, headed by a detachment of grenadiers and a hearse, followed by carriages bearing the members of the French Assemblée Legislative. An official delegation of Jones's fellow masons from the Lodge of the Nine Sisters accompanied by Colonel Samuel Blackden of South Carolina brought up the rear. Gouverneur

Morris did not attend as he had a dinner appointment that evening. Jones was buried in the Protestant cemetery outside the city gates. His body was placed in alcohol in a sealed lead coffin, paid for by the French, in the belief that one day America would recognize its debt to Jones.

20   Novelist Booth Tarkington, from Indiana, lived at this address from 1905 to 1908. Here he wrote *The Guest of Quesnay.* He had already written *The Gentleman from Indiana* (1899). A few years after leaving this address, he wrote to a friend about Rue de Tournon. His letter exemplifies the wonder that many Americans feel about the richness of the history of Paris.

> It was the top number of that wonderful little street. No one could live long enough to get all its story, from the time when the Luxembourg was a Roman camp, Molière played where Foyot's is now. From the Rue de Tournon Daudet went out in his overcoatless dress suit. Renan lived there. Balzac lives there. Just around the corner were the haunts of Aramis and Company. The old streets of the Musketeers are there yet, with most of the names, at least, unchanged since young D'Artagnan found himself in that row over the baldric of Porthos, the handkerchief of Aramis, and the shoulder of Athos... I dined often at Foyot's and found there a waiter whom I put into "The Guest of Quesnay" transferring him to the "Trois Pigeons," and calling him Amédée... Ah! the Rue de Tournon! I still haunt that neighborhood in my thoughts of Paris, but the last time I saw it was in 1911, when I went to that corner and looked up at the stone balcony that used to be mine and wondered who was living there.

Until the building at number 33 was torn down in 1938, it housed a very popular restaurant first opened in 1848 by Louis-Philippe's chef Foyot.

Place du Trocadéro (16th) Métro: Trocadéro

Palais de Chaillot. Duke Ellington and his band played here on 2–3 April 1939. The concerts were a tremendous success. The program included "Rockin' in Rhythm," "Black and Tan Fantasy," "Mood Indigo," the concertos "Clarinet Lament," "Echoes of Harlem," and "Trumpet in Spades," featuring Cootie, Barney, and Tex. Lawrence Brown played "Sophisticated Lady" and Juan Tizol performed his own "Caravan." Duke Ellington played variations on Rachmaninov's Prelude in C sharp minor and "Merry-Go-Round" and

"Dinah in a Jam." Ellington was awed by the excellent acoustics in an auditorium built 100 feet below ground in anticipation of German air raids.

Rue Tronchet (8th) Map F

24 Hôtel Madeleine-Elysées, formerly Hôtel des Etrangers. In 1853, George Catlin lived here alone. Penniless, he wandered the streets of Paris, describing himself as "destitute, despondent and deaf, but still without bitterness."

Avenue Trudaine (9th)

(13) Mary Cassatt, the most important 19th-century American woman painter, moved into an apartment here with her parents in 1878. She had settled in Paris in 1874, having spent five years in Paris as a child. A friend of Degas, she began to exhibit with the Impressionists in the 1870s. In her later work she reintroduced the mother and child theme, giving the subject a dignity little seen since the madonnas of the Renaissance. *Little Girl in a Blue Armchair* (1878) reflects the influence of Degas, Renoir, and Manet. Her studio was at nearby 6 Boulevard de Clichy, in a building which no longer exists.

Jardin des Tuileries (1st) Map F

During the late 18th and 19th centuries these gardens, like those of the nearby Palais-Royal, were *un lieu de galanterie* frequented by ladies of easy virtue. Visitors who had known London commented that the harlot's cry so common to that great city was delightfully absent in Paris, where women indicated their availability in a far more subtle and coquettish fashion.

In his diary for 25 August 1810, Aaron Burr recorded crossing through these gardens, where "on my way home the devil put in my way Flora, ... went to *sa chambre ... elle est jolie, bonne, voluptueuse.*" Burr spent two hours with her for seven francs. The following day he recorded in his *Journal:* "Went to bed last night full of penitence and contrition. Full of Apprehensions too." Later, cheered by a clean bill of health, Burr introduced his young friend John Vanderlyn to Flora. This time the charge was but three francs for two hours. Much of Burr's scanty funds were spent upon the

Floras of Paris. He recorded deciding to return to Paris from Sceaux by foot, a distance of eight miles, thus saving two francs for "une fille de joie."

ᴔ

In 1840, Elizabeth Cady Stanton, feminist and author of the *Woman's Bible* (1895), arrived in London to attend the World Anti-Slavery Society Meeting, which opened in Freemason's Hall on 12 June. To her astonishment and to that of the many other women who had come from all parts of the civilized world, if the English were interested in granting slaves their freedom, they were not about to extend similar privileges to the women present. Not only were the women delegates not permitted to speak during the entire twelve-day convention, but they were forced to sit "in a low curtained seat like a church choir" so that their physical presence not upset the grave moral reasonings being carried on by the men. But Stanton's deepest anger was directed against the British Protestant clergy who were the most violent in their opposition to the women's delegations. As she noted sarcastically: "The clergymen seemed to have God and his angels especially in their care and keeping, and were in agony lest the women should do or say something to shock the heavenly host.... It was really pitiful to hear the narrow minded bigots, pretending to be teachers and leaders of men."

It was a relief to arrive in Paris. Accustomed to the restraint and solemnity of American Sundays, Stanton discovered that in Paris the Sabbath was "gay and charming." She later recalled: "The first time I entered into some of the festivities, I really expected to be struck by lightning. The libraries, art galleries, concert halls, and theaters were all open to the people. Bands of music were playing in the parks, where whole families with their luncheons spent the day.... A wonderful contrast with that gloomy day in London."

While Stanton enjoyed listening to the old soldiers at the Hôtel des Invalides recall their years with Napoleon and visiting Notre-Dame and the Louvre, her most lasting impressions of Paris were the gardens with their amenities for children. Upon her return to America she wrote about the Jardin des Tuileries:

> The extensive and beautiful grounds were always gay with crowds of happy people. These gardens were a great resort for nurses and children and were furnished with all manner of novel appliances for their amusement, including beautiful little carriages drawn by four goats with girls or boys driving, boats sailing in the air,

seemingly propelled by oars, and hobby horses flying round on whirligigs with boys vainly trying to catch each other. No people have ever taken the trouble to invent so many amusements for children as have the French. The people enjoyed being always in the open air, night and day. The parks are crowded with amusement seekers, some reading and playing games, some sewing, knitting, playing on musical instruments, dancing, sitting around tables in bevies eating, drinking, and gayly chatting.

Rue de Turenne (3rd) Métro: St.-Paul

29 Samuel Morse took modest quarters in this private house in September 1831 and was joined by his friend, sculptor Horatio Greenough. James Fenimore Cooper frequently called on them.

Rue de l'Université (7th) Maps A & C

2-4 Formerly Hôtel d'Entragues. On Saturday evening, 21 December 1776, Benjamin Franklin took rooms at this hotel with his two grandsons. They stayed here until 8 January 1777, when they moved down the street to Rue Jacob. It was Franklin's third and last visit to France, and it was also his longest, for he would stay until 1785.

Franklin and his party had left Philadelphia on 26 October 1776 and had driven by carriage to Chester, fifteen miles south of the city on the Delaware River. The following morning they took another carriage three miles to Marcus Point, where they quietly boarded the *Reprisal*. Such precautions were necessary for it would have been impossible for someone as famous as Franklin to have sailed from Philadelphia without the knowledge of the British. The *Reprisal* took exactly one month to reach the French coast, and by 7 December Franklin was in Nantes, where he was the guest of the French shipping merchants Penet and Pliarne.

Franklin's arrival in Paris was immediately noted by the British ambassador Lord Stormont. Thanks to paid informants, Stormont had a complete list of Franklin's guests, and after a few days he reported to Lord Weymouth in the Foreign Office in Whitehall that Franklin's early popularity was already beginning to wane, since "nothing in this country," wrote the ambassador, "is more than a day's wonder." But Stormont was wrong, and over the years Franklin's popularity continued to grow. It was from this hotel, on 28 December 1776, that Franklin and his two fellow commissioners,

Arthur Lee and Silas Deane, paid a visit to the French minister of foreign affairs, the Comte de Vergennes, at Versailles. From the outset they were assured of the protection of the French court, and over the years a strong sense of respect developed between Franklin and the French minister.

9 Hôtel Lenox, formerly a pension. T.S. Eliot arrived in France in the summer of 1910 when he was 22, and he moved into a pension at this address in the fall. He attended seven lectures given by Bergson at the Collège de France that winter. His French tutor and friend was the 24-year-old Alain Fournier, who would soon publish *Le Grand Meaulnes,* a major French novel of the 20th century. Eliot described his time in Paris "on the old man's money" as the most romantic year of his life. The following July he began working on "The Love Song of J. Alfred Prufrock," which appeared in *Poetry* in June 1915.

21 Albert Gallatin was the American minister to France from 1815 until 1823 and spent the first two years at this address. Born in Geneva, Gallatin came to America at 19. He served in the House of Representatives from 1795 until 1801 and became leader of the Republican or Jeffersonian minority. In 1813, as secretary of the treasury under Jefferson, he led the mission to negotiate the Treaty of Ghent, which ended the war with Great Britain. He was one of the most brilliant and successful of the Jeffersonian statesmen. He and his American wife believed in frugality, modesty, personal discipline, and self-examination. However, his 18-year-old son James, who was his secretary and kept a journal, was determined to live life to the fullest. For 30 July 1816, young James Gallatin recorded:

> I have been all day interviewing servants—tall and short, fat and thin—until I can hardly speak. After sorting out what I considered the best, I had them draw up for father's approval, which I am glad to say he gave. Major-domo—Callon by name, a very fine person; two house footmen, Edouard and Alfred; two carriage footmen, Louis and Jean; Chef, Monsieur Ratifar, such a great personage (he brings his own kitchen staff); three maids, all pretty—I chose them. I don't know what mamma will say when she sees them. I hate to look at ugly women.
>
> The house is really very fine *entre cours et jardin* [between courtyard and garden]. Furniture old but very good. We have to supply our own plate and linen. We have to make some

alterations, so mamma and Frances have gone to the Lussacs at Versailles. I have my own valet, Lucien, aged twenty-five—a very important person he thinks himself, valet to a Secretary of Embassy. He will call me "Excellence."

Some three weeks later he was ready to encounter *le beau monde:*

August 23—I drove my new "curricle" for the first time today. I do not know which was the most proud, myself, Lucien, or the horse. It is rather difficult to drive a spirited horse and to keep taking off one's hat every moment. I have to be on the *qui vive* [alert] not to fail to return a salute; I will do better when I get to know people's faces better, but now I find it most difficult. I saw many lovely ladies, and I flatter myself some of them saw me. I find they notice much more when I am driving than when I am on foot. Moral—always drive.

I have just come back from walking the gardens of the Palais Royal. How pretty Frenchwomen are! I know I shall get into all sorts of scrapes.

22   Hôtel de l'Université. Tennessee Williams was glad to get back to Paris in July 1948 after ten miserable days working with John Gielgud on the London production of the *Glass Menagerie.* He joined Gore Vidal at this accommodating hotel. "The management is ideal," he told a friend. "They frankly state that they prefer young bachelors 'a little bit pederastical' is how they put it—and that is all they have. I have two huge rooms, windows ceiling to floor and mirrors same size, for only 1000 francs a day." ($2.00 at the time.) It was a hot summer and Williams went down the street to the swimming baths on the Seine. "The Bains Deligny contain some rare beauties," he continued, "and one finds at the Boeuf [sur le Toit] the handsomest kept boys of Europe like jewels in Tiffany's windows—to be admired but not touched." Williams gave a big party which soon filled with uninvited guests, French actors and actresses all hoping to get roles in Jean Cocteau's proposed stage version of *A Streetcar Named Desire.* Jean-Paul Sartre had been invited, but instead he chose to sit all alone in the bar of the nearby Hotel Pont-Royal. When one of the guests who knew him went to fetch him, the high prophet of Existentialism refused to budge. "Very French," recalled Gore Vidal. "Williams was pissed off." The following day, Cocteau invited Williams and Gore to lunch at the Grand Véfour to discuss the role of Stanley Kowalski for his current friend, Jean Marais. Gore, who acted as translator, noted that Marais "looked beautiful but sleepy.... Between Tennessee's solemn analysis of the play and Cocteau's rhetoric about theater (the long arms flailed like semaphores denoting some dangerous last junction) no one made any sense except Marais." The handsome young French actor simply wanted to know if he would have to use a Polish accent while playing Kowalski. The luncheon was all for nought. Cocteau broke up with Marais and produced *Streetcar* with naked blacks acting out the rape of Blanche in pantomime. The following month, Williams returned to America on board the *Queen Mary* with fellow hotel guest Truman Capote.

24   Hôtel de Senneterre. This magnificent *hôtel,* built in 1670, had a series of owners before being purchased in 1778 by Comte Henri-Charles de Senneterre for 160,000 livres. His daughter married the Maréchal de France Louis de Conflans, Marquis d'Armentières. (The name Armentières became famous with American soldiers in 1917 in the song "Mademoiselle from Armentières, parlez-vous?") At the start of the French Revolution the family emigrated except for the Marquise d'Armentières, who stayed on only to be guillotined on 27 July 1794. In such cases, the house became national property and was awarded as a prize in the public lottery—tickets 50 livres each. The winner of the Hôtel Senneterre sold it to an American, William Vans. Thus Vans, a simple merchant who had just arrived in Le Havre where he had married a French girl, became the owner of a major *hôtel* in Paris. Such were the fortunes of the revolution. Vans was typical of those American merchants who brought desperately needed wheat to France in 1794 and 1795, and who stayed on as traders, delighted to be living in homes ten times the size of anything they could have afforded back home. However, with the reestablishment of civil order and fiscal responsibility by Napoleon, the days of speculation in a depreciated French currency were over, and by 1805 most American merchants had returned home. In 1807, Charles de Conflans, the young son of Louis de Conflans, returned to France and appealed to the government for the return of his home. The appeal was denied. With the Restoration in 1815, Charles de Conflans sued the owner, who sold back the family property in 1822. During the late 19th century, the front of the mansion was modernized; however, the original doors have been preserved. In 1908, the city of Paris bought the building to demolish it. The French government objected, bought it from the city, and installed the Ministry of Commerce. Such is the history of one *hôtel particulier.*

(50) Site of the Hôtel de l'Intendance. Edna St. Vincent Millay lived here in May and June 1921. She was working on *The Ballad of the Harp-Weaver,* which won the Pulitzer Prize the following year.

78 Hôtel Hocquart. This hotel served as headquarters for the American Commission to the Peace Conference from December 1918 to July 1919. The Treaty of Versailles was signed on 28 June. The hotel is now being restored.

82 Hôtel de Plouville. American minister plenipotentiary William C. Rives lived here from 1830 to 1832. Rives signed the Convention of the United States with France on 4 July 1831, which ended the troublesome spoils claims arising from the Napoleonic wars and the mutual seizing of shipping in the Caribbean. Rives's American guests included the sculptor Horatio Greenough, Samuel Morse, Martin Van Buren, and James Fenimore Cooper.

(90) Madame de Staël's daughter Albertine lived here with her husband, the Duc de Broglie. Her salon was famous and among her American guests in 1827 was James Fenimore Cooper, who found the duchess "decidedly the sweetest, and to my taste, the most attractive woman I have seen in Paris." Cooper's father had, in 1804, helped Mme de Staël in the administration of a 23,000-acre estate in St. Lawrence County, New York, bequeathed to her by her father.

(169) Mark Twain took a house here in the beginning of November 1894. His wife Clara Clemens and their daughter Susy were happy during the six months they spent here. The house (250 dollars a month) had four bedrooms and reminded them of their home in Hartford. Later Mark Twain wrote of his lodgings:

> It was a lovely house; large rambling, quaint, charmingly furnished and decorated, built upon no particular plan, delightfully uncertain and full of surprises. You were always getting lost in it, and finding nooks and corners which you did not know were there and whose presence you had not suspected before. It was built by a rich French artist, and he had also furnished it and decorated it himself. The studio was coziness itself. With us it served as a drawing-room, sitting-room, living-room, dancing-room—we used it for everything. We couldn't get enough of it. It

is odd that it should have been so cozy, for it was 40 feet long, 40 feet high, and 30 feet wide, with a vast fireplace on each side, in the middle, and a musicians' gallery at one end.

Before leaving America, Mark Twain had invested 200,000 dollars in a newspaper typesetting machine. On 21 December, he received a letter telling him that the typesetter had failed the *Chicago Herald* test. This spelled virtual bankruptcy. The following day, after a sleepless night, he wrote to financier Henry Huttleston Rogers: "I seemed to be expecting your letter, and also prepared and resigned; but Lord, it shows how little we know ourselves and how easily we can deceive ourselves. It hit me like a thunderclap. It knocked every rag of sense out of my head, and I went flying here and there and yonder." The next news from America was even worse. Not only had he lost all his money, but he had incurred liabilities. Ever a writer and lecturer, Mark Twain finished the *Personal Recollections of Joan of Arc,* toured the world giving lectures, and paid off his debts within four years.

Rue du Val-de-Grâce (5th) Map D

8 Man Ray took a studio here in 1929. He was now a successful fashion photographer and could afford one studio for photography and another for painting.

Rue de Varenne (7th) Map C

53 Edith Wharton and her husband moved into number 53 in 1908, having decided to settle permanently in France. In the same house was a fellow American and longtime Paris resident, Walter Van Rensselaer Berry, who has been described as the "epitome of elegance in the Jamesian manner." When Berry died in 1927, he left his superb private library of 8,500 books to his nephew and fellow Parisian Harry Crosby. However, in his will he noted the gift of the entire library "except such items as my good friend, Edith Wharton, may care to choose." Alas, Edith Wharton chose almost every item, which led to a bitter struggle with Crosby. The final score was 500 books to Wharton, the rest to Crosby. Wharton purchased a house outside Paris near the forest of Montmorency, where she moved in 1918. Her finest novel, *The Age of Innocence* (1920), won the Pulitzer Prize.

58　　When the Whartons sublet the spacious apartment of George Vanderbilt in 1906, Edith Wharton was already an established novelist, fresh with the success of *The House of Mirth* (1905). Her writing reflected the influence of Henry James, who was a frequent visitor at her home on the Rue de Varenne.

69　　Le Ministère de la Recherche et de la Technologie, formerly Hôtel de Clermont et d'Orsay. In 1786, 30-year-old painter John Trumbull went to visit the house of Comte d'Orsay, where the opulence and elegance of the surroundings struck him:

> Tuesday, August 7th. Went to the house of the Count D'Orsay, said to be one of the most superb in Paris; it is in truth overloaded with elegance; the furniture is expensive and rich, to a fault; the eye can find no rest; the windows, in one of the apartments looking upon the garden, are of plate glass, only two pieces in each. The picture room contains the most beautiful collection of perfect little things that I have ever seen together; the Visitation of the Virgin, by Rubens—the taking down from the Cross, by Rembrandt—an Infant Saviour, by Vandyck—are superb. Teniers, Paul Potter, Wouvermans, Mieris, Metzu, Netscher, Van Oort, etc. etc., have precious specimens here. Small bronze copies of the finest antique statues, the choicest porcelain, etc. etc. literally crowd every apartment. The dining room is magnificent, ornamented with marble copies of some of the best antiques; the columns which separate the windows are of green and white marble; the windows are of plate glass, of prodigious size; but in my opinion, this room has one inexcusable fault,—it looks upon the court yard, where is all the dirty business of the stables, etc., objects far from pleasant to contemplate, in convivial hours.

77　　Musée Rodin. The former Hôtel de Biron, constructed in 1731, had a long and colorful history before being taken over by the church as a *pensionnat* for girls. Beginning in 1908, artists such as Rainer Maria Rilke, Isadora Duncan, Matisse, and Rodin were given permission to work and live here. In 1910, the French government bought the building and permitted Rodin to stay on the condition that he leave his works to the state, which would conserve them in this building. Hence the Musée Rodin. Among Rodin's American students was Malvina Hoffman, who worked for him from 1910 until his death in 1917.

✣

On 30 January 1937, Helen Keller was accorded a unique privilege: to touch the Rodin sculptures. The museum closed one hour early, the silk cords protecting the statues were taken down, and Helen Keller, standing on a chair, was able to explore Rodin's world. She felt *The Thinker,* "primal, tense, his chin resting on a toil worn hand. In every limb," continued Keller, "I felt the throes of emerging mind." She told George Borglum, the American sculptor who was accompanying her, that she recognized in the statue the same force as the one that had shaken her when Teacher had spelled "water" and she discovered that everything had a name. Keller touched Balzac's mighty forehead, but most revealing of all were the six burghers of Calais, who had given themselves up to the English so that their city might be saved. She ran her fingers on their haggard cheeks, exclaiming: "It is a work sadder to touch than a grave, because it is a conquered city typified."

78   Hôtel de Villeroi. Thomas Jefferson was a frequent guest of the handsome Comtesse de Tessé, the aunt of Adrienne Lafayette. The house was built in the 1720s, complete with delightful gardens and an intimate, private theater with seats for 110 guests. The Comtesse de Tessé, who was the same age as Jefferson, shared his interest in gardening, architecture, and politics. During the Revolution, the furniture, mirrors, and interior woodwork were sold for 58,000 livres and the building was used by the Ministry of War. Today, it is occupied by the Ministry of Agriculture and hidden from the street by other government buildings.

Rue de Vaugirard (6th) Map B

1 bis   Hôtel Trianon Palace. Richard Wright, author of *Uncle Tom's Children* (1938) and *Native Son* (1940), left America in May 1946 after a bitter fight with the State Department to obtain a passport. While staying in this hotel he discovered that he was an important person in France. He was received at the Hôtel de Ville and named an honorary citizen, and the following year he settled in France permanently. Shortly after his arrival he wrote, "Paris is all I ever hoped to think it was, with a clear sky, buildings so beautiful with age that one wonders how they happen to be, and with people so assured and friendly and confident that it took many centuries of living to give them such poise. There is such an absence of race hate that it seems a little unreal."

4   Formerly Hôtel de Lisbonne. This hotel, which is just off the Boulevard St.-Michel, has been home to many American journalists, especially those who worked at the Paris *Tribune*. William L. Shirer, who lived here in September 1925, wrote,

> The rooms were rather spacious. In each was a large writing table and bookcase well lit by French windows that extended from the floor to the high ceiling, a comfortable double bed, a dresser, a washbasin beneath a large mirror, and the inevitable *bidet,* which had to serve as a bathtub since there was no bathroom in the place (there had been one on the first floor, but the proprietor used its tub as a coalbin).

What more could one ask for in a hotel for 250 francs or 10 dollars per month? A more comfortable toilet. "There was a so-called 'stand-up' toilet by the stairwell on each floor. But it took some practice and a great deal of dexterity to use it.... The trick was to achieve a proper balance without kneeling over and then, at the end, keeping your balance, to reach high for the nail on the soggy wall from which old cut-up newspapers hung." Shirer went on to say that in his all travels in Europe, he had never encountered these Turkish stand-ups, not even in Turkey. But he did come across one in a regal chamber in Jawalabad, in the palace of the king of Afghanistan. A French archeologist in his group found it "very primitive."

Edgar (Ned) Calmer moved into the Lisbonne in 1927 and lived there on and off for the next seven years while he worked for the Paris *Tribune* and the Paris *Herald*. He joined his fellow *Tribune* staff members, Eugene Jolas and Elliot Paul, in editing *transition*. In November 1933, he befriended Ernest Hemingway, who was horrified to learn that Calmer's 2-year-old daughter had not been baptized. The child was baptized shortly afterwards with Hemingway as godfather. Calmer's first novel, *Beyond the Street,* was published by Harcourt, Brace in 1934. That December, Hemingway recommended the 27-year-old author for a Guggenheim grant. The request was turned down, and Hemingway admitted that no one he recommended ever got a Guggenheim. Calmer, who later worked for CBS, wrote a book about the Hôtel de Lisbonne, *All the Summer Days* (1961).

16   Mary Putnam took a room here on the sixth floor in fall 1868. A medical student, she worked in the wards of the city hospitals. Like the other members of her family, she was a fine writer. She was also well attuned to the nuances of both the French and English societies:

> After actually seeing French people, and finding how well founded is their reputation for *esprit,* the English according to the glimpses I get of them, occasionally, seem intensely insipid. I encounter frequently along the rue de Rivoli whole families of English girls, all dressed alike, all wearing the same expression, all meek, subdued, conventional as a pack of sheep. In the anatomical class is a young Englishman who is the centre of amusement for the whole class, who get a great deal of fun out of him, without in the least infringing upon politeness. He seems a good innocent youth too, but so daisy-like, sandy and English. I always imagine him on his return to London seated at his father's substantial mahogany table, surrounded by his four well educated sisters, and relating his terrific adventures in Paris,—and how finally he will say, as he tries to eye a glass of port with the air of a connoisseur, "Oh, by the way, there was a woman in our class—Yes there was, 'pon my honor, and by Jove she always answered just as well as us fellows." This is a modest statement, as it would be difficult not to know ten times as much anatomy as the youth in question.

Mary Putnam was obviously attached to her father, and he was concerned that he might lose his only daughter to a European marriage. But he need not have worried, for Mary Putnam was as level-headed in the question of romance and marriage as she was in the study of medicine:

> You need not be afraid that I shall become "especially interested" in any one here. In the first place I have no personal acquaintance, and in the second, such acquaintance with Frenchmen, who devote their gallantry in one direction, fall in love in another and marry in still a third, thus dividing their attentions among *femmes d'esprit,* pretty women and women with a substantial "dot,"—such acquaintance is by no means dangerous. I have no particular desire to marry at any time; nevertheless, if at home, I should ever come across a physician, intelligent, refined, more enthusiastic for his science than me, but who would like me, and for whom I should entertain about the same feeling that I have for Haven, I think I would marry such a person if he asked me, and would leave me full liberty to exercise my profession. Otherwise,—no . . .

When she returned to New York City in 1872, after six years in Paris, she married Dr. Abraham Jacobi. She pursued a distinguished medical career at the Woman's Medical College of the New York Infirmary and also became the first woman member of several medical societies.

(30)   Site of the Hôtel Savoy. Twenty-one-year-old Aaron Copland arrived in Paris on 16 June 1921. He spent a week here before leaving for the American School of Music in Fontainebleau. Copland attended as many concerts as possible, including Cocteau's ballet *Les Mariés de la Tour Eiffel*. He was astounded by the active and vociferous stance of the French audience, having never heard an audience boo or hiss before.

(32)   Ford Madox Ford had an apartment here which he loaned rent-free to Allen Tate, his wife, novelist Caroline Gordon, and their friend, poet Leonie Adams. Allen Tate had received a Guggenheim grant for 1928-29, and the trio took over the apartment in January 1929 for six months when Ford left for the United States. Tate had been one of the founders of the *Fugitive* (1922-25), a magazine that represented a Southern literary group of political conservatives. His biography of Stonewall Jackson appeared in 1928, and he completed his biography of Jefferson Davis here on Rue de Vaugirard. He met Gertrude Stein and Sylvia Beach. He was upset by F. Scott Fitzgerald who, upon being introduced, asked him: "Do you enjoy sleeping with your wife?" Tate replied: "It's none of your damn business." Nor was he consoled on learning that Fitzgerald asked all married men this question. Tate accompanied Hemingway to the bicycle races on Sundays at the Vélodrome d'Hiver, but French influence did not appear in his work until the publication of *The Mediterranean and Other Poems* in 1936. Tate's experiences in France were never particularly satisfactory and were interludes in a literary career devoted to the American South.

46   Association des Etudiants Protestants. Thomas Eakins arrived in Paris in October 1866 at the age of 22. He was accepted at the Ecole des Beaux-Arts and took a room here directly opposite the Luxembourg Palace. He assured his mother: "My room is not as large as my bed chamber at home [Mt. Vernon Street, Philadelphia], but it is large enough and has a big window in it, which gives plenty of light. The walls are papered, and the ceiling is nicely white-washed. The floor is of stone or rather a sort of brick painted red, but a big piece of carpet in the centre of the room covers half of it." It

was customary in America during the 19th century to carpet bedroom floors; Americans arriving in Paris frequently asked to see every hotel room until they found one with a carpet. Young Eakins assured his mother that his room contained "no bugs and not even fleas which bother Americans very much in Paris." Waking up in the morning was no problem: "The soldiers... of the Luxembourg wake me up at the right time in the morning with their trumpets and drums." Eakin's letter was accompanied by sketches and a full text. "My room is well furnished, and the principal piece is of course the bed. It is kept clean and tidy. The French bedsteads all seem to have curtains. They add to the beauty, and help keep out the light... there is a big flat pillow half the size of the bed which goes down at the foot and covers the legs after one is in bed. It is not a bad idea, for when the feet are right warm there's no necessity for a heavy bunch of bed-clothes." Like all hotel bedrooms, Eakins' had a stove in the corner of his room:

> It is necessary to build a fire every two or three days to dry the room and purify it, even if you are not going to sit in it. To make a fire you take a little ball of resinous shavings. These balls are about as long as one's finger and twice as thick. You light it and put a bunch... of little sticks on top and then a couple of big pieces over them and then pull down the gate in front. After the fire is well started you can put up the gate... and throw some coke in on top of the wood. The next thing I've drawn is a mahogany box with a door and drawer to it. I think that you would have a good deal of trouble guessing its use if I hadn't left the door a little open.

50   Hôtel de la Trémoïlle. In 1798, Joel Barlow bought this house for 430,000 francs. He was attracted by the frontage, 140 feet overlooking the Jardin du Luxembourg, and especially by the front gate, the most magnificent he had seen in Paris. (The gateway has now been classified an historical monument.) Entering the gateway, Barlow found himself in a courtyard with wings on either side running from the building on the street toward the main house. An elegant vestibule opened onto a large salon with seventeen-foot ceilings, which connected to the library. There were eleven bedrooms, six with fireplaces on the first floor. The cellars could hold 500 barrels of wine, the stables twelve horses, and the courtyard five carriages. The gardens, *de style anglais,* were shaded by fruit trees and ornamental shrubs. Barlow lived here with his wife Baldwin and their bosom friend Robert Fulton. Unable to afford a full house of servants or to furnish the entire house, Barlow nevertheless built up a collection of books which upon his return constituted one of the finest libraries in America. Barlow introduced Fulton, who had no formal education, to the world of French, Italian, and German literature. Together they read philosophy and studied higher mathematics, chemistry, and physics. They also tinkered with Fulton's newest idea, the submarine. In 1804, Barlow returned to America after a seventeen-year absence.

58   Scott and Zelda Fitzgerald took over this apartment on 2 May 1928 and spent their first summer on the Left Bank. The apartment belonged to their friends Gerald and Sara Murphy, with whom they had already stayed in their Villa America at Cap d'Antibes. Murphy immediately arranged for Zelda to study with Lubov Egorova, a former prima ballerina and a teacher with Diaghilev's Ballet Russe. Fitzgerald continued to delay working on *Tender is the Night* (1934) and took refuge in a series of stories about his midwestern boyhood, which he had begun in March in Delaware. It was here, in this large, elegant, but cheerless apartment, that Fitzgerald wrote two of the Basil Duke Lee stories.

70   Institut Catholique. A former convent of the Carmelites, this site had vast grounds which stretched from Rue du Regard to Rue du Cherche-Midi. On 11 August 1792, the convent was seized and converted into a prison. One month later, 115 priests were taken from the convent and executed. The Carmelites returned after the Revolution and rented out rooms in some of the buildings on the property. John Vanderlyn was living here in 1810. He had gone to Rome five years earlier, where he painted his most important historical picture, *Marius Amidst the Ruins of Carthage* (M.H. de Young Memorial Museum, San Francisco), which won a gold medal in the Academy exhibit in Paris in 1808. (Legend has it that Napoleon chose this painting for the prize.) On 26 February 1810, Aaron Burr, now a penniless exile, arrived at Vanderlyn's door. He recorded in his *Journal:* "Found Vanderlyn. He is the same as ci-devant. Took breakfast with him. An hour looking at his pictures. Marius on the Ruins of Carthage obtained the gold medal in 1808. I see nothing in that line to exceed it. Other admirable things, both original and copied."

Before Vanderlyn left France for home in 1815, he sketched the gardens of Versailles. He transferred these sketches onto 3,000 feet of canvas and, back in New York, he had a small rotunda built where he showed this and other panoramas. He had probably gotten the idea from Robert Fulton. The show had a brief popularity, and in the winter he took it on tour in the South. His historical paintings found little market in America however, and he died in 1852, embittered and impoverished.

89 Poet Lawrence Ferlinghetti was 28 when he arrived in Paris in 1948. He took two rooms here below street level for 26 dollars for one year. Later he opened the City Lights Bookshop in San Francisco.

Rue Vavin (6th) Map D

(40) Sculptor Frédéric-Auguste Bartholdi had a studio at 40 Rue Vavin, at the corner of the Boulevard Raspail, from 1871 until 1893. In his studio the 37-year-old sculptor began his plans for the Statue of Liberty. He visited New York in 1871, and promptly wrote: "I have found a superb site. I've made a sketch of the statue as it will be. It is Bedloe's Island in the middle of the bay. It is an island owned by the government and held commonly by all the states; it faces the Narrows which are for all intents and purposes the gateway to America." In his Paris studio he built the first model of the statue. Today, the nine-foot model can be seen in the museum of the Ecole des Arts et Métiers. A second copy is in the Luxembourg gardens, where Bartholdi used to like to walk.

50 Harold Stearns lived here in 1926. He had been the *Baltimore Sun*'s Paris correspondent for five years, and also worked for the European edition of the *New York Herald*. In the Paris *Tribune* of 3 May 1925, Eugene Jolas described him as the "enfant terrible of American journalism," but by 1926 his reputation was rapidly becoming that of a boring hanger-on in cafés. A former intellectual leader of American youth (*America and the Young Intellectual,* 1921) and an inspiration to the postwar generation, Stearns fell to writing under the name "Peter Pickem," forecasting horse races for the Paris *Tribune,* a job he held until he left France in 1930. Ernest Hemingway portrayed him as the indigent Harvey Stone in *The Sun Also Rises.* Stearns returned to America, where to the surprise of almost everyone he wrote *Rediscovering America* (1934), which was received with critical acclaim. In *America: A Reappraisal* (1937) he reversed the position which had made him famous earlier, defending America against its Marxist critics, most of them home-bred. The irony was that Stearns had urged all young Americans of talent to emigrate if they wished to be creative, but only wrote well himself in the United States.

Place Vendôme (1st) Map F

1   Hôtel Vendôme. In 1936, between finishing *Swing Time* with Ginger Rogers and beginning *Shall We Dance,* Fred Astaire took a brief vacation in Europe, spending a week with his wife in Paris. They picked this small hotel in order to avoid publicity and newspaper reporters.

3-5   IBM Building, formerly Hôtel Bristol. Every spring from 1890 until 1910 John Pierpont Morgan had the same corner suite on the first floor in this hotel run by his father's ex-butler. The Morgan bank had extensive dealings in France, which included a loan of 50 million dollars to the French government at the time of the Franco-Prussian War (1870-71). This was considered one of the most spectacular financial operations of the time. Morgan was an assiduous art collector, and the hotel was besieged by art dealers when he stayed here. His collection is housed in the Pierpont Morgan wing of New York's Metropolitan Museum, of which he was president.

4-6   Formerly Hôtel du Rhin (entrance through number 6). John Slidell arrived in Paris in February 1862 to take up his post as Confederate commissioner to France. He was accompanied by his wife and secretary, and was greeted by American Confederate sympathizers who chanted:

> Bienvenu, notr' grand Slidell! Au coeur loyal et l'âme fidèle!
>
> [Welcome our great Slidell! He has a loyal heart and a faithful soul!]

His credentials had been signed the previous summer by Jefferson Davis, but the trip over had taken longer than anticipated. Slidell set sail on the British packet *Trent,* and on 8 November 1861 the ship was boarded by crew from the U.S. warship *San Jacinto.* Slidell was taken off the ship and interned in Boston. Americans in the northern states greeted this action with wild applause, whereas the British government sent a stiff note of protest and demanded his immediate release. The prospect of war with Great Britain was not welcome, and Slidell was released and permitted to resume his journey. During the Civil War there was a large body of Confederate sympathizers in Paris, particularly among the upper classes. The expression *Nos frères de Louisiane* was heard everywhere.

15   Hôtel Ritz. This building dates from 1705 and was taken over by César Ritz in 1898 and turned into the most luxurious hotel in Paris at that time. Franklin and Eleanor Roosevelt stayed here in 1919. FDR attended the peace conference as Secretary of the Navy.

From August 1944 until the summer of 1945, the Ritz was requisitioned for high ranking officers and important guests. One of the first guests was Fred Astaire, who was on tour with the USO. He recalled in his autobiographical *Steps in Time* that during the winter the hotel had no heat and no hot water, but it was a vast improvement over sleeping on makeshift theater stages and in the back of army trucks. Arthur Sulzberger, a *New York Times* reporter, was billeted here during the summer of 1945. He lived in a two-bath, five-room suite. On the day that the hotel was returned to private management, he was told that the suite would cost two hundred dollars per day. He left that afternoon.

One winter day in 1956, when Ernest Hemingway stopped by for a drink in the hotel, the baggage man asked him to remove his trunks, which had been in the hotel storage room since 1927. In them Hemingway found his notes which became the basis for *A Moveable Feast*.

16   The Obelisk Press. Jack Kahane, an Englishman living in France, accepted Henry Miller's *Tropic of Cancer* in October 1932 and published it in September 1934, having taken more time to produce it, noted the exasperated author, than he had taken to write it. The Obelisk Press published *Aller Retour* (Siana Series) and *Scenario* the following year. Additional books by Miller included *Black Spring* (1936), *Max and the White Phagocytes* (Seurat Series), and finally *Tropic of Capricorn* (1939). Kahane's office was in the back and looked onto the interior courtyard.

17   Thomas Jefferson' dined here as the guest of the very wealthy Monsieur Chalut de Vérin, a farmer-general (tax collector). Vérin's art collection filled several rooms on the ground floor.

Rue Vercingétorix (14th)

(50)   Painter Stuart Davis took a studio here in 1928 for a year. Many years later Davis recalled: "I liked Paris the minute I got there. Everything was human-sized. The pressure of American anti-art was removed. You could starve to death quicker there but you had the illusion that the artist was a human being and not just a bum."

Davis had exhibited in the New York Armory Show of 1913 at the age of 19. Disenchanted with the teaching of Robert Henri in New York and the Ashcan School of realism, Davis was the first American to master the formal basis of Cubism. His first abstract paintings were the "egg beater" series of 1927. His work had flat planes, clean mechanical angles and curves, set off by sharp silhouettes, and reflected the influence of Léger. In Paris, Davis recorded city scenes and did a series of local street scenes such as the *Rue Lippe.* Davis had written that "the process of making a painting is the art of defining two-dimensional space on a plane surface." He had thus eliminated the third dimension which most other American artists were still struggling to capture at the time. He returned to New York in August 1929 and said that he wished to "spike the disheartening rumor that there were hundreds of talented young artists in Paris who completely outclassed their American equivalents." On the contrary, he felt that the "work being done here was comparable in every way with the best of the work over there by contemporary artists." It was probably true, and was indeed a comforting statement, but the Depression of the following years cast gloom over the American art world. Most artists survived thanks to the government's WPA program.

Rue de Verneuil (7th) Map A

6   In 1924 Eugene Jolas became an editor with the Paris *Tribune,* where he did his best to replace Ford Madox Ford. Jolas' column "Rambles through Literary Paris" introduced American readers to French writers André Gide, Jean Giraudoux, Philippe Soupault, and André Breton. To French readers he presented Eugene O'Neill, Sherwood Anderson, Ezra Pound, and James Joyce. Jolas' most important contribution was launching the literary review *transition,* which he coedited with a fellow editor from the *Tribune,* Elliot Paul. They began *transition* here in Jolas' apartment on Rue de Verneuil before moving the editorial office to Rue Fabert.

29   Hôtel de Verneuil, formerly *un hôtel particulier.* Princess Gallitzin, widow of the privy counselor Prince Michael Andreevich Gallitzin, lived here with her five children. She enjoyed Americans, who were frequent guests at her famous soirées. On 24 December 1826, she invited James Fenimore Cooper to accompany her to a service in a Greek Orthodox church on the following Sunday, and then to attend a family birthday celebration in her home. Cooper wrote a highly amusing reply in French, pointing out that since he did not feel well, he had to save his energy and choose between church and the soirée, between the chance of being canonized and being entertained, between spiritual loss and earthly rewards. He chose the birthday celebration. A few months later, Cooper, his wife, and the princess were invited to a ball given by Count Pozzo di Borgo. Since Mrs. Cooper was indisposed, the princess asked Cooper to be her escort. He was told to come at nine. The author described his reception at the Rue de Verneuil in a letter:

> So I went. I was ushered into the dressing room of the good lady, and ordered to take a seat behind a skreen and before a good fire, while she continued her toilette—My situation was droll enough. There was I on one side of the skreen, and her highness and her two maids on the other, she dressing and I toasting my toes, and both chatting as freely as if we were in a well-filled salon.

53   Harriet Beecher Stowe arrived in Paris for the first time early in June 1853. *Uncle Tom's Cabin,* published the previous year, had already sold 300,000 copies. In *Sunny Memories of Foreign Lands,* published when she returned to America, she recounted that on Rue de Verneuil she lived in a mansion belonging to a certain Marquis de Briges:

> We entered by a ponderous old gateway, opened by the concierge, passed through a large paved quadrangle, traversed a short hall, and found ourselves, in a large cheerful parlour, looking out into a small flower garden.... In five minutes we were at home. French life is different from any other. Elsewhere you do as the world pleases; here you do as you please yourself.

Many Americans who have either lived in or visited France have described their first attempts to converse in French. The brilliant opening sentence brings in reply a torrent of French words, cascade upon cascade of sounds reinforced by gesticulations. All Americans agree; there is only one thing to do. Keep going. Don't pause. Don't think. Keep talking. Before you know it, you're speaking French. Among the best descriptions of that terrifying moment is Harriet Stowe's:

> When I first began I would think of some sentence till I could say it without stopping, and courageously deliver myself to some guest or acquaintance. But it was like pulling the string of a shower-bath. Delighted at my correct sentence, and supposing me *au fait* [up to it], they poured upon me such a deluge of French that I held my breath in dismay. Considering, however, that nothing is to be gained by half-way measures, I resolved upon a desperate game. Launching in, I talked away right and left, up hill and down,— jumping over genders, cases, nouns, and adjectives, floundering through swamps and morasses, in a perfect steeple-chase of words. Thanks to the proverbial politeness of my friends, I came off covered with glory; the more mistakes I made the more complacent they grew.

Rue Vieille-du-Temple (4th) Métro: St.-Paul

47   Hôtel des Ambassadeurs de Hollande. It was here on 9 October 1776 that Caron de Beaumarchais established his arms trading company, Roderigue Hortalez et Cie, and in his spare time wrote *The Marriage of Figaro.* More than one month before the American Declaration of Independence, the French government decided to send secret aid to the Americans. On 10 June 1776, Beaumarchais received one million livres from the French treasury by order of Louis XVI, and a similar sum from Spain. This enabled him to set up his company and sell arms, cannon, munitions, and military supplies to the young republic, and to provide it with credit when necessary. When the American purchasing agent for Congress Silas Deane arrived in Paris in July 1776, the French Minister for Foreign Affairs Vergennes told him that while France could not help America officially, Beaumarchais could. The two men met many times in the following months, and Beaumarchais kept Vergennes abreast of their arrangements. On 14 October 1776, in this hotel, Deane and Beaumarchais signed a major contract to provide military equipment, arms, and cannon sufficient for an army of 30,000 men. It was agreed in writing that Beaumarchais would be repaid in tobacco shipped by Congress. Credit of nine months as of the date of arrival of the arms was extended. Between December 1776 and September 1777, eight ships left France for America, one of which was seized by the British in the West Indies. They carried arms and cannon from the Royal French arsenals and French artillery officers, sailing under false names and passports, to help with the artillery.

In London, upon learning of the agreement, the American agent Arthur Lee, one of four Lee brothers from Virginia, was furious. In February 1776, he had talked with Beaumarchais in London about possible French aid and now discovered that Silas Deane had signed the contract which he had suggested earlier. Lee sent a special messenger to Congress telling them that the arms which Deane and Beaumarchais were shipping to America were in reality a well-concealed gift from the French king and should not be paid for. Indeed, continued Lee, if bills were submitted, both Deane and Beaumarchais would be guilty of fraud. The charge was most serious, but it took time to reach Congress, which wisely decided to see if any arms were going to arrive and if they were accompanied by bills. After all, the first aim of Congress was to win the war and for this it needed arms.

In Paris, Beaumarchais was blissfully unaware of such charges and was busy visiting French arsenals, obtaining gunpowder from reluctant French naval port commanders, and hurrying along suppliers of material for uniforms. As word of his operation spread, professional soldiers anxious to serve in any way came here in hope of obtaining free passage to America on one of Beaumarchais's ships. One such was Baron Frederick Wilhelm von Steuben, a former staff officer of Frederick the Great, who had held an important command in the Seven Years War. Although Benjamin Franklin had given him a letter of introduction to General Washington, it was left to Beaumarchais to provide him with his passage and money for living expenses. As Steuben spoke no English, Beaumarchais found him a 17-year-old secretary and interpreter, Pierre Duponceau. The two men dined in this house with Beaumarchais on the evening of 11 September 1777. The following morning they left for Marseille where they boarded the eighth and last of Beaumarchais's ships to leave for America. Setting sail on 26 September, the ship dropped anchor off Portsmouth, New Hampshire, on 1 December. They reached Valley Forge on 23 February 1778 and were welcomed by Washington. Steuben quickly recognized the courage of the American soldiers, but he also noticed the lack of discipline. He then wrote what became a famous manual, the "blue book" entitled *Regulations for the Order and Discipline of the Troops of the United States.* He molded the Continental Army into a disciplined force. Steuben commanded in the trenches at Yorktown, and on retirement was awarded large tracts of land in several states by Congress. He died in the United States in 1794. Steubenville, Ohio, was named for him. Duponceau served at Valley Forge, and when he left the army moved to Philadelphia where he became a lawyer. He died there in 1835, having served as president of the American Philosophical Society. Other volunteers who called here and whose passage was provided by Beaumarchais included a 23-year-old French engineer, Pierre L'Enfant, who later designed the plans for the cities of Washington and Detroit.

The charges sent to Congress by Arthur Lee bore fruit, although of an unexpected nature. Silas Deane was recalled. The French government, which trusted Deane but distrusted Arthur Lee, showed its disapproval by inviting Deane to return to America on board a French ship accompanied by the French minister. Deane was questioned at length by Congress but no decision was reached. Arthur Lee was then recalled and Congress split into two warring factions. Although the French minister in Philadelphia informed Congress that the arms sent to America were not a gift, a number of congressmen remained suspicious, and Beaumarchais's payment was delayed indefinitely. In 1786, Congress got wind of the secret payment by Louis XVI to Beaumarchais of one million francs. The French government refused to answer a direct question put by a member of Congress as to whether or not Beaumarchais had received money from the king. It was a French internal affair. Congress refused to act. In 1794, the French revolutionary government revealed the secret payment to Beaumarchais of one million livres, a payment quite unknown to Silas Deane, and one which appeared to justify the charges made by Arthur Lee. Beaumarchais died in 1799, bitter and deeply hurt by Congress's refusal even to recognize his contribution to the revolution, let alone repay him. The cost of the arms, munitions, and shipping were well above six million francs. With the French Restoration, the Beaumarchais heirs again asked for payment of the four million franc debt. In 1818, the French minister told Congress that Roderigue Hortalez had been a legitimate French business concern and that the money given to Beaumarchais by the French king had nothing to do with the sum owed. After endless inquiries, Congress settled on a payment to the heirs of 800,000 francs in 1835.

Rue du Vieux-Colombier (6th) Map B

21 In the heart of the Left Bank, the Club du Vieux-Colombier, or "le vieux-co" as it was called, was one of the homes of Existentialism and jazz following the end of World War II. Jazz was not simply the music of the moment, it was symbolic of America and freedom after the German occupation. Above all, in France, it was the music of youth. Sidney Bechet began playing his clarinet in the Vieux-Colombier with Claude Luter's band in fall 1949. He settled in France, he said, because he felt "that it was nearer to Africa." Other musicians at the club included drummer Kenny Clarke and trumpeter Bill Coleman. Bechet died in Paris in 1959.

Avenue de Villiers (17th) Métro: Malesherbes

45 Isadora Duncan and her brother Raymond took a large studio here in 1900. It accommodated twenty guests, so Isadora gave subscription concerts, dancing barefoot in her Greek tunic, complemented by colored scarves draped from her shoulders. Her audience included Winnaretta Singer and her husband Prince de Polignac, painter and lithographer Eugène Carrière, dramatist Victorien Sardou, and Loïe Fuller.

In *My Life* Duncan recalled meeting Rodin in his study on Rue de l'Université, a meeting which terminated in Duncan's studio on Avenue de Villiers:

> Rodin was short, square, powerful, with close-cropped head and plentiful beard. He showed his works with the simplicity of the great. Sometimes he murmured the names for his statues, but one felt that names meant little to him. He ran his hands over them and caressed them. I remember thinking that beneath his hands the marble seemed to flow like molten lead. Finally he took a small quantity of clay and pressed it between his palms. He breathed hard as he did so. The heat streamed from him like a radiant furnace. In a few moments he had formed a woman's breast, that palpitated beneath his fingers.
>
> He took me by the hand, took a cab and came to my studio. There I quickly changed into my tunic and danced for him.
>
> Then I stopped to explain to him my theories for a new dance, but soon I realised that he was not listening. He gazed at

me with lowered lids, his eyes blazing, and then, with the same expression that he had before his works, he came toward me. He ran his hands over my neck, breast, stroked my arms and ran his hands over my hips, my bare legs and feet. He began to knead my whole body as if it were clay, while from him emanated heat that scorched and melted me. My whole desire was to yield to him my entire being and, indeed, I would have done so if it had not been that my absurd up-bringing caused me to become frightened and I withdrew, threw my dress over my tunic and sent him away bewildered. What a pity! How often I have regretted this childish miscomprehension which lost to me the divine chance of giving my virginity to the Great God Pan himself, to the Mighty Rodin. Surely Art and all Life would have been richer thereby.

Rue Vivienne (2nd) Map F

(15)   Site of the Hôtel des Etrangers. Nathaniel Parker Willis, 25, arrived in Paris in 1831 as correspondent for the *New York Mirror.* He was driven here in a fiacre from les Messageries on Rue Notre-Dame-des-Victoires and insisted on a bedroom with a carpet:

> As one is a specimen of all, I may as well describe the Hôtel des Etrangers, Rue Vivienne, which, by the way, I take the liberty at the same time to recommend to my friends. It is the precise centre for the convenience of sight-seeing, admirably kept, and, being nearly opposite Galignani's, that bookstore of Europe, is a very pleasant resort for the half hour before dinner, or a rainy day.
>
> The fiacre stopped before an arched passage, and a fellow in livery, who had followed me from the Messagerie (probably in the double character of porter and police agent, as my passport was yet to be demanded), took my trunk into a small office on the left, over which was written Concierge. This person, who is a kind of respectable doorkeeper, addressed me in broken English, without waiting for the evidence of my tongue that I was a foreigner, and, after inquiring at what price I would have room, introduced me to the landlady, who took me across a large court (the houses are built round the yard always in France), to the corresponding story of the house. The room was quite pretty, with its looking-glasses and curtains, but there was no carpet, and the fireplace was ten feet deep. I asked to see another, and another, and another; they were all curtains, and looking-glasses, and stone floors! There is no wearying a Frenchwoman, and I pushed my modesty till I found a chamber to my taste—a nutshell, to be sure, but carpeted—and bowing my polite housekeeper out, I rang for breakfast and was at home in Paris!

There are few things bought with money that are more delightful than a French breakfast. If you take it at your room, it appears in the shape of two small vessels, one of coffee and one of hot milk, two kinds of bread, with a thin, printed slice of butter, and one or two of some thirty dishes from which you choose, the latter flavored exquisitely enough to make one wish to be always at breakfast, but cooked and composed I know not how or of what. The coffee has an aroma peculiarly exquisite, something quite different from any I ever tasted before; and the petit-pain, a slender biscuit between bread and cake, is, when crisp and warm, a delightful accompaniment. All this costs about one third as much as the beefsteaks and coffee in America, at the same time that you are waited upon with a civility that is worth three times the money.

18   The Galignani family ran a publishing house, a bookstore, and a reading room here from 1804 until 1886, when they moved to their present location at 224 Rue de Rivoli. The reading room or *salon de lecture* was a regular stopping place for all American and English visitors. Isaac Appleton Jewett left the following description of these salons:

> You can go through hardly one of the great streets of Paris, without seeing half a dozen times, the words, *Salon de Lecture.* These salons are the great central resorts of Parisian newsreaders. Pausing before one of them, you perceive its windows quite covered with the names of forty or fifty journals to be found within.

In 1814, the house of Galignani published a *New Paris Guide or Stranger's Companion through the French Metropolis* which, beginning with the 1824 edition, became the standard English guide to Paris. Few American tourists were without this guide, which was published every year from 1824 until 1894. It gave information on the best fare in restaurants and the prices to expect. It listed those cafés one could safely take a wife and family, and others to which one could accompany a lady friend. It described hospitals, prisons, churches, theaters, historical monuments, gardens and parks, and gave advice concerning the citizens of Paris, their customs, qualities and occasional faults. Washington Irving worked as an editor for Galignani, and in 1824 they published his *Salmagundi; or, The Whim-Whams and Opinions of Launcelot Langstaff Esq. and Others,* a series of satirical essays.

(49)   Site of the Salle Musard. On Friday, 26 May 1837, Dr. Willard Parker and a friend visited this new concert hall, which had opened the previous year. Parker recorded in his *Journal:*

> The Hall is large—capable of containing 3,000 persons and 200 musicians. The room is brilliantly lighted—walls richly painted. The Hall is the 1/2 of a circle. The House was very full—90 instruments compose the concert Musard. The composer conducts the whole. They meet *every evening.* Franc for admission. We got home at 11. The music was not to be surpassed.

For two months in 1844, Tom Thumb performed in afternoon and evening shows put on by P.T. Barnum. The first day's receipts were over 5,500 francs, the promoter recording that he could have doubled that sum in a larger hall, but he was nevertheless compelled to "take a cab to carry my bag of silver home at night."

Quai Voltaire (7th) Map **A**

17   Before returning to the United States in 1796, James Monroe appointed Fulwar Skipwith as consul general. Skipwith bought number 17 to use as his consulate. While he looked after the interests of his fellow Americans, he did not neglect his own, and over the next few years he acquired numbers 12, 13, and 14, which he rented out. He was still living here in 1801.

On 1 November 1927, Virgil Thomson took over the attic and stayed here until 1940. Gertrude Stein had found him this apartment, and he immediately went to work on an opera, *Four Saints in Three Acts,* with libretto by Stein. He was overjoyed to be living at last in his own flat. His financial worries were solved by a new patron, Mrs. Chester Whitin Lasell. Over the next years Thomson acquired an increasing number of friends, and his Friday soirées were well known.

19   Hôtel du Quai Voltaire. Novelist Willa Cather stayed here for two months in 1920 while she worked on *One of Ours,* set in France (Pulitzer Prize, 1922). This hotel was rich in literary associations; Baudelaire lived here while working on *Les Fleurs du Mal,* and Richard Wagner finished the *Meister Singer* here.

Bibliography

Beach, Sylvia. *Shakespeare and Company.* New York: Harcourt Brace, 1959. Modest and a joy to read.

Dulles, Foster Rhea. *Americans Abroad.* Ann Arbor, Michigan: University of Michigan Press, 1964. American tourists during two centuries of European travel.

Duncan, Isadora. *My Life.* New York: Boni & Liveright, 1927.

Fitch, Noel Riley. *Sylvia Beach and the Lost Generation.* New York: W.W. Norton & Company, 1983. Authoritative and entertaining.

Flanner, Janet. *Paris Was Yesterday 1925-1939.* New York: Viking, 1972. Articles from the *New Yorker.* A delight to read.

Ford, Hugh. *Published in Paris: American and British Writers, Printers, and Publishers in Paris, 1920-39.* New York: MacMillan, 1975.

Gajdusek, Robert E. *Hemingway's Paris.* New York: Scribners, 1978. Delightful photographs set against quotations from Hemingway's and other writers' works.

Hemingway, Ernest. *A Moveable Feast.* New York: Scribners, 1964.

Hillairet, Jacques. *Dictionnaire Historique des Rues de Paris.* 7th ed., 3 vols. Paris: Les Editions de Minuit, 1978. Indispensable to any serious study of Paris. Consulted daily and sometimes hourly during the years it took to research *Americans in Paris.*

McAlmon, Robert. *Being Geniuses Together 1920-1930.* Revised with additional material by Kay Boyle. Garden City, New York: Doubleday, 1969. The title says everything.

Mellow, James R. *Charmed Circle Gertrude Stein & Company.* New York & Washington, Praeger Publishers, 1974.

Rice, Jr., Howard C. *Thomas Jefferson's Paris.* Princeton, New Jersey: Princeton University Press, 1976. Scholarly, urbane, entertaining, and lovely to look at.

Rood, Karen Lane, ed. *Dictionary of Literary Biography,* vol. 4. *American Writers in Paris, 1920-1939.* Detroit, Michigan: Gale Research Company, 1980. Rich in facts and trivia.

Shirer, William L. *20th Century Journey: A Memoir of a Life and the Times.* New York: Simon and Schuster, 1976. Unfortunately only part of this highly entertaining memoir deals with Paris. But the rest is well worth reading.

Stein, Gertrude. *The Autobiography of Alice B. Toklas.* New York: Random House, 1933.

Wickes, George. *Americans in Paris.* Garden City, New York: Doubleday, 1969. Informative.

Acknowledgments

Grateful acknowledgment is made to the following publishers and individuals for permission to include selections reprinted from:

Shakespeare and Company by Sylvia Beach, by permission of Harcourt Brace Jovanovich, Inc. Copyright © 1956, 1959 by Sylvia Beach; *An American Artist's Story* by George Biddle, by permission of Harold Ober Associates Incorporated. Copyright © 1939 by George Biddle; *That Summer in Paris* by Morley Callaghan, by permission of Penguin Books. Copyright © 1963 by Morley Callaghan; *Six Nonlectures* by E.E. Cummings, by permission of the Harvard University Press. Copyright © 1953 by E.E. Cummings; "myself, walking in Dragon st" is reprinted from *ViVa,* poems by E.E. Cummings, by permission of Liveright Publishing Corporation. Copyright 1931, 1959 by E.E. Cummings. Copyright © 1979, 1973 by the Trustees for the E.E. Cummings Trust. Copyright © 1979, 1973 by George James Firmage; *The Fourteenth Chronicle: Letters and Diaries of John Dos Passos,* edited by Townsend Ludington, by permission of Gambit, Inc. Copyright © 1973 by Elizabeth H. Dos Passos and Townsend Ludington; *My Life* by Isadora Duncan, by permission of Liveright Publishing Corporation. Copyright 1927 by Boni & Liveright, Inc. Copyright renewed 1955 by Liveright Publishing Corporation; *Paris Was Yesterday 1925-1939* by Janet Flanner, by permission of Viking Penguin Inc. Copyright 1925-1939 (inclusive) © 1972 by The New Yorker Magazine, Inc. Copyright 1934, 1935, 1950, copyright © renewed 1962, 1963, 1968 by Janet Flanner; *Selected Letters of William Faulkner,* edited by Joseph Blotner, by permission of Random House, Inc. Copyright © 1977 by Joseph Blotner; article by William Randolph Hearst, September 3, 1930. Copyright © 1930 by The New York Times Company. Reprinted by permission; excerpts from *Ernest Hemingway; Selected Letters; 1917-1961,* edited by Carlos Baker are reprinted with the permission of Charles Scribner's Sons. Copyright © 1981 The Ernest Hemingway Foundation, Inc.; © 1981 by Carlos Baker; *Letters of Archibald MacLeish,* edited by R.H. Winnick, by permission of Houghton Mifflin Company. Copyright © 1983 by the Estate of Archibald MacLeish and by R.H. Winnick; *Letters of Edna St. Vincent Millay,* edited by Allan Ross MacDougall, by permission of Harper & Row, Publishers, Inc. Copyright © 1952 by Norma Millay Ellis; *Remember to Remember* by Henry Miller, by permission of New Directions. Copyright © 1947 by New Directions Publishing Corporation; extracts from letters of Henry Miller are reprinted by permission of Tony and Valentine Miller, and Barbara Sylvas Miller; *Ship of Fools* by Katherine Anne Porter, by permission of Little, Brown and Company. Copyright © 1962 by Katherine Anne Porter; Ezra Pound, *Pound/Ford, The Story of a Literary Friendship,* edited by Brita Lindberg-Seyersted, by permission of New Directions Publishing Corporation. Copyright © 1982 by the Trustees of the Ezra Pound Literary Property Trust; *20th Century Journey* by

Picture Credits

1. Collection Viollet, Paris. 2. Photo N.D. Roger-Viollet, Paris. 3. Roger Viollet Juxtaposée, Paris. 4. Roger-Viollet Juxtaposée, Paris. 5. Photo Harlingue-Viollet, Paris. 6. Collection Viollet, Paris. 7. The Baltimore Museum of Art, The Cone Archives, Baltimore, Maryland. 8 and 9. Collection of American Literature, the Beinecke Rare Book and Manuscript Library, Yale University. 10, 11, 12 and 13. Princeton University Library, Sylvia Beach Collection, New Jersey. 14. André Kertész. 15. (top) Musée National d'Art Moderne, Centre Georges Pomidou © by ADAGP, Paris 1984; (bottom) Bibliothèque Nationale Paris. 16. Princeton University Library, Sylvia Beach Collection, New Jersey.

1. André Kertész. 2 and 3. (left) Princeton University Library, Sylvia Beach Collection, New Jersey; (center and right) Musée National d'Art Moderne Centre Georges Pompidou, © by ADAGP, Paris 1984. 4 and 5. Collection Viollet, Paris; (insert) The Bettmann Archive, New York. 6 and 7. Roger-Viollet Juxtaposée, Paris. 8, 9, 10 and 11. French Embassy Press and Information Division. 12. Collection Viollet, Paris. 13. (top) Photo Roger-Viollet, Paris; (bottom) Roger-Viollet Juxtaposée, Paris. 14. Roger Viollet Juxtaposée, Paris. 15. Associated Press Photo. 16. Photo Harlingue-Viollet, Paris.

Index

Americans are in boldface.

Académie des Beaux-Arts, 53
Académie Colorossi, 65, 66, 92
Académie Française, 53
Académie de la Grande-Chaumière, 92
Académie des Inscriptions et Belles Lettres, 52, 53
Académie Julian, 63-66, 178-79
Académie Matisse, 99-100, 233-34
Académie des Sciences, 53, 117, 156, 222
Académie des Sciences Morales et Politiques, 53
Académie Whistler, 235
Adams, Abigail, 10-12, 107
Adams, Henry, 46-47, 80, 205
Adams, John, 10-12, 16, 19, 29, 106-7, 117, 171, 187, 193-94, 197-98
Adams, John Quincy, 10, 96, 97, 201
Adams, Leonie, 256
Adler, George, 208
Agee, James, 75
Albany Evening Journal, 118
Alcott, Louisa May, 126
Alcott, May, 126
D'Alembert, 5
Allée des Cygnes, 94-95
Alliance Française, 143
Allston, Washington, 119
Amato, Pasquale, 42
American Academy of Music, Fontainebleau, 13, 111, 256
American Ambulance Corps, 62, 84, 241
American Cathedral, 69, 89
American Church, 165
American Legionnaires, 115-16
American Monthly Magazine, 153
American-Polish Committee, 213-14
American Revolution, 11, 15, 17, 20, 52, 100, 193-95, 242, 264-67
American School, 223
Anderson, Margaret, 16, 31
Anderson, Sherwood, 30, 45, 66, 79, 83, 104, 106, 142, 262

André, Jules-Louis, 27
Antheil, George, 77, 104, 111, 136, 160-61, 192
Apollinaire, Guillaume, 100, 104, 140
Arago, Dominique, 53, 222
Aragon, Louis, 112, 120, 161, 192
Arc du Carrousel, 88
Arc de Triomphe, 42, 88, 229
Armstrong, Louis, 78
Arp, Hans, 75, 223
Assemblée Nationale, 171
Association des Etudiants Protestants, 256
Astaire, Adele, 51
Astaire, Fred, 51, 110, 260, 261
Astor, John Jacob, 25, 147
Atlantic Monthly, 17, 68, 77, 142, 222
Auric, Georges, 14, 74, 77, 110
Auriol, Vincent, 114
Austin, Charley, 202-3

Bache, Benjamin Franklin, 193
Bacon, Robert, 152
Bains Chinois, 103-4
Baker, Josephine, 4, 15, 57, 76, 83-84, 87, 125, 135-36, 203, 210
Bakewell, John, 27
Bal Mabille, 137-38
Balbastre, Claude, 96
Baldwin, James, 107, 163, 215
Ballet Russe, 137, 184, 258
Baltimore Sun, 259
Barlow, Joel, 12, 13, 57-58, 104-5, 157, 257-58
Barnes, Djuna, 59, 158
Barney, Natalie Clifford, 18, 104, 222
Barnum, Phineas T., 203, 270
Barnum and Bailey, 38
Barras, Admiral, 20
Barrie, Sir James, 114
Bartholdi, Frédéric-Auguste, 44-45, 73, 94, 259
Baruch, Bernard, 61, 125

Bassiano, Princess, 136
Baths, Public, 103-4, 187
Beach, Cyprian, 16, 165
Beach, Sylvester Woodbridge, 165
Beach, Sylvia, 16, 55, 66, 77, 83, 136, 142,
    157, 158-61, 163, 165, 192, 225, 256
Beardsley, Aubrey, 13
Beat generation, 91
Beaumarchais, Pierre Caron de, 5, 11, 16-17,
    197, 264-67
Beauvoir, Simone de, 158, 216
Beaux, Cecilia, 64
Bechet, Sidney, 135, 267
Beckett, Samuel, 59, 75, 163
Beckwith, J. Carroll, 139, 152
Beerbohm, Max, 24
Bell, Alexander Graham, 222
Benét, Stephen Vincent, 66, 116-17, 222
Bennett, Arnold, 125
Bennett, James Gordon, 41
Bennett, Robert Russell, 14
Benson, Frank, 179
Benton, Thomas Hart, 65
Béranger, 211
Berendt, Rachel, 104
Berenson, Bernard, 104
Berger, Arthur, 14
Bergson, Henri, 247
Bernhardt, Sarah, 43
Bernstein, Leonard, 14
Berry, Walter Van Rensselaer, 36, 251
Bibliothèque Nationale, 55, 120, 198-99, 211
Biddle, George, 8, 65
Bigelow, John, 24, 39, 165
Bingham, William, 11
Bird, William, 6, 7, 66
Bishop, Elizabeth, 159
Bishop, John, 157
Bishop, Morris, 185
Black Manikin Press, 59
Black Sun Press, 36, 115
Blackbirds, 86
Blackden, Colonel Samuel, 242
Blitzstein, Marc, 14, 59
Bois de Boulogne, 12, 38, 90, 237
Bonaparte, Jérome, 95
Bonheur, Rosa, 237

Bonnat, Léon, 9, 26
Bonneville, Nicolas, 157
Borglum, Gutzon, 20, 253
Bori, Lucrezia, 42
Bouillard, Dr. Jean-Baptiste, 227, 228
Boulanger, Gustave, 64, 178, 179
Boulanger, Nadia, 13-14, 19, 33, 64, 111, 128,
    192
Bourdelle, Antoine, 7, 135
Bourget, Paul, 209
Bowles, Paul, 14
Boyle, Kay, 59, 75, 216, 217
Bradley, William Aspenwall, 222
Braggiotti, Mario, 109-10
Brancusi, Constantin, 24, 223, 230
Braque, Georges, 223
Breer, Robert, 66, 92
Brenner, Victor, 53
Breton, André, 59, 112, 161, 262
Bréville, 196
Brewster, Kingman, 214
Bricard, Sophie, 134-35
Bricktop, 4, 77, 130
Broglie, Duc de, 96, 250
Bromfield, Louis, 222
Brooks, Rev. Phillips, 232
Brown, Arthur, 27
Brown, Gladys, 144
Brown, John, 217
Brown, Lawrence, 243
Brown, Panama Al, 210
Brown, William Slater, 67, 84-85
Bruce, David, 214
Bruce, Patrick Henry, 99-100, 233
Buber, Martin, 75
Buchwald, Art, 22, 130, 143, 163, 165
Buffon, Georges, 89
Bulfinch, Charles, 4
Burnett, Whit, 230
Burr, Aaron, 25, 56, 95, 177, 244-45, 258
Burroughs, William, 91, 163
Butler, Nicholas Murray, 114

Cabanel, Alexandre, 26
Cabell, Joseph C., 200

Eakins, Thomas, 9, 25-26, 165, 256-57
Earle, Dr. Pliny, 155-57
Eaton, Wyatt, 178
Ecole Alsacienne, 113, 153
Ecole des Beaux-Arts, 8, 9, 25-29, 50, 63-64, 165, 179, 222-23, 256
Ecole de Médecine, 69-71, 131, 205, 226
Ecole Militaire, 37, 39
Ecole Normale de Musique, 33
Eddy, Arthur J., 152
Edison, Thomas, 54, 72-73, 162, 202, 236-37
Edström, David, 60
Edwards, Hilton, 72
Egorova, Lubov, 258
Eiffel, Alexandre-Gustave, 44, 72-73, 236
Eisenhower, Dwight D., 42
Eliot, T.S., 86, 104, 136, 159, 161, 230, 247
Ellerman, Bryher, 158-60
Ellerman, Sir John, 158-60
Ellington, Duke, 72, 77, 90, 127, 243-44
Elliott, John, 121
Eluard, Paul, 59, 74, 120
Elwell, Herbert, 111
Emerson, Ellen, 17
Emerson, Ralph Waldo, 5, 17, 29, 154, 158, 178, 197, 211
Erlanger, Philippe, 74
Ernst, Max, 59, 120, 163
Eugénie, Empress, 82
Evans, Dr. Thomas, 80-83

Fairbanks, Douglas, 50
Falguière, Jean, 7, 28
Falke, Pierre, 146
Falla, Manuel de, 91
Fantin-Latour, Henri, 78
Farley, Lillian, 3
Farrell, James T., 59, 163
Faulkner, William, 47, 53, 158, 233
Fauré, Gabriel, 90, 111
Ferlinghetti, Lawrence, 233, 259
Ferrar, Geraldine, 42
Ficke, Arthur, 143
Fine, Irving, 14
Finney, Ross Lee, 14

Fish, Hamilton, 165
Fitzgerald, F. Scott, 31, 60, 66, 83, 145, 146, 183-84, 239-40, 256, 258
Fitzgerald, Zelda, 183-84, 239-40, 258
Flanner, Janet "Genet", 30-31, 104, 136, 215, 216, 222
Flaubert, Gustave, 34, 77, 141
Foch, Maréchal, 61
Folies-Bergère, Théâtre des, 83
Fontaine, Pierre, 53
Ford, Ford Madox, 6, 161, 215, 229-30, 256, 262
Foucault, Jean-Bernard, 181
Foujita, 35
Fournier, Alain, 247
Foyer International des Etudiantes, 225
Fraenkel, Michael, 240
Franco-Prussian War, 82, 162, 260
Frankenheimer, John, 163
Franklin, Benjamin, 5, 11, 19, 29-30, 32, 37, 40, 48-49, 52, 53, 93, 106, 117, 193-95, 197, 246-47, 265
Franklin, William Temple, 182, 193
Frascati (gaming house), 202
Fremstad, Olive, 42, 162
French Revolution, 5, 15, 48, 57, 69, 95, 123, 154, 157, 195, 201, 225, 242, 249, 253, 258
Frey, Jacques, 109-10
Frieseke, Frederick C., 65
Frost, Arthur B., 233
Frost, Robert, 158
Froullé bookseller, 93
Fuller, Loïe, 75, 135, 202, 267
Fuller, Margaret, 171, 211
Fulton, Robert, 12-13, 114, 147, 148-49, 157, 177-78, 223, 257-58, 259

Galantière, Lewis, 185
Galerie Arnaud, 223
Galerie Daniel Cordier, 128
Galerie Denise René, 92
Galerie Ileana Sonnabend, 93-94
Galerie des Machines, 38, 39, 73
Galerie Maeght, 223

Reid, Mrs. Whitelaw, 45
Reid Hall, 45
Réjane, 76
Renoir, Auguste, 90, 100, 124, 244
Restaurants
  L'Auberge du Centre, 60
  Foyot, 243
  Le Grand Véfour, 174-75, 248
  Au Père Tranquille, 185
  Le Pré aux Clercs, 30
  Les Trois-Frères Provençaux, 175-77
  Véry, 174-75
Reubell, Henrietta, 86-87
Reverdy, Paul, 161
Revolution of February 1848, 29, 44, 196
La Revue Nègre, 15, 86, 135, 203
Ribicoff, Abraham, 163
Rice, Elmer, 32, 115-16
Rilke, Rainer Maria, 252
Rives, William C., 250
Robeson, Paul, 159
Robinson, Theodore, 27, 179
Rochambeau, General, 20
Rockefeller, John D., 61, 125
Rodgers, Richard, 41-42, 127
Rodin, Auguste, 252, 267-68
Rodin Museum, 20, 252-53
Rogers, Ginger, 260
Roosevelt, Eleanor, 90, 197, 216, 261
Roosevelt, Franklin D., 53, 90, 197, 216, 261
Roosevelt, Theodore, 41, 69, 102
Root, Waverly, 121
Rorem, Ned, 74
Rosenquist, Jim, 93
Ross, Harold, 31
Rossi, Carmen, 235
Rothschild, Baron Edmond de, 127
Rousseau, Jean-Jacques, 5, 171, 180
Roussel, Albert, 14
Rubinstein, Helena, 22, 59-60, 192
Rudge, Olga, 77, 160
Rummel, Walter, 186
Russell, Morgan, 233

Sacco and Vanzetti, 116, 137, 140
Saint-Exupéry, Antoine de, 36

St. Gaudens, Augustus, 7, 26, 28, 77, 80, 107-8, 151, 152
St. Louis Globe Democrat, 162
Salle Gaveau, 111
Salle Musart, 270
Salle Pleyel, 77, 90, 192
Sand, George, 34, 211, 217
Sandburg, Carl, 59
Sanderson, Sybyl, 75
Sardou, Victorien, 76, 267
Sargent, John Singer, 21-22, 90, 111, 139-40, 143, 152
Saroyan, William, 236
Sartre, Jean-Paul, 216, 248
Satie, Erik, 77, 111, 120
Saunderson, John, 124
Schola Cantorum, 221
Schönberg, Arnold, 14
Scioto Land Company, 57
Scott, Sir Walter, 2, 201
Scotti, Antonio, 44
Scudder, Janet, 7, 28, 45
Secession, 67
Seeger, Alan, 67-68
Seldes, Gilbert, 91
Sessions, Roger, 14
Sevareid, Eric, 235
Shakespear, Dorothy, 18, 151
Shakespeare and Company, 66, 158, 159-61, 192, 233
Shapero, Harold, 14
Shaw, George Bernard, 114
Shaw, Irwin, 22-23
Sheldon, Frederick, 118
Shirer, William L., 71, 79-80, 98, 112, 136, 142, 187-88, 222, 240, 254
Short, William, 97
Shriver, Eunice, 163
Shriver, Sargent, 163
Siegmeister, Elie, 14
Sign of the Black Manikin, 59
Singer, Isaac, 125-26
Singer, Winnaretta, 90-91, 126, 267
Sisley, Alfred, 179
Skinner, Cornelia Otis, 184, 216
Skinner, Otis, 216
Skipwith, Fulwar, 95, 270

MAPS
OF
PARIS

Map A Saint-Germain-des-Prés

1. Jefferson, Bulfinch, Trumbull
   9 quai Anatole-France
2. Farley
   7 quai Anatole-France
3. Rives 82 r. de l'Université
4. Stowe 53 r. de Verneuil
5. Davidson, MacLeish
   44 r. du Bac
6. Capote
   7 r. Montalembert
7. Gallatin
   21 r. de l'Université
8. Eliot 9 r. de l'Université
9. Williams
   22 r. de l'Université
10. Vans 24 r. de l'Université
11. Cooper 29 r. de Verneuil
12. Crosby 19 r. de Lille
13. Pound 9 r. de Beaune
14. James, Lowell, Emerson
    7 r. de Beaune
15. Cather 19 quai Voltaire
16. Skipwith, Thomson
    17 quai Voltaire
17. Wright 9 r. de Lille
18. Jolas 6 r. de Verneuil
19. Franklin
    2-4 r. de l'Université
20. Franklin, Jay, Adams
    56 r. Jacob
21. Franklin 52 r. Jacob
22. Irving, Anderson,
    Hemingway 44 r. Jacob
23. Miller 24 r. Bonaparte

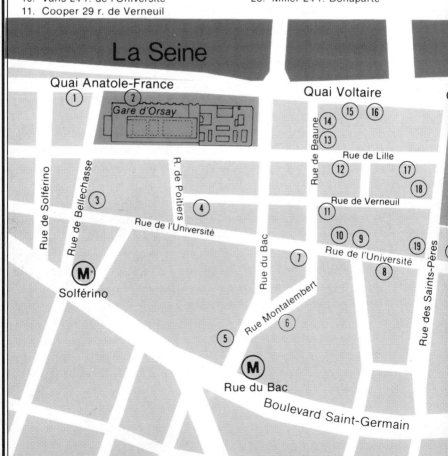

Map B Jardin du Luxembourg

1. Ferlinghetti
   89 r. de Vaugirard
2. St.-Gaudens
   3bis r. Jean-Ferrandi
3. Wright 4 r. Régis
4. Cooper
   12 r. de l'Abbé Grégoire
5. Williams, West
   43-5 blvd Raspail
6. Bechet
   21 r. du Vieux-Colombier
7. American artists
   31 r. du Dragon
8. Whistler 64 r. des Sts-Pères
9. Millay 65 r. des Sts-Pères
10. Pound 59 r. des Sts-Pères
11. Lehr 52 r. des Sts-Pères
12. Wilder, Tunney
    151 blvd St.-Germain
13. Vanderlyn, Burr
    70 r. de Vaugirard
14. Stein, Toklas
    27 r. de Fleurus
15. Stein 58 r. Madame
16. Fitzgerald 58 r. de Vaugirard
17. Barlow, Fulton
    50 r. de Vaugirard
18. Hemingway 6 r. Férou
19. Ray 2bis r. Férou
20. Trumbull Eglise St.-Sulpice
21. Whistler 13 r. Férou
22. Eakins 46 r. de Vaugirard
23. Faulkner 26 r. Servandoni
24. Tarkington 20 r. de Tournon
25. Paine, Morris, Monroe
    Palais du Luxembourg
26. Jones 19 r. de Tournon
27. Parker 13 r. St.-Sulpice
28. Paine 2 r. de l'Odéon
29. McAlmon 8 r. de l'Odéon
30. Beach, Antheil
    12 r. de l'Odéon
31. Earle, Tate 6 pl. de l'Odéon
32. Jefferson, Irving
    Théâtre National de l'Odéon
33. Whistler, Van Doren
    5 r. Corneille
34. Putnam 16 r. de Vaugirard
35. Shirer, Calmer
    4 r. de Vaugirard
36. Wright 1bis r. de Vaugirard
37. Longfellow
    49 r. Monsieur-le-Prince
38. Putnam
    39 r. Monsieur-le-Prince
39. Whistler
    22 r. Monsieur-le-Prince
40. Wright, King
    14 r. Monsieur-le-Prince
41. Beach 8 r. Dupuytren
42. Putnam
    12 r. de l'Ecole-de-Médecine
43. Longfellow 5 r. Racine
44. Hoffman, Duncan,
    Hemingway
    Jardin du Luxembourg

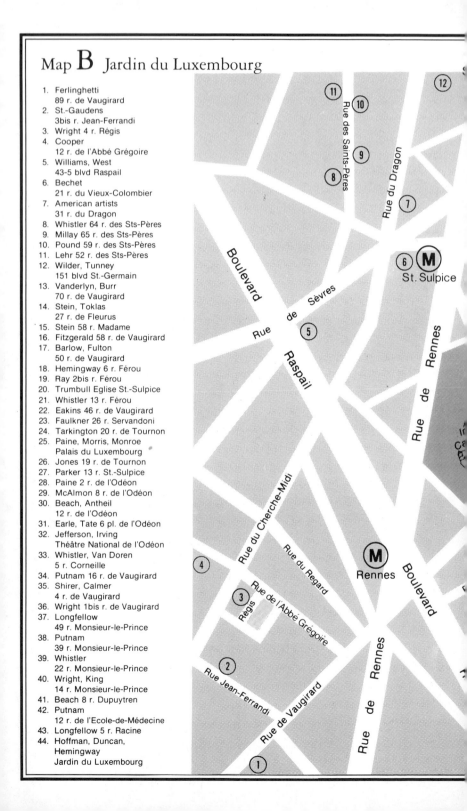

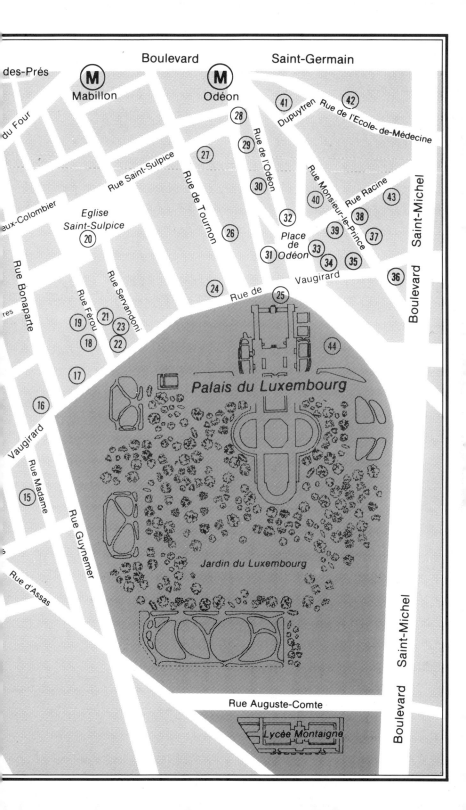

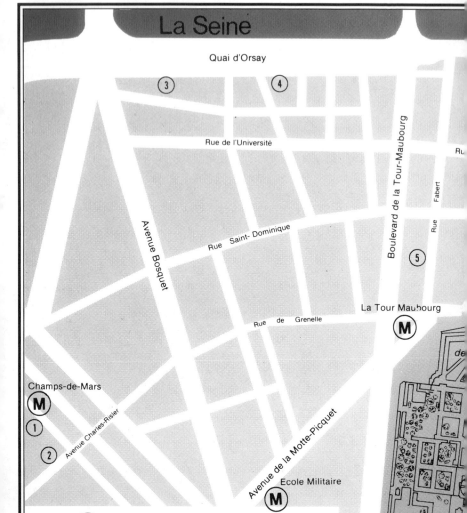

La Seine

Quai d'Orsay

Rue de l'Université

Rue Saint-Dominique

Avenue Bosquet

Boulevard de la Tour-Maubourg

Rue Fabert

Rue de Grenelle

La Tour Maubourg (M)

Champs-de-Mars (M)

Avenue Charles-Risler

Avenue de la Motte-Picquet

Ecole Militaire (M)

Map C Invalides

1. Barnum & Bailey Circus
   Champs-de-Mars
2. Cooper, Buffalo Bill
   Champs-de-Mars
3. Buchwald 83 quai d'Orsay
4. King 65 quai d'Orsay
5. Jolas, Paul 40 r. Fabert
6. Trumbull, Morris, Stanton,
   Roosevelt
   Esplanade des Invalides
7. Cooper 59 r. St.-Dominique
8. Kennedy 37 quai d'Orsay
9. Adams, Fuller
   Place du Palais-Bourbon
10. MacLeish 23 r. Las-Cases
11. Skipwith 102 r. de Grenelle

12. Jefferson
    104-6 r. de Grenelle
13. Adams 105 r. de Grenelle
14. Hoffman, Keller
    77 r. de Varenne
15. Trumbull 69 r. de Varenne
16. Jefferson 78 r. de Varenne
17. Wharton 58 r. de Varenne
18. Wharton 53 r. de Varenne
19. Whistler 110 r. du Bac
20. Porter 13 r. Monsieur
21. Bruce 33 blvd des Invalides
22. Ray 5 ave. de Lowendal

Avenue de Tourvil

Lowendal

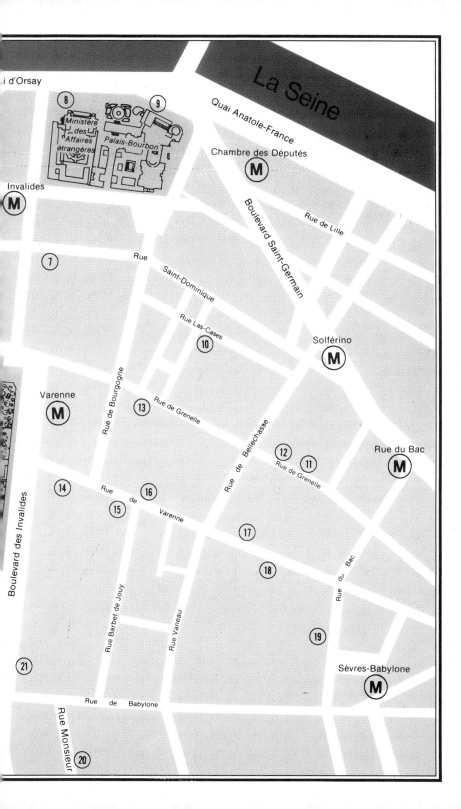

Map D Montparnasse

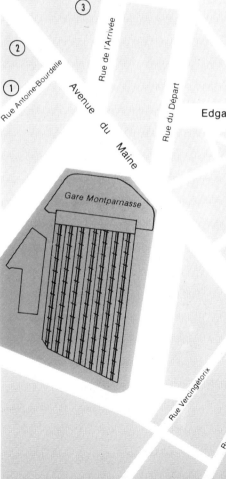

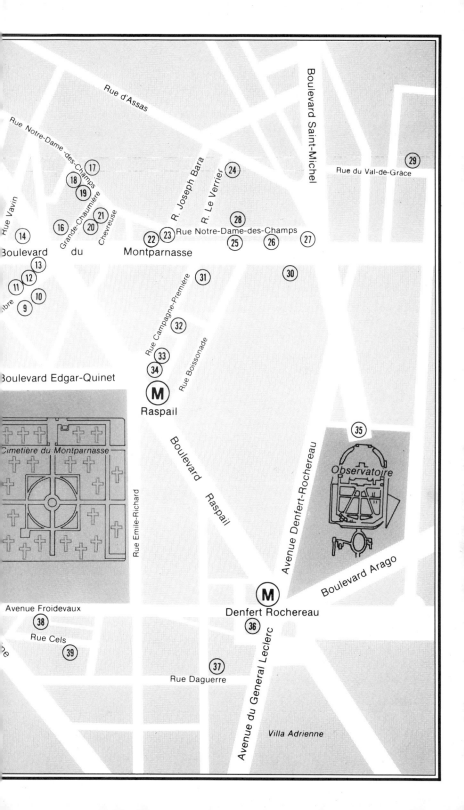

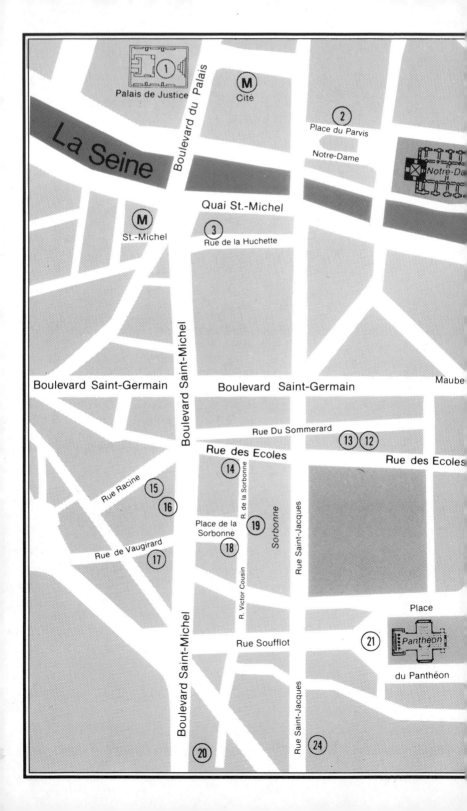

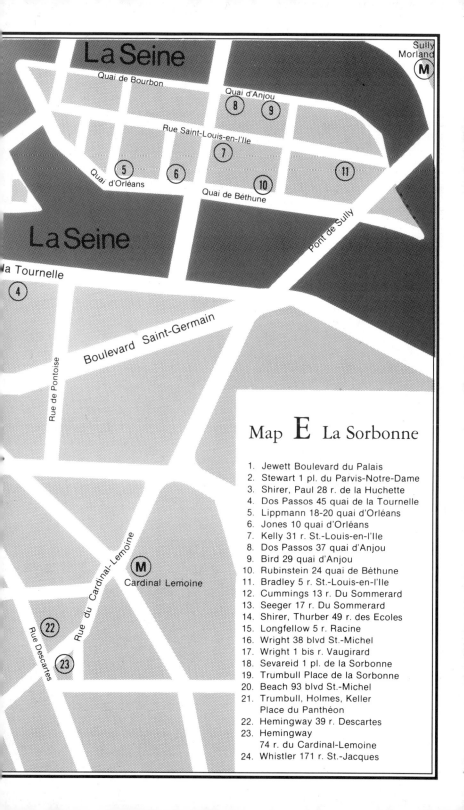

Map E La Sorbonne

1. Jewett Boulevard du Palais
2. Stewart 1 pl. du Parvis-Notre-Dame
3. Shirer, Paul 28 r. de la Huchette
4. Dos Passos 45 quai de la Tournelle
5. Lippmann 18-20 quai d'Orléans
6. Jones 10 quai d'Orléans
7. Kelly 31 r. St.-Louis-en-l'Ile
8. Dos Passos 37 quai d'Anjou
9. Bird 29 quai d'Anjou
10. Rubinstein 24 quai de Béthune
11. Bradley 5 r. St.-Louis-en-l'Ile
12. Cummings 13 r. Du Sommerard
13. Seeger 17 r. Du Sommerard
14. Shirer, Thurber 49 r. des Ecoles
15. Longfellow 5 r. Racine
16. Wright 38 blvd St.-Michel
17. Wright 1 bis r. Vaugirard
18. Sevareid 1 pl. de la Sorbonne
19. Trumbull Place de la Sorbonne
20. Beach 93 blvd St.-Michel
21. Trumbull, Holmes, Keller
    Place du Panthéon
22. Hemingway 39 r. Descartes
23. Hemingway
    74 r. du Cardinal-Lemoine
24. Whistler 171 r. St.-Jacques

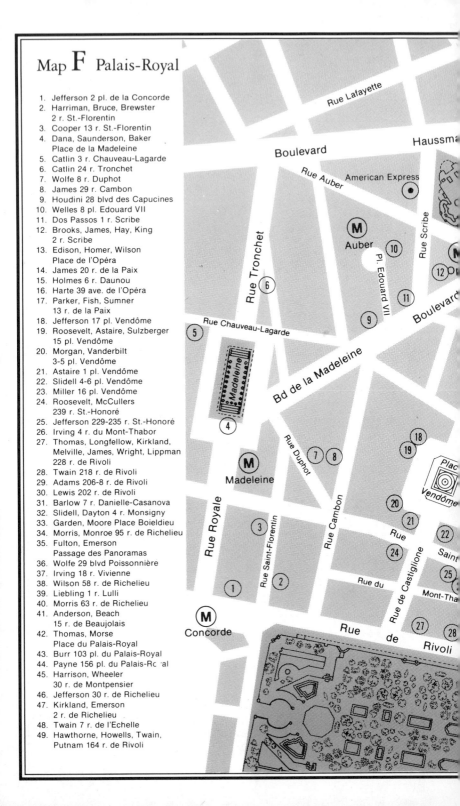

Map F Palais-Royal

1. Jefferson 2 pl. de la Concorde
2. Harriman, Bruce, Brewster
   2 r. St.-Florentin
3. Cooper 13 r. St.-Florentin
4. Dana, Saunderson, Baker
   Place de la Madeleine
5. Catlin 3 r. Chauveau-Lagarde
6. Catlin 24 r. Tronchet
7. Wolfe 8 r. Duphot
8. James 29 r. Cambon
9. Houdini 28 blvd des Capucines
10. Welles 8 pl. Edouard VII
11. Dos Passos 1 r. Scribe
12. Brooks, James, Hay, King
    2 r. Scribe
13. Edison, Homer, Wilson
    Place de l'Opéra
14. James 20 r. de la Paix
15. Holmes 6 r. Daunou
16. Harte 39 ave. de l'Opéra
17. Parker, Fish, Sumner
    13 r. de la Paix
18. Jefferson 17 pl. Vendôme
19. Roosevelt, Astaire, Sulzberger
    15 pl. Vendôme
20. Morgan, Vanderbilt
    3-5 pl. Vendôme
21. Astaire 1 pl. Vendôme
22. Slidell 4-6 pl. Vendôme
23. Miller 16 pl. Vendôme
24. Roosevelt, McCullers
    239 r. St.-Honoré
25. Jefferson 229-235 r. St.-Honoré
26. Irving 4 r. du Mont-Thabor
27. Thomas, Longfellow, Kirkland,
    Melville, James, Wright, Lippman
    228 r. de Rivoli
28. Twain 218 r. de Rivoli
29. Adams 206-8 r. de Rivoli
30. Lewis 202 r. de Rivoli
31. Barlow 7 r. Danielle-Casanova
32. Slidell, Dayton 4 r. Monsigny
33. Garden, Moore Place Boieldieu
34. Morris, Monroe 95 r. de Richelieu
35. Fulton, Emerson
    Passage des Panoramas
36. Wolfe 29 blvd Poissonnière
37. Irving 18 r. Vivienne
38. Wilson 58 r. de Richelieu
39. Liebling 1 r. Lulli
40. Morris 63 r. de Richelieu
41. Anderson, Beach
    15 r. de Beaujolais
42. Thomas, Morse
    Place du Palais-Royal
43. Burr 103 pl. du Palais-Royal
44. Payne 156 pl. du Palais-Royal
45. Harrison, Wheeler
    30 r. de Montpensier
46. Jefferson 30 r. de Richelieu
47. Kirkland, Emerson
    2 r. de Richelieu
48. Twain 7 r. de l'Echelle
49. Hawthorne, Howells, Twain,
    Putnam 164 r. de Rivoli

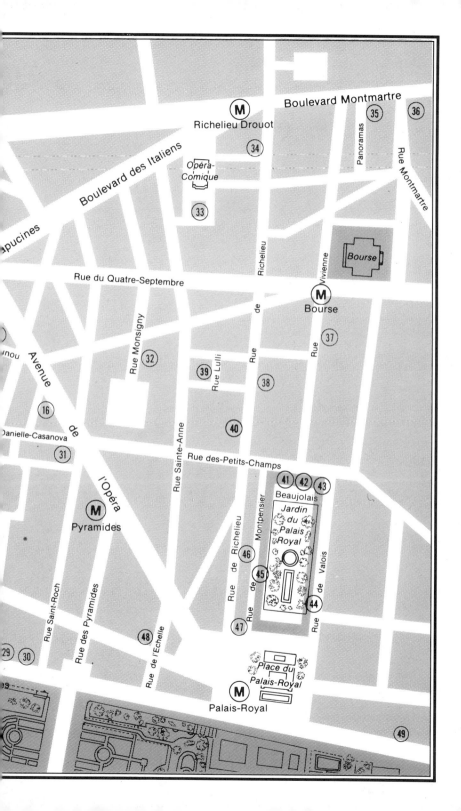

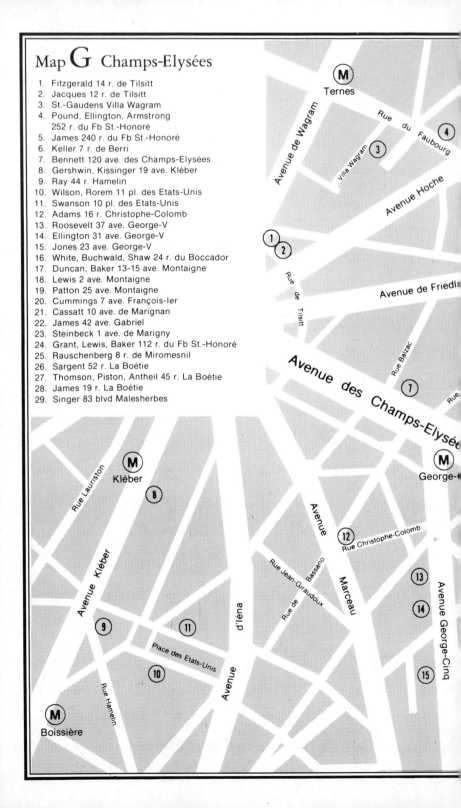

Map G Champs-Elysées

1. Fitzgerald 14 r. de Tilsitt
2. Jacques 12 r. de Tilsitt
3. St.-Gaudens Villa Wagram
4. Pound, Ellington, Armstrong
   252 r. du Fb St.-Honoré
5. James 240 r. du Fb St.-Honoré
6. Keller 7 r. de Berri
7. Bennett 120 ave. des Champs-Elysées
8. Gershwin, Kissinger 19 ave. Kléber
9. Ray 44 r. Hamelin
10. Wilson, Rorem 11 pl. des Etats-Unis
11. Swanson 10 pl. des Etats-Unis
12. Adams 16 r. Christophe-Colomb
13. Roosevelt 37 ave. George-V
14. Ellington 31 ave. George-V
15. Jones 23 ave. George-V
16. White, Buchwald, Shaw 24 r. du Boccador
17. Duncan, Baker 13-15 ave. Montaigne
18. Lewis 2 ave. Montaigne
19. Patton 25 ave. Montaigne
20. Cummings 7 ave. François-Ier
21. Cassatt 10 ave. de Marignan
22. James 42 ave. Gabriel
23. Steinbeck 1 ave. de Marigny
24. Grant, Lewis, Baker 112 r. du Fb St.-Honoré
25. Rauschenberg 8 r. de Miromesnil
26. Sargent 52 r. La Boétie
27. Thomson, Piston, Antheil 45 r. La Boétie
28. James 19 r. La Boétie
29. Singer 83 blvd Malesherbes

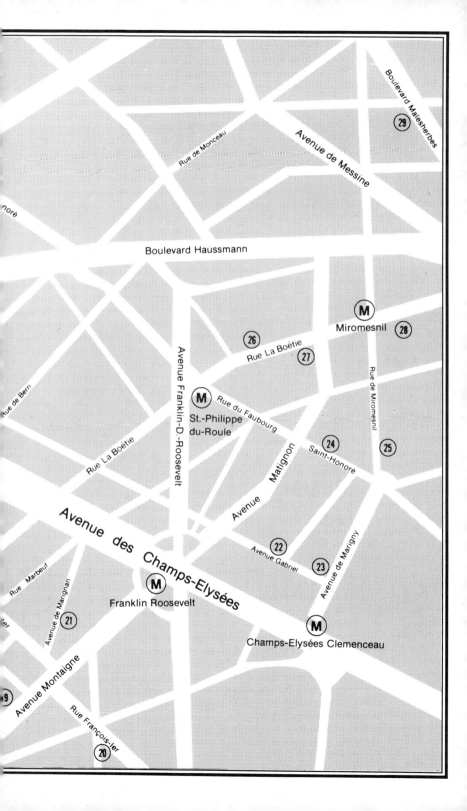